D0251158

CyberShock

CyberShock

**Surviving Hackers, Phreakers,
Identity Thieves, Internet Terrorists
and Weapons of Mass Disruption**

by Winn Schwartau

Thunder's Mouth Press
New York

Published by
Thunder's Mouth Press
841 Broadway, Fourth Floor
New York NY 10003

5-2000

Library of Congress Cataloging-in-Publication Data

Schwartau, Winn.
    CyberShock / by Winn Schwartau.
        p.   cm.
    ISBN 1-56025-246-4
    1. Computer security.   2. Computer hackers.   3. Computer crimes.
    I. Title.
    QA76.9.A25 S3537 2000
    005.8 21—dc21

                                                                    99–046073

Designed by Kathleen Lake, Neuwirth & Associates

Distributed by Publishers Group West

Manufactured in the United States of America

Dedication

My mom taught me write . . . from wrong.

Sherra, my wife, tolerates the 7 X 24 clickety-clicks of a writer.

Adam, my son, finally became a big reader.

Ashley, my daughter, wants to be a writer; not so fast young lady.

My in-laws for feeding me the fodder I need for some of my stories. Thanks.

Anti-Dedication

I talk about a lot of products in *Cybershock*. Some I speak about positively, some disparagingly. The former are not endorsements. The latter not 100% disses, just my opinion—so forget the lawsuits.

The people I talk about—some of you should consider yourself lucky I didn't tell everyone more of the truth. Most of you will be quite pleased, though. My publisher is concerned that the photos of the hackers imply that they are whore-mongering, drug-taking criminals. No. These are just photos of conferences. The feds aren't taking drugs. The group shots are mere group shots of hackers; no hidden implications. Chill and enjoy.

Contents

Acknowledgments   x

Foreword by John "Cap'n Crunch" Draper   xiii

Introduction   xxi

Part I: The Hackers   1

The Great New Global Society   3

Whole Lotta Hacking Goin' On   19

CyberGraffiti   25

Who Are the Hackers?   33

CyberChrist at the Hacker Con: Las Vegas, Nevada, USA   53

Hactivism: Political Hacking   69

An American Alien Hacks Through Customs   79

Part II: Protecting Kids, Family, and Your Privacy   83

In Cyberspace You're Guilty Until Proven Innocent   85

Protecting Your Kids and Family from Hackers   111

Spam   130

Scam Spam: Fraud   141

Part III: How They Hack   153

Getting Anonymous   155

Password Hacking   165

Hack and Sniff   176

Scanning, Breaking, and Entering: Anatomy
      of a Friendly Hack   180

War Dialing: Hacking the Phones   195

Trojan Hacking   201

Hacking for $ 206

Viruses, Hoaxes, and Other Animals   212

Crypto Hacking   229

Steganography: Hiding in Plain Site (Sight?)   253

Hacking for Evidence   258

Part IV: "We're Sorry, but the Computers Are Down"   273

Denial of Service: Taking Down the Net   275

Schwartau to Congress: HERF This   284

Weapons of Mass Disruption   286

Part V: Anti-Hacking Tips and Tricks   313

Hiring Hackers   315

Catching Hackers   325

Defensive Hacking: Firewalls   336

Corporate Anti-Hacking: It Ain't the Technology   346

Lying to Hackers Is OK by Me   357

Part VI: Law Enforcement, Vigilantism, and National Security   365

Hacking and Law Enforcement   367

Corporate Vigilantism: Strike Back or Lay Back?   374

Infrastructure Is Us: The National Response to Hacking   390

Something Other Than War   408

Part VII: The Future   419

    Luddite's Lament   421

    The Future of Microsoft   425

    Messing with the Collective Mind: PsyOps   428

    Extreme Hacking   432

    The Toaster Rebellion of '08   438

    Postscript   448

Appendix   450

    Top Hacker Sites   450

    Top 50 Security Sites   451

    Other Works by Winn Schwartau   453

    Index   455

Acknowledgments

There are a ton of people who helped out with this book. A ton of people could be 10 at 200 pounds each, or twenty skinny 100-pound kids or a whole slew of friends around the world. Whatever.
Here's a few of them–in alphabetical order:

If I forgot to mention anyone, I apologize but it's my publisher's fault. He's rushing me.
Winn Schwartau 010100, 12:02 AM

Adam (My son)
Air Force Office of Special Investigations
Anonymous (Great Book)
Ashley (The Girl)
Betty O'Hearn
Bill Church (Spies R Us)
Bob Ayers (Got out of US alive)
Bruce Schneier (Numero Uno Crypto Geek)
Carolyn Meinel (For Fodder)
Chris Goggans
CIA (For trying to recruit me and failing)
Dave Shriner (Mr. Herf)
DefCon (Jeopardy)
Digital Ebola
DISA Representatives
Electronic Disturbance Theater
Evil Dr. Delam (Hack me Not)
FBI (Especially my students)
Frans Mulschlegel
Fred Cohen
Fred Villella
General Jim McCarthy
General John Meyers

George Phillips (Remember the Sheraton)

Hackers who hacked me and my family who will never, ever, hack again.

Information Warfare Readers: All 200,000 of you
InfowarCon Attendees: 1993 and on
ISS
James Ken Campbell (Weapons of Mass Destruction)
Jeff Moss
Jerry Kovacich (The Beer)
Jim Christy
Jim Kates
Jim Settle
JP
Ken Mellem
Ken Williams
Kermit (STU III)
KGB (Good Vodka and Interviews)
Legion of the Underground
Mark Hardy (For almost taking off her blouse)
New York City Police Department
New York State Police
Office of the Secretary of Defense
Optik Lenz
Peter Shipley (The War)
Peter Wayener
Punkis
R. Loxley
Ronald Rosenberg
Sara Gordon (Viri Guru)
Secure Computing Corporation
Seven (For not hacking)
Sherra (Clickety-click)
Sir Dystic (Cult of the Dead Cow)
Sun Tzu
Suzanne Gorman (She Beat It)
US Secretary of Agriculture, Dan Glickman (Quotes)
White Wolf Survival

And everyone else I forgot who will never let me forget it. You all deserve much credit for the support you have given me over the years. Thanks ever so much.

Winn Schwartau

Foreword

by John "Cap'n Crunch" Draper

I was one of the original phone hackers from the early 70s.

I earned this distinction by accident because of my knowledge of electronics, and because of a Blue Box I had built.

It all started when I was minding my own business and got a call from a blind kid who had either dialed a wrong number or was scanning random numbers looking for interesting results. This guy's voice was amazingly similar to the voice of a friend I was expecting a call from.

Soon, I realized I was talking to the wrong person, but what attracted my attention was when he called himself a "phone phreak," or a person who experiments with phones.

Phone phreaks will dial random numbers to see where they go or try dialing unused prefixes to find "ring back" codes—numbers you can dial to test the bell of your phone. There are all sorts of test numbers you can dial.

I had recently been discharged from the military and amused myself by calling other remote military establishments on the military Autovon network. This is a private internal phone network that allows one military base to phone another without going through the "private sector" phone system.

We even used it to "phone home" when we got an operator to place an "outside call" for us. Although this practice wasn't officially allowed, sympathetic operators do place outside calls from remote sites.

I learned my new phone phreak friend's name was Denny; the number he gave me to reach him later turned out to be unusable, so I shrugged it off as a wrong number.

A few weeks later, I was experimenting with a new antenna design. I drove around the city testing the range and reception while transmitting music on the FM band. When I got back and was ready to shut the transmission off I gave out my phone number on the air, asking anyone who was listening to give me a call.

Denny called me again and let me know that he was picking up my transmissions on the radio, which were being received very clearly about three miles away. I recognized his unique DJ-sounding voice, and asked him if he had called me before; I gave him the number he gave me earlier to refresh his memory. He said that number was a "loop" number, a special test number.

Denny then told me about phone phreaks and invited me to visit him. This launched my phone phreak career.

I had just been introduced to a whole new group of people—blind people who, with their sensitive ears, were able to hear every click and pop to determine which relay switches were opening and closing during the setup of a phone call.

When I first entered the room where Denny lived, the lights were off. Blind people don't need them. There were three other people in the room.

One was a musician with perfect pitch, another was a DJ wannabe with a DJ voice, and a third person I don't really recall.

They taught me how easy it was to make free calls. I couldn't believe it. Just by sending tones down the line, nothing else, it was possible to take total control of the internal network of the telephone company—for free—and call anywhere an operator can. It was that easy.

Someone suggested I use a "handle" or "nickname."

I said "OK, just call me 'Cap'n Crunch'."

The name stuck.

Back in those days, the worst thing that happened was Don Ballanger getting busted. He was busted for building and selling Blue Boxes for organized crime; he had made a fatal mistake: using long-distance information circuits to get connected to the trunks. Bitter about getting busted, Don contacted Ron Rosenbaum, an independent writer who eventually wrote an article called "The Secrets of the Little Blue Box," published in the 1971 October issue of *Esquire*.

Ron Rosenbaum got much of the information in the article from the blind kids. '

The kids agreed to be interviewed by Rosenbaum as long as their names weren't used, so their parents would not find out. I talked to Ron and asked him not to publish the article but he did it anyway. Most of the stuff he published in the *Esquire* article came from the blind kids; I furnished very little information to Ron. My comments on that article are on my web site: www.webcrunchers.com/crunch.

The *Forbes* article was responsible for launching a large federal grand jury to investigate how extensively this sensitive telephone information had gotten around.

By about this time, perhaps 1,000 people knew about the problems and flaws in Ma Bell, the AT&T telephone monopoly of the 1970s. Steve Wozniak read the *Esquire* article with great interest, as he had designed one of the original Blue Boxes, but the frequencies given in the *Esquire* article were wrong.

This didn't stop the Woz. He was a good researcher, and spends a LOT of time in the university libraries.

The Woz finally came across the *Bell System Technical Journal*, which published the actual frequencies, which, oddly enough, were remarkably close to the frequencies mentioned in the *Esquire* article. The Woz knew he had it right, but he didn't know how to use the Blue Box. He knew how to design the electronics and get the tones correct, but didn't know how to access the line or what he had to do to dial into a number that would give him access to a trunk.

As he quickly learned, using a blue box was very easy. You just dialed any toll free number, such as an 800 number, sent a 2600 Hz tone down the line, and listened for a "ker-chink" sound. If you didn't hear that sound, then it wasn't possible to use it.

If you did hear the tone, you would dial a number like: KP-212-555-1212-ST . . . KP being an opening tone, ST being a closing tone. The call would go through, and as far as the billing equipment goes, you had just dialed an 800 number. There was no record of the call to the 212 number above, unless the phone company put a "pen-register," or monitor, on the line. Those are very expensive pieces of equipment, and could only monitor a single line at a time.

I knew that when I walked out of Woz's dorm my ass was cooked and I couldn't do anything about it. One reason was that the Woz box was digital. Its tones were not pure, so it had a specific "signature" that made them more easily detectable when they were used. This made it easy for the telephone company police to catch Rich, one of Denny's friends who had purchased a Woz box. Rich was picked up by the police and forced to testify before a grand jury where my name came up, and it was evident to them that I was the key person they wanted. This was derived from grand jury testimony and the fact that my phone number was found in just about everyone's address book.

The Woz, on the other hand, had nothing to do with the blind kids. He lived in a dorm, where they couldn't trace the calls to him, so he stayed out of harm's way.

In May 1972, I was arrested by the FBI. The connection to my name (Cap'n Crunch), my phone number, and the *Esquire* article plainly depicted me as the leader of the phreaks, which then made me Numero Uno as far as the FBI and police were concerned. The blind kids looked up to me as their leader.

So the FBI figured they got their man.

But I was really a very small fish when there were so many people out there who could do things as sinister as shutting down the entire telephone network.

Today, everything is computerized, and hackers are doing "hard time" in direct contact with terrorists, thieves, organized crime syndicates, and other people who shouldn't know how to manipulate the phones illegally. Granted, it takes a lot of knowledge to shut down a system, but given enough time it is certainly possible to teach the dumbest criminal a few tricks for causing some serious damage.

I was sentenced to four months in Lompoc federal prison near Vandenburg Air Force Base. This provided me with ample opportunity to teach ten to fifteen very eager to learn inmates everything I knew. From word I have gotten, three of them turned out to be excellent hackers, and to this day have never been arrested again.

The authorities are just sweeping this issue under the rug, hoping that nobody will notice the filth. Shutting down a telephone switch can be done really easily, from any remote terminal, provided you have the right access codes.

Over the years, older analog telephone equipment has been replaced with digital computerized equipment, and Blue Boxes don't work much anymore.

As the older equipment was being replaced with digital equipment, computers were playing a larger role in controlling and switching calls, as well as in maintenance work. Computers allow all the new services, like Caller ID, conference calls, and other features, which were hard to implement on mechanical switches.

As computers were used more, it wasn't necessary to have any of the switching offices manned anymore, so the phone companies installed remote access to the switches: a security problem, of course. A worker just dials into a terminal and connects to the switch remotely. Of course, all transactions with the computer are logged, but hackers have ways of hiding their activities. For instance, a remote request to forward a phone line would not be noticed as much as another request to switch a normal phone number to a WATS (free) line.

Either way, the hacker achieves the same effect: he is able to make a free call by forwarding some random line to the person or party he wants to call.

Today, even small companies have their own private phone systems, called Private Branch Exchanges (PBX). These are computerized and have all those annoying voice menus like "Press 1 for Sales," "Press 2 for Customer Service," and so forth. These PBXs have other features, such as permitting key employees to access outgoing phone lines that allow someone (hopefully working for the company) to place company-related phone calls from home, and bill the call to the company. These outside access numbers are easy to find, and their codes are often not changed from the manufacturer's default codes, which every good hacker/phreak knows.

Over time, fewer and fewer people knew about the new computers the phone companies were installing, and since the breakup of Ma Bell, other switching companies have entered the market, creating a whole new set of rules for phone hackers. So, rather than just Western Electric Equipment, there are many more manufacturers of switching systems available to smaller and more localized phone companies.

In the last thirty years, phone hacking (phreaking) has merged with computer hacking. Hacking today occurs on many smaller playing fields, rather than on one big one like the old phone company, AT&T. There is a much greater variety of things hackers can do now. More equipment and software means there are so many more hacks needed to get into systems. But, because most of this equipment can be purchased through independent companies, it is very easy for a hacker to pose as a customer.

He can glean lots of useful information on the system, such as how to maintain the switch, test it, etc., which all require maintenance access to the switch through software. Hackers even rewrite the telephone system code and install it on a switch remotely. The switches were designed that way so they can be easily maintained.

OK, I told you what we did back then and what happens today.

So how do we try and stop it? I can only make a recommendation: Minimize exposure of hackers to criminals.

Hackers can and will continue to do some serious damage to systems, but to treat them like criminals and put them in direct contact with criminals is certainly not the thing you want to do.

It's probably too late now. I guess just about EVERY criminal element is looking to use hacking techniques to further their goals. Of course, the more the press covers hackers, the more important hacking the Internet will seem for anyone wanting to use it in less-than-noble ways.

Jails are the perfect venue for transferring hacking knowledge. Inmates have a LOT of spare time on their hands, and a patient teacher can teach just about anyone anything, given enough time. And they do.

Instead of jailing hackers, perhaps they should do "community service" by using their skills to make systems more secure. This would be a good start. This approach has worked on some occasions, and jailing hackers is just going to make things worse.

With the huge attacks against the Pentagon, threats to the infrastructure, and direct attacks on military systems in the war in Kosovo, there are serious national security issues not only for the military, but for our financial institutions. Hacking opens up a whole new form of terrorism.

The vulnerable computers that are connected to the Internet are used for administrative purposes. Protected by simple passwords, these systems can be hacked by an "enemy of the state" and services can be disrupted. Threats from outside the network should be considered very seriously. Our systems are accessible from a lot of places outside the country.

I think the government should put up systems to hack, encourage hackers to try and break in, and reward them with lots of cash, equipment, software, etc. Many private companies are doing this now, and are getting good results.

CyberShock will give you lots and lots of tips and tricks to improve your personal and company security.

As for the future, hackers are always going to be around, and there isn't anything that anyone can do about it—except deal with it. Hackers can and will be bitter—especially if they get busted—and bitter hackers can do a lot of damage indeed if they put their minds to it.

We also have to understand that no matter how advanced systems get, there are going to be holes in them, and hackers are going to exploit them. If the authorities take a hardnose attitude, then it is my opinion that hackers will retaliate more and do nastier things than they otherwise would. If hackers can be put to work in community service, to help secure systems as punishment, I think we would be better off in the long run.

My recommendation for budding hackers? Simple: Don't get caught.

You can hack legally if you offer your services to a company or agency that trusts you. The main thing here is trust. Most companies are always going to be reluctant to turn a hacker loose on their system, at least not without tight supervision.

What am I doing almost thirty years later? I'm currently working on setting up a Software Development lab in India. With it, we will offer much lower software development costs to the I.T. industry.

I am also working on the Mac port for SpeakFreely, a Net Phone program for voice communication over the Internet, which can be done using 28.8kb connections.

And of course answering all the email I get. So visit my site at http://www.webcrunchers.com/crunch.

In the meantime, enjoy Winn Schwartau's thoroughly entertaining and informative overview of hacking and hackers.

John "Cap'n Crunch" Draper
December 1999

Introduction

CyberShock is not for everyone.
This book will have absolutely no value for you if:

- You or your company are not connected to the Internet.
- You have no money in the bank. Any bank.
- You don't use credit cards.
- You don't use the telephone, a cell phone, or other communications devices. In other words, you don't phone home or call mom.
- You don't drive, use trains or airplanes.
- You never plan on going to the hospital.
- You don't own a home.
- You never want credit or a loan.
- You don't shop, or if you grow your own food.
- You don't rely upon the power company for electricity.

Or if you are the super-technical geek type[1] who knows a whole lot more about programming and software code than I do.
Do you meet that criteria?
If not, you or your children might want to go to hacker camp.
Hear this, technocrats:
CyberShock is not meant to be a primer on hacking for hacker wannabes or for budding technical types. There are dozens of high qual-

---

[1] No offense.

CampCaen is a real offering. I don't know if the rest is real or spoofed. Doesn't matter either way. It's fun.

ity technical books which talk about hacking and information security in the deep technical terms you want.

This book is for everyone else, namely you: the other 5.99 billion people on the planet who have no idea what PCCIP, TCP/IP, CGI, FTP, DES, or API mean, and who probably don't care.

And even if you are the technical type, you probably have an Aunt Libby or Cousin Bill or a truck driver in-law who may recognize a computer when they see one, but even that stretches their expertise. This is not an insult in the least; it's a fact of life that the vast majority of Americans and people everywhere are simply not technical by nature.

Today, you don't have to be an underground hacker or a professional computer engineer to be affected by *CyberShock*. Folklore and rumor about the Internet is at an all-time high.

The media makes it sound like the world is collapsing around us because of these punkster hackers who mess with banks and telephones and government computers. What's with that?

Like any average person, you want the TV remote to flip channels, the microwave to heat leftovers, and the ATM to dispense cash upon demand. When the cable company or electric company can't answer billing questions because "the computers are down," either blind acceptance or exasperation are the normal responses.

> *"What do you mean the computers are down? I'm on my lunch break and this is the only time I can call!"*
> *"You will have to call back later."*
> Click.

With the Y2K scare, millions of people have been suddenly thrust into becoming aware of their reliance upon computers for their very existence, a fact that gets lost in the maelstrom of day-to-day living. Headlines about the potential for Y2K disasters, the seemingly constant flux of headline hacking, and virulent computer viruses spreading global havoc have also served as a wake-up call to America and industrialized-information-age societies worldwide.

> *"My bank statement is wrong. . . . Can you fix it?"*
> *"But the computer says it's right. Can you prove that the computer is wrong?"*

The Internet is here and trouble has started. The rules change daily. New hacks occur by the hundred or thousand every month. The power of technology doubles every 9–18 months[2] and its march forward sees no end.

CyberShock is a non-technical manual for coping with these changes.

The links and references included for your use contain vast amounts of information—more than you could ever digest in a lifetime—and still that information is incomplete.

So, then we ask ourselves what can we do about hacking? As you will learn, in order to solve the problem, first you have to understand the problem.

This is your chance to really learn what is going on . . . out there . . . virtually and really . . . in Cyberspace . . . the Internet.

CyberShock. It affects you, too.

> Winn Schwartau
> January 1, 2000, 12:01AM.
> The lights are on.

▶ Real, Honest, Case Stories Of The Non-Technically Inclined

▶ Case #1

1st Person: "Do you know anything about this fax machine?"

2nd Person: "A little. What's wrong?"

1st Person: "Well, I sent a fax, and the recipient called back to say all she received was a cover sheet and a blank page. I tried it again, and the same thing happened."

2nd Person: "How did you load the sheet?"

---

[2] Moore's Law.

1st Person: "It's a pretty sensitive memo, and I didn't want anyone else to read it by accident, so I folded it so only the recipient would open it and read it."

▶ Case #2

Tech Support: "What does the screen say now?"
Person: "It says, 'hit enter when ready'."
Tech Support: "Well?"
Person: "How do I know when it's ready?"

▶ Case #3

I was working the help desk. One day one of the computer operators called me and asked if anything "bad" would happen if she dropped coins into the openings of her PC. I asked her if this was something she was thinking of doing. She said, "never mind" and hung up. So I got out my trusty tool kit and paid her a visit. I opened her CPU case and sure enough, there was forty cents.

▶ Case #4

"Hello, Tech Support; may I help you?"
"Yes, well, I'm having trouble with WordPerfect."
"What sort of trouble?"
"Well, I was just typing along, and all of a sudden the words went away."
"Went away?"
"They disappeared."
"Hmm. So what does your screen look like now?"
"Nothing."
"Nothing?"
"It's blank; it won't accept anything when I type."
"Are you still in WordPerfect, or did you get out?"
"How do I tell?"
[Uh-oh. Well, let's give it a try anyway.] "Can you see the C:\ prompt on the screen?"
"What's a sea-prompt?"

[Uh-huh, thought so. Let's try a different tack.] "Never mind. Can you move the cursor around on the screen?"

"There isn't any cursor. I told you, it won't accept anything I type."

[Ah—at least s/he knows what a cursor is. Sounds like a hardware problem. I wonder if s/he's kicked out his/her monitor's power plug.] "Does your monitor have a power indicator?"

"What's a monitor?"

"It's the thing with the screen on it that looks like a TV. Does it have a little light that tells you when it's on?"

"I don't know."

"Well, then look on the back of the monitor and find where the power cord goes into it. Can you see that?"

[sound of rustling and jostling] [muffled] "Yes, I think so."

"Great! Follow the cord to the plug, and tell me if it's plugged into the wall."

[pause] "Yes, it is."

[Hmm. Well, that's interesting. I doubt s/he would have accidentally turned it off, and I don't want to send him/her hunting for the power switch because I don't know what kind of monitor s/he has and it's bound to have more than one switch on it. Maybe the video cable is loose or something.] "When you were behind the monitor, did you notice that there were two cables plugged into the back of it, not just one?"

"No."

"Well, there are. I need you to look back there again and find the other cable."

[muffled] "Okay, here it is."

"Follow it for me, and tell me if it's plugged securely into the back of your computer."

[still muffled] "I can't reach."

"Uh-huh. Well, can you see if it is?"

[clear again] "No."

"Even if you maybe put your knee on something and lean way over?"

"Oh, it's not because I don't have the right angle—it's because it's dark."

"Dark?"

"Yes—the office light is off, and the only light I have is coming in from the window."

"Well, turn on the office light then."

"I can't."

"No? Why not?"

"Because there's a power outage."

"A power—!?!" [AAAAAAARGH!] "A power outage? Aha! Okay, we've got it licked now. Do you still have the boxes and manuals and packing stuff your computer came in?"

"Well, yes, I keep them in the closet."

"Good! Go get them, and unplug your system and pack it up just like it was when you got it. Then take it back to the store you bought it from."

"Really? Is it that bad?"

"Yes, I'm afraid it is."

"Well, all right then, I suppose. What do I tell them?"

"Tell them you're TOO STUPID TO OWN A COMPUTER!" [slam]

I know none of you are that bad . . . right? Right? OK? Right?

The Hackers

Hackers. Who the heck are they?

Are they really drug-driven denizens and techno-anarchists, as many in the media portray them?

Or instead, like the Cold War DEW system used to warn of incoming Soviet missiles, are they really just the Early Warning System for Cyberspace and the Internet? Good guys or cyber-terrorists?

Take a gander at just how widespread the hacking phenomenon is, how many different kinds of people are involved, and see if you agree or disagree with their motivations for hacking. I know that over the years my views have changed. Hopefully this (reasonably) dispassionate overview of the world of hacking will let you form your own opinions.

The Great New Global Society

The only constant in modern society is change. Get used to it.

Unknown

Y ou've heard about them.

You've read the headlines.

Hackers.

Maybe you work for a company that has been hacked.

Or worse yet, maybe you yourself or your family or friends have been the victim of hacking.

But sure enough, if you haven't been hacked yet, there is little doubt that you will be. As you will learn, it's fairly inevitable.

The first thing I am going to ask you to do is to get rid of all of your preconceived notions about hacking. Forget what you've read in your local newspaper or seen on CNN. Some of it is right but a lot of it is wrong. I am going to ask you to keep an open mind, for you will discover that hacking is not really what you thought it was after all. Hacking is about something very different—society—and it has much greater consequences for us all than you probably could ever have imagined.

In fact, hacking is so big a deal, I recently sat through a senior military briefing that ended with the comment, "We will all be long gone before we figure out what to do about hacking. And, to add insult to injury, the whole hacking scene is going to get a hell of a lot worse before it gets any better. I think abject chaos is the best description I can offer." The NSA official asked not to be identified.

I don't mean to scare you right off the bat here; there is plenty of time for that. But, if you are already part of the twenty-first century, which you are, you should be concerned at a minimum, and maybe, just maybe, very, very scared.

By accident of birth, and the luck of being born prior to the onset of

3

the twenty-first century, you are faced with the reality of hacking. Consider that your tax dollars are partially spent by the government and law enforcement to thwart hacking, which certainly takes away from other worthy or not-so-worthy causes: ergo, you have already been victimized by the incredible rise in criminal hacking.

If, instead, you had been born at the end of the eighteenth century, you would have been part of another revolution—the Industrial Revolution—when western civilizations began the transition from an agrarian-based society to one of great machines, a brand-new society where boats moved by steam instead of sails and oars; where powerfully huge, fire-breathing iron horses were propelled down thin rails of steel much faster than any air-breathing animal could run; where in the United Kingdom, and then the United States, the loom threatened to replace entire populations who for thousands of years had made cloth by hand.

Or if you had been born at the end of the nineteenth century, you would have been part of the inchoate information age, when electricity was thrust upon us, radically influencing every facet of our lives. Electrical power distribution had an even more profound effect on civilization than had Gutenberg's printing press had over 300 years earlier. Electricity made the telegraph and telephone possible. It allowed the genius Nicolai Tesla to build the first radio, and thereby introduce communication by radio waves. (Marconi fans, you've been living the fantasy of history book error for too long!) This age allowed the entrepreneurial spirit of Edison to invent light bulbs and the phonograph, and to drive his staff of inventors to the point of exhaustion and create dozens of devices that defined the early twentieth century.

But the fact is you were born in the twentieth century. If you are reading this now, you are part of perhaps the most radical change in the history of human evolution—and not all of it is necessarily good news.

We have created a Global Society where economists don't yet understand the Global Economy. The old axiom, "when a butterfly flaps its wings in China, a tornado will spin in Oklahoma" becomes even more true today as disparate cultures, peoples and societies attempt to merge into planetary unity, despite all of our differences.

Our unquestioned reliance upon technology for the most mundane of tasks reeks of nonchalance, arrogance and apathy. The global network consists of Computers Everywhere: moving the money, moving the planes, turning on the power, turning on the water, powering the games, and educating our children. Computers Everywhere.

At the heart of this new Great Global Society, though, is a hoard of characters which are defining the future as much as living it: hackers.

To Live It Is to Know It

Hackers are an extremely complex and terrifically misunderstood component of modern society. No amount of explanation, including this book, is sufficient for you to really "grok" what a hacker is or what his motivations are. To understand hacking, one must hack—at least a little.

Like love, sex, or any other deeply experienced feeling or emotion, words alone are an incomplete description. In the truest sense of the word, hacking is experiential: one must feel it to appreciate it. Hacking is empirical; there is no formula to follow. There is no magic button which one can press to become a hacker. The better hackers learn their trade by direct experience, by endless sharing with other people of similar interests, and by trial and error.

Even then, once the thrill of hacking is experienced, that feeling is still only one of a myriad set of emotions and feelings that accompany the tapping of the keyboard which takes countless weeks and months to appreciate.

In our souls, many of us are hackers by our very nature.

At a financial seminar I gave in the New York area, dozens of professional banking and brokerage managers attentively listened to story after story and read slide after slide as I attempted to give them a feel for what hacking was about. This particular group was a tough audience; most of them didn't want to be there but it was a job requirement to attend.

So I decided to try an experiment.

During a break, I sat behind a computer and poked around for a couple of minutes, speaking very loudly as I struck each key.

"Good!" A few people looked my way and then returned to their conversation.

"OK, got in there . . ." A few more glances over to where I was sitting. "Perfect. They left the front door open." A couple of folks stepped closer.

"Hey, they never changed the manufacturer's default passwords. Looking good," I exclaimed, waving a proud fist in the air. More folks came to watch.

"Whacha doin'?" one asked with more interest than he had shown all day.

"Seein' if I can break in . . ." I answered. By now a handful of folks were coming over to see what I was doing. The room quieted as I kept pounding away at the keyboard. No one could see the screen as I typed but I had their attention.

I yelled out the Archimedes "aha!" and shouted, "Hey, we just broke into the White House. Anyone want to see?" Half of the room anxiously rushed over to see what I had just done.

"Lemme see, what you got?"

"Anything about Monica?"

"Can you get into Hillary's email?"

The onslaught confirmed my experiment. The entire audience consisted of closet voyeurs who, just like any hacker, wanted to peer behind closed doors where they had no business being. Voyeurism is a part of all of us, to a lesser or greater extent, and looking into the secretive chambers of the White House is very tempting.

Although some of the group were visibly disappointed that I had not actually hacked into the White House, most of them got the point. They experienced the anticipation, perhaps even the minor thrill of expectation as they waited for great national secrets to be exposed in front of their eyes. And then some of them experienced the adrenalin letdown as the truth became apparent: I was merely messing with their minds in hopes of giving them an emotional glimmer into hacking.

This was not an isolated case. At one of the InfowarCon[1] conferences I ran in Brussels, Belgium, we billed the final session of the day as "Live Hacking." The intention was to show people, in a controlled environment, what was actually involved in breaking into computers. Even though this was the last event of the conference, scheduled from 3:30–5:00 PM on a Friday afternoon, the conference hall was packed to the rafters.

Two associates of mine, Chris Goggans and Bob Stratton of Secure Design International (www.sdii.com), coordinated the session. They had received permission from the administrators of the target computer networks to perform a live break-in. They figured that if the SDII crew could break in, they would learn about the holes in their networks and sew them up. It was a fair trade.

As the session began, the three hundred attendees inched their way forward to where Chris and Bob had set up their equipment, despite the large screen projection of their activities to the auditorium. People clearly wanted to be close to the action. The first demonstration was to show how hacking techniques would not work against a university computer server that was well protected and whose systems administrator they knew. But something went wrong.

With their first hacking trick, they broke in—accidentally! It turned out that the computer was not so well secured, and the audience cheered while Chris and Bob immediately shut down the hacked connection. This was not supposed to happen—and, strictly speaking, they had unwittingly crossed a legal boundary. But the audience was in hacker

---

[1] www.infowar.com

heaven. Most of them had never seen a live hack and they were so struck by what they had seen that the session did not end until well after dark that evening. The audience had vicariously experienced, first hand, what hacking was about. Nonetheless, it is doubtful that any of the corporate and military attendees went on to become hackers. Their jobs are to defend against computer intruders.

I don't believe that a true hacker can be created. I tend to believe they are born. Or, perhaps more accurately, certain people have hackerlike inclinations and then it is up to them to learn how to behave.

Hacking is an intense experience. Someone cannot one day say, "Hey, hacking is cool. I want to be a hacker," and then go do it. I get dozens of emails from people who ask how to break into this or that system. These folks want the Hacking Handbook handed to them so they can follow from Step 1 to Step 10 and call themselves a hacker. Rubbish! As you will learn, this class of computer user is derogatorily known as a Script Kiddie or Wannabe, or by even more obscene names with the same meaning. These are not hackers in the true sense of the word.

The intensity of hacking comes from the dedication required to learn the ropes. Hackers spend months and years learning about computers, operating systems, networks, programming, and software. The image of colorfully creative coifs, painful piercings, and poorly dressed hackers drinking gallons of Jolt cola, absently munching on pizza, and conducting marathon hacking sessions for twenty-four to thirty-six or more hours is not too far from truth. That is the dedication required to get inside the mind of the computer, know the nuances of the network, and have the personal wherewithal and stamina to continue despite failure after failure. Because, at one point, the skilled hacker will prevail, and the network will be his.

The truly skilled, creative, and original hacker will spend his every available waking moment in the pursuit of knowledge—and access to computers—no matter his true motives. He will learn from his mistakes, be cautious in his endeavors, and perfect his techniques. Perhaps he will build better hacking tools to speed up his tasks, automate the redundant steps, and build alternatives for attacking different kinds of computers.

And all of this takes time. A lot of time. Many hackers today spend countless hours looking for weaknesses and vulnerabilities in computer operating systems like Windows-9X, NT, or the many flavors of Unix. Others will acquire software programs, take them apart, and analyze them line by line to find programming errors that they can exploit.

Imagine that you are given a copy of your local phone directory and you are told that there is one wrong phone number in it. Go find it. How long would that take? Where would you begin? What steps would you follow? What techniques would you develop to achieve that task, short of reading every number, calling it and verifying it? The truly skilled hacker will find the most efficient way, build the tools he needs, and wait for the answer to arrive.

If this seems like a lot of effort, it is. It takes a tremendous amount of effort and dedication to dig deep into the computer network and find out what's right and what's wrong. Most of us cannot sustain that personal level of intensity for years on end, but hackers do.

What Was the Most Successful Hack In History?

Remember the movie "Apollo XIII"? The capsule was spinning out of control. The astronauts were up there freezing their *tuchises* off and their air supply was going bad. Things did not look good. Down here on Terra Firma in Houston, a NASA manager lugged a big box into a room full of exhausted engineers. He dumped an assortment of odd-looking parts onto the table. "Gentlemen," he said, "this is what they have up there. That's all they have. Now, figure out how to save their lives."

They pulled, prodded, taped, and turned an unlikely collection of misshapen bits and pieces into a makeshift air filter which provided oxygen. But they also had a major power problem. There wasn't enough power in the command module to do everything they needed for a safe reentry. What to do? Astronaut Ken Mattingly spent countless frustrating hours in the ground-based simulator measuring the power drain under every conceivable combination. Finally, after a thousand attempts, they found the one sequence that would work.

That was the ultimate in hacking: Making a terrifically complex system do something it was not intended to do by the designers.

I tend to view engineering as hacking. Or maybe it's the other way around. I grew up as an engineer. My father and mother were both engineers, so I guess I came by it naturally. I remember taking apart a radio to see how it worked. My father said, "All you've done is take it apart. If you want to know how it works, you have to put it back together." The tears of a six-year-old subsided and I spent weeks putting the radio back together. The intensity of that experience taught me how a radio worked and also provided the first lesson in the amount of dedication I needed to become an engineer, as well as how much frustration is associated with it.

When engineers are handed a task, say to build a special communications system for a fighting soldier out in the field, they are faced with daunting constraints:

1. The performance of the system must meet extremely rigid standards as defined by the military.

2. It must work in deserts, swamps, and at the North Pole.
3. Communications must be intelligible all of the time.
4. It has to be secure so the enemy cannot listen in.
5. It must be able to transmit and receive signals for a certain number of miles.
6. It must be simple to use, as we don't expect soldiers to be engineers.
7. It must be simple to repair so that a field technician can fix it quickly.
8. It must be battery operated and have enough power to operate for at least forty-eight hours without a recharge.

Simple, eh? Oh, yeah, there is one more criterion: It can't weigh more than six pounds, battery included.

Engineers will struggle for months and longer to find new ways to meet these tough specifications, and they will try anything and everything they can come up with to meet the challenge. Remember the early space shuttle? The heat-resistant tiles kept falling off, which would mean a fiery death to returning astronauts. NASA engineers finally got it—with the help of inventive teenagers.

Electric cars. How do we build one that lasts longer than sixty or eighty miles between charges? They're still working on that by researching new battery technologies. How do we make chips smaller and smaller, pack their silicon backs with millions of new transistors, yet avoid the associated heat that is generated?

What about building a bigger bridge? A faster commercial aircraft? Miracle drugs with fewer side effects? Cleaner power? Transparent aluminum? Cheaper water desalinization? These are some of the most compelling engineering problems as we enter the twenty-first century, and we will face more year after year. The people who tackle these problems in earnest, the engineers, are themselves hackers, and unfortunately, most hacker stories and headlines forget that point. Successful hackers and engineers rely upon an innate ability: out of the box thinking.

I had the opportunity to meet one of the greatest minds of the twentieth century, Buckminster Fuller. He coined a term which is equally apt for both engineers (of any discipline) and hackers: *ephemeralization*.

Ephemeralization is doing more with less.

How do you shovel ten gallons of manure into a five-gallon hat? There's a way if someone wants to really think about it. Apollo XIII's experience certainly demonstrated ephemeralization at its best. And so does creative hacking. When we see teenagers with incredible hacking skills, keep in mind they are using no more tools than you or I can buy at CompUSA, through any catalog, or acquire on the Internet. It's what they do with it afterwards that makes the difference, along with the dedication, time, and intensity with which they are willing to attack the problem.

Hacking in its more generic sense has been going on for decades. Didn't Galileo expend massive amounts of effort in redefining man's place in the cosmos? Great mathematicians spend lifetimes to perfect one proof. Salk? Pauling? Great minds dedicated to solving problems either thought unsolvable or answering questions never before asked. Hackers do this every day.

Microsoft would like the public to believe that it writes quality software, but most know that they can't for a simple reason: they cannot test every possible combination of events and environments the software will encounter in real life. Security is very, very tough, and doesn't lend itself to maintaining $100 billion companies.

So hackers do the testing for us.

They find the holes, the weaknesses and the vulnerabilities. Unfortunately some hackers are not benign and they will try to exploit their discoveries to the detriment of their victims. Other hackers, as you will discover, have an engineer's purity and their goal is self-improvement, knowledge, and the betterment of the computer, Internet security, and the Great Global Society they are creating.

Even non-engineering types—including you!—have experienced hacker-like emotions. The car enthusiast who wants to extract every last bit of horsepower from his engine or make his vehicle get just a bit more mileage per gallon follows the same path as the engineer and the hacker, but he does it inside his garage and his results affect him and him alone. How much time and effort will he spend? I grew up in New York City and didn't drive until I was twenty-two, but when I spent my teenage summers in suburban Michigan, my cousin Terry was forever rebuilding his car in hopes of better performance.

Chess players are notorious for spending hours gazing at a single problem on their chess board. Their mind invisibly works through the myriad permutations until they arrive at an acceptable move. Mental hacking? Perhaps; the rigor is the same, the medium is different.

Soon after Marconi and Tesla pioneered wireless communications, radio enthusiasts took up the cause. Average folks caught the radio fever. Crystal and antenna in hand, they experimented. What frequencies exhibit the best transmission characteristics? How does the weather affect communications? Can you bounce signals off of clouds or the ionosphere to transmit farther? How do you reduce the amount of static?

Amateur radio fans came to be known as hams and experimented unfettered for nearly two decades before the US Navy found that the hams were interfering with military communications. Regulation was the next step. Peace was made when the US Government allocated specific frequencies for hams and hams alone.

Today, I see the parallels and I wonder where we will end up in twenty or fifty years' time. Will the best and the brightest of the hackers go down in history as great contributors to the evolution of computers? Or will nonsense headlines prevail, in which an entire culture is indicted due to the rambunctiousness of a few?

To further understand the complexity of the hacker and the hacking phenomenon, we need to put the technology into the context of history.

I precariously date the onset of modern computer hacking to the mid-1960s, but no matter what date I choose, I will be chided. Several significant events occurred roughly simultaneously:

1. AT&T was the phone company. Period. No competition. The 1960s represented the first time the average phone customer could make long distance calls without the assistance of an operator. National and, to a lesser extent, real-time international connectivity had begun.

2. Computers, those ten-ton, room-filling behemoths, had gone mainstream in corporate America. Despite Tom Watson's prediction of a worldwide market for three computers, IBM owned the mainframe computer business by far.

3. The first of the baby boomers were making their presence in society felt.

4. The Vietnam War divided our nation as no other event had since the Civil War.

Baby boomers, the children of World War II, myself included, were not to be the ones who really popularized hacking, although many of my generation have certainly contributed to it. Something else happened as we built the future.

Society flattened.

Quick history lesson.[2] The Phoenicians ruled the seas for a while. The

---

[2]Western History. China and the East were a mystery back then, too.

Egyptians had their day as did the Greeks. The Romans built an empire around the Mediterranean and England. The Dark Ages saw power rise and fall rapidly as kingdoms and serfdoms fought it out with the Northern marauders from Germany, the Russian steppes, and what would become Scandanavia.

As the Renaissance evolved, we saw Spain and France fight for global influence and control of commerce. Then England built what many regard as the greatest empire of all time. From India to the South Pacific to the New World, the king's power was unquestioned. These were all superpowers who essentially controlled the planet for their time.

Then there was America. Upstart colonies who had the temerity to tell King George to go away and stay away. We kicked out the French (with wads of money), beat the hell out of Mexico, and took over small islands in the Caribbean. Then we made the single best real-estate purchase in the history of the world: We bought Alaska from the Russians fifty years before the fall of the czar.

Although we were isolationist by national policy, World War II thrust the United States into superpower status. Two wars took place 10,000 miles apart, and we kicked ass in both. But then the Soviets got their feelings hurt, driven by thousands of years of Russian paranoia, and suddenly there were two superpowers in a nuclear stalemate. We may look back upon the Cold War as the Good Ol' Days because, despite the threat of planetary thermonuclear extinction, there was relative peace. Neither of us really wanted to push the button. Our agenda was power and money. Their agenda was power.

On the scale of global influence there were two huge spikes; the Soviets and the Americans competed on the military scale, but America reigned supreme on the economic scale.

The fall of the Soviet Union represented a profound change: the US was now the solitary military superpower, but perhaps devoid of will to use that power. Economically, the American spike of power was beginning to dissipate. The American goal to spread democracy and capitalism to billions of previously quiet non-consumers had competition from Europe and the Pacific Rim.

Japan, Inc. was making great strides in its exports while our trade balance suffered because of our massive import habit. China, with a potential future consumer base of 1.3 billion people, took back Hong Kong[3] and is now flush with hard currency. The Southeast Asian coun-

---

[3]A remaining bastion of the British Empire.

tries both produce and consume, further eroding American domination of the world's economy.

The economic scale is flattening. While no one doubts our economic strength, the G-8 is a shared international effort at promoting global wealth, and America doesn't run the show anymore. The European Union, with a population more than twice that of the States, is flexing its earned muscle. I am no economist, but at current growth rates, the US will become a second-rate international player within thirty years. In industrial corporations and the military, power is wielded in a top-down, hierarchical manner. The president tells the vice-presidents who tell the directors who tell the managers who tell the supervisors who finally tell the factory floor workers what to do. (In the military it's from general to grunt.) Such were managed companies and, to a similar extent, managed socialized societies. "We will decide what is good for you and you will like it."

Then the 1980s struck. A couple of recessions and the overpopulated middle management of yore felt the noose and were cattle-prodded into unemployment. Tens of millions of folks who felt they had a job for life, just like their daddy did, were suddenly thrust into the psychological mayhem of absolute freedom.

Now let's add the Internet.

Everyone can reach anyone else who is connected. At first it was just the geeks and some government weenies and professors at engineering departments. They all came from the same culture and there was peace. Corporations were spending furiously to add technology to make themselves competitive, but at the same time their new look echoed the Internet community as a whole: no longer was a president in his ivory tower. He was connected to everyone else, too. He could communicate directly with his troops, all the way down the pyramid of power, and they could communicate with him.

What occurred was empowerment of the individual, both within and outside of the corporation. Tens of millions of displaced workers found new lives as entrepreneurs within the massive information technology industry or as corporate telecommuters who worked from home.

The technology of the Internet flattened society at the same time as the econo-political landscape of Planet Earth reshaped itself. An accident of history or serendipity to be sure, but the changes are so incredibly profound we have no idea how things will turn out.

Empowerment is what this book is all about: putting incredible power in the hands of the individual, the foreign competitor, and for-

merly uninfluencial nation-states. The Internet—the great equalizer—
has flattened society by increasing the power that each of us have. Personal influence wasn't squashed by a lightning bolt from Zeus, it was
strengthened by minimizing the nation-state and through the free distribution of powerful technology.

Corporations are replacing the nation-state on the power curve, and
there is little that the nation-state can do about it; the nature of the
multinational company is not allegiance to a flag, but to its global stock-
holders. The military's mission of protecting a country's interest is being
displaced as those interests lie everywhere at once. What do you protect
when the $$$ are mere quantum uncertainties travelling along thin
strands of silicon and copper?

Now, let's add kids to the equation; not great monolithic money-hun-
gry corporations grabbing pieces of the Global Pie in a financial thirst-
hungry frenzy, just kids. Little kids.

Kids Will Be Kids

Kids will do as other kids do and have done so since the day the apes
learned to beat the hell out of each other with marrow-filled bones.

Kids are the cruelest people, we say. It's in their nature as they grow.
It's also in the nature of parents to stay as oblivious as they can when
their children are doing things they don't understand. How may parents
need their kid's help to install "parental" content-filtering software?

As a preteen, my idea of fun was using my imagination. I lived in New
York City, a couple of blocks from Central Park. On the weekend and
during the summer, I would wander over alone or with friends, hook up
with other kids, and we would play. Not with high definition LCD video
screens of little Japanese cartoonish characters bounding about, but with
sticks and leaves and tremendous amounts of imagination. A tree became
a fort. A boulder was a distant city to be besieged. The concrete path
served as an impassable white-rapids river. Let the games begin!

Of course we played pranks, too. The local butcher hated us. "Do
you have pigs' feet?"

He'd answer "Yes."

To which we ever-so-brilliantly came back with, "Wear shoes and no
one will notice."

As technical teenage mavens of the 60s, we were rebellious but the
effects were fairly local. During tenth grade we took over our high
school's PA system and announced that the school day was ending early.
Thirty-two hundred happy kids made a swift exodus to the A-train, and
baffled teachers and administrators realized they had lost control. I
never got caught for that one.

Then there was the instant banana peel that I saw demonstrated on Johnny Carson one night. It was supposed to be 1,000 times more slippery than ice. We bought some, covered the science hallway with it and rang the end-of-period bell. Hundreds of kids slipped and slided their way to ground zero and crawled out of the school.

I later made the front page of the *New York Daily News*, arm in arm with Carol, breaking into school during a three-month-long teachers' strike. My worst offense was locking the principal in his closet "till the war in Vietnam ended" or "they let us wear jeans to school." That lasted about a half hour until the SWAT team came swinging and liberated our fearless leader. Thankfully they were gentle and no one got really hurt.

In the grand scheme of things, these were minor pranks. I defend nothing more than my youthful exuberance, my anti-'Nam politics, and the statute of limitations. Was I right?

No . . .

Maybe . . .

Back then the rules were different.

We didn't have thirteen-year-old middle schoolers planning mass murder. Was that a *prank*? Maybe. But being tried as an adult and life in prison is the political response by a disgusted citizenry. How much teenage angst and attitude is enough to warrant prison for seventy years? Jeez, I hope I am raising my rugrats better than that.

But the world has changed.

The monumental novel, *Lord of the Flies*, portrayed a cadre of boys marooned on an island without parental supervision. The macabre results of youthful isolation echo the most atavistic and Neanderthal instincts in man: survival of the fittest, ostracism of the weak, and brutal competitive enforcement of capricious rules.

That is the nature of the Internet. Flame wars target people with unpopular views, attack the weak networks, ignore the web sites with nothing to offer, and support an ecommerce engine bound to continue creating untold billions in paper wealth as we learn how to coexist with this global network we have built.

The Just Do It generation of empowered youth versus the older Just Watch It generation of couch parents is battling for the control of mindshare and behavior in a world where the rules are being written as we go.

Americans curse Hollywood for blood-and-guts action movies. Video games are more gory than the 6 PM news during Vietnam. The media sells more advertising with mass murder than with Good News. What are our children learning when the evening news has to cope with the

Adam, my son, at two.

phrase "oral sex" and the President of the United States in the same sentence?

Hacking is about more than just kids, to be sure, but as today's ten-year-olds hit the Net, what is their behavior? It's the *Lord of the Flies*.

"Mom, can I have a computer?"

"Sure, Bobby, why?"

"It'll help me with my homework and school projects."

The teachers told Mom the same thing. "Sure, I guess so. But your father and I can't help you a whole lot . . ."

"That's OK, Mom. I know what to do." And you can bet Bobby and his friends have a pretty darn good idea of what they are going to do when their homework is put aside.

Empowered preteens and teens. Raging hormones, massive attitudes, made pugilistic by exposure to life . . . and connected to every place on Planet Earth all at once. The power at the fingertips of any Net-savvy kid today is greater than the electronic power of entire nation-states twenty-five years ago. In a world of no restraint and broken homes, what about the rules of civilized behavior? The Net doesn't follow the rules of generations past. It's designing its own rules and the kids are acting like kids—with the most incredible empowerment in human history.

Today's one- and two-year-olds will be even more immersed in the technology and have more power than today's teens, and since nobody can claim to know what the Internet or our Global Village will look like in a decade, we are *punting*.[4]

And so we end up back where we began: with hackers, the great enablers and dis-enablers of the Internet and Cyberspace.

As you're about to find out, they're everywhere.

▶ The Information Disenfranchised

The dilapidated slums of Northeast Washington DC grimly rot in stark contrast to the primrose cleanliness and American godliness of the Mall.

---

[4]My son has been PC fluent since he was 18 months old.

Bounded at one end by the Capitol building and, a mile and a half away, the Lincoln Memorial on the Potomac River, the midpoint spire is the 555-foot-high Washington Monument. The White House, Smithsonian, National Gallery, and dozens of classically inspired, stony-faced official edifices complete the image of America that we like to portray. This is where much of the work of government occurs.

Driving past the harsh poverty surrounding New York Avenue is a daily reminder to Maryland commuters that many Americans still are not connected to each other and have assumed the role of the Information Disenfranchised. In modern societies, where tens of millions of us suffer from an information glut, the impoverished Information Disenfranchised represent the other extreme end of the socio-technical spectrum: they live in the wrong zip code, use antiquated telecommunications services, and survive from day to day on the most pedestrian of all payment mechanisms, cash.

How would you feel if you received no junk mail? None. Not a single "get rich quick" offer, no pre-approved credit cards or solicitations of twenty-nine dollar carpet cleaning. I know that 70 percent of the mail I receive is junk mail; snail-mail-spam. And I throw out the vast majority of it as do 98 percent of people who receive their own zip-code-income-filtered junk mail. But what if AT&T or MCI didn't want your business? What if Mastercard just ignored you entirely? What they're saying is "We Really Don't Want You."

That is the information-void condition that the lowest economic 20 percent of America experience.

Despite Al Gore's hope and promise to wire everybody to the Internet (which he of course invented) and give them equal opportunity, getting connected still requires some money for a computer, software, modem and monthly fees. It's not *expensive* by middle-class standards, but when the choice is to eat or surf the Internet, guess which comes first?

These are the people whom we are leaving behind and who need the incredible power of the Net as much as we do, if not more. Free on-line libraries mean that the poor don't need a car to get to the physical public library. On-line education rather than a night school cuts costs and the need for babysitters. Job-searching across the country empowers everyone on-line. It seems that the on-line onslaught of discount coupons and offers of free goods are tailored to the financially comfortable and not the millions of poverty-enshrouded inner-city and Appalachian citizens.

So while we talk about hacking and anti-hacking, I like to put on my *I Have A Social Conscience* hat and remember that industrial- and information-age countries have forgotten masses whom we dare not leave behind as we grow our twenty-first century reality.[5]

In the early days of the Internet, back in the late 80s, the original hackers and academicians were loath to invite we newbies onto their electronic playground. We were clueless lamers who deserved every flame mail we received because—well, because we were lamers. With barely a million folks on what was the Net in 1988–1990, the original hackers and on-line denizens feared a population explosion of clueless non-technical hoards. Their worst fears were met with CompuServe, America Online, and the World Wide Web, when the unwashed non-technical mouse-clicking user was invited to get connected by the marketers.

With somewhere in the neighborhood of 400 million people on the Net worldwide[6], it's only going to get busier.

The Information Disenfranchised are going to get on the Net sooner or later, and the question is, will they remain disenfranchised or will they be "equalized" by the Net? Spam doesn't know if you are black, pink, purple or polka-dotted. A web site doesn't know if you are a gazillionaire or can barely feed your family in LA's barrio.

The Internet is proclaimed to be the Great Equalizer for every member of society. Maybe it is. The original bellicose arrogance of early Netizens was annoying to say the least—they wanted the rest of us to go away. Is society going to do the same thing to the current millions who are information disenfranchised?

The Net is amazingly self-regulating. It is a borderless society all its own, devoid of conventional rules and regulations. Let's only hope that, as the technology migrates to the lower socioeconomic strata, the increasingly commercial nature of the Internet doesn't chase away those people who can most benefit from its power.

And, let's hope that government, in its infinite wisdom, doesn't create some twisted way to enforce equality. The Internet can take care of that all by itself.

---

[5] Just look at the failed World Trade Organization talks in November, 1999 in Seattle.
[6] Hey! It's a number. I can't defend it but it's around the middle of the estimates.

Whole Lotta
Hacking Goin' On

In April of 1998, the Department of Defense announced that it had been hacked 250,000 times in one week.

The media ate that story up with a vengeance. It was as though hacking was some new invention suddenly thrust upon an unsuspecting public, which of course it wasn't. But this event marked the first time the DoD openly admitted to attacks on such a vast scale.

In my 1997 book, *Information Warfare*, I estimated that hacking and computer crime cost America between $100 and $300 billion dollars each year. I had taken lots of separate industry estimates (phone fraud, chemical industry, viruses, on-line credit card fraud, software piracy, etc.) and added them together. In 1998, the FBI said that they also estimated losses to the American economy in the $100–$300 billion range.

Things just seem to be getting worse.

First of all there is a big difference between hacking and criminal hacking, but the techniques are the same. When the Pentagon or a company finds itself under some sort of hacker attack, they do not know if the attack is from a relatively benign teenager in his bedroom or from a transnational criminal organization intent on causing extensive financial damage.

The key word here is *intent*, because the techniques of the casual, ankle-biting hacker are the same used by true criminals or even terrorists who might be targeting our national infrastructures. In fact the problem is actually worse, because the effects of a hacker, a criminal, or a software glitch are often indistinguishable. In 2000, we are only at the first stages of being able to examine technical attacks with a hope of determining intent.

OK, so we know a lot of hacking is going on. How much?

That question resounded loudly within the mind of Bob Ayers, a top security expert with the Defense Information Systems Agency (DISA), the DoD arm tasked with providing security for the entire defense infrastructure. In the early 1990s many of us were sounding the clarion, warning of massive impending cyber-attacks as the technology proliferated and our reliance upon the technology became firmly entrenched.

But we had very little hard data. Reliable reports of attacks coming from the private sector were few and far between for fear of public embarrassment, encouraging more attacks, loss of confidence by investors and customers, as well as the specter of government overseers poking their bureaucratic noses into private-sector affairs.

We all needed data to gather support from top-level management, industry, and political leaders so appropriate defenses could be put into place—an endless battle that still continues and will for decades to come.

DISA's Ayers decided that they needed to have a way to measure the extent of hacking, and more importantly, the vulnerability of the DoD to hacker attacks, no matter the motivation. In 1994, Bob and his crew of experts began a long series of tests that would last into 1996. Their method was to attack DoD sites themselves, using only common hacker tools available on the Internet.

The attacks were friendly, looking for weaknesses in the thousands of DoD networks, and they applied a set of rules they had to follow.

1. They would only attack DoD sites that asked to have their security tested. They would not attack any DoD networks without explicit permission. This was a massive exercise in *ethical hacking*.

2. Once network administrators asked for their security to be tested, Bob's crew sent them the latest updates, revisions, patches, and fixes to make their networks as secure as they could. Whether these fixes were implemented or not is an unanswered question.

The results of the DISA study provided a benchmark which helped spur the security industry and the Pentagon into an active, defensive mode.

1. They attacked approximately 30,000 networks.

2. They successfully penetrated and took control of 88 percent of those networks, despite the efforts to get administrators to protect themselves. But that wasn't the bad news.

3. Of the successful attacks, network administrators only detected or noticed that they were under attack 5 percent of the time. That's it. When we think of the military guarding bases with ship-shape Marines carrying loaded rifles—ready to shoot if necessary—hopefully they can identify and stop a potential intruder. That's detection (of the bad guys) at the base perimeter. Imagine if the military's radar systems could only identify 5 percent of an enemy's incoming planes or missiles. That was the state of the art for the DoD according to Ayers' DISA study. But there was still more bad news.

4. Of the 5 percent (of the 88 percent) of the attacks that were detected, only 4 percent of them were reported to authorities. That meant that the vast majority of network administrators did not bother to tell their higher-ups that their networks had experienced an intrusion.

5. When all of these numbers were added up, the results were scary: for every hacker attack/event that the DoD knew about, there were 400 more that went unreported. That's a 40,000 percent difference. In meetings with the US Army's 902 Military Intelligence Group, their studies found the ratio to be only 1 in 1,000 attacks were reported.

The US military has since taken the issue a great deal more seriously and in 1998 President Clinton authorized $1.5 billion to protect US infrastructure and Pentagon resources. On October 1, 1999, four-star general John Meyers took over as the chief of cyber-defense at the Pentagon. It was the first time such a senior officer has taken the reigns.

According to the FBI, crime is down. Way down. Even though there were 13.2 million serious crimes reported in 1997—1.6 million violent ones, 18,000 murders, and millions of others—these figures represent an overall decline of 13 percent since 1988. But cyber-crime is certainly on the rise.

In 1996, Warroom Research, in cooperation with the US Senate Permanent Subcommittee on Investigations conducted a study on computer crime, one of the first studies to quantify the extent of the problem.[7] Two hundred thirty-six large companies responded to the survey and the following results emerged:

1. 58% detected attempts by outsiders to gain access to their computers in the prior twelve months.
2. 30% didn't know if they had been attacked. That's scary too.
3. 58% of the firms detected more than 11 "successful attacks."
4. The kinds of attacks were quite varied:
   a. 40 sniffers were installed
   b. 34 stole password files
   c. 88 probed/scanned the system
   d. 64 introduced viruses
   e. 108 downloaded data or trade secrets
   f. 38 were denial-of-service attacks
5. Only 27% said that insiders were not involved, implying that between 63–73% did involve insiders. 10% reported that it was unknown whether or not insiders were involved.
6. Only 28 of the 129 insiders were subsequently fired, suspended or referred to law enforcement.

The Warroom study also examined the financial losses incurred. Note that these figures are from only a couple of hundred companies. The extent nationally and internationally must be significantly higher.

1. 16% of insider attacks cost the firm more than $1 million for each incident.
2. 69% of insider attacks cost more than $50,000 each.
3. 17% of outsider attacks cost the firm more than $1 million for each incident.
4. 66% of outsider attacks cost the victim firm more than $50,000 each.

Only a handful of the crimes in the study were reported to law enforcement for the reasons mentioned earlier. The fear of reporting is

---

[7]www.warroomresearch.com/wrr/survetstudies/996ISS_Survey_SummaryResults.htm

so prevalent that over 90 percent of the surveyed firms said they would only report cyber-attacks if it was mandated by law, if everyone else reported their incidents, or if they could report anonymously. As you will see, these pervasive feelings influence a company's behavior and how it responds to computer crime.

The Department of Energy's Computer Incident Advisory Capability team received only 169 security incidents (hacking, etc.) in all of 1997. From October to March of the following year, though, incidents increased from forty per month to over eighty per month, a staggering increase in less than a year.[8]

In March of 1999, the results of an FBI-sponsored study were announced.[9] The "1999 Computer Crime and Security Survey" also queried private corporations, financial institutions, and government agencies. All areas of computer crime are on a steep increase:

- System penetrations by outsiders were experienced by 30% of those surveyed.
- The Internet as source of the attack rose from 37% in 1996 to 57% in 1999.
- Insider attacks were reported by 55% of respondees.
- Only 31% of the companies experiencing loss could quantify it. 163 organizations cited combined losses of $123 million.
- 23 firms reported combined losses of $43 million in proprietary information theft.
- 27 financial organizations showed losses of $38 million in fraud.
- 33% of respondees said they didn't know if they had been attacked from the Internet.
- External attacks were varied:
  - 98% experienced vandalism
  - 93% experienced denial-of-service attacks
  - 27% found financial fraud
  - The cost to the company of the average attack was $198,583

The findings from the Survey's press release is daunting in its implications. The study "confirms trends established over the last three annual

---

[8]Contract #W-7405-Eng-48, Lawrence Livermore National Laboratory
[9]www.gocsi.com/prelea990301.htm

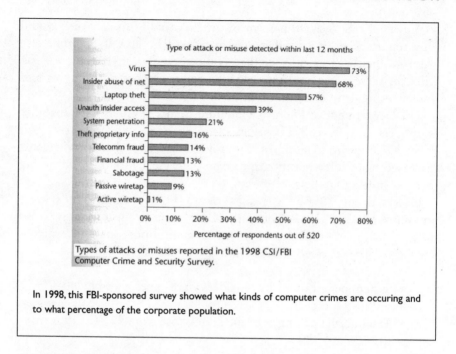

Type of attack or misuse detected within last 12 months

Virus	73%
Insider abuse of net	68%
Laptop theft	57%
Unauth insider access	39%
System penetration	21%
Theft proprietary info	16%
Telecomm fraud	14%
Financial fraud	13%
Sabotage	13%
Passive wiretap	9%
Active wiretap	1%

Percentage of respondents out of 520

Types of attacks or misuses reported in the 1998 CSI/FBI Computer Crime and Security Survey.

In 1998, this FBI-sponsored survey showed what kinds of computer crimes are occuring and to what percentage of the corporate population.

surveys. It is clear that computer crime and other information security breaches pose a growing threat to US economic competitiveness and the rule of law in cyberspace. It is also clear that the financial cost is tangible and alarming."

- 62% of the organizations were attacked from the outside
- 90% experienced virus contamination
- 19% were sabotaged
- 32% were hit with denial-of-service attacks

Michael Vatis, director of the FBI's National Infrastructure Protection Center, said that the study "confirms the need for industry and government to work together to address the growing problem of computer intrusion and computer crime generally. Only by sharing information about incidents, threats and exploited vulnerabilities can we begin to stem the rising tide of illegal activity on networks and protect our nation's critical infrastructure from destructive cyber-attacks."[10]

It's a jungle out there.

---

[10]ibid.

CyberGraffiti

There are hackers and there are hackers. Not every computer crime is an attempt to dislodge a nation or embezzle millions from a major corporation.

When I was a kid, the subways in New York City were the canvas for spray-painting graffiti artists—many of whom actually had artistic talent beyond their inane and obscene messages. In the 1950s, *Kilroy Was Here!* and its associated fingers and nose hanging over a fence filled white-picket neighborhoods with a touch of humor. *Taki 183* became the arcane message of the 1970s subway system.

Graffiti of the 1980s became increasingly political, racial, and social. Then the New York government found a solvent to easily dispense with the spray-paint graffiti.

The 1990s. Graffiti. Well, web sites seem like a perfectly good place to start, eh? The home page of any web address (URL)[11] is an electronic canvas which sends a message. A billboard if you will. Graffiti on billboards, graffiti on web sites, same difference, different medium.

Hacking web sites is great fun for many hackers because it is so easy. Microsoft NT is notoriously insecure and new NT hacks appear weekly. With the scripting tools on the Net, making a statement by putting graffiti on a web page (especially the home page) is widely viewed as "almost not a crime." But in reality, the graffiti artists are committing felonies.

---

[11]Web addresses are designated by URLs, or Uniform Resource Locators. The name of a web site, like www.website.com is a URL.

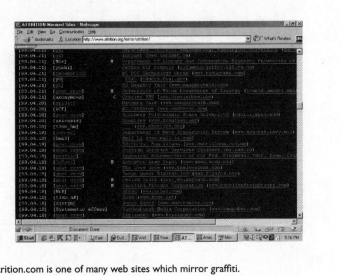

www.attrition.com is one of many web sites which mirror graffiti.

There is no telling how many thousands or more web sites have been spray-painted with some opposing messages, but if you check at hacker web sites like www.attrition.com you will see long listings of hacked sites with graffiti-laden pages for viewing.

The CIA is an attractive target for decades of embarrassing headlines. What do you mean you didn't know that Pakistan and India were in the nuclear weapons club? You really didn't suspect Aldridge Ames even though he lived a million-dollar lifestyle? China's espionage programs against the US were a big surprise, you say?

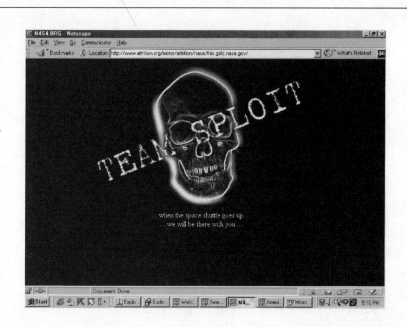

NASA has horrendous security and I wonder if it will ever get any better. Dominated by scientists who believe in the open exchange of information, to them security means controls and censorship and they battle it all the way. Team Sploit is one of those hacker groups who think it's cool to do this to as many sites as they can.

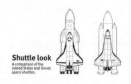

Shuttle look
A companion of the United States and Soviet space shuttles.

How many billions of dollars of US taxpayer–paid research into the design and construction of the Soviet Shuttleski? It wasn't so much on-line spying as just good old-fashioned spying. Today, advanced plans for aeronautics and other projects are stored on computer networks. How many seconds would it take to steal an entire set of plans? You will soon find out that time is critical!

Much of the graffiti is far too graphic for a book like this, but spend a half hour at www.attrition.com and you will get an eyeful. Some graffiti is, however, very entertaining, even if you don't agree with its message.

Unlike *Kilroy Was Here*, the electronic graffiti phrase of choice is *U R Owned* or some variation. This means that the hacker who broke in and sprayed electronic drivel on your home page thinks you are a lamer and your security is so bad you deserved it. YOU ARE OWNED! Arrogance is so much of the teenage-hacker mindset.

The LAPD is not known to be kinder and gentler, even to hackers. The racist overtone is obvious.

Hopefully the Vatican and the Pope have a sense of humor.

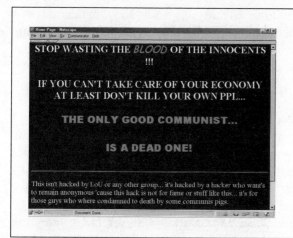

Anti-China sentiments have been running high. Later you will read about the LoU hacker declaration of war against China.

Not much more graphic than MTV, so I chose to include this hacker-written pro-environmental graffiti page.

On the other hand, NASA must drastically improve their security for the obvious reasons, as above. No one is exempt from web graffiti.

So, go on down to your favorite hacker site, find the Hacked Web Page mirrors and take a gander. It's not a bad way to spend a rainy afternoon, but be warned that the material is often heavy R-rated. Hackers know no bounds.

I think you get the idea. The hacking problem is big. No, make that huge. But despite all of the studies, we really don't know exactly how huge. Is it $100 million or $100 billion? Does it matter?

As the 1990s came to an end, you saw the mainstream media talk more and more about hacking and cybercrimes as they increased at a terrifying rate. The costs are in hard dollars, yes, but they also take a mental toll on the human psyche. A dead body, while terribly unpleasant, is a known, tangible result of a crime. With cybercrime there are so many facets—the vast majority of them intangible—that we don't know how to quantify properly. The background of fear, uncertainty, and doubt (FUD) that surround cybercrime shows up in many ways.

Many of us are reluctant to use cyber-banking for fear of personal loss. Corporations are scared to connect mission critical systems to the Internet. The Pentagon wants to disconnect altogether. A large number of Americans won't put their credit card on the Internet when in reality there is more danger of loss when a credit card slip is left in a garbage can at the local greasy spoon. A US naval ship had to be towed back to its base when a Microsoft NT server failed, creating more military FUD.

Now, remember those 250,000 "attacks" against the Pentagon in 1998? Were there really that many? No, not at all. Those "attacks" were conducted by two teenagers with a scanner, a hacker tool which examines the outer edges of a network by asking it a lot of questions such as "are you there," "what services are working," and "what sort of systems are you using." These are automated tools which can run for hours on end without human intervention. By scanning hundreds of Internet addresses in this manner, and considering each and every scanning query an attack, the Pentagon arrived at its astounding figure.

Hopefully this book will help provide a balance for you, so you can separate the chaff from the "real deal." Yes, the Internet can be a very bad neighborhood, and no, we don't have all of the answers yet, but there are a lot of very dedicated people working to solve the myriad problems we face.

Don't buy into the hysteria of an Internet gone mad, nor be naïve enough to travel through Cyberspace without looking in the rearview mirror, wearing seat belts, and using your high beams for guidance. Tread lightly and behave responsibly. It won't make you victim-proof, but it will make you a lot less likely to become a victim.

Now that you know the facts and figures, let's move to see who these hackers are and what they're really doing.

▶ Linux is Da Bomb

Most hackers I know hate Bill Gates.
Most hackers I know hate Microsoft.
Most hackers I know hate Windows.

Welcome to SPOGGE
(rhymes with rogue)

Society for Prevention of Gates Getting Everything
(It is a tongue-in-cheek rebellion against Bill Gates and Microsoft Corporation getting all the money.)
Home of the Roaring Rodent.

SPOGGIE™

The SPOGGE Page. The Society for the Prevention of Gates Getting Everything. It speaks for itself. Not a bad spoof and a great general store! www.galaxymall.com/retail/spogge/ index.html

Most hackers I know hate Redmond, Washington.

Most hackers I know are in love with Unix, a computer operating system originally developed in the mid 1980s.

Like a manual-shift car, Unix gives the power-user a lot more control over what he does, but then again, you have to know what you're doing to take full advantage of its features. Rather than driving a GUI (Graphical User Interface) like Windows, lots of hackers and engineers prefer the touch and feel of driving the software on their own—step by step. It might be a bit more unwieldy, but they do have total control.

Microsoft, despite its protestations, has a virtual monopoly on both operating systems and software applications. I am as guilty as the rest; I use Microsoft Office 97 and I will likely upgrade each time a new useful version appears. I am not a Microsoft fan, but I am a fan of my editors being able to read what I write and of having compatibility with my business associates. So, Microsoft it is.

But now, a real challenge to Microsoft's hegemony has arisen. Linux represents about 5 percent of the market as of early 1999, which scares the living bejeezus out of Gates and Company, and that figure will assuredly increase. For the first time, a product is actually taking the Microsoft Office suite to task. It is called Star Office for Linux. It offers the word processing, spreadsheet, and presentation software previously owned by Microsoft, and the files are compatible.

If you'd like to try something a bit different, get a legitimate copy of Red Hat Linux and Star Office and tell Bill Gates he's over the top with this monopoly thing. In mid-1999, Sun Microsystems bought Star Office and made it available for free. Go to www.sun.com for your copy. For the budding hacker, Linux is da bomb.

Linux Resources

- Red Hat Linux www.macmillansoftware.com
- Open Linux 2.2 included Star Office
  www.calderasystems.com
- www.linux.com
- www.microsfot.com (note spelling)
- www.sun.com

Hacked Web Sites/Graffiti

- http://www.2600.com/hacked_pages/
- http://www.csci.ca/breach.htm
- http://www.euronet.nl/users/jasmine/root/
  digitalunderground/hackedwebsites.html
- http://www.hackernews/com/archive/crackarch.html
- http://www.hektik.com/hacked/
- http://www.onething.com/archive/
- http://www.rootshell.com/hacked_sites/
- http://www.turkeynews.net/Hacked/
- http://www.unc.edu/courses/jomc191/defaced.html

Who Are the Hackers?

The other day a reporter from the *Weekly Gazette* in beautiful downtown Knoblick, Kentucky called me.

He asked, "What's a hacker?" Two thoughts competed for my attention. First: The people in Knoblick, Kentucky don't get out much and this reporter who normally covers farming news for his paper really didn't have the slightest clue. Second: Any of a dozen intelligence agencies were playing a trick on me.

The truth turned out to be yet a third option I had not yet considered: He was simply confused.

The reporter asked a ton of questions. "You know, whenever I read about hackers I really don't know who they are. What is it about them that makes them different? How old are they? What is their background? Why do they hack?"

If you read about hackers in the national media, you get a quite distorted view of what hackers are really about. Only criminal hackers make the front page of the paper, which follows the media dictum, If It Bleeds, It Leads.[12]

The media made Kevin Mitnick a national icon for hacking.[13] Sure,

---

[12] Most people are engrossed by the macabre.

[13] The Kevin Mitnick saga is long and has been extensively covered. Search on "Kevin Mitnick" and look for the aboveground media coverage from CNN, ZDNet, *Wired Magazine* and the *New York Times*. The feds have him portrayed as the ultimate criminal hacker. Then get the other side of the story from the hacking community that believe he is nothing more than a curious kid (thirty years old) who is a scapegoat for stupid law enforcement officials and companies who have no idea how to protect their networks. He got out of jail, January, 2000.

Kevin did a lot of bad things with computers and telephones, and he has been in and out of trouble with the law.[14]

So, I spent some time with the Knoblick reporter and tried to explain aspects of the complex culture of techno-geeks and hacking. When the paper came out, the quotes attributed to me included, "Hackers are criminals who break into computers." Arrgggh! Not even close, Mr. Greenjeans. Not even close.

The reporter had asked a lousy question. Well, maybe it's not so much a lousy question as it is an unanswerable question that doesn't neatly fit the sound-byte reporting of Knoblick's high-speed media machine. There is no absolute, single accurate answer to define the hacking community. Besides, this is a new century and what we learned in the 90s was not to stereotype people. And if any one portion of society is un-stereotypable, it is the hackers.

The best definition I have heard for hacking comes from a Dutchman, Rop Gongjjrip, ex-hacker and former publisher of Amsterdam's *Hacktic*, an early hacking magazine. Rop exudes the highest set of morals and ethics I have ever encountered in the community and he is now a successful businessman. I always found it amusing that the Amsterdam police had a hard time watching and believing in Rop's migration to legitimacy. When hacking was made illegal in Holland, he quit. Rop was also named in a sensitive US document from Livermore National Laboratories as a potentially dangerous hacker. Hogwash.

Rop told me, "Hacking is the abuse of technology," and I was an immediate convert to that point of view. To abuse technology is to push it to its limits, to the outer limits of its capabilities to see what happens. A car enthusiast will push his vehicle to the Red Line of performance until the whole auto is shaking; he will attempt to improve upon the manufacturer's efforts and tweak the timing or the gear ratios or diddle with air/gas mixtures until he has squeezed every last ounce of performance from the engine. That's hacking.

I often ask audiences to tell me about the greatest hack in history.

They suggest the Morris Internet Worm of 1988,[15] the NATO or CIA or FBI web page hacks, and an assortment of other reasonably notable

---

[14]His exploits were so well-exploited that *Times* reporter John Markoff and alleged Mitnick victim Tsotumo Shimamura wrote an absolutely awful book called *Takedown* which is subsequently being turned into a movie.
[15]Robert Morris Jr. is blamed with releasing a virus-like Worm which brought much of the Internet of the day to a grinding halt. He said it was an accident. Search on "Robert Morris."

events. I counter that the greatest hack in history was memorialized in the film "Apollo XIII."

Popular techno-lore says that Steve Jobs and Steve Wozniak, the creators and founders of Apple Computer, Inc., were hackers who made and sold Blue Boxes which allowed folks to make free telephone calls. But the truth is, a reasonably good engineer in any discipline at all is a hacker. Airplane designers, chemists, forensics specialists—they all require knowledge, capability and creativity to be the best that they can be—and that is hacking. A friend of mine works at a nuclear weapons laboratory. His job is to hack the nukes. He comes up with every conceivable method to break into the bomb, cause it to go off without authorization, and compromise its electronic security mechanisms. I hope he is very, very good at his job.

The sound-byte-laden popular opinion that hackers are criminals is just plain wrong. I hope that by the end of this book you will see that the hacker/techno/computer community is merely an echo of the spectrum of society as a whole, each with its evil dark side as well as its balancing and more prevalent benevolent good side.

Creating a taxonomy for hackers is a cruel task. No matter what I do, what I say, and where I draw the lines, I will be criticized. The range of opinions are so widespread that consensus is not achievable. Nonetheless, some attempt is better than no attempt, so I'll try to offer a reasonable classification of the hacking community. Keep in mind a few things:

1. Just as in the Internet and much of the new information society, nothing is static. What was true when I wrote this in late 1999 may evolve or mutate into something else in 2000 or 2001. This is a dynamic culture, a dynamic period of history, and the one constant we know is that everything will change.

2. This is not an attempt at a fixed taxonomy, rather a beginning for us to use and build upon.

3. The lines are gray. There is no white and black dividing line between each category; it's a slippery slope with many overlapping characteristics from one to the next. The only exception there might be is the line between legal and criminal behavior, but even that is extremely complex.

Hackers (Haxorz, Haxors)

The best guess from law enforcement and opinion-driven surveys is that there are somewhere between 500,000 and 5 million hackers worldwide. I hate this kind of survey because it assumes the word "hacker" means whatever the reader wants it to mean. I use the term hacker to include anyone truly proficient in software coding (programming), debugging systems, or identifying vulnerabilities and weaknesses in networks and computers.

At hacker conventions anywhere from 100 to 3,000 people show up, most of them proudly wearing the hacker moniker. When you query the crowd though, and ask the older folks (older than thirty years) in shorts and t-shirts, they'll tell you that only 5 percent of the attendees are any good, and that the rest are hangers-on, looky-loos, script kiddies, or bozos in search of a TV crew.

When psychologists analyze the hacker community, they come up with quite a laundry list of personalities as well, not all of them complimentary. However, again, such analyses tend to look at the loud media-driven hacking views, not the quiet, behind-the-scenes hackers who in fact may be more dangerous and malicious than those that crave attention.

1. Hackers are largely males from age 12–28. Apply a bell curve and it will do just fine, with a concentration in the late teens and early twenties. I know lots of hackers in their thirties, too, but the hacker population is being fed by preteens with technology at their fingertips. Women just don't seem to be as interested in the technology as the guys do, which certainly echoes the male–female ratio of science and math education in colleges and at technical jobs in the workplace. In the sciences, the male of the species dominates. Something to do with the right brain, left brain thing.

2. Dysfunctional upbringings and families are extremely common. With a national divorce rate of 50 percent, it's no surprise that unsupervised kids, especially those without a male role model, will tests the limits of acceptable behavior.

3. Drugs and alcohol abuse are also common in this crowd. They do drugs I have never even heard of. Of course, the older hackers grew up, and either moderation or abstinence are much more the norm.

4. Hackers tend to be very smart but they also tend to perform below par in school. Smart kids in the public school system are all too often pegged as troublemakers because their boredom level is so high. My son is bright, and is often bored with the tedium of multiplication tables he has known since kindergarten.

5. Many have addictive personalities, which partially explains why so many of them can sit for endless hours at their keyboard and monitor. Consider that the world's greatest psychologists are hired by gaming companies like Nintendo. Their goal is to create games using risk/reward activities which are inherently addictive. Hacking is certainly a risk/reward endeavor, but the downside is also greater than losing at Pac-Man.

6. According to psychologists, many hackers exhibit Narcissistic Personality Disorder. They crave the attention they didn't receive while growing up in broken homes. Like so many children, younger hackers act in ways that will attract attention, gain peer approval (bragging rights) and maybe land their exploits on the front page of the *New York Times*.

7. A lot of hackers are still children. I'm talking about the twenty-to-thirtysomethings who still have no life, no wife, no mortgage, and who live in a fantasy world of Unix and ASCII instead of diapers and PTA. The Peter Pan syndrome for so many of these terribly skilled yet immature men and women is a life-limiting handicap from which they need recovery.

Cliff Stoll, author of *The Cuckoo's Egg*, added one item to this list: "And," he assured me, "they can't get a date!" No matter, their priorities are different.

Arrogance is a key trait among hackers—perhaps understandably so. Hackers are different. Braggadocio runs rampant and claims of new exploits are often exaggerated beyond the believable.

"Hey, I broke into the White House, man."

"Sure. How did you do it?"

"Not gonna tell you. You're a lamer."

Never mind that www.WhiteHouse.Gov is a stand-alone web server that sits isolated from all other networks in an office where the Secret Service investigates any threatening email to the president.

"Hey, we got into the Pakistani nuclear weapons program server."

"No you didn't you lying sack of shit."

"The hell we didn't. It was easy, the Pakis are real lamers. No clue on how to protect their server."

"So what did you get?"

"Nuclear test data."

"Lemme see it . . ."

"No, man. I'm saving it if I ever need it."

"Right."

The closet nature of many hackers is driven by their emotional need for bragging rights and recognition. Many hackers want to claim credit for their successes but also avoid the details to support their claims. The competitive nature of the hacker underground keeps many alleged exploits and hacks within small cadres of hacking friends and also creates a sense of distrust when such claims are made. The final problem many hackers face is that if they do announce a notorious hack they performed, and then support it, they could face the ugly specter of gun-waving law enforcement visiting them at 5:00 AM.

Not all hackers fit every trait or act in such an immature way, but the psychologists who study hacking say that the profiles they create are an aid in predicting computer crime and hacking, and in narrowing down the list of potential suspects during an investigation.

Under the banner of *hacker* lies a finer granularity of people and groups:

Elite (Uber-Hacker)

Elite (also spelled 31it3 in hacker ASCII) represents the crème de la crème of the hacking community. Or so they say. Some hackers are elite by their very longevity. Others are called elite because of a particularly successful hack they did. Other elite hackers openly publish a hack or discover a significant weakness in a system. One cannot call one's self elite; the moniker must be given by others as a sign of respect. There is a degree of arrogance that goes hand in hand with becoming an elite hacker. Of all the hackers out there, only a handful have achieved the elite or uber-hacker status.

White Hats

These are hackers who may have operated illegally at one time or another but have since sworn off their past. Or maybe they never did anything illegal ever and just hack for the love of hacking. They are engineers.

Some may have actually done substantial damage to systems, broken into important US computers, or abused communications services. But that's all in the past, white hat hackers say. *All* in the past. "I've grown up and want to do good security work. I don't hack anymore."

However, psychologists agree that once a teenager or young adult has acquired the skills, it may be very difficult for him to stop breaking into computers. It's the nature of the beast. I have found this to be partially true.

Right or wrong, when a young person admits to having done malicious or criminal hacking in the past, it is a tough call to decide if he's really through with it. One hacker I know got nabbed by the feds, then claimed to clean up his act, only to walk onto the premises of a big financial company with a complete set of lock picks. How much contrition is there?

It comes down to ethics and morality. The rules seem to be different with computer crime than with physical crime. The argument goes, "If I don't do any damage, why should it be a crime?" This is the same argument that has been used to defend "educational" hacking. If a hacker wants to learn abut a new operating system or network, how else can he do it but to break into a distant computer and play around until he learns it? If the victim company experiences computer problems as a result, the educational defense goes out the window. Besides, according to US federal law, possessing passwords to a system without permission or entering a computer without permission is a felony.

Consider the following case: A family goes shopping. They leave their front door open. Along comes some harmless person who notices the open door, walks into the house and looks around. He doesn't touch anything and then leaves the house exactly as he found it. Is that ethical? Moral? Is it legal?

These are some of the fundamental questions that society faces today. How do we handle an entire component of society that operates by a set of rules that they designed independent of the "establishment" rules and mores?[16]

White hat hackers claim to have made the transition. They say they function by the accepted norms of society. Some of them mean it. Others are providing lip service for naïve ears.

---

[16]This is the same question the US military faces. In September 1999, Chinese colonels wrote a book called *Unrestricted War*. The Chinese maintain that since they could not beat the US in conventional war as defined by the West, they now declare civilian targets and private infrastructure as legitimate targets.

Black Hats

If black hats are any good, you don't know who they are. They hide very well and do not have the ego drive to be openly recognized. They work alone or with very small groups of people whom they trust implicitly. Typically the black hat is up to no good. He is working for his own advantage, according to his own rules, and without regard to the effects of his deeds.

Many hacking groups operate as anonymously as possible. That's part of the game, making it harder to detect their activities and catch them. When the Hacking For Girlies broke into the *New York Times* in 1998, they only identified themselves by that name. Otherwise, they could go to jail. Breaking the law is a darn good reason not to announce your real name and address. But, in hacker parlance, many of these black hats are media-whores: They want the attention and the recognition, without the jail time. Occasionally the media interviews these hackers, giving them the desired publicity, but with their true identities hidden.

The agenda of black hats is varied:

1. They might be promoting a social movement or cause: environmental, anti-nuclear, anti-McDonald's, for Kurds or freedom in China.

2. They may have a vendetta against a person or organization. An increased number of attacks against the Department of Defense occurred during the Kosovo crisis. The FBI also found itself under direct attack as a result of their anti-hacker efforts and arrests in 1999.

3. They may be bored and in need of something interesting to do.

4. Maybe it's just to be mean. Again, we see an echo of modern society manifesting itself as pugilistic behavior just for the sake of being a pain in the ass. Many black hats allow their asshole gene to furiously multiply, infecting their other cells to the point that their usefulness is stifled by overwhelming arrogance and attitude.

5. Some black hats are merely criminal hackers whose agenda is profit-oriented. Kevin Mitnick is accused of this in his litany of criminal charges.

Ethical Hackers

Ethical hackers are generally white hats who are hired to test the security of companies. In many cases they have to be heavily insured, sometimes bonded, and strict rules are enforced. No renegade activities are permitted.

Crackers

Crackers are criminal hackers. Since so much hacking is truly useful to the information technology community as a whole, it's difficult to label all hacking as "bad." Groups like the L0pht, Cult of the Dead Cow, and Dis.Org openly hack, but they hack within controlled environments, and most decry criminal hacking in any form. Security professionals and software vendors may hate having their security problems exposed in such an "in your face" manner, but perhaps history will judge these hacking efforts in a positive light. The balance between openness and secrecy is a fine-edged sword.

Hacking does cross into blatantly illegal behavior, which the US (and other countries) have strictly defined.

1. If you possess passwords to a computer or network that you do not have permission to use, you have broken a US federal law and perhaps many others.

2. If you actually enter a computer system without permission, even if there are no security controls or password blocking mechanisms, you have also committed a felony.

Hackers who engage in this behavior are called crackers. They actually break into the systems that they have learned how to penetrate. They may do no damage there, but the law makes no distinction. If damage is done, there will be even more charges if the cracker is caught.

Phreaks (Phreakers)

Before computers there were telephones. In the old days, rotary dial telephones ruled. Three slots for a nickel, dime, and quarter.

My corner drugstore had one of these phones when I was kid and that's where I learned how to make free phone calls. I cut a piece of stiff construction board about twelve inches long and three-eighths of an inch wide. Then I carefully slid the strip down the dime slot as far as it would go. If I wanted to make a call, I'd pick up the phone, get a dial tone and put a penny into the nickel slot. The phone registered the penny as a dime, the call was made, and I got my penny back.

That was an amateur form of phreaking: telephone hacking. The term comes from the anti-war efforts of the late 1960s when Abbie Hoffman and his followers (and hippies in general) referred to themselves as Freaks. The "ph" was from phone. Voilà Phreaks.

Telephone company security used to be more abysmal than it is today. I sat with a hacker named billsf in Holland one day in the early 1990s and he demonstrated. He had access to the local Dutch phone company controls and made a free call to it.

"Now, I am connecting to a telephone switch in Italy . . ." Dial, dial. Still no charges. "Now I am going to Moscow where they really have no security." Dial, dial. India. Singapore. Sydney, Australia, San Francisco, New York, London, and then the other phone on his desk rang.

"Pick it up." I did and the voice, delayed by about two seconds, was billsf's.

The telephone system was the first global computer and it was a legitimate political target. AT&T ruled as a monopoly. ITT was publicly indicted as being part of some CIA disaster in Chile. They had too much money, too much power and anything that rang of the establishment during the Vietnam era was fair game. Revolution, man. Are you ready?

While telco security is far improved today, phreaks still go after them because of their infinite connectivity, although with the Internet and IP (Internet Protocol) taking over, there is less than there was. Using the telephones as an element of social engineering, though, and using large companies' private telephone systems as launching pads for other exploits is still common.

Teleabuse and fraud, including cellular fraud, accounts for billions of dollars in losses annually. Cellular hacking, an outgrowth of phreaking, made news as criminal endeavors "cloned" the chips inside of stolen cellular telephone signals and created massive Phone Home operations within immigrant communities.

Simply, when you make a cell call, your identifying information is broadcast with your voice. Cell scanners can pick up this information, store it, and then phreak/engineers program new chips with your identifying codes in it and run up huge phone bills—which go straight to you.

Script Kiddies, Wannabes, Push-Button Hackers

The South Korean Defense Department called and told me that they might have have some interesting contract work for my company, but first they needed some information. They wanted me to send them every security exploit I knew of. Then we could talk business. No, I didn't send them anything, but their approach echoed that of what many serious hackers and security engineers call script kiddies(z).

This category of hackers is reserved for those who do not develop their own hacking tools, do not analyze code, cannot program, and do not really understand what information security is all about. The script kiddies scour hacking sites for tools developed by other people, download them, use them, and call themselves hackers. No one really knows what percentage of the hacking community fit here, but based upon what I have heard, it appears to be in the 95+ percent arena.

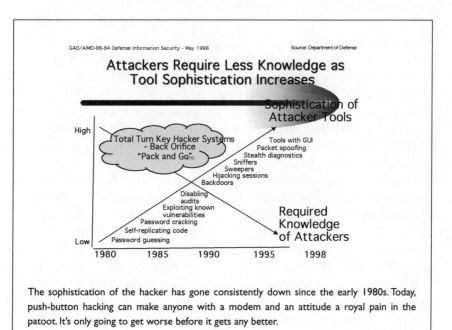

The sophistication of the hacker has gone consistently down since the early 1980s. Today, push-button hacking can make anyone with a modem and an attitude a royal pain in the patoot. It's only going to get worse before it gets any better.

Certainly many of the script kiddies are computer science students who want to learn about security and networking. That is part of the reason that exploits are published: Educate the vendors and the community, and increase the state of the art.

However, a large percentage of the script kiddies merely download the tools and then attempt to use them in attack mode. That is why so many thousands and perhaps millions of "attacks" occur every year and are on the increase. I don't mean to denigrate those who are truly trying to use such tools and software for education, but mindlessly going after the White House, the Pentagon, and US Airways is stupid—and in many case stupidly criminal.

If you want to play with hacking tools, fine. But use it on your own networks which you control, or on networks where you have been given permission to hack.

The script kiddies make it difficult for security professionals and law enforcement to tell the difference between a real attack and some automated information-gathering lark by a bunch of middle-school kids from Barnblack, Arkansas. Their activities make it easier for the real computer criminal to get away with his hacks. The noise level is so high that separating the chaff from serious cyber-assaults is tough. Script kiddies are pretty much held in low esteem by hackers, software engineers, large companies, and law enforcement.

Warez Dudez

These guys have been around forever. Their goal in life is to get free software. They don't want to pay Gates and Company a dime. They want their latest *Doom* or *Dungeons and Dragons* for free. Back in the early 1980s, lots of Apple software was copy-protected to counter software piracy. Nintendo puts extensive anti-piracy mechanisms into their products. Warez dudez want them all, and they want to give it away for free to their friends, too.

There is a legitimate discussion on the nature of freeware or open source software: Should software be free? Linux is a notable open source software success where the operating system was written and free distribution was encouraged. The business would follow on later. Netscape helped pioneer the business of giving away free software and others have followed suit.

But in general, a software company wants to be paid for its software. According to the Software Publishers Association (often called the Software Police) an estimated 50 percent of all software worldwide is bootleg. In Hong Kong, around the Far East, in Russia and other emerging countries, you can buy every piece of software Microsoft has ever written for 100 dollars. Forget about getting support because it's illegal software, and beware of viruses and trojans, but still you can buy it.

Not too long ago Warez bulletin boards openly published their bootleg deeds, but with the SPA in cooperation with law enforcement and major software vendors, copyright violations are being vigorously prosecuted.

Criminals

"Why would criminals hack?"

I prefer the question, "Why would criminals *not* hack?" If thousands of kids are successfully causing mayhem, why shouldn't organized crime (and smaller criminals, too) use the same tools, which have proved to be so highly effective?

Citibank was victimized for millions of dollars by a man from St. Petersburg, Russia—and he was caught. Drug cartels are using advanced and legally available encryption to hide their activities.

The true criminal is not going to use only on-line hacking in the furtherance of his riches. He is going to resort to the old tried-and-true techniques that have served him so well in the past: extortion, blackmail, and physical breaking and entering. Hacking is a skill to be added to their arsenal just as is having a list of good getaway drivers.

As more sophisticated hacking tools are developed, criminals are going to employ them for their own goals. But the best hack is to get an insider to work with you—in any way you can.

On-line espionage is part of the criminal equation. The FBI has more espionage cases on their plate now than ever before and many of the cases are highly technical in nature. Translation: They involve hacking.

Just keep in mind that if there is a way to make a criminal's job easier and safer, he is going to use it. Thinking any less of your adversary is naïve and dangerous.

Terrorist Hacking (International, US-centric)

One step up from profit-oriented criminals is the terrorist. Again, the question we have to ask is "Why would they *not* use hacking if it helps them?"

Anti-terrorist experts have added hacking and the Internet to the other weapons of mass destruction such as nuclear, biological, and chemical threats. Pakistan runs a "terrorist" information warfare educational center on the Internet, allegedly headquartered in London. Mid-East factions have called the Internet "a weapon to be mastered."

When queried about what worries federal law enforcement the most, the off-the-record answer in a quiet restaurant is "the US militia." Ruby Ridge and Waco bring up images of extreme Americans scared of their government. I am not debating their cause here, but by living in the US they have easier access to even more technology than their overseas counterparts. After all, they are Americans!

Law enforcement has serious concerns that extreme US militia groups might resort to intense cyber-assaults against the government and critical US infrastructures such as transportation, power, and emergency services.

I remember the former head of the FBI in New York, Jim Kallstrom, talking about terrorism; he discussed cases where they had caught an operative terrorist cell getting ready to shoot down airplanes at O'Hare airport in Chicago, and another one planning to poison the water supply of a Northeast city.

Terrorism generally conjures images of bombs and indiscriminate death. However, depending upon the goals of the terrorist, other means might well suffice. Using cryptography and anonymity certainly advances their abilities. Using offensive hacking tools in large-scale attacks in combination with effective pointed messaging on the Internet might serve a similar purpose.

Nation-state Hacking

When the National Security Agency ran a test to see how much damage North Korea could do to the United States using only cyber-weapons, the "bad guys" were able to shut down significant portions of American life within seven days. In an exercise called *Eligible Receiver*, they only used the hacker tools from the Internet and attacked with a vengeance.

They went after banks, Wall Street, the airlines, water and oil distribution, as well as communications systems, and the effects were astounding to the military and civilian leaders who participated or observed the exercise.

In Peter Schweizer's book *Friendly Spies*, he discusses the German national hacking project, RAHAB, established in 1988. The goal was to map the world's electronic highways and see what systems could be attacked, information gathered and put to use by German industry and government.

In 1990, the former French leader of their CIA, Count de Maranches, published *The Third World War* and revealed the extent of French spying against the US. Notably, he omitted details of any hacking efforts on their part.

At an intelligence conference in Washington DC, I asked a former Soviet KGB colonel, "Has the Soviet Union or Russia engaged in any foreign hacking and what do you do?" The colonel leaned over to his KGB associates, chatted in Russian for a moment, then replied in a thick accent, "If we have, we will not tell you about it." During the Cold War, the Russians aggressively targeted 3,500 US technologies every year, with a focus on military applications. Since the Cold War, the spying continues but with a bent for commercial usage.

According to the FBI, at least 122 countries now have on-line intelligence and spying capabilities. Again, keep asking yourself why they would not be engaged in such activities considering how low the risk is of getting caught, much less extradicted and prosecuted under US law.

Yes, Virginia, there is a *world* of hacking going on.

US Information Warriors

Does the US government itself hack? Here are some data points:

1. In 1995-6, I developed offensive hacking scenarios for the US military. It was called ECO-D, or Economic Deactivation, and was a model on how to use hacking techniques to project US power when needed. Oddly enough, the model I used was eerily similar to the 1999 Yugoslavian situation.

2. Many hackers I know have been contracted by the US Government because of their superior skills. Many are still actively engaged with the military.

3. Many of these "training sessions" occur at US bases overseas.

4. The Pentagon "struck back" at hackers from the Electronic Disruption Theater in September of 1998.

5. The US absolutely has the capability to hack its adversaries.

6. In May of 1999, MSNBC reported that the US was looking for ways to attack the financial holdings of the Serbian leader, Milosovic.

From 1994 to the present the US has developed very high levels of hacking skills; it would be supremely dumb if they hadn't. The Air Force Information Warfare Center in San Antonio, Texas is often credited with the highest skill sets. Several of their senior staff left and have commercialized products developed at the center. The Naval Warfare Center is aggressively working on defensive approaches to hacking. Every branch of the military is hotly pursuing ways to stay competitive in a world of asymmetric warfare: war where the other guys play by a different set of rules than the rest of us. Under the guise of information warfare or information operation, contracts abound on how to defend against cyber-attacks, but the offensive capabilities are shrouded in secrecy.

Of course we have offensive capability, and a lot of it comes from the hackers. Why not use what works?

Classified programs run by government contractors are developing extensive offensive hacking tools which in all likelihood exceed the power of on-line hacking tools. They understandably want to keep their capabilities secret from the bad guys, but many insiders swear that they can't do much more than hackers can themselves. Which is not bad, especially if you feed your good-guy US information warriors with powerful computers, slabs and slabs of money, and virtually assured anonymity. You'll get the best minds money can buy.

Hacker Gangs

Most hackers are fiercely individualistic by nature, but there is also a great deal of camaraderie despite their differences. Children play in packs, companies need multiple people with multiple talents to get business done, and so it is with hacker gangs. The term "gang" is more extreme than hacker groups, and may only show the differing motives, but still groups of hackers do get together and hack as teams. There are literally hundreds of these groups.

1. Hacking for Girlies took responsibility for the highly publicized *New York Times* hack which targeted *Times* writer John Markoff as well as *Happy Hacker* author Carolyn Meinel.

Hacking for Girliez (HFG) gained notoriety after the *New York Times* web hack of late 1998.

2. The Legion of the Underground (LoU) announced it was declaring war on China for its humanitarian violations.

3. The MoD, Masters of Destruction (or Deception) was involved in a hacker war with the Legion of Doom for years, ending in many of the MoD members being incarcerated.

4. The CHAOS Computer Club in Germany has shown libertarian political bents.

5. Dis.Org claims to be purely ethical and interested in security endeavors, with many of its members in legitimate corporate positions.

6. The L0pht is a Boston-based group who have testified before Congress, and are known for writing password-cracking schemes. They offer security consulting.

Don't get the idea that a mean hacker group name in any way indicates whether they are white hat or black hat or anything else for that matter. Hacker names and hacker group names are all about image and posturing for image. Eric Bloodaxe. Cheshire Catalyst. Captain Crunch. What do they say about the person behind the name? *2600 Magazine* publisher Eric Corley has used Emmanuel Goldstein from Orwell's *1984* as his public name since 1984. What's in a name. Sir Dystic. Se7en. Spiderwoman. Dr. Delam. Lou Cipher. These are alter egos at work, much like we all adopted during the CB craze of the 1970s. Smokey and the Bandit sped down southern back roads. Phiber Optic hacked his way to jail. Then there's the little white Jewish kid who used the moniker SuperNigger.

Names. Just names.

Hacking groups also compete for recognition by the conventional media yet decry their "clueless" reporting. They occasionally go to war like the MoD and LoD did in the early 1990s. Today's hacker battles often target Carolyn Meinel, who attracts her hacker detractors in droves and actually runs on-line hacking war games on her web site.[17]

Like killer gangs the Crips and the Bloods of the Los Angeles barrios, hacker groups manifest common interest, mutual support, and dislike of other groups. But, unlike Crips and Bloods, they don't carry Uzis.

Drive-by hacking is thankfully one hell of a lot less offensive or deadly than drive-by shootings. You will hear throughout this book about various groups who are aligned for their particular reasons and motivations. Before rendering judgment, though, you might just want to go check out their web sites and let them speak for themselves.

Be Very Scared. Be Very, Very Scared.

If all of this begins to sound like all-out war, in many ways it is. A new kind of war, to be sure, but conflict all the same.

---

[17] www.happyhacker.org
www.techbroker.com

As in any conflict, in order to be able to defend yourself, you have to know how the bad guys will be coming after you. What tools/weapons will they use? How do they think? What are their capabilities? What other conditions will influence their behavior?

The hacker community is serving a larger purpose than merely breaking and entering computers for giggles. The serious white hat hackers provide a worldwide test bed for security weaknesses of the myriad systems upon which society depends for its very survival.

So please, don't think that all hackers are bad. Yeah, some are a royal pain in the ass—yup! But as in any community they are in the minority and by and large are not the sophisticated elite hackers, who generally want to help not hurt. At the same time, do not underestimate what a dedicated, well-financed technical adversary can achieve in short order.

This hacker overview is far from complete. Entire theses are written about the culture and it is worth the effort to do some additional reading. The US military is performing extensive studies into the psychology of hackers and what makes them tick, then using that information to detect hacker attacks and find the perpetrators.

The hacker culture is very rich and complex, and the divisions I have used are certainly gray and artificial, but we need to have some basis from which to work. For example, other hacker categories occasionally used to include trainspotters, whose sole goal is to break into as many systems as possible for bragging rights. Kilroys leave a sign they have been there. Lamers . . . well lamers are lamers, as you will see.

Every time I go to a web site or read the news or speak to folks in the underground or in officialdom, I learn something new. So should you. Do not be content with my explanations—go on out there and form your own opinions.

We security people and writers live on the fringe of hackerdom, but just 'cause we do doesn't mean what we say is 100 percent right. Just because the US Attorney General indicts a hacker doesn't mean he is a criminal. Craig Neidorf was indicted by the feds for publishing supposedly secret internal Bell South documents worth hundreds of thousands of dollars in the hacker zine *Phrack*. His family spent a fortune on his defense until the feds dropped the charges. It turned out the information was also in a Bell South pamphlet with a price tag of something like $12.95. Who's the real criminal there? Right.

The hugely expensive law enforcement sting, Operation Sun Devil, goes down in history as an embarrassing sweep of supposed hackers and confiscation of their computers; it was of no value to the public.

Despite more than two decades of personal computers and various forms of the Internet, and years of the web, the non-technical politicians, the rigid mind-sets of lawyers and some law enforcement officials only exacerbate the myths and lies about hackers and hacking.

Should you be scared? Yes. Absolutely. But not so much of the freaky looking purple-haired kid down the street.

Hopefully by the end of this book you will know who to be scared of, what the real personal, corporate, and national hacking issues are, and what you can do about it.

So, don't panic yet. Wait till you've finished this book.

Welcome to the world of hacking and anti-hacking. Cyberwar. The offense and defense of Cyberspace. This is *CyberShock*.

▶ Look Who's Hacking?

Amateur Hacking	Professional Hacking
Who?	**Who?**
Kids	Foreign Nations
Teens	Competitors
Miscreants	Technical Mercenaries
Students	Nation-State & Corps.
Non-Affiliated	Former Intelligence
Mostly Males 12–28	Foreign Military
Troublemakers	Terrorist Groups
Security Interest	Political/Social Sects
Vendors/Developers	Religious Fringe
Global	US Government
Why?	**Why?**
Thrill	Economic Gain
Bragging Rights/Ego	Mercenary Jobs
Learning	National Strength
Harassment	Competitive Intelligence
Boredom	Political Power
Occasional Profit	Religious Influence
Security Enhancement	Prelude to Conflict/Conflict
Embarrass Vendors	Sanctions

Resources?	Resources?
Individual	Terrorists in Cells
Generally Splintered Groups	Formal Organization
No $$$	Lots of $$$
Ready Technology/COTS	$1–$10 million for National effort
Some Programming Skills	Any tecnology at all, w/Govt.
NT, Unix but few other technical skills	Any skill set required
Limited Pool of Talent	Large Pool of Talent
No Training	Professionally Trained

CyberChrist at the Hacker Con

Las Vegas, Nevada, USA

When adrenaline-driven teenage computer hackers sporting *Scientology Kills* t-shirts are body-pierced with enough metal in their tongues, eyebrows, and genitals to shift a compass's magnetic north reading, people tend to notice.

When trailer-park trash suddenly see themselves at the summit of life's gene pool in the presence of these visually disturbing individuals, you gotta know the party's about to begin.

And again I got hired to run Hacker Jeopardy at the July DefCon, the premier hacking convention in the world. Only problem is, how will these two cultures mesh?

Hurtling down Industrial Drive in a sparkling white Chrysler Sebring JXI convertible with only fifty-four miles on the odometer, we pass behind the great Las Vegas hotels. The 118 degree air parches my eyeballs to the point where I am willing to flush them out with the hot beer we ripped from a fat tourist's hands while at a red light.

CyberChrist is behind the wheel, recklessly meandering in and out of the vast traffic flows that Las Vegas was not designed to handle. Jorge, the Irish Mexican hacker, holds a senior engineering position at a major ISP when he is sober. He is sitting next to CyberChrist muttering Jim Morrison's motto in a thick Russian accent: "Drink, sing, drink, sleep, drink, die," as he swigs from the Stoli bottle. "Hot vodka is better than no vodka," he shouts to a disbelieving family of fourteen on their annual trek to Lady Luck from Who Cares, Oklahoma. My two-bedroom suitcase doesn't fit in the Sebring's trunk, so it gets put into the back seat where I am jammed next to an overweight green-neophyte-tenderfoot sales guy from a DC-based software company with more money then sense. We are embarrassingly glued together from the waist down, and we each try to skirt a silly millimeter farther from each other to insure our long-term heterosexuality.

"It's there!" CyberChrist screams over the bass-booming sound system which is blasting BTO's *Takin' Care of Business*.

"Kto?" Russian for "huh?" The vodka bottle is momentarily separated from Jorge's mouth.

"There. That's the Plaza," CyberChrist says with disdain. After all, he has rented a 1,600-square-foot palace suite at the pinnacle of the Luxor pyramid. I don't for a moment believe it costs 10,000 dollars a night, even with hookers included, but at DefCon, self-delusion is an absolute requisite for survival and getting one's soundbytes on CNN.

The Plaza Hotel was built in 1423, or so it seems. It sits at the ass-end of Freemont Street in downtown Las Vegas, about ten miles from the decent hotels on the Strip. Sometimes the Freemont area is called Glitter Gulch for its gaudy displays of neon and incandescence. In 1984, I was hired by ESPN and Kaypro Computers (remember them, kids?) to give away one million dollars on television and we got stuck at the Plaza then, too. And despite the desk clerk's insistence that the Plaza has gone through a major upgrade and interior improvement, I know for sure the carpet is the same as it was two decades ago. Seedy would be a compliment.

The first person we see exiting the hotel's entrance is a fifty-something homeless black man wearing Rasta hair encrusted with a lifetime of filth and neglect. At least he was wearing a sparkling new pair of Air Jordans. The Plaza's restaurant is based upon aluminum diner architecture. Food crumbs and unknown sticky liquids have been left as a reminder of meals past. But again I am assured that the food is excellent. The casino crowd stepped right out of a Carl Hiaasen novel centered in any impoverished part of Florida. I mean no disrespect, and I come to chastise myself, for even the poor folks and dregs of society need their own place to gamble. And that place is the Plaza Hotel, which loudly boasts "The Loosest Penny Slots in Vegas" and 25-cent craps. At the Plaza, the high rollers go to the two dollar blackjack tables. Phew!

My hotel room has no closet. No shit. No closet. But it does have a fabulous view south to the Strip, up to the 1,000-foot roller-coaster-capped Stratosphere, and to the surrounding mountains which provide a purple backdrop to dancing UFOs from nearby Area 51. My bathroom is five feet long, and forty-two inches wide. The plastic marble sink sits in the main part of the room, and the previous guests were kind enough to leave me two shriveled pieces of soap encrusted with fossilized pubic hairs. I look for the shampoo, and ask the impish Thai cleaning ladies, who vigorously shake their heads and sputter, "no shampoo, no shampoo."

Wonderful. The artworks on the walls are framed pictures of flowers cut out from ancient yellowed editions of the *Saturday Evening Post*. The room, other than the decaying soap, is clean, though. I specified that I wanted a clean room when I checked in. I told them I had stayed here before and the concierge got a worried look on his face.

No self-respecting hacker would go to a hacker con without the basic necessities.

Because DefCon had been virtually blackballed from the better hotels on the right side of the tracks in Las Vegas, it needed to find a new victim facility, and I guess this was the best they could do on a year's notice.

As I gambled that evening, I ran into DaCobbs, a friend from England (so he says . . .) and his wife, who is much more huggable than he is. She's some sort of spook with the National Reconnaissance Office in that one billion dollar building near Dulles Airport no one knew about till it was "outed" on "60 Minutes" one serene post-golf Sunday evening.

"They're gonna trash this place!" he says gleefully. "They're going to bloody well trash it . . ."

"They have to," I agree as the dealer shovels to my "21" a huge pile of Ruble-worthless chips with a faded tawdry picture of Jackie Gaughan, the Plaza's owner, on them. "It's a necessity. This is the worst hotel of them all."

In fact, the DefCon hackers do *so* much mind-fucking at these events, of the last five hotels that hosted DefCon (The Sands, Sahara, Tropicana, Monte Carlo and Aladdin) three were subsequently destroyed by the wrecking ball. You make the connection.

The bellman is forced to stop at the bar to pick up a dozen one dollar Heinekens for CyberChrist. And I warn him, "One year this Muslim family had flown in a few hundred close friends from around the world.

The hotel put the Muslim wedding right next to the DefCon dress-black-with-fangs Vampire Party playing the most god-awful head-bangers music at volumes they could hear in Hell. The wedding was cancelled." The bellman nervously winced.

I go on. "Then there was the time they dumped the furniture and beds from an entire floor into one room so they had enough room for their computers." But the bellboy only smiled. "There's more! They even . . ."

"I have the weekend off. But I'll be sure to spread the word." Previous DefCons have always experienced over-the-top behavior such as the con's promoter, Dark Tangent, being hustled to the airport in a big hurry because half of the Las Vegas Police Department were after him for allegedly having kids at a stripper event. Or maybe the stripping got to be more than stripping. Hell, I wasn't there. Or maybe you missed the time when "Pete" got tossed by security for fighting within eyeshot of the casino floor. Yeah, that's a party I want to attend. Another DefCon was about to begin.

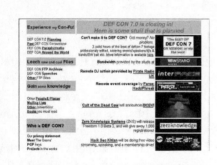

DefCon has come a long way since beginning at the first hotel it was ever thrown out of. Commercialism—hey, no red-blooded American can help it! www.defcon.org. The 1999 DefCon was a massive event, 3,000 strong, held on the right side of the tracks with little trouble.

Las Vegas has the distinction of being home to the largest of the largest conventions and exhibitions in the world.

Las Vegas: whatever you want, no matter how decadent, blasphemous, illegal or immoral, at any hour, is yours for the asking, if you have cash or a clean piece of plastic. Comdex is the world's largest computer convention, where 150,000 techno-dweebs and silk-suited glib techno-marketers display their wares to a public who is still paying off the 20 percent per annum debt on last year's greatest new electronic gismo, which is now rendered thoroughly obsolete. The Consumer Electronic Show does for consumer electronics what the First Amendment does for pornography.

And there is DefCon.

I have been hosting Haxor Jeopardy in the searing Las Vegas heat since 1994. Amidst hacker riots, purse-swinging wives whose husbands are taking off Bad Kitty's top (www.badkitty.com), Muslim weddings, and throngs of police ringing the room to keep the peace, Haxor Jeopardy is never boring. I don't know whom to credit with this spoof. Thanks, though!

It's indulgence gone wild, Vegas notwithstanding, if previous cons are any example. But now put a couple thousand techno-anarchists together in Sin City, USA, stir in liberal doses of illicit controlled pharmaceutical substances, and we have a party that Hunter Thompson would be proud to attend.

DefCon is raucous, so there is intense security once the hotel realizes what it has gotten itself into. By then the hackers have locked onto the same frequencies that the hotel's private walkie-talkie radios use so they always know where the cops are. Helpful at awkward times.

There are underage children who aren't supposed to drink drinking, and overage children who shouldn't drink drinking too much. Drugs are discreetly prevalent and hookers are the norm. But the technology is ablaze, powered by nicotine, caffeine and assorted adrenaline encouragement, in the form of huge ad hoc networks of laptops and more and more curious equipment from times past.

The music is abominable—but then again, I used to be a record producer in the heyday of rock'n'roll, so color me biased. As for dress code, if you have ever wanted to attempt a fashion statement, here's your chance. If no one notices you, you have failed.

All the while, as this anarchistic renegade regiment marches to the tune of a 24-hour city, they are under complete surveillance by the authorities. Authorities like the FBI, the Secret Service, telephone security, maybe even Interpol.

And how did the "man" arrive in tow behind the techno-slovens that belong behind bars?

They were invited.

After all, they're only hackers. I wanted to see teens and X generationers with their eyes so star sapphire–glazed over that I could trade them for chips at the craps table. Does the truth live up to the fiction?

DefCon hackers. And they seem so normal . . .

God, I hope so. It'd be downright awful and un-American if 3,000 crazed hackers didn't get into at least some serious trouble.

The Cell Hacking Party

I got invited to see a cell hacking demo; a highly illegal one at 1 AM. Sure! No names, they said. OK. No problem. In one of the several thousand hotel rooms at the Sahara was a pile of equipment to make an underbudgeted FBI surveillance team insanely jealous. There in the middle of the ridiculously filthy room that gave the maid a case of the shudders, sat a log-periodic antenna poised atop a husky adjustable photographic-style tripod. A hunk of wire was attached to a cell phone's antenna jack, along with a second cell phone/scanner and a modified Oki 900 cell phone, and some speakers to broadcast the cell conversation the hackers were intercepting. I don't know how many laws they were breaking. (The leader of this group was put away by the Feds in late 1999.)

A half dozen "kids" sat around enthralled, each begging for his turn to, as Hacker Jon put it, "harass cellular users. Pure and simple. Harassment. Stomp on the son of a bitch," he laughed, joined in by the others.

When a "good" conversation was detected, they entered the channel into the broadcasting cell phone and spoke. And talk they did. Stomping, they called it. For those on the receiving end of the harassment, it must have sounded like the overbearing voice of God telling Noah how to build the ark.

The hacker/phreaks particularly enjoyed breaking in on fighting couples. (I counted six impending divorces.) Almost without exception the man was in a car and the lady was at a fixed location, presumably home.

Him:	Where the hell have you been?
Her:	Nowhere.
Him:	Bullshit.
Her:	Really honey . . . (Defensive.)
Him:	Who's with you? (Intense anger.)
Hacker:	Don't believe her. She's a whore.
Him:	What was that?
Her:	What?
Him:	That voice.
Her:	What voice? (*She* can't hear the hacker.)
Hacker:	Me you asshole. Can't you see she's playing you for a fool.
Him:	I know she is. (The poor sap agrees.)
Her:	What's that, honey?
Him:	I know he's there with you.
Her:	Who? (Incredulous.)
Him:	That guy . . . whoever you're 'shagging' when I'm at work.
Hacker:	Yeah, it's me.
Him:	Shit! Who the hell is there?
Her:	No one!
Him:	I can hear him, he's there. You're both making fun of me . . .
Hacker:	She's laughing at you, man.
Him:	No shit. Who the hell are you?
Hacker:	The guy who takes care of her when you can't, asshole.
Him:	That's it.
Click!	

Drug dealers aren't immune to these antics.

Buyer:	Where's the meet?
Dealer:	By the 7 Eleven on Tropicana.
Buyer:	You got the stuff?
Dealer:	You got the cash?
Buyer:	Yeah, dude.
Dealer:	Be sure you do.
Hacker:	He doesn't have the cash, my man. He's gonna rip you off. What?!
	What?! (This time both sides heard the intruder's voice.)

Buyer:	Who is that?
Dealer:	What's that about a rip-off?
Buyer:	This ain't no rip-off man.
Hacker:	Yes it is. Tell 'em the truth. You gonna take his drugs and shoot his ass. Right? Tell 'em.
Dealer:	You gonna rip me off?
Buyer:	No, man!
Dealer:	Your homeboy says you gonna try and rip me off?
Buyer:	What homeboy?
Hacker:	Me, you bozo drug freak. Don't you know that shit can kill you?

Click!

Good samaritanism pays off upon occasion. This time it's CyberChrist to the rescue.

Her:	Honey, hurry up.
Him:	I'm on the freeway. I'm coming.
Hacker:	He's late. Let's save her ass.
Him:	What was that?
Her:	What did you say, honey?
Hacker:	He said he was going to save your ass.
Him:	Who did?
Her:	The guy on the radio. (Technical ignorance abounds.)
Hacker:	Me. You're late and she's scared so we're gonna beat you there and make her safe.
Him:	Who the hell is that?
Her:	Who?
Him:	The guy with you?
Her:	There's no one here.
Him:	He says he's gonna beat me there and pick you up.
Hacker:	Damn right we are.
Her:	Hey, this is cool. Who's there?
Hacker:	CyberChrist talking to you from Silicon Heaven.
Her:	No shit. Really?
Hacker:	Yeah, (choke, laugh) really.
Him:	What's happening, honey?
Her:	I don't know, for sure. He says it's God.
Him:	God!?!?
Hacker:	Close enough. Listen, you sound alright. Go get your woman, man. Keep her safe.

Him: No problem. Uh, thanks.
Click!

Around 4 AM, the hacker/phreaks definitely helped out law enforcement. One end of the conversation was coming from inside a hotel, maybe even the Sahara. The other from another cell phone, most likely in the lobby.

Her: What do you look like?
Him: I'm five foot nine, thinning brown hair, and 180 pounds. I wear round glasses and . . .
Her: I get the idea. Where are you now?
Him: I'm coming down the elevator now. What do you look like?
Her: I'm six foot one in my heels, have long blond spiked hair and black fishnet stockings.
Hacker: Don't go man. It's a bust.
Him: What?
Hacker: Don't go, it's a bust. You don't want your name in the papers, do ya?
Her: What the fuck?
Him: There's a guy who says this is a bust.
Her: Bust? What bust?
Hacker: That's the clue, man. She's denying it. Of course it's a bust. Is it worth a night in jail to not get laid?
           (He whispers not too quietly to another male companion.)
           Shit. There's some guy on the phone who says it's a bust. What should we do?)
Hacker: I'm telling you man, don't go.
Him: This ain't worth it. I'm going back.
Click!

A couple of hours later the same hooker was overheard talking to one of her workmates.

Then this jerk says it's a bust. Cost me 300 dollars in lost business.
You, too? Same shit been going on all night long.
What the . . . ?

Hackers. That's what.

The FBI Speaks

Andy Black was the man who investigated Vladimir Levin and the Citibank hacker heist in the early 1990s. He is part of the FBI's San Francisco Computer Crime Squad. And now he is speaking at DefCon about how to catch hackers. Massive attendance for his speech; police ringing the room just in case the hackers turn violent, which they never do, with a small handful of notable exceptions.

The most often asked question at one of these sessions is, "Where can I get a job?" Andy politely hands out applications to join the FBI. I don't know how many get filled out or how many, if any, are taken seriously, but it is a great PR move to keep the hackers pacified: "Yes, your government does want your help—if you're made of the right stuff."

Andy started his speech with a joke. Or half a joke that is. He held up an FBI t-shirt as a prize. "The best answer to this question wins the shirt." Silence, waiting for the FBI to speak. "How many FBI agents does it take to screw in a lightbulb?"

Hands up everywhere. Andy calls on one.

"Two."

The audience was silent. Andy stares and looks disbelievingly at the kid. Two? Next.

"Fourteen. One to turn what's left of the bulb after the other thirteen shoot it." Mild laughter. And so it went. Dumb and dumber. Andy called on me.

"FBI agents don't screw in lightbulbs. They screw in hot tubs!" I won the t-shirt hands down. This is the gentler, kinder, post–Ruby Ridge FBI.

Arizona prosecutor Gail Thackeray and her hacker friends. They swear she drank them all under the table. I wasn't there, but she has earned a sailor's reputation.

The Information Call: Hackers on Planet Earth, New York

Emmanuel Goldstein, publisher of *2600, The Hacker Quarterly* is very funny. He also knows a lot about social engineering.

"Sometimes you have to call the phone company back. Sometimes you have to call over and over to get what you want. You have to keep in mind that the people at the other end of the phone are generally not as intelligent as a powered-down computer." He proceeded to prove the point in front of a thousand hackers, the media, and telephone security. Sort of Candid Camera. You just don't know what these guys will pull.

Ring, ring.

Shhhhh. Ssshhh. Quiet. Shhhh.

"Directory Assistance."

"I need some information."

"How can I help you?"

"Is this where I get numbers?"

"What number would you like?"

"Information."

"This is information."

"You said directory assistance."

"This is."

"But I need information."

"What information do you need?"

"For information."

"This is information."

"What's the number?"

"For what?"

"Information."

"This is directory assistance."

"I need the number for information."

Pause. Pause.

"What number do you want?"

"For information."

Pause. Guffaws, some stifled, some less so. Funny stuff.

"Hold on please."

Pause.

"Supervisor. May I help you?"

"Hi."

"Hi."

Pause.

"Can I help you?"

"I need the number for information."

"This is directory assistance."

"Hi."

"Hi."

"What's the number for information?"

"This is information."

"What about directory assistance?"

"This is directory assistance."

"But I need information."

"This is information."

"Oh, OK. What's the number for information?"

Pause.

"Ah, 411."

"That's it?"

"No. 555-1212 works too."

"So there's two numbers for information?"

"Yes."

"Which one is better?" How this audience kept its cool was beyond me. Me and my compatriots were beside ourselves.

Pause.

"Neither."

"Then why are there two?"

Pause.

"I don't know."

"OK. So I can use 411 or 555-1212."

"That's right."

"And which one should I use?"

Pause.

"411 is faster." Huge guffaws. Ssshhhh. Ssshhhh.

"Oh. What about the ones?"

"Ones?"

"The ones."

"Which ones?"

"The ones at the front of the number."

"Oh, those ones. You don't need ones. Just 411 or 555-1212."

"My friends say they get to use ones." Big laugh. Shhhhhh.

"That's only for long distance."

"To where?" How does he keep a straight face?

Pause.

"If you wanted 914 information you'd use a one."

"If I wanted to go where?"

"To 914?"

"Where's that?"

"Westchester."

"Oh, Westchester. I have friends there."

Pause.

"Hello?"

"Yes?"

"So I use ones?"

"Yes. A one for the 914 area."

"How?"

Pause.

"Put a one before the number."

"Like 1914. Right?"

"1-914-555-1212."

"All of those numbers?"

"Yes."

"That's three ones."

"That's the area code."

"I've heard about those. They confuse me." Rumbling chuckles and laughs throughout the hall.

Pause.

She slowly and carefully explained what an area code is to the howlingly irreverent amusement of the entire crowd except for the telco narcs in attendance.

"Thanks. So I can call information and get a number?"

"That's right."

"And there's two numbers I can use?"

"Yes."

"So I got two numbers on one call?"

"Yeah . . ."

"Wow. Thanks. Have a nice day."

Spot the Fed: DefCon

"Hey kids, now it's time for another round of Spot The Fed. Here's your chance to win one of these wonderful *I Spotted A Fed* t-shirts. And all you have to do is ID a fed and it's yours. Look around you. Is he a fed? Is she under cover or under the covers? Heh, heh. Spot the Fed and win a prize. This one-size-fits-all XXX large t-shirt is yours if you Spot the Fed." Jeff Moss was hawking the game.

I had to keep silent. I hang out on both sides and have a reputation to maintain. I knew who the feds were and that would have been cheating.

"Hey, I see one," screeched a female voice from the left side of the 700+–seat ballroom.

Feds get Spotted during the Spot the Fed Contest, DefCon II

Chaos! Where? Where? Where's the fed? Like when Mark McGuire hits one toward the center field fence and 70,000 screaming fans stand on their seats to get a better view of a ball 1/4 mile away flying at 150 miles per hour, this crowd stood like lemmings to espy the fed. Where's the fed?

Promoter Jeff jumped off the stage in anxious anticipation that yet another repressive anti-freedom law enforcement person had blown his cover. Where's the fed? Jeff is searching for the accuser and the accused. Where's the fed? Craned necks as far as the eye can see; no better than rubberneckers on Highway 95 looking for pools of blood and misplaced body parts—they half expected a Fed to be as distinctly obvious as road-kill. No such luck. They look like you and me. (Not me.) Where's the fed?

He's getting closer, closer to the fed. Is it a fed? Are you a fed? C'mon, fess up. You're a fed. Nailed. Busted.

Here's your T-shirt. More fun than Monty Hall bringing out aliens' autopsy remnants from behind Door #3. Good clean fun. But they didn't get 'em all. A couple of feds were real good at hiding themselves. Must have been dressed like an Hawaiian surf bum or miserable banshee from Hellfire, Oregon. Kudos to those feds I know that never got spotted.

Next year, guys. There's always next year.

SummerCon: Atlanta

CIA Agent Steele (he prefers to be called a case officer) is as rowdy as everyone else. The hotel bar officially closed at midnight, but a couple of hundred in cash to the bartender and the hackers had their own private after-hours club. "Semper Fi!" Steele screams from a table top. "Hackers are God!" A smattering of applause, drunken acknowledgement, and back to the beer.

The next morning, Steele's head-throbbing session, titled "Talk to a Real Live Spy!" is well attended. Morning meaning 1 PM. They bombard him with unanswerable questions:

"Who did the Russians trade you for?"

"Tell us where the aliens are hidden?"

"Who's the mole in the CIA today?"

"What about those Chinese, huh? What's with letting them spy on us?"

Entertaining and lengthy. Steele's one-hour session drags to two and off he's dragged for more questions in the bar. But during Steele's oration, someone was having fun with the hotel's elevators.

The Robinsons invited about 200 people to their daughter Amy's wedding to Scott Mavers. Trouble was, they picked the hacker weekend to get married; it was a wedding no one would ever forget. The wedding was to be held on the penthouse floor, twelve stories up from the ground. But the elevators . . . they wouldn't go to the penthouse anymore. They would only go from the ground floor to the basement and back . . . and the hotel couldn't reach the Otis repairman . . . and we are terribly sorry but Grandma Ethel and Great Granddad Morris are going to have to walk upstairs, there's really nothing we can do . . . and yes we are very sorry . . . yes, Mrs. Robinson, we will have the emergency medical services on call. Damned hackers! The hotel staff had to carry up three octogenarian-laden wheelchairs, and they didn't even receive a tip for the back-breaking slavery. Hackers.

While the Robinsons were still hoofing and heaving up the stairways, teenage hacker Misfit was consuming vast quantities of alcohol at 3 PM. Misfit passed out, cold, on a couch, and a dozen of his hacker friends thought it would be very funny if they moved Misfit from the comfort of the couch to the chilled concrete floor of the maintenance room. Which they did, but the elevator deal had finally woken hotel security up to the fact that there were hackers in the hotel—lots of hackers—and they somehow ended up in the maintenance room and found Misfit, who was subsequently arrested by the Atlanta Police Department, still dead-to-the-world drunk. Hackers #43 and #54 tried to explain that no, he was put in the room by other hackers to sleep it off and don't arrest him . . . but the police knew there were hackers everywhere and they had to arrest somebody . . . and those elevators and the poor Robinsons. Cousin Ellie needed oxygen, so the cops who didn't arrest Misfit ran up twelve flights and helped her out, and the cops stayed for the day.

Checkout was on Sunday. The hotel had survived, sort of. The pool was filled with things that don't belong in a pool, some of them fitfully mangled after a hundred-foot fall. Good riddance. Here are your bills. Mine was $0. Zero. So were Bill's and Chris's and Mike's—all of our bills were zero. Except for CIA Agent Steele. Seems he got billed for everyone else's room, phone and bar charges.

Oh, yeah, he also got saddled with the bill for the wedding.

Resources

- www.defcon.org is home to the hacker convention.
- www.2600.com is home to the HOPE conventions.
- Search on "CyberChrist" on www.inforwar.com for two extended stories about CyberChrist himself and the goings on at hacker conventions. Heavy R-rated: beware!
- Search on "Hacker Conventions"

▶ The Top Ten Signs Your Coworker Is a Computer Hacker[18]

10. You ticked him off once and your next phone bill was for $20,000.
9. He's won the Publisher's Clearing House sweepstakes 3 years running.
8. When asked for his phone number, he gives it in hex.
7. Seems strangely calm whenever the office LAN goes down. .
6. Somehow gets HBO on his PC at work.
5. Mumbled, "Oh, puh-leeez" ninety-five times during the movie *The Net*.
4. Massive 401k contribution made in half-cent increments.
3. His video-dating profile lists "public-key encryption" among turn-ons.
2. For his welcome voice on AOL, you hear, "Good Morning, Mr. President."
1. You hear him murmur, "Let's see you use that Visa now, *Professor I-don't-give-'A's-in-Computer-Science!*"

---

[18] I want to thank Dave Gurolski, one of the spokepeople at ISS for this list. We used it on the road for several months. Thanks Dave.

Hactivism

Political Hacking[19]

Cyber-civil Disobedience

During the question-and-answer period after a speech to 800 raving New York hackers in the summer of 1994, I made what I considered at the time to be an innocuous off-hand comment:

> "If my generation had had the technical toys you guys have, the 80s never would have happened."

They hooted and hollered in approval as the older attendees pondered the implications.

Thirty years ago, millions of Americans shouted their convictions and anti-war sentiments by marching in the streets and engaging in variously creative forms of civil disobedience. Today, anti-nuclear activists and environmentalists have maintained the tradition, while repeat-offender anti-abortionists seemingly wear the badge of both misdemeanor and murder arrests with pride. But the visceral images of huge traffic-jamming Vietnam-era protests broadcast live on the evening news will be the ones indelibly etched in our minds and history books.

In the 1990s, due to ever-unpopular White House stances on encryption, privacy, and Internet taxation, the Clinton Administration similarly invited demonstrable outcries, but with the modern twist of technology-driven protest.

---

[19]The original version of this article appeared in *Information Week* in 1994. Most people thought the idea was too extreme ever to occur. Read on.

White House support for the Justice Department's Digital Telephony Bill further exacerbated an already disgruntled cyberpublic. Law enforcement wanted to continue its court-authorized surveillance activities despite, critics say, no proven need for expensive and possibly invasive anti-privacy technology and legislation. In general, the administration's handling of Cyberspace has been severely questioned and criticized, from the board room to the university to millions of on-line users.

President Clinton's conceptual endorsement of an electronic National ID Card may prove to be the needed fodder to create an explosive critical mass of popular dissatisfaction. So what is a disgruntled citizenry to do?

Cyber-civil disobedience is timely, poignant, and potentially highly effective.

Thirty years ago, youthful and academic demographics flavored the anti-war movement: predictable-looking people predictably demonstrating against their government's policies while always aware the TV cameras were rolling. Today, administration policies are loathed by a wide cross section of America that traverses most social, economic, and age barriers.

Thirty years ago, a demonstration or protest required organization and the congregation of huge numbers of people, all within the limits of the necessary police permit. Signs and slogans and chants prefaced the occasional Mayor Dalylike headline-grabbing overreactions.

Today, the netherworld of Cyberspace offers an unrestricted, unregulated and certainly unorganized refuge as an alternative to conventional assembly. Cyberspace provides the ideal mechanism for cyber-civil disobedience, the protest means of choice for the Information Age. Cyber-civil disobedience is waged by remote control, over vast distances, yet the effects can be highly focused against selected targets.

And, best yet, there isn't a policeman guarding each and every portal to the information superhighway, waiting to haul a civil disobedient off to the slammer.

Phil Zimmerman would probably disagree on this last point. Facing the potential of years in prison, he was under investigation for violating US export control laws that govern encryption schemes. My book, *The Complete Internet Business Toolkit*, (New York: VNR, 1996) was banned from export from the United States because it contained dozens of cryptographic programs. Forty-two or more months in the slammer for taking my book on a trans-Atlantic flight.

One widely discussed act of mass civil disobedience would be the intentional violation of encryption export laws by tens or hundreds of thousands of people, rendering attempted export policy enforcement virtually impotent. All the protestors have to do is make a copy of their favorite encryption scheme and place it on the Net, electronically mail it to their buddies overseas, or even just post it on a domestic BBS. All of these acts are, depending upon your interpretation, against the law. Precedent-setting cyber-civil disobedience on this scale gives the government the unenviable and unpopular choice of either selective enforcement or policy revision.

Cyber-civil disobedience is easily disguised. If, for example, the electronic mailboxes of selected, and presumably offensive, government services are overloaded with lengthy unnecessary garbage-laden messages, they literally collapse under the weight of popular opinion. Such widespread shrapnelling of targeted systems by millions of cyber-civil disobedients could effectively shut down non-critical electronic government services whose demise would act as highly visible media-magnets. Cyber-events are news and news spreads the word: the protesters need the publicity for enlistment of more sympathizers.

Rotary dial telephones that once used to ring in one's opinion are today replaced with tens of millions of home PCs connected to tens of millions of modems. Using a little piece of software known as an auto-dialer, it would only take a few thousand distant and invisible confederates to shut down a company's or agency's PBX, or president@ whitehouse.gov, and thus their ability to communicate. With a larger "demonstration" of cyber-civil disobedience, entire telephone exchanges would only be capable of responding to would-be callers with, "All circuits are busy."

With an electronic US population of an estimated 70 million, a high percentage of which are cyber-aware, the capability for cyber-civil disobedience is within the realm of short-term possibility, if not probability. Network systems have limited bandwidth, an obvious weak point that a cyber-civil disobedient can easily exploit to the detriment of the service provider and its customers.

Whether it's Right to Lifers shutting down an abortion clinic's ability to communicate, extreme environmentalists striking in Cyberspace instead of the woods, or an angry public venting electronic frustration at its government, the capability for cyber-civil disobedience is real and within the power of millions of people.

Washington should keep in mind that for an Information Age population to aggressively voice its discontent, America doesn't have to take to the streets.

Cyber-civil Warfare

I initially wrote about hactivism and cyber-civil disobedience, in no way trying to incite or encourage immediate action. I received a fair amount of hate mail from folks decrying the premise that the Internet would ever be used for such purposes.

Well, somebody was listening.

In November and December of 1995, protesting French and Italian citizens targeted their respective governments' Internet presence to voice their dissatisfaction with official actions and policies.

On February 29, 1996, the White House was to be the target of an immense "broadcast storm" of email, each containing a copy of the Bill of Rights. The goal was to shut down part of whitehouse.gov and alert President Clinton that much of the Internet community was fearful that administration cyber-policies were inconsistent with the Constitution. The results, however, were ineffective, as apparently not enough people participated.

Then, in March of 1996, Mexicans called for Internet strikes similar to those in Europe. In May of 1996, someone or some group blasted broadcast storms to the alt.religion.scientology usernet news group in an apparent attempt to stifle critics of the Church through a denial of service attack. But that was only the beginning. Hackers have their own approach.

At all hacker conventions, a lot of drinking occurs. A lot. And SummerCon is no different. During one of the early AM drink fests, one thoroughly inebriated hacker came up to me.[20]

"I need your help, Winn. You gotta get CNN here right away!" I listened between the slurps and slurs of his speech.

"Why?"

"Well isn't it obvious?" he exclaimed, his arms randomly pointing at the barroom chaos. "We're gonna declare war on France!" he shouted with pride.

Trying to appear nonplussed, I merely asked, "Oh really? Why?"

"Isn't it obvious?" I shook my head, no, it's not obvious to me, but then again he was living in another reality. "They've been stealing American secrets for years and our government doesn't have the guts to do anything about it, but we do! Will you get CNN here now!" He seemed exasperated with my inability to comprehend what was obvious to him.

"Ah, are you really sure about this?"

"Damn right I am! We want to do it live on national TV." No matter

---

[20] I have substantially cleared up the language to cater to your reading sensibilities.

it was 4:15 on a Sunday morning. "We own France!" A familiar phrase often repeated on web site graffiti hacks: U R OwNeD!

I had known this hacker for a few years and, when sober, he is relentlessly good-natured. Drunk, he is also relentlessly good-natured, but with an agenda his more placid personality hides. "I think you might have some trouble with that," I said.

"No way. We already own . . ." and he listed a number of French companies and French government agencies that they claimed to have hacked into and built back doors so they could return at will; this is called rooting a system.

"OK," I said sublimely. "But don't you think you might get arrested?"

"Who would arrest us for being good Americans? Who? Who?" he demanded.

"Well, how about the FBI for one?"

He looked around the room. "They're not here. Besides, there's no law against hacking the French."

He passed out shortly thereafter, but I checked into it with my friend Jim Settle, chief of the FBI's Computer Crime Squad in Washington, and he said, "Hell, we'd arrest him anyway, then figure out what to do. I know there's a law somewhere."

Hack Attacks

Hactivism had begun and 1998 will go down as the watershed year that empowered political groups to take action on the Internet.

- After www.armyinkashmir.com was set up to denounce Pakistan's "proxy war" and "narcotics terrorism" in Kashmir, it was hacked.
- In June 1998 an Indian nuclear facility was hacked after the country set off an atomic bomb in a weapons test.
- In August, crackers helped focus attention on the plight of Chinese Indonesians.
- The Hong Kong Blondes hacked mainland China's police networks, tipping off anybody it found lined up for political arrest.
- In September, the Electronic Disruption Theater, in support of the Mexican Zapatistas, launched a denial-of-service attack against an information site at the Pentagon.
- The most prominent attack in 1998 was against the *New York Times* (www.nytimes.com) in October. A hacker

group calling themselves HFG or "Hacking for Girlies"
claimed responsibility. They were supporters of Kevin Mitnick, a hacker convicted of computer-related fraud. When
the *NYT* rebooted their servers, the hackers retook control.
The attack took place because Slut Puppy and his partner-
in-crime Master Pimp were "bored."[21] The graffiti-ridden
web site attacked John Markoff, reporter for the *New York
Times*, who helped with the Mitnick investigation, and
attacked Carolyn Meinel, whose book *The Happy Hacker*
made her unpopular with the underground community.

Most of the 1998 attacks were merely web graffiti attacks which
underscored the notion that everyone and everything on the Internet is
both vulnerable and fair game. But 1999 was the year it became almost
commonplace. The NATO efforts against Serbia created a huge wave of
electronic protests.

- According to the Russian newspaper *Segodnya* on 31
  March, unknown hackers hacked into NATO's informa-
  tion server, www.nato.int. The site was down for at least a
  half hour in this "Net victory." The report said the Rand
  Corporation, a defense-oriented think tank, was next.
- In January 1999 the web site for Philadelphia mayoral candidate John White was "faked," allegedly by an opponent.
  False quotes were attributed to White about how minority
  voters ought to consolidate political power.
- The White House web site was hacked for its pro-NATO
  stance, as was the US Senate.
- Constant floods of email to the NATO email servers shut
  down email for extended periods of time.

In 1976, Indonesia annexed East Timor, although the action was
never recognised by the United Nations. The East Timorese set up a virtual country on a Dublin-based server and has been under constant
attack.[22]

Certainly the most newsworthy hacker attacks in the first half of
1999 are related to the Kosovo conflict in Serbia. In my youth we had
the Vietnam War on TV for six o'clock dinner. Now we are seeing real

---

[21]12/15/98, Hackers for Girlies interview, THE WORLD OF SLUT PUPPY AND
MASTER PIMP. By Adam L. Penenberg, *Forbes*.
[22]http://www.techweb.com/wire/story/TWB19990202S0002

warlike activities appear on the Internet—at every hour of the day. The Internet doesn't sleep.

In late March of 1999, NATO's web site was attacked by Belgrade-based hackers, who saturated the site with emails and queries that prevented access to the site, which contains information about NATO and updated press releases on NATO's movements in Yugoslavia. The *Los Angeles Times* said that at the same time crackers called MacroHard Group attacked a site called World-Albania.com and replaced the site's information with a link to a banned Belgrade radio station.

This activity doesn't mess up NATO's ability to conduct operation, but after a hundred media organizations pick up on it, it becomes a huge issue. It isn't the hack itself—it's the CNN after-effect. Web-attacks like this become a very effective tool for propaganda when in fact the actual technical attacks are fairly minor.

Hactivism in 1999 has continued unabated. A June 1999 "demonstration" against financial institutions in England was coordinated with massive cyber-attacks. Anti-capitalist, environmental, and anti-nuke groups took credit.

How and Why the Electronic Disturbance Theater Challenged the Pentagon

The battle between the Electronic Disturbance Theater and the Pentagon may go down in history as a defining moment. This was the first time that the US military launched a cyber-counteroffensive against people within the United States—that we know about. As can be expected, the military isn't talking, and I was met with blunt "no comments" from officialdom. However, some Pentagon folks have spoken on the condition of anonymity. And of course, the Electronic Disturbance Theater, the EDT, is speaking loud and clear.

First of all, conventional media, in its usual dumbed-down nontechnical perspective, insists that the Pentagon was attacked by hackers.

"Technically, it was not a hack," says Ricardo Dominguez, one of the four members of the EDT. "The Zapatista FloodNet is a network traffic tool multiplier that can be thought of as a weak denial-of-service tool or a strong collective presence tool." The ethos behind the preannounced event at the Pentagon's electronic doors was a "conceptual art performance work using the targeted site as a context—an art medium—which engenders a symbolic performance action." An Internet art form of protest.

"We were fortunate to see it coming," a Pentagon staffer said. How could they not? It was announced in advance by the EDT. "It allowed us to prepare for it and respond accordingly." Respond accordingly to what is the question though. What is the policy of the Pentagon to "striking back" at an on-line assault? None that we can find at this time and none the military will acknowledge—officially.

Nonetheless, from all appearances, the Defense Technical Information Center (DTIC) found itself under assault by the Electronic Disturbance Theater and reacted in a renegade fashion, without legal internal consultation as to the ramifications of their actions.

The Pentagon has not publicly described the nature of the attack against them.

Despite their official silence, this is what I am told happened:

The Zapatista FloodNet is "network art, where the [target] site's search engines are used symbolically against" the target. According to the EDT's Dominguez, in the "September 9, 1998 action, FloodNet caused persistent re-searching of the targeted site local search engine every nine seconds." The civil disobedients initiated countless searches for words like "justice" and "honor"—"which are NOT FOUND by search service (sic) at the targeted site." Overloading the search engine, bandwidth, and performance of the target systems might seem to be the overarching goal, but there is much more behind the EDT motivations.

The political rationale of many of the EDT's network-art-events is a call to action and awareness of the Chiapas, Mexico "aggressive" military stand-off against the Zapatista National Liberation Army. The US has provided extensive support as part of our War on Drugs, which branded the Pentagon a legitimate target as anti-Zapatista. Regardless of the motivation, the actions of Dominguez and the EDT were bandwidth- and service-hogging, which spawned the hair-trigger response from the Pentagon's DITC. The Defense Information Systems Agency (DISA) likely offered significant support in structuring, if indeed not actually launching, the electronic counteroffensive. DITC is an electronic library of sorts, but DISA has been actively involved in both defensive and offensive cyber-tools and development for well over a decade. In addition, DISA and ASSIST (Automated System Security Incident Team) a CERT-like military organization, got in touch with the security department at New York University, which housed the EDT pages at that time.

The Pentagon gave away a lot of its rapid response capability in this seemingly minor skirmish, which is one reason why they have kept so quiet on the subject. Clearly, their response was a political oops!

Upon detection of the EDT's FloodNet assault, the Pentagon responded with a "truly effective denial-of-service attack," says the

EDT. The on-line "protesters were redirected to a Pentagon applet called "hostileapplet" which crashed their browsers." This Java applet fired a "series of rapidly appearing Java coffee cups across the bottom of the [browser] screen coupled with the phrase 'ACK'. FloodNet froze." So it would seem that the Pentagon response, a denial-of-service attack, worked, but the EDT was ready.

Bret Stalbaum, a San Jose, California member of the Electronic Disturbance Theater stopped the Pentagon's counteroffensive by "changing the html to avoid the pages where they—the Pentagon—had put the applet." If the Pentagon utilized a file called "hostileapplet" one must naturally ask if there is a "hostileapplet2" and "hostileapplet3" and "hostileapplet4" and so on. How deep does the Pentagon's arms arsenal of offensive software go? No one is talking. But with only a little imagination, it's not too hard to figure out. $1 billion + 1,000 programmers + national security = a lot of powerful offensive software.

After the Pentagon's brusque and effective response, the EDT intimated that it would consider a lawsuit against the government. The group is now in discussion with a Seattle-based attorney who himself "wants to join" the EDT. "When we do make a decision," Dominguez promised me, "we will let you know. Until then don't assume anything."

But then there's Posse Comitatus, an 1878 law which bans the use of the military from domestic law enforcement. Can, or more importantly, should the military be launching cyber-counteroffensives against virtual or physical locations within the United States? The EDT says, "It may be the only doctrine that is on our side" in any possible future legal tussle with the US Government. "But, they will argue that they were disarming us and that it was not a strike."

FloodNet was released to the public at 12:01 AM on January 1, 1999, indeed a potentially disturbing event that could even further empower push-button hackers and clueless punks with an attitude. As for the EDT? "We will continue to develop tools, tactics, and theory for the development of html activism and the larger umbrella of hactivism." These methods are to be used by communities suffering under armed aggression who normally have "no means and are without voice."

"Remember," Dominguez says, "FloodNet was not created by hackers or terrorists, but by artists and activists who wanted to create a simple point & click tool that would bring civil disobedience to the html community."

Resources

- www.Zdnet.com, www.nwfusion.com and do a search on "Hactivism"
- Search on "Hactivism" for the latest
- "Electronic Civil Disobedience" by the Critical Arts Ensemble. ISBN 1-57027-056-2
- "The Electronic Disturbance" by the Critical Arts Ensemble. ISBN 1-57027-006-6
- www.infowar.com/class_3/cybciv.html-ssi
- www.thing.net/~rdom/ecd/EDTECD.html
- http://lists.tao.ca

An American Alien Hacks Through Customs

A Lesson in Customs for the Net-savvy Traveller

OK, OK, so some people think I'm a Net Personality, but really! Phil Zimmerman was nearly put in jail for four years by the feds for violating US crypto export laws. Dan Farmer made headlines for making SATAN. All I did was write a few books about war. I mean, really!

With a fever of 102 degrees and my nose dripping with a contagion I had acquired in Poland a few days before, I handed the US customs official the official I'm Carrying No Illegal Drugs form. "Anything to declare?" he asked indifferently.

"A bottle of Bulgarian merlot," I snorted while wiping my reddened proboscis on a sweaty denim shirt sleeve. At that, he pointed me towards the darkened, most-feared section of the vast customs receiving station, Secondary Inspection.

Over to the X ray machine I trundled my ailing body, a pair of wheeled suitcases, two laptop computers, a maze of wires, telco equipment, and an assortment of materials that were soon to be my undoing.

The month prior I had in fact cracked three ribs in an oversized London bathtub, so I had no choice but to ask the next customs man in the Welcome to America gauntlet to hoist my 60 kilo luggage for me. They stopped the X ray conveyer belt and doubled then tripled and then yes, quadrupled the ion storm power bombarding my belongings; all in search of a hidden compartment hiding a golden corkscrew for the merlot. They peered, and twisted their heads to the side, and invited other inspectors to crane their necks and point at the insidiously obvious contraband I was attempting to bring into the United States.

"Tertiary Inspection," they declared, and my luggage was hoisted this time onto a long slick aluminum tray some three feet wide that was perfectly suited to carry out bovine autopsies.

And there waiting for me was a snarling young peach-fuzzed customs inspector with an attitude and a gun. His hands were covered with Living Playtex gloves to protect him from any of the myriad diseases we Netizens carry home with us. He had heard about boot sector viruses, obviously.

He asked, and I explained what sort of work I do: Internet security, information warfare, espionage stuff. The usual from any of my books. Inspector Fuhrman (like Mark of bloody-glove OJ fame?) wouldn't give me his name or badge number but he was chock full of inane questions that one expects from bad 1970s B movies about spies.

"And the government lets you do that?" he quizzically asked with the Dan Quayle–like ogle-eyed stare of a deer petrified by speeding headlights.

Huh? I thought to myself and my face must have mirrored abject disbelief. "Yeah, I work for the government, too," I offered haltingly. Was this a trick question disguised behind half a bottle of red wine and non-prescription European cold medicine?

"Do you work for the Soviet Union?" he asked in all earnestness while digging through my carry-on case, pulling out stacks of file folders and bellowing "Aha!" upon discovering a book entitled, *Economic Espionage in America*. "So, do you?" he asked again.

"That would be kind of tough," I answered with my own attitude, "since they went out of business six years ago." I crossed my arms in defiance of Fuhrman's job-for-life stupidity.

He poked deeper into my cache of hidden troves and popped out with three declassified Department of Defense reports on security. "And what about these . . . these . . . I suppose the government thinks it's OK to carry these around . . ." he stammered. I merely nodded. (*Hey, Inspector Fuhrman, what about that guy over there? Yeah, him. The one with the turban and an Uzi barrel sticking out of it?*)

Fuhrman held each file up and dangled it from over his head, peering inside and waiting for kilograms of white powder to come cascading out; after all, I had just come from London, England. Idiot.

And so it went. Piece by piece. Paper by paper. And the incredulous question too-oft repeated to be believed: "The government really lets you do this?" And my mental response, *Yes, Fuhrman, there is a First Amendment and you are stepping all over it.*

He found my light reading materials and questioned my legal right to read them, or even possess them. *Weapons of Intelligence and Conflict in the Information Age.* I wrote it, yet Fuhrman, here, intimated such documents represented a national security threat. *Autonomous Mobile*

Cyber Weapons. He stared hard at that one. *Surviving Denial of Service on the Internet. The Ping of Death Page.* "And the government really lets you do this?" he droned for the umpteenth time.

He held up a single sheet of paper that had caught his eye and scanned it carefully before handing it to me. "And what's this?" A half a second later I replied as snidely as I could, "A Reuters news release," and tossed it back. *(Hey, Inspector, what about that lady, that one with the chicken under her arms who is frothing at the mouth?)*

Now, behind Fuhrman stood a handful of other customs inspectors, including the helpful Inspector Earl Mullins. While Fuhrman spirited away a tall pile of other insidious Net-techy documents to a nearby office, Mullins approached. "We tried to tell him to leave you alone, but he's new . . ."

"And an idiot who thinks he's caught himself the next Aldrich Ames," I added. Mullins didn't disagree.

My collection of videotapes didn't go unnoticed, either. "The Hacker Attack." "The Information Bomb." "Hackers Breaking Into the Pentagon." "This stuff is legal?" He chortled. "And they let you do it?"

Then it was on to my drugs. Blood pressure medicine. Aspirin. Afrin. And gobs and gobs of available-only-in-the-UK mints. "What are these for?" he demanded. "Bad breath," I said leaning away from Fuhrman to make the point. And then . . . then . . . then . . . then he found The Watch. It's a curious, very heavy, silver Darth Vaderish wristwatch with cantilevers and buttons and strange symbols reminiscent of those on the cover of the *Alien Coverup* book I was also carrying.

"I suppose this is a laser beam," he snorted while feeling around the contours for a button to push.

"Don't touch that!" I yelled and dove backwards, cowering for fear that the Watch's gigawatt beam might instantly vaporize me. He jolted and bolted momentarily, but he failed to see the humor in the situation. The Inspectors behind him giggled mercilessly at his expense. *(Hey, Inspector! What about that family over there tugging that Libyan fruit tree? Don't you want to talk with them, too?)*

Now that every paper and folder and file and book and dirty sock and piece of underwear of mine was spread along the twenty-foot length of the autopsy table, Fuhrman ordered, "Give me your passport," and he gallumphed over to the office to process my name amongst the distant digitial files of known terrorists. "Call the White House," I offered. "They know who I am."

"Don't you know that they're closed today?" Jesus, how stupid could I be. It was Sunday. Of course the government was closed.

The other inspectors merely shook their heads in embarrassment at

Fuhrman's shenanigans. He still refused to give me his name but Supervisory Inspector Ms. Torres curtly handed me back my passport, and ushered Fuhrman with a gentle shove on the tush over to the Dunce's Corner for admonishment.

Now, I never did quite figure out what national secrets I was bringing into Tampa, Florida, the United States of America; nor why Customs Inspector John Lider (ha, gotcha!) decided to spend an hour harassing me. But I did learn a lot more by what Inspector Lider didn't do.

I had two laptop computers loaded with gigs of files of infinitely more interest than my book on aliens or my copy of *Internet Underground*. Not once did Lider-Fuhrman show the least interest in the best place to secret information away: On a laptop, emblazoned with the hacker motto: I Love (heart) *Your* Computer. No, no interest there.

Nor was there any recognition of a 630MB CD-ROM containing almost 5,500 security tools and 70+ cryptographic programs on it, even though the disk was clearly labeled, "Banned From Export Out of the United States." (No longer a crime, by the way. It is legal to carry crypto for your own personal international use.)

While in Poland, I had been given a set of a half dozen more CDs with hacking and cracking programs, security tools, crypto, and God knows what else: I haven't had the chance to look yet. But one might expect the astute customs inspector to at least show a cursory interest in a set of CDs and documents *written in Polish*!

But alas, no, not our Lider-Fuhrman, no.

So, for the Net-savvy traveller, or even the occasional industrial spy, a few words of advice.

1. Put all of the good stuff on your hard disk. The hard disk is inside of a computer. They don't know that yet.
2. Label the computer, "Contraband."
3. Cyrillic CD-ROMs are not subject to duty. Détente is in.
4. Bring in several million dollars in cybercash on a floppy disk.
5. Taxing magnetic bytes is still a few months off.
6. When you come to the US, use Tampa Airport, ask for Customs Inspector Lider. Don't call him Fuhrman, though. He still might be sensitive about this whole affair.
7. Be prepared to repack your own dirty clothes. That's not in their job description.

II

Protecting Kids, Family, and Your Privacy

My family has been hacked. My kids, wife, in-laws, and cousins—not to mention my neighbors. Personal privacy, especially due to the Internet, is at an all-time low.

What are we going to do about it?

Hacking is more than just breaking into big military computers; it's also about you, your kids, and friends. But with identity theft, guilt by electronic association, and everything about each one of us published on the Internet, in what some refer to as the "Wild Wild West" of Cyberspace, what can you do to protect yourself? Some of the answers are here . . . but I will tell you now, it's up to you: No one else will help. Read on!

In Cyberspace You're Guilty Until Proven Innocent

How would you like to have your life so thoroughly and totally turned upside down that normal functioning became a daily frustration, or worse yet, something to be feared?

What if your life were so completely altered that you didn't even recognize yourself? And what if your very existence was so much of a mess that you couldn't get a job, lease a car, rent an apartment, or buy a house? What if you couldn't get a phone, cable service, or even health insurance? And then imagine every credit agency on the planet was after you for incredible sums of money you didn't spend, or that the police were looking at you for crimes you didn't commit? What kind of life is that?

That is the kind of life that tens of thousands of Americans suffer every year, through no fault of their own.

Bill Waters was an ace Korean War fighter pilot. A Southern gentleman, he led a rich life; he saved and invested so he could enjoy a comfortable retirement. His wife, Gail, volunteered her time with charity work and they were both very active in their church. At 66, life was good.

Then it all came crashing down around them.

It started with a letter from GMAC, General Motors Acceptance Corporation. They wanted to know why Bill had not made payments on the three expensive cars he had bought three months earlier. "We know you may have overlooked this responsibility, and in order to preserve your excellent credit rating . . ."

We have all received letters like that, but Bill and Gail were mystified. What cars? They wrote back and said there must be some mistake. They had not bought any cars . . . much less financed them. From the old school, they paid cash. Shortly thereafter, a national jewelry chain wrote the Waters a similar letter asking for payments on more than $50,000 in gems and gold. "Where is your payment?"

GMAC wrote back and said that as far as the finance company was concerned, the Waters owed the $70,000 for the three cars, and unless payments were made immediately, legal proceedings would commence.

Credit card companies started writing letters too, demanding payments on more than $100,000 in charges that Bill and Gail had made. They felt helpless. His blood pressure began to soar, his nerves made sleep difficult, and they were both fearful of what was going to happen next. Over a period of about six months, they were hit with bills in excess of $250,000, and despite their letters stating that the charges were not theirs, the lawsuits against the Waters began.

The incredible stress sent Bill to the hospital. The companies wanted their money—not excuses. The Waters contacted the bank they had been with for years and it turned out that they, too, wanted money for a line of credit the Waters had placed against their very expensive home in Chatanooga, Tennessee.

Six weeks later, Bill Waters was dead. A massive stroke and a heart attack caused by stress had killed him.

Bill Waters was my cousin.

None of the bills were theirs. They had become the victim of identity theft: criminal hackers had adopted Bill Waters' electronic identity and gone on a spending spree totalling more than $350,000. The criminals had chosen their victim very carefully:

- The Waters had excellent credit with very high limits.
- They owned an expensive home, free and clear.
- They had substantial savings and investments in banks and brokerage firms.
- They owned two late-model cars with no liens on them.
- They travelled first class and stayed at top-of-the-line hotels.
- They had no children.

How had the criminals picked their latest victim so well? Research. They performed extensive research into the Waters' background, their lifestyle, and their assets. They knew what they were looking for: an older well-to-do couple who would probably resort to polite letter-writing to dispute the charges rather than make a huge stink. In fact, Gail only began to ask for help from law enforcement after Bill had entered the hospital from which he would not return.

*   *   *

Clearly we have a national problem here, as tens of thousands of Americans experience similar horrors but are generally not aware of the trouble brewing around them until it reaches mammoth proportions.

The phrase "In Cyberspace You're Guilty Until Proven Innocent" is a modern truism. Congress has seen fit to do nothing to rectify the situation; huge corporations fight attempts to ameliorate the deterioration of privacy in American life. It's a creeping invasion of your and my lives that has gone on for nearly fifty years and continues to get worse every day.

Each of our lives are inextricably defined by the contents of computers. The average American and some information about him resides within about 50,000 different computers and is exchanged, bartered, sold, or updated about ten times per day. Our lives are defined—and judged—by the contents of these machines.

The government has its share of computers in which some of your most private secrets are kept. IRS computers hold every aspect of your financial being, yet IRS employees have consistently abused that information by selling it or selectively accessing private files and feeding it to criminals for profit, or to the media for exploitation. And now the IRS is increasing its efforts to require on-line tax filing—across the Internet. Veterans are enmeshed within the VA computers. The Social Security Administration retains a piece of your financial future. The list is long: FHA mortgages require extensive justification, law enforcement computers and networks store your transgressions, voter registration knows your latest private address, unlisted phone numbers, and political affiliations. County records store your real estate, car, boat, and airplane ownership for anyone to legally access.

Corporate America knows even more about you. They know your buying habits, where you travel, what you spend, and how well you pay your bills. Your bank knows every single non-cash transaction you make, the source of all of your deposits, and a plethora of personal information about you, your family, and your life. Credit card companies sell your name to anyone who is looking for potential purchasers of thousands of products. And marketing companies know you better than you know yourself. They can, with the aid of sophisticated software and a history of what you have bought in the past, predict how well you will react to direct mail or telephone solicitations for highly targeted sales campaigns.

Is this really what you want your life to be? An open book for criminals and marketing exploitation? Today it is. Would you, for example, put on your letterhead or stationery the following information?

- Address and last five addresses
- Social Security number
- Income and sources of income
- Taxes paid
- Criminal records
- Financial status
- Charitable donations
- Everything you own or have owned
- Credit card numbers
- Exactly what you bought from whom in the last twelve months
- Where you travelled, with whom, and what you did

No, neither would I, but given the absolute lack of privacy we have in the United States today, that is just the information anyone with a keyboard can have in minutes. Dozens of on-line services have popped up in the last few years that provide that exact service and no one is doing a damn thing about it. It will indeed take an act of Congress to give back to Americans what we have lost in the last half of this century for lack of concern and the special-interest dollars that pour into political campaigns.

The problems are complex:

1. Companies are not required by law to protect the confidential records that contain sensitive and private information about us. There is little legal recourse for violations, except in the most extreme cases, such as Bill Waters'.

2. The government has no standards for protecting private information. The military goes to great effort to properly secure Classified, Secret, and Top Secret information, but there are no provisions for adequate handling of information not put into those categories as a matter of national security. (The military is finding itself in a similar situation as the individual. Toilet paper supplies, machine parts, software procurement, and travel orders, for example, are unclassified information, and therefore not controlled by the same security restrictions as if they were classified. However, unless those processes occur without interruption, the US could find itself less than prepared in time of national emergency; our combat readiness can suffer.)

3. The concept of public records hasn't changed in more than 200 years. The object back then was to ride a horse down a tree-covered dirt road, enter the wooden courthouse, and look up in a hand-written ledger who had bought the hundred acres of land over the grassy knoll. Today, public records are availabe on the Internet for free or for a small fee to an information service. The original intent has been undermined by technology that allows for incredible abuses.

4. There is no law or control over who may have access to your private information. For example, credit reports are supposed to be very private. You may have found that out by applying for a loan and being told by the lending institution that you may not have a copy of your own credit report. That confounds common sense, but that's the way it is. To make matters worse, if you tell one of the credit reporting agencies you own a condominium or house and want to rent it, for a small fee you will receive a credit report computer terminal and get the full report on anyone at all . . . whether they are applying for credit or a lease, or not.

5. Your medical records are available to doctors, hospitals, and insurance companies, but not to you. If a data clerk accidentally hits the wrong key and the records say you have HIV, you are never told about it. If you discover, perhaps, that you are turned down for life or health insurance even though you've never been sick in your life, you will soon discover that you cannot access those records or correct them. The excuse that businesses like the Medical Information Bureau offer is that they are private company records owned by them, not the individual. Again, this is beyond absurd.

6. Organizations may buy or sell your name and associated information without your consent or knowledge. Is this right? I don't think it is.

Computers are making this situation worse every day. Or perhaps it is more accurate to say that people who want to abuse other people are using the technology for their own profits—the hell with everyone else. In early 1999, Florida decided to sell the photographs of every driver in the state to a marketing company in New Hampshire. The company said they were building a system to permit retail sales establishments to verify the identity of credit card purchasers by downloading the cardholder's picture.

Public outcry short-circuited the project, but the state legislature was obviously clueless about the dangers: a person's photograph is the last remaining piece of the puzzle needed to achieve total identity theft. CD-ROMs of every driver and automobile in Florida, Oregon, and Texas have been made available since the mid-1990s as a way for states to increase their revenues—privacy be damned!

Stealing a life is hacking in every sense of the word—except that in most cases it is not necessary to break into computers to accomplish the task. Private detectives and intelligence agents developed the basic techniques that are now used by criminals and malicious hackers alike.

Let's assume that the motivation is profit—theft—just as it was with Bill Waters. First, the thief wants to get a list of possible candidates, or victims. By comparing public charts of income versus zip codes, the list of target neighborhoods is narrowed down. Zip code 90210, Beverly Hills, is obviously a high-income area, as are thousands of others. Older folks make better victims, so lists from the AARP, a retirees' organization, targeted for the richer zip codes will further refine the victim roster. It is a simple matter to also get the phone number of the potential victims. Reverse lookup directories will supply an address to a phone number. People finders on the Internet will give address, email, and other contact information.

At this point, more legwork is necessary. Perhaps a drive by the top twenty names will verify the financial assumptions made by the computer analysis. Now, a credit report on each will tell the criminal if the person has good credit, room on his charge cards, and how much he owns of various assets. This will determine the size of the "take" for the criminal.

The identifying feature by which most of us live today is our social security number. The credit report will have that, past addresses, and other information that is ostensibly private between you and the financial institution. But, most importantly, the criminal will now have enough information to convince many people that he is you.

- Name
- Address
- Past addresses
- Phone
- Social Security number

If it were me acting as criminal, I would want to test the waters, so to speak, and learn more about my victim. For a score of $250,000 or more, the extra effort is well worth it.

The phone company is a good start, as they have probably the most abysmal security procedures in the known universe. The identity thief calls up and pretends to be the victim.

"Hi, this is Mr. Victim, and I've just had a small stroke."

"Oh, I am so sorry."

"Thanks, but I'm all right. Just need some rest."

"How can I help you?"

"I'm going to be staying with relatives to recuperate, and I wanted to know if you could send my telephone bill to me there. Would that be OK?"

"Sure, Mr Victim. I just need to verify your identity for security purposes."

"Good. I am glad that you're being so careful."

"Thank you, we try. What is your current address?"

Given.

"What is your phone number?"

Given.

"What is your Social Security number?"

Done.

"What address would you like the bill sent to?"

The criminal gives an address in-care-of the ersatz relative's name.

What does this do? It allows the criminal to call numbers on the bill so he can speak with the victim's friends or relatives and learn a great deal more.

"Hello, Mrs. Smith. My name is Tom Jones from AAA Travel, and we've been trying to reach Mr. Victim. He has a refund coming to him. Do you know where he is?"

"Hello, Mrs. Smith. My name is Tom Jones from Publishers Clearinghouse and Mr. Victim is on our final list and he left your name as a contact . . ."

"Hello, Mrs. Smith. My name is Tom Jones from Big Health Company, and Mr. Victim said I could ask you a few questions about him . . ."

The fine art of social engineering strikes again.

The next step turns the tables. Call the victims to learn about their gullibility factor. After all, these are seniors with money.

"Hello, Mr. Victim. My name is Tom Jones from American Investors, and Mrs. Smith said I should call you about a way you can double your investment in just six months." The criminal will learn through a few seemingly innocuous phone calls everything he needs to know about his victim to enhance his chances of a big rip-off.

Identity theft is simple, and that's why it is done so often by enterprising criminal entrepreneurs.

Acquiring the victim's driver's license is pretty straightforward, too. On the Internet, you can download full-color templates of drivers' licenses from all fifty states. In most states you can acquire the real driver's license information to make the identity theft all the more complete. All that's left to be done is fill in the information, add a picture of the imposter, and even add the Social Security number in those states that employ such horrific violations of personal privacy. (Listen up, Virginia!) Poof, there are two of you.

Once your identity has been stolen, you may unknowingly buy houses, cars, run up interminable debt, or even commit crimes.

Imagine you are driving down the street and your taillight is out. You get pulled over by a sheriff. He asks you for your license and registration. He goes back to his police car, which is outfitted with a computer. He enters the information from your license which is transmitted back to the local police station which in turn is tied into state police and Department of Motor Vehicles computers. Many municipalities also tie into national law enforcement computers such as the FBI's NCIC (National Crime Information Center).

In a couple of minutes, the officer comes back to your car, except his gun is unholstered or he is holding it in his hands. "Get out of the car, sir."

"Huh? What's the problem, officer?"

"Out of the car, now," he orders with his gun pointed your way.

You get out, are handcuffed and hauled off to the hoosegow.

Are you going to make your early morning meeting or pick the kids up from school? No way. Because the police are believing the contents of the computers over your protestations.

The Ins and Outs of On-line People-hacking

In the good old days, pre-1990, personal data searches were time-intensive and required lots of phone calls, written letters, and travel. But the Internet changed all of that. Today, your life is an open electronic book to those who want to know everything about you—no matter their purpose.

There are, of course, legitimate purposes for doing investigations into individuals. Law enforcement needs to profile suspects—understandably so. It would be nice if stockbrokers or banking personnel were arrest-free, especially of arrests involving financial crime. Employers may have some legitimate need to know about a potential hire's background. I don't think that many of us would dispute proper background checks with a real purpose and subsequent protection of that information.

However, deep background investigations can and do occur without your knowledge or consent—thanks to the Internet and huge data bases of information assembled by enterprising information brokers, who sell it in parcelled bits. Again without asking your permission—and that is the crime, even though these firms are operating with the full protection of the law.

Broadly, there are two kinds of records. The first is public records such as marriages, lawsuits, drivers' information, real estate holding, voter registration (including unlisted phone numbers), many criminal activities, bankruptcies, creditors, financial, health, and so on. Because of the cost to state and local government in providing electronic versions of the paper records, private companies have taken up the task of converting them and then offering the data for a fee to investigators.

The second broad class of personal information is non-public records such as telephone logs, utility bills, military service, banking and tax documents, medical files, credit card transactions, and travel and shipping records, to name a few. The professional information broker and the criminal, though, have little trouble extracting highly confidential information from any of these sources, all in the name of background checks. I find it especially bothersome how the information brokerage industry has so little regard for individual privacy, that they are so willing to violate it for money, and that there is little or no legislative or legal oversight.

Some of the larger, and as they put it, more reputable, information brokers claim that they won't sell information unless it's to legitimate private investigators, major corporate subscribers, lawyers, or law enforcement. Nonetheless, their weak defensive arguments aside, anyone with a checkbook or credit card can drive right through the unregulated gaping hole of No-Privacy.

You or I or a criminal can still acquire what the big companies say they do not make available to Joe Six-Pack by merely hiring an on-line investigator or cyber–private investigator (or attorney with minimal scruples) to do the dirty work. It may cost a few bucks, but when financial gain, vengeance, stalking, or other malicious activity is the goal, what's a couple of hundred bucks anyway?

Third-party information brokers, for a fee, will sell that which you are generally unable to gather on your own. There is no shortage of tricksters, harassers, criminals and ne'er-do-wells who full well understand better than you or I how to take advantage of these services, to the detriment of the personal privacy and security of all Americans. A quick scan of your local Yellow Pages and a couple of phone calls will prove the point. Big Bill, one of my neighbors, is engaged in exactly this form of information brokering and he and I have had endless debates over the usefulness (his position) or putritude (my position) of what he and his kind do for a living.

Major information brokers often enter into strategic relationships with firms that can enhance their business, such as CDB with Equifax, the credit reporting agency. If you take a look, many of these firms provide no real, physical address, preferring the anonymity of a PO Box. Why? They don't want disgusted Americans beating down their doors in protest.

Public records are just that, and will remain public probably for a long time, unless someone in Washington changes the laws to reflect the new reality of pervasive abuse such systems offer. Regulation over the use of private information and oversight of those engaged in the information brokering industry would be a good first step. Some of the larger groups involved in the sale of public (and other) information include:

www.cbd.com	CBD-Infotek 800.992.7889
www.dbt.net	DBT Online
www.knowx.com	
www.esperian.com	The credit agency (real estate primarily)
www.bisi.com	Background Information Services
www.merlindata.com	Merlin Information Services 800.367.6646
www.openonline.com	Online Professional Electronic Network
www.dnis.com	DCS Information Systems 800.299.DNIS
www.bigfoot.com	Verifies telephone numbers and addresses
www.pimall.com	The PI mall for private investigators
www.nali.com	The National Association of Legal Investigators 800.266.6254

Under the belief (which may well have no basis in fact) that information brokers only sell legal public records, the astute investigator will then resort to quasi-legal and anti-ethical means. Private investigators have friends in law enforcement who often will help out with private information. Bank security staff are often ex-law enforcement and have consistently helped out with extra-legal information gathering.

And then, there is always lying. The well-honed hacker tricks of social engineering have been perfected by the better PIs, who know how to extract extensive information from utility and phone companies, shipping firms, banks, and brokerage companies; in short, anyone with the information that they need.

Is Your Fiancé an Axe-murderer?

I know I have received dozens of unsolicited (spamlike) emails from individuals and organizations that offer unlimited personal data–searching for a fee. Or they offer complete background checks for $49 or a book on how to do it yourself for $29. They promise the sky and attempt to sound like information brokers who will solve your every problem. They tease the recipient with "Do You Really Know Your Wife?" or "What's Your Employee Hiding?" in the subject line.

In every case I have seen so far, there is an email address for ordering, or a PO Box in Funktown, Louisiana to send in your check. There is never a phone number or real address. There has never been a phone listing for the name of the business they use. For what it's worth, I have responded to at least twenty of these solicitations via email. I said that I am a security guy and would like to do an article on them or include them in this book. The score? Zero responses.

These are scams, pure and simple. Any real business will offer a phone, a human to talk to, and a means of verifying their legitimacy. Forget these characters. They are out to fleece you, or deliver a sheath of useless fuzzy Xeroxed papers with the same information you can get for free on the Internet.

It Oughta Be a Crime

Companies, especially large national companies, don't have a clue.

The other day I called AT&T, you know, the long distance company. I needed a second cell phone for my wife. The mobile service operator looked up my account and I told her just to add the second phone to it.

"Fine, sir. Everything is in order, I just need your Social Security Number."

Red flags shot up faster than a Patriot missile.

"Why do you need that?"

"The order entry screen has a field for it."

"You don't need it," I countered. "You have no legitimate business need for my SSN."

We argued, and she only regurgitated the same old story that the software required the magical nine-digit number which, when abused, can unravel lives.

"Hold on for a supervisor, please," she said with distinct rancor.

"Supervisor, may I help you?"

"Yes, ma'am," I said with as much sweetness as I could muster, and I told her my problem.

"Sir, the software won't accept your order without your Social . . ." to which I again countered that there was no business need for AT&T to have it in their records. Only the IRS, my bank, my employer, and certain government agencies have a legitimate need for it.

She paused, and asked me to hold on. In a minute I was on the phone with yet another, higher-up supervisor, and we went through the same routine again.

"Please tell, me," I begged, "why do you need it?"

"It's for security, sir. It's how we identify you when you call in."

I cringed. Here is AT&T, one of America's largest companies, telling me and undoubtedly millions of others, that their Social Security Number is their only and best way of providing individual security for their phone records. How incredibly ridiculous.

"OK. Here it is. 414-39-4096."

"Thank you. Your order has been placed." I wrote down the number I had made up for future reference since all the number was used for was identification.

A couple of hours later, another AT&T representative called.

"Sir, the Social Security Number you gave us belongs to someone who is dead. Can you read it back to me, please?"

Aha! They lied! "How do you know it's for a dead person?"

"We checked."

"But I was told that the number is only for identification. What does it matter which nine digits are used?"

The AT&T rep stuttered. "Ah, it is . . . but we have to verify identity." Programmed bullshit coming out of her mouth.

"You have been billing me for months, I have been paying you for months. The bills arrive here and you put the charges on my American Express card. What is the identity question?"

She stuttered and paused again. "Without your Social Security Number, sir, you cannot have a new cell phone. It's company policy."

"Are you going to disconnect my other service?"

"Why, of course not, sir. You are a valued customer."

I quickly cancelled my AT&T service and went with a carrier who did not require an invasion of privacy to use their phones. Calls to the AT&T public relations office went unanswered.

Wondering how far this abuse went, I contacted my bank about their remote banking services. You know the kind, where you can use the telephone, dial up and query your account and such. It turned out that they, too, use a Social Security Number as the ultimate means of determining a customer's identity. The account is password-protected with a four-digit code which permits unlimited attempts at getting in, a hacker's delight. In short, next to no security.

I spoke to the bank vice president and asked that my remote banking identification code be changed from my Social Security Number to another nine-digit code that I select. They told me that their system couldn't accomodate that, but that excuse lacked any rationale: nine digits is nine digits is nine digits.

Astonished at what I was learning, I faxed the chairman of the bank and spelled out my concerns over their lack of security controls. Within minutes, the head of bank security called me; he was a former Secret Service agent and had been with the bank for only a few months. We talked and he commented, "Holy . . . I had no idea." He was acutely aware from his experience that a Social Security Number in the wrong hands could spell disaster; he knew about identity theft and criminal hacking tricks of the trade.

"What do you suggest?" he asked.

We chatted about the various kinds of user-authentication products that are available, but they also require extensive and expensive systems modifications. "It looks to me that the designers chose the easy way out with no regard for privacy or security," I said, and he agreed.

"The simplest way is to alter bank procedure and policy to allow customers who care about security to choose their own nine-digit code. You also need to restrict the number of unsuccessful password attempts to two or three to eliminate account hacking."

Time will tell if this conversation has any effect.[1]

And in the meantime, I shut down my remote banking.

Note that when you call up your credit card companies, they, too, will ask for your address and phone number as primary identification. But

---

[1]Eight months later, this big Southern bank still employs the same abysmal process.

they will also ask for your Social Security Number as proof positive that you are you. Unfortunately, as you are learning, with a tiny bit of effort, a criminal or hacker can easily impersonate you on the telephone and start fouling up your life.

What you can do:

We're not going to change the way things are done overnight, but there are several things you can try to increase your personal electronic security.

1. Call those companies who use your SSN as ID and work your way up the management hierarchy. Find someone intelligent, get their name and employee ID number. Ask that your SSN be removed as your final ID code and that another nine digits be used. I have found several companies that do not have to report to the IRS have been willing to modify the code. Don't give up. Keep trying, as it is in your best interest to avoid becoming a victim to either identity theft or other forms of crime. Sure, your worst-case exposure on credit-card fraud is fifty dollars, but who needs the hassle?

2. If you don't get a satisfactory response, write a letter or send a fax or email to the president of the company. Be nice. Spell out your concerns and reasons coherently. Include your efforts to repair the situation. You may or may not get a response. And yes, this will take some time and effort.

3. If you are so inclined, get the Social Security Number of the bank president or his secretary from the resources available on the Internet. This is perfectly legal and it might prod them a little. I have seen some people go as far as including the credit report of the company official. Your call.

4. Let other people know that they should be worried about this national abuse and have them take action, too. As Arlo Guthrie said in *Alice's Restaurant*, when one person complains, it's a pain in the butt. When thousands take action, it's a movement. And just maybe, we citizens can get something positive accomplished.

5. Find companies to do business with that understand security and the invasive nature of using your SSN as identification.

6. And if they really, really insist, despite your best protestations that they have to use your SSN as final and ultimate identifica-

tion, have them put in your records that you will only give out the last four digits on the phone. It's better than nothing.

Ultimately, new laws are needed and this is the responsibility of state and federal lawmakers. Write your congressman. Fax him. Call him. Make him aware of the problem. A new law could be very simple and solve a big problem:

"Organizations are not permitted to use an individual's Social Security Number for identification or other business purposes unless required to by law."

It's that easy. Now, all we need is for someone in Congress to care.

Can You Prevent Identity Theft?

In a word, no. The computers are too interconnected, company policies are not designed to cater to personal privacy and security, and most importantly, everything about you and your life is available on the Internet or for a small fee from information brokers. However, you can take some steps to mitigate the damage if you do ever become a victim.

1. Don't throw sensitive papers into the garbage. Dumpster diving, or going through your garbage, is a standard hacking trick by criminals.

2. Ask how companies handle sensitive information and what their security and identification precautions are. Insist on answers that make sense.

3. Avoid pickpockets. The fifty-dollar limit on your credit cards isn't the issue; you likely carry a full set of identification that enables someone to quickly adapt your electronic identity.

4. Do not put your SSN or phone number on checks. If it's there now, order new checks and shred the others.

5. Some credit cards are now available with a picture. Ask.

6. Make passwords hard to guess and as long as you can.

7. Scrutinize all credit card, telephone and other bills for unauthorized activity. Report it immediately.

8. Never, ever give out personal information on the phone to people you don't know. Telephone solicitation is a great criminal scam. Be especially cautious about cellular phones.

9. Order your credit report a couple of times per year to see what the computers say about you. This is the one area that Congress has seen fit to address with the Fair Credit Reporting Act. Immediately correct any mistakes in writing to the credit agencies.

10. Get your name off of unsolicited credit offers. Your name is being sold daily to direct marketers.

11. Don't fill in personal information on forms, registrations, or warranties. They don't need it. They want to sell it.

In short, you have to take the initiative yourself, even if it means hiring a professional to help you through the process and, in the worst case, to restore your good name. Monitoring your electronic existence is crucial.

Organizations can also take positive steps to increase personal privacy and security of their employees and customers. But they need to care first.

1. Perform in-depth background checks on staff who will have access to personal employee and customer information.

2. Keep private information in locked file cabinets and encrypt the file if stored on computers.

3. Use something other than SSNs for personnel and customer identification.

4. Use photos for company ID cards.

5. Restrict access to the Internet and fax machines for those employees with access to sensitive data.

6. Avoid leaving confidential information on voicemail, cell phones, pagers, answering machines, or in email.

7. Use physically secure printers and fax machines when proprietary information must be output.

8. Design a corporate policy detailing how to handle personal and private customer and employee information.

9. Advertise your corporate privacy policy and procedures to your staff and on your web site.

10. Train your employees to the danger of identity theft and fraud.

11. Don't share or sell information about your customers without their permission. It's wrong. It may be legal, but it's still wrong.

12. Only acquire and use that information which is required to do business—no more.

13. Make absolutely sure that the person with whom you are dealing is really who they claim to be.

14. Don't use an SSN for identification.[2]

At the Desktop

Your Internet connection and web browser are both a source of facility and insecurity, so here are a couple of things to think about before letting your kids or yourself loose out there. (You will learn more about personal desktop protection in the chapter on Firewalls, Viruses, and Trojan Horses, on page 336.)

Java is a new computer language that will work on any kind of computer, no matter what system it is. But Java presents a few problems. Occasionally you will notice on your browser that Java is running. This means that the site you are visiting is sending you a small program, written in Java, to run on your desktop. What is inside of that program, though? Do you know? Mobile code (software programs that move from computer to computer) can be very destructive.

In the following examples, I was on the America Online web site.

The screen gives the choice of believing whether AOL is sending you malicious code or not. Obviously, it's not in their best interest to do so, so you're probably all right. You can, though, choose to grant their Java code access to your computer or deny it.

---

[2]Many thanks to Mari Frank and Beth Givens for their fine books and suggestions. For a more thorough guide, see the references at the end of the chapter.

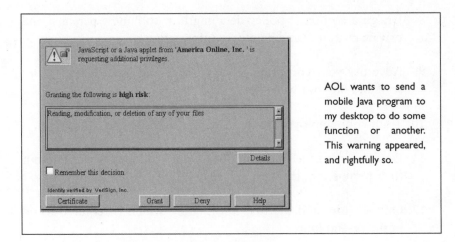

AOL wants to send a mobile Java program to my desktop to do some function or another. This warning appeared, and rightfully so.

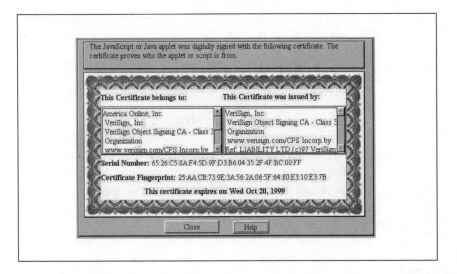

Now, note that in the lower left, it says, "Identity verified by Verisign, Inc." Verisign offers "certificates," or CAs, which are cryptographic proof of who sent the message, or in this case, Java code.

This Verisign certificate appears and gives you enough details so that if you really, really wanted to, you could go through the pain of verifying its authenticity on your own. But for most folks this is plenty. In theory, AOL's Java code could scour your hard disk for all sorts of privacy-related information, but we all hope not.

Now we are going to talk about encryption and other security in the coming chapters, so here are a couple of quick lessons to help you with your own desktop security.

In the lower left-hand corner of Netscape browsers you will see a lock. If the lock is open, then the communications between you and the web site are unencrypted, or subject to eavesdropping. When ecommerce is used, such as at Amazon.com or other places you might make a web purchase, generally the lock will close, meaning encryption is protecting the contents of the transmission. Microsoft does it with a Profile Assistant which gives you control over the transaction and how much security you would like to use.

If you hear the term SSL, or Secure Sockets Layer, and if the site you are connected to uses it, that means they are using encryption to protect your communications and/or transactions. Feel good about this.

Cookies

Sometimes you will go to a web site that repeatedly asks you for a password and user ID but you get sick and tired of entering it every time. Web sites now use "cookies," which are small bits of information that they place onto your computer. In both Netscape and Microsoft Internet Explorer you can choose whether to let cookies on to your machine, when, and by whom. Generally, accepting cookies from reputable sites is no problem, as is accepting Java. But, if you are out there in the great unknown, landing on planets where you don't know if the life forms are hostile or not, you may want to play it a bit safer.

Internet Explorer allows you to set up Internet zones to delineate how you act depending upon where you surf.

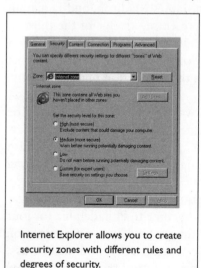

Internet Explorer allows you to create security zones with different rules and degrees of security.

To be fair to both Netscape and Microsoft, here are the respective security options they offer.

Please!

Spend five minutes—that's all it takes—to go through the security options in either or both of these products on your computer. The Help files are pretty good and do point you to additional help if you need it. Security is being updated all the time, so if you upgrade your browser or get a new one, check to see what additional features have been added. If there is any doubt in

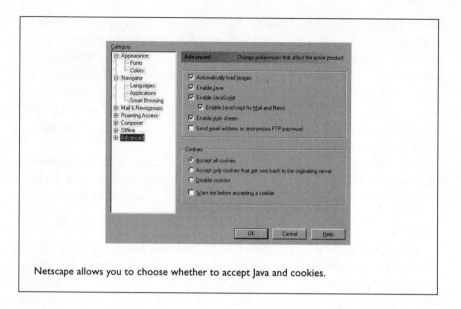

Netscape allows you to choose whether to accept Java and cookies.

your mind, err on the side of caution; be conservative until you are more comfortable with living on the edge.

An Electronic Bill of Rights

On May 14, 1787, George Washington, James Madison, and Benjamin Franklin joined fifty-two other men representing twelve of the thirteen states to, in the words of Alexander Hamilton, "render the Constitution of the Federal Government." The Constitutional Convention met through September of that year, writing the instruction manual on how to run the United States of America.

Two hundred years ago, the world was a very different place. The war with England was over and the United States (plural) were preparing for peace. They needed to forge unity amongst themselves, establish the new country as a viable international partner, and build a strong defense for a secure future.

Weaknesses in the original Constitution (the Articles of Confederation) prompted the new nation's leaders to come to Philadelphia for four months of emotional debate. Their ultimate goal was a Constitution which would reflect a balance between monarchy and democracy. Despite vast differences among the participants and their views on how to fashion a new nation, they succeeded at their task. Signed by only thirty-nine of the original fifty-five delegates, the Constitution of the United States became the supreme law of the land on June 21, 1788, with its ratification by nine of the thirteen states. Due to deficiencies in state and individual rights, the First Congress submitted twelve amendments to the Constitution to the states in 1789. The ten surviving amendments, known as the Bill of Rights, are viewed as the ultimate safeguards of our personal freedom and liberty, perhaps even more so than the original body of the Constitution itself.

These two documents, the Constitution and the Bill of Rights, have carried this nation forward for over two hundred years and have suffered only seventeen changes. Today, however, we see that our national migration into Cyberspace represents such a fundamental change in our national character, and in our connection to the physical world, that the existing tentacles of laws and legislation are not automatically sufficient. The United States again finds itself at a crossroads.

The Constitution was written for and by an agrarian society that relied upon oil for lamps, manual looms for clothes, and horses and sails for transportation. It was written at a time when loading a musket took the better part of a minute and communications could take days or weeks, not fractions of a second. The Constitution was written to establish a new nation on Earth (a physical place that can be found on a map), not in Cyberspace (a virtual, intangible place, the borders of which defy conventional cartography). The framers provided the means to amend the Constitution as needed, but they could never have imagined the technological advancements of today's world.

Thomas Jefferson wisely recognized that fact. He wrote,

> *I am not an advocate for frequent changes in laws and constitutions, but law and institutions must go hand in hand with the progress of the human mind. As that becomes more developed, more enlightened, as new discoveries are made, new truths discovered, and manners and opinions change, with the advance of circumstances, institutions must advance also to keep pace with the times. We might as well require a man to wear still the coat that fitted him when a boy as civilized society to remain under the regimen of their barbarous ancestors.*[3]

In Jefferson's day, the Constitution provided a workable alternative to anarchy, but as every day passes, we find that we are outgrowing our

---

[3]Private letter to Samuel Kercheval from Monticello, July 12 1816 and inscribed on the wall of the Jefferson Memorial, Washington, DC.

country's overcoat as we lead the world into Cyberspace. The world is a very different place from the one in which this country was founded over two hundred years ago.

The fundamental concepts of a real place versus a virtual place are profoundly different. Two hundred years ago people lived in a tangible world, where they could touch and feel their property and money. Today, we trust that the computer has got it all straight. Two hundred years ago ownership meant physical possession: A man's property could be measured between sticks in the ground. Today, possession of financial wealth is determined by reliable electron excitation, ownership has become a quantum uncertainty, and place is as untouchable as Alice's netherworld. You will never be able to drive a car down the information highway!

Cyberspace just doesn't accommodate many of the existing models we have generated to run modern society for two centuries. Can the traffic rules from horse-and-buggy days be applied to a high-speed interstate system or to urban congestion? Do the procedures of the old Pony Express have any real applicability to a modern postal service that delivers nearly 200 billion pieces of mail each year? Can the rules of a preindustrial agrarian society be reasonably expected to fill the needs of a postindustrial society in which information is the prime commodity of value? Stretching existing laws and judicial interpretation through awkward convolutions hasn't worked. Some fundamental changes are called for.

We find ourselves in a position similar to our ancestors', who wanted to create a model for the future success of the newly established country. It is now time to build a policy for *our* time in history; to establish rules and guidelines that are congruous with the fabric of Cyberspace. The United States has always met the challenges before it, and we are today presented with unprecedented opportunity to, as Richard Nixon might say, "seize the moment." Standing before us is the opportunity to lead our nation, and perhaps the world, into an era of success, achievement, benevolence, and greater prosperity than civilization has ever seen.

At the base of that new model must be citizens' rights and an Electronic Bill of Rights, which must be as simple as the original in concept. In 1994 I published the first version in *Information Warfare: Chaos on the Electronic Superhighway*, subsequently adapted for republication in the 2nd Edition of *Information Warfare*, revised in 1996. This abbreviated version was published in *Federal Computer Week* in mid-1997 and was subsequently adapted by Vice President Al Gore.[4] It is a simple yet bold proposal, requiring political strength, vision, and the love of one's

---

[4]He gave no credit to anyone for this invention, which must have followed his invention of the Internet.

constituency more than oneself. The six-point Electronic Bill of Rights takes into account the realities of modern technology and overarching legislative wisdom.

1. I own my name. My name is mine to do with as I please. Not yours.

2. You, as a business, may use my name for the purpose of our transaction only. You may not sell, barter, or otherwise market my name or any information about me or that transaction without my explicit permission.

3. If you need to keep my name in files for the purpose of ongoing business, you will protect it from abuse, illicit access, or accidental release.

4. If you have any files containing my name, you must notify me of the existence of those files, send me copies upon request, and provide a reasonable means to add, delete, or correct information. I am entitled to periodic updates when I request.

5. The government will create a new data classification called "Personal but Unclassified," and set standards for its protection in both the private sector and for legitimate government needs.

6. I will have civil and criminal recourse against persons and organizations, private and government, who either violate my Electronic Rights or permit them to be violated.

These simple principles will bring back much of the privacy that has been eroded away since the dawn of the computer age. It places a common sense limit to how my name may be used, and will add credibility and accuracy to existing data bases. It works in real corporations, in the virtual e-economy, and for children, too.

These simple principles, though, will also cause a backlash by those organizations who do not believe in the privacy rights of the individual and who make their living by twisting the concepts of public records and unregulated data bases for their personal profit.

But more importantly, these simple principles will help us find the leaders in Washington who understand how critical and fundamental these rights are and should be. These new leaders will find the political courage to finally make Cyberspace a much, much safer place to play, live, and do business.

The US Does In Fact Guarantee Individual Privacy

Too many people incorrectly believe that personal privacy is not, nor
has ever been considered a basic human right. I hope to expose this for
the fallacy it is. Indeed, privacy is a basic human right despite the popular narrow-sighted view to the contrary.

True, the word privacy does not exist in the US Constitution or in its
amendments. It is from that weak position, however, that people argue
that we should therefore not expect privacy: because the Constitution
does not offer it. Placate not my offended sensibilities, though, by stating that "we have the right to seek privacy, but there can be no guarantee that we will find it." So what?

I feel sickened that professionals dangle the Constitution as the ultimate
arbiter of what rights we have, should have, and should not expect to have.
Having been involved in many governmental, military and social international affairs over the years, I would suggest that we in the US do in fact
have rights that most of us ignore, or worse yet, are even unaware we have.

To discover those rights, all one has to do is to examine a single yet
profound document that the US Government signed on behalf of its citizens: that is you, me and users of the Internet, too.

On December 10, 1948, the United States of America signed the Universal Declaration of Human Rights, one of the most powerful and
underlying proclamations ever made and agreed to by the vast majority
of the nations on the planet. The General Assembly of the United
Nations was the adapter of these rights to which so many Internet-fluent
advocates seem to be ignorant. I happen to keep a copy next to my desk
and have done so for over a decade.

The document's opening paragraph sets the stage for global human
rights by declaring that "every individual and every organ of society . . .
shall strive by teaching and education to promote respect for these
rights . . . and to secure their universal and effective recognition and
observance." Good thoughts, good words. If privacy is one of those
rights, then where are the US-based educational offerings? Permit me to
demonstrate that the United States has indeed imbued its citizens with
certain rights to privacy:

Article 12 of the Universal Declaration of Human Rights says, "No
one shall be subjected to arbitrary interference with his *privacy*, family,
home or correspondence, nor to attacks upon his honour and reputation. Everyone has the right to the protection of the law against such
interference or attacks." And everyone (in the UN sense of the word)
includes the citizens of the United States.

Privacy—despite the Constitution's earlier denial of its existence—is clearly an important concept to the global framers in a post–World War II world. Yet, despite that signatory support, where are the Congressional efforts to develop privacy in this country as has been done in Canada, the UK and other civilized countries? Where, indeed!

I find it especially intriguing that the concept of privacy is adjuncted by the word "correspondence," which in 1948 meant the mail or radio communications but today would easily encompass other electronic transmission such as email. That would imply that recent efforts on the part of the private sector to vacuum up private information from the Internet, from public sites, from direct marketers and from credit card companies, to name a few, are in direct violation of the spirit of the Universal Declaration of Human Rights—which the US guarantees we citizens since they are a signatory to it.

Sounds to me like we signed up for personal privacy but in the last fifty years have forgotten to do anything about it.

Let's see if collectively we can kick some legislative butt and get Washington to recognize privacy as a basic American right.

Search This

Identity theft, identity fraud, privacy, Social Security Number, private investigators, information brokers, public records, credit, credit card scams.

Reporting Identity Theft

- Equifax: 800.685.1111 (The credit agencies hate fraud almost as much as you do, and contacting them will assist in short-circuiting some damage to your electronic reputation.)
- Experian (TRW): 800.397.3742
- Trans Union: 800.680.7289
- US Postal Service: 800.275.8777 (Anyone using the mail for fraud violates federal law.)
- US Social Security Administration: 800.772.1213
- FBI and US Secret Service: Check your local phone book.

Resources

- *The Privacy Rights Handbook*, Beth Givens, and the *Privacy Rights Clearinghouse*, Avon Books. ISBN: 0-380-78684-2
- *Privacy Piracy*, Mari Frank & Beth Givens, an Office Depot IDEAbook. Spring, 1999.
- www.identitytheft.org (Mari Frank's web site)
- www.privacyrights.com (Beth Givens' remarkable organization)
- www.pirg.com—California Public Interest Research Group
- www.goa.gov, report #: GCD-98-100BR
- www.equifax.com/consumer/faqs/fraud/fraud.html
- www.experian.com (Visit "Ask Max")
- www.tuc.com/consumer/fraudvictim.asp
- www.treas.gov/usss (Secret Service); www.fbi.gov (FBI)
- *From Victim to Victor: A Step-by-Step Guide for Ending the Nightmare of Identity Theft*, Mari Frank, Porpoise Press. ISBN: 1-892126-01-X
- *Check It Out: How to Find Out Practically Anything About Anyone in Your Life*, Edmund J. Pankau, Contemporary Books. ISBN: 0-8092-2900-5
- *The Sourcebook of Online Public Record Experts*, Carl Ernst, BRB Publications. 800.929.3811
- *How to Locate Anyone Who Is or Has Been in the Military*, Richard Johnson, MIE Publishing. 800.937.2133
- *The Private Investigators's Guide to the Internet*, Joseph Seanor, TI Pubs, Inc. 512.420.9292
- www.idfraud.com
- www.cdt.org—Center for Democracy and Technology (privacy advocates)
- www.cpsr.org—Computer Professionals for Social Responsibility
- ww.eff.org—Electronic Frontier Foundation
- www.nvc.org—National Victim Center
- Medical Information Bureau—617.426.3660 (See if you can get your own records.)

Protecting Your Kids and Family from Hackers

On-line chat rooms are like having a conversation with someone by writing on the bathroom walls.

There are some sick people out there.

I mean really sick, twisted, demented people who prey upon our children for their own depraved reasons. And as parents, we do our absolute best to keep our children far from their kind. I should know.

My young teenage nephew was befriended by an adult "good neighbor" and, unbeknownst to my in-laws, their son was sexually abused for years, until he committed suicide. The pedophile is in jail for life, in isolation from the other prisoners who would kill him for his crimes.

When sex offenders are released from jail, community disgust demands that they be publicly identified when they attempt to move into a neighborhood. Those who do survive prison are often so vilified by being 'outed' they have a terribly difficult time trying to put their lives together again.[5]

Society is developing the awareness and collective will to protect children from the outrages of sexual abuse in the physical world. We do not tolerate any forms of pedophilia or child pornography: We rightfully

---

[5]Authorities lean towards the belief that once a sex offender or pedophile it is almost impossible to change one's ways without substantial professional help, castration, or extreme drugs.

revere our children, and most parents will go to any length to protect them.

But what about Cyberspace? What is going on there? When parents know less about the computer than the kids, who's the boss? When kids are often fearful to admit an on-line encounter of a sexual nature to their parents, how is a parent to help? When kids are targeted by ruthless on-line marketing organizations to whip out their parent's credit cards and fill out forms asking for very personal information, how do we respond?

▶ Time/CNN Poll

April 27-29, 1999. Teens surveyed were 13 to 17 years old. *Time Magazine*, May 10, 1999, p. 40.

The results speak for themselves:

- 82% of teens surveyed use the Internet.
- 44% have been to an X-rated site.
- 25% have visited hate group web sites.
- 14% have seen sites where they are taught how to build bombs.
- 62% said their parents knew little or nothing about the web sites they visit.
- 43% of parents have no Internet-use rules for their kids to follow.
- 69% of the kids don't follow the rules or have none to follow.
- 72% of girls (57% of boys) suspect they have 'chatted' with people who are pretending to be someone they are not.
- 58% of girls (39% of boys) have been asked to provide personal information like telephone number and address.

Kids aren't stupid, though, especially the techno-savvy ones. While hormones may be raging and rebellion constantly tests the limits of authority, they have a fundamental grasp on reality.

- 83% of those surveyed trust their parents a "great deal."
- Only 13 percent, though, trust what they read on the Internet a "great deal."
- Cynically, and echoing much of adult skepticism, only 39% trust the conventional media a "great deal."

Besides the miscreants who troll the Internet for children (motive notwithstanding), what are our children doing on-line themselves? For the first time in history, much of what our children are exposed to is hidden from our view. With latchkey kids and both parents working, who's watching what they do? When I was a preteen, I came home from school and spent about two hours alone before my mother got off of work. My choices for activity were limited.

- Homework. I was expected to do my homework before mom came home. No excuses and we didn't have a dog to eat it.
- The radio. Harmless Cousin Brucie lyrics on WABC-AM, bouncing teenybopper music, and the Beatles. The most offensive lyrics of the day were by the Rolling Stones in a song called "Let's Spend the Night Together." Oooh . . . how risqué!
- Television consisted of three network channels and a handful of local channels that offered movies like *The African Queen* and *Godzilla*. Cartoons were *Rocky and Bullwinkle*.
- Read, write, think without chaotic external stimulus. I did a lot of that since there's only so many *Crusader Rabbit* reruns.

Today, the overstimulated preteens and teenagers face quite a different set of choices than I did, and it's not all technology.

- Homework. When the schools give it, parents have to care enough to see if it was completed. In order to achieve a higher graduation rate and less failure to proceed from one grade to the next, the response of national educators has been to lower standards. Good move for America.
- Radio. Lyrics range from love-struck sublime and oldies stations to brutal gangsta-rap lyrics where sexual violence is unabashedly celebrated. My teen daughter is thankfully offended by the extreme "foul-mouthed music" that is played over the airwaves despite FCC guidelines.
- Video games. OK, *Pokemon* is fairly benign, but it conditions kids to be obsessive. The game researchers and psychologists employ "operant conditioning," a stimulus-response-reward cycle, to make the game as engrossing as possible to kids. This approach has a powerful effect on behavior. At the other end of the video game spectrum are *Doom* and *Quake*, in which kids are rewarded for murdering cybervictims in full glorious color. *Carmaged-*

don rewards gamers for mowing down pedestrians. *Duke Nukem* features pig-humans in police vests, and don't forget the host of intensely violent martial arts games. Good way to spend an afternoon.

- Videos and television. A quick walk to Blockbuster Video offers the latest rage of violence and gratuitous sex, much of it targeted at the teen audience, even if they are rated R. At home, with 100+ channels, the *Fishing Highlights* channel is probably not a teen's first choice. They will naturally gravitate to the materials we wish they woudn't see; but that's being a teenager. While *Playboy* magazine was the most blatant material available in my youth, cable television gets about as graphic as it can—with nothing left to the imagination. Even MTV celebrates teenage sexuality in the most graphic ways it can without being pulled off the air.

- The Internet. The sex. The incredible amount of sex on the Internet isn't just about loving sex between spouses. It offers vast amounts of sex between anyone or any group of people with the urge. The "push" advertising is compelling to the teenage libido, especially with offers of "Free!" and all too graphic sales pitches on both the web and on Usenet. But it gets worse. Interspecies sex is morally disgusting, yet alluring pictures of naked women with horses, dogs and chimpanzees are an attempt to appeal to the sickos in society—and to youngsters on the prowl for taboo.

Beyond sex, what are your kids learning on the Internet? How to hate ethnic minorities, religious sects of differing values, their government, and police? Racist America has taken to the Net for disseminating their hateful messages, propaganda, and lies. While the CNN poll said only 39 percent of teens believe the conventional media, how easy is it to sell hate to angst-filled preadults? How much of the racist messages will get through?

The two Columbine high school students who killed thirteen people on April 20, 1999, in Littleton, Colorado, frequented violent hate sites on the Internet, built their own of similar ilk, and even produced a movie which echoed the tragedy they created. Who was watching them? Astoundingly, other Columbine parents felt "they had no business learning what their kids were doing on the Internet."[6]

---

[6]*St. Petersburg Times*, June 6, 1999, p. 6D.

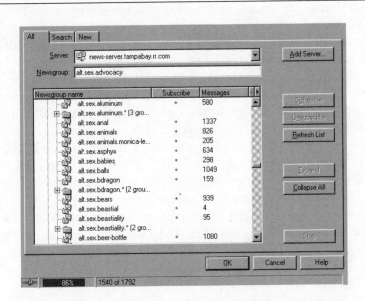

Tens of thousands of highly graphic words and pictures can be found on the thousands of sex-oriented news groups. These are just a click away on any browser and are free.

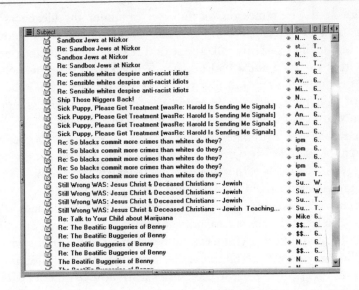

White power and various hate groups populate much of Usenet, too.

And therein, according to most experts, lies the problem. forty percent of American teenagers are on the Internet today, a number that is expected to double by 2001. But with a parental attitude of non-involvement, we see an echo of what is wrong with America and other information-rich societies today: our children are growing up with greatly diminished parental guidelines and supervision. Is it any wonder that much of what occurs on the Internet today is a reflection of the foreboding 1954 novel, *Lord of the Flies*?

Without parents to instill values in their kids, without an educational system that understands the medium, without any restraints by the media-producing industries, is it really any wonder that kids left to their own devices are attracted to extreme behavior?

Some people find it easy to blame the Internet for their kids' woes and choose to unplug them altogether. The Internet is at fault for its free-wheeling, anything-goes content, and thus it should be avoided at all costs. The Internet is what is wrong with society today. Blame the Internet. But that's just not true.

The Internet is a reflection of society itself. Don't worry, I am not going to get into a Dan Quayle family values rant, for family values are as different as families. The problem is values. Lack of values; lack of values taught, and lack of values instilled by both words and actions. Is the violence on TV and in the PG-13 movies any different than playing *Doom*? Isn't sex-filled prime-time TV a permission slip for kids to explore sexual extremes on the Internet or under the bleachers? And what about President Clinton's exploits forcing Dan Rather, Peter Jennings and CNN to openly talk about oral sex on the six o'clock news? I know that my wife and I had our hands filled with inventive explanations for our eight-year-old. But that's not the Internet, that's the President of the United States. The Monica tapes provided no less a graphic discourse on sex than any adult magazine or the Internet.

Many parents legitimately argue that the sex doesn't bother them; kids will be kids. What worries them is the constant, seemingly acceptable levels of violence that we are bombarded with daily. That is a parental choice for them to make. But the key word is choice.

Parents who do not involve themselves in the things their kids are exposed to have *chosen not to make a choice*, which leaves the children to be educated by other children and develop a sense of right/wrong all on their own. As we can all remember from our youth, children can be the most cruel people in the world as they learn how to interact with their peers. Without parental guidance and an occasional tug on their freedom-tether, what have we wrought? A generation we don't understand that is infinitely more techno-savvy than the vast majority of their elders.

I have heard parents say over and over, "*What can I do? My kids picked the computer, they built the computer, they hooked the family up to the Internet, and they fix it when it breaks. What hope do I have of controlling what they're doing?*" That is abdication of responsibility. Period. Choosing not to be involved. Ignorance is not a valid excuse. Ignorance of the law is not a legal defense, and technical naïveté is not an excuse for poor parenting.

Parents are capable of learning the technology. Take a course at a local adult education center. Hundreds of video training tapes will walk you through every aspect of computers and the Internet so you can learn at home at your own pace. And you have a very valuable source at home: your kids. Have them teach you how to take a computer apart and put it back together. They can show you the ins and outs of the Net. This approach does a lot more than just teach you techy stuff. It can help you build the bonds of trust and responsibility that parents and kids need.

Some parents feel that the government should be responsible. "Ban the X-rated sites. Get sex and racist-hate sites off the Internet altogether and things will be just fine. People who put bomb-building instructions on the Internet should go to jail. If it's offensive, it should be illegal."

Well, dear parents who hold this opinion, you have a couple of huge problems that you should thoroughly think through before continuing to espouse this view.

1. Wait! I remember J. Edgar Hoover and his distorted vision of national law enforcement. I see the current FBI director, Louis Freeh, advocating the potential banning of personal cryptography. He worries about the specter of terrorism on US soil and considers what personal freedoms we may have to give up to remain safe. We could always tell Congress, "Hey, you decide," but giving 500 lawyers such power is the ultimate in hypocrisy. The Internet community will never let this happen, so forget it.

2. In the United States we have a little thing called the First Amendment. That gives you and me and everyone else the right to say what we believe, with very little exception. No, you can't yell fire in a crowded theater, you can't joke about bombs at airports, you can't libel people, and you can't threaten the president. Other than that, just about anything goes. The concept of *morally acceptable to community standards* is a moving target. Consider that the two-piece bathing suit was invented and first worn to a shocked public only in 1946. At the turn of the century, a woman's exposed ankle was considered to be very sexy. Now we

have *Baywatch*, globally viewed by more people than any TV show in history with bare derrières on prime time. Most of what is available for viewing or reading on the Internet also comes in books and magazines, and can be found at the library.

3. Whose values of censorship should we employ? Yours? Mine? OK, we agree to ban bestiality. Fine. Pedophelia is a no-no, too, we agree. Now how about Nazi sites? Should we ban those? And explicit video-action sex on streaming downloads from thousands of web sites? Sites that advocate terrorism against the US? Are those OK? What about extreme religious attitudes that are anathema to our Western culture? And while we're at it, let's get the Catholic Church and Islamic sites banned 'cause they offend me. Your ideals of censorship or mine? Censorship is a slippery slope. Once it begins, there is no end, depending upon who is in control. At the end of the day, if I am in control of censorship, I end up with an Internet built just for me. How sad if we choose to forego responsibility so we can bowl an extra seven frames.

4. The Internet is international. Sure, we Americans invented it and we are the driving force behind a global economic engine called ecommerce, but the Net is for everyone. As John Berry Barlow, cofounder of the Electronic Frontier Foundation (EFF) said, "US law is just a local ordinance." Think about speed traps or ancient blue laws in the South. They affect no one but themselves and the errant speeder; there is no impact on New York or Chicago. On the Internet, US laws affect US citizens and those people within the physical confines of this country. Our laws do not apply elsewhere across the globe. Politicians in Minnesota are leading an effort to ban gambling from the Internet, so most gambling sites are headquartered in Latin America. The age of consent is lower than the US's eighteen years of age in Japan, Holland, and many other countries. International agreement, reciprocity, and common law is a distant vision, if achievable at all.

Protecting your kids from the potential ravages of the Internet, their own inherent curiosity, and their occasional misplaced trust *is* achievable. As with information security and protecting networks from hackers, there is no perfect answer; it doesn't exist. But you can protect your children a far sight more than they can protect themselves. In the physical world you set rules for your home and you expect your kids to abide by them. Same thing on the Internet. You have to set rules and be willing to enforce the rules when it's called for. The Internet is a highly dynamic medium, always changing, so you will also need to employ flexibility and fairness. There is no black and white.

Don't expect me to set rules for your family; nor should you automatically adapt the rules of another family. The rules you decide as a family are your rules, no one else's. Perhaps the following list of things you can do will be helpful in choosing what sort of behavior and technology is acceptable to you.

1. America Online (AOL) offers a "kids only" account which blocks young users from everything except monitored chat rooms and web sites deemed to be kid-friendly. Check with AOL for their current offerings. Perhaps getting rid of your local ISP and running with AOL, the Big Boy of the Net, will solve some immediate problems. On the other hand, if your kids are computer literate, they may know how to set up their own accounts without your knowledge.

2. Check with other ISPs, especially the large national ones, and see what sort of kid-friendly filters or special areas they have. Local ISPs tend to be small and they view their job as only providing access to the Internet—and then you're on your own.

3. Ask your neighbors (the ones who seem to speak computer), your church, and your kids' schools what they recommend. Perhaps they have new answers that have been developed since this book was published. Whatever you decide today could change tomorrow. Remember that the Internet as we know it today, the World Wide Web, was only invented in 1994 and heavily populated since 1998. It's going to change a lot, only none of us know how.

4. At home, consider placing the kids' computer in a family area where you can instantly see what they're doing. In my home of eleven computers, servers, printer room, and network (yeah, we have a lot of technology) the kids' machine is in the dining room, right off the kitchen and in the path to the family washroom. The mere presence of parents, even unspoken vigilance, can have a tremendous effect on their on-line activities. I have watched my daughter set up virtual worlds with a dozen or more of her friends in multiple chat rooms which are echoed on all of their computers. Once in a while we'll sit down with her and see who is on-line. We'll even type/chat with her friends 'cause they're

good kids. Be watchful, though, for secret codes such as 1,2,3,4, which can mean "parental unit nearby," or 1,2,3,4,5, which can mean "parental unit is annoyingly standing over my shoulder, so chill on what you're saying." Of course, you can always scroll on the chat window to see what conversation preceded your invasion. One popular chat facility on the Internet is called IRC, or Internet Relay Chat. Hundreds of IRC "channels" exist but they are absolutely unmonitored and can get extremely raucous or obscene. My preference is for my kids to set up private chat rooms with their friends.

5. Talk to your children. Yeah, talk to them. Discuss honestly and openly what they're doing on the Net, and what your concerns are. They learn about the mechanics of sex from health classes in school, but not about proper behavior. Discuss with your kids your real worries and what they think would be an equitable way to develop both trust and a reasonable degree of confidence that they are adhering to your guidelines. Kids don't want parents to look over their shoulders or read their diaries; privacy is important in personal development. But kids must also realize that parents have an ethical and legal responsibility to protect their offspring. Don't expect one half-hour meeting with your kids to solve your every worry. Make it a regular dialogue.

6. Disconnect from the Internet altogether. I hate this option, but it does exist. The Internet offers kids a tremendous amount of access to everything they could ever want to know, and it would be a terrible mistake to take that away from them, but perhaps in the most extreme cases it is necessary. One family we know allows only one hour of television per week for the whole family. In my opinion that's more than a little extreme, but I understood that they wanted to do family things more. However, making kids grow up in electronic- or media-isolation is a questionable response. Children need exposure to the real world in order to survive and succeed in it, and no, we cannot protect them against everything. Parents who worry too much: Chill out a little. Many child psychiatrists say that if we overprotect them and deny them access to the same things their friends have, they can rebel worse than if they had access to the forbidden fruits of television or the Internet. Lastly, if you do choose to disconnect, you have to confiscate the modem in addition to cutting up the wire.

7. Three popular programs can help you keep your kids' activities within bounds. Net Nanny, Surfwatch, and Cybersitter provide automatic filters which will block web surfing to inappropriate sites. None are perfect, and this is only one possible approach. Check out www.cyberangels.org/safetyandprivacy/chart.html for a comparison of major filters. The problems with contents filters are many:

- They do not block all bad sites, as new ones appear all of the time. You will need to go to the vendor's site and update the filter program fairly often to keep it reasonably current.
- Keyword blocking is a major impediment. The word "butt" may be a restricted word, but "butt" can also mean cigarettes. "Sex" and "breasts" might be filtered words but then breast cancer, breast-feeding and sex education might be blocked, or even sites on "sextuplets" or "Sussex, England." Innocent sites are victims.
- Some filters are political or agenda-driven. The filter vendor might ban viewpoints they don't agree with, information on specific politics or religious beliefs that are counter to their beliefs but are not offensive to most sensibilities.
- Your children might be able to disable the programs, especially if they had to help you install them.

8. Cybersnoop is exactly what it says. It tracks all web activities and stores them in a tamperproof file which, in theory, only parents can track. If your kid is good enough to hack/crack Cybersnoop, he is smart enough to behave responsibly. www.pearlsw.com

9. Your web browsers also create files of Internet history. In Microsoft Internet Explorer you can find the details in the History file. In Netscape Navigator, open the "cache" files. You may wish to set the size of these files to 20MB or more for a longer archive.

10. Many parents read their kids' email. Others decry this as an invasion of privacy like reading a diary or listening in on a telephone call. The difference is, you know who is writing the diary and your kids know (hopefully!) who they are speaking to. Anybody can pretend to be anybody on the Internet. We accidentally read

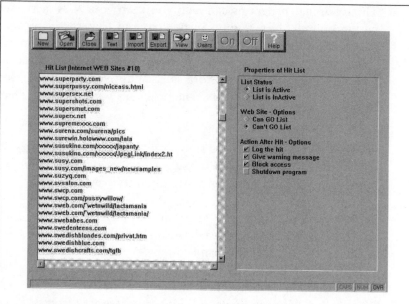

Net Nanny offers complete adult management flexibility to filter web sites, Usenet groups, and words and phrases. Updating the files is a parental responsibility.

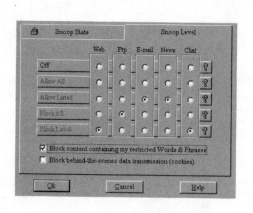

CyberSnoop's master configuration menu lets parents choose which Internet features, services, and sites may be used. Parents, playing with the evaluation program for a little while is well worth the effort. Maybe even have your kids help out. We made it a family safety effort.

one of our fourteen-year-old daughter's emails and were shocked at what a boy had written her. We then checked the outgoing mail she sent in response and smiled. She told the sender she didn't want to hear or read talk like that and to stop or she would tell. We were pleased, but still are tempted to look once in a while. Maybe an agreement with your child that you will spot-check

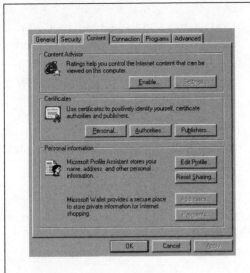

With Internet Explorer you can set some guidelines for what you will allow into your computer. Spend a few minutes with your browser and examine its security capabilities.

email once in a while is enough. If they tell their friends what you are doing (or threatening to do) it may be enough to keep things tame. Remember, though, it's your job to keep your kids safe according to your rules.

11. Educate your kids. You tell them not to talk to strangers. Everyone on the Internet is a stranger unless you really, really know who is at the other end of the wire. Impersonation of little boys and girls is the norm for on-line pedophiles. Police pretend to be little girls in order to identify perverts and they have been very successful in capturing them. Think bathroom walls.

12. Make sure your kids never ever give out personal information like their real name, phone number, address, or other identifying information best kept private.

13. You might want to initiate a web or Usenet search using your child's real name or his/her on-line handle. Use several different search engines. By reading what they are saying or what is being said about them you have an excellent clue as to what they are doing on the Internet.

14. If your child receives inappropriate pictures or messages from strangers, be prepared to report it to your local police or through

the many on-line kids'-safety sites, such as Cyberangel. Keep in mind, though, that the materials may simply be spam to a list that was sold to an on-line marketer. However, if your child receives several of these, it is possible he was visiting inappropriate sites in the first place and his email address was captured as a marketing target.

15. Do not respond to provocative flame mail that attempts to suck you into verbal on-line battles. Only losers engage in this despicable behavior.

16. Choose a genderless screen name. Cutie_Suzie is too enticing for on-line sickos. Macho_Mike might attract the wrong kind of people, too. Bear in mind, though, that everyone else might be genderless and not who they seem. (Bathroom walls.)

17. Do not flirt on-line unless you are prepared for the consequences. Even if you really think you know who you're talking to, the best advice is extreme caution.

18. If you end up in an uncomfortable situation, log off.

In closing: Parents, it is up to you. No one is going to do it for you. You are just going to have to get over the idea that someone else will solve your kids-versus-the-Internet problem; they won't and they can't.

It's up to you and your children, as a team, to create a healthy dialogue and a safe surfing Internet experience. And remember, they are kids. They will make mistakes and you can't protect them from everything.

On-line Stalking

Susan and Mike owned a lovely home, had two children—one of each kind—from her first marriage, and life was wonderful in their suburban paradise. Until the first email arrived.

```
You are in terrible danger. Beware.
```

Susan told Mike about it and he just dismissed it out of hand with the correct advice, "Ignore it." The following day Susan got another email.

```
You didn't heed my warning. This is your last chance to avoid
something awful. I warned you before.
```

Mike calmed Susan's nerves by explaining the odds were that this was just some power-ego-driven nutcase they didn't know. He looked at the return email address and it was from Hotmail, one of those free, anonymous web-based email services. The next day brought another message.

```
Your kids are now in danger. You should watch over Evan and
Michelle more carefully.
```

No amount of Mike's calming efforts deterred Susan from going to the police. Her children were being threatened. But the police said they couldn't do anything for two reasons. There were no "real world" threats of bodily harm, and besides, they weren't capable of investigating on-line crime. "Let us know if anything happens," was the best they offered.

While Mike worked late on Friday evening, Susan received a phone call. The voice was electronically masked to sound evil; a cross between Darth Vader and the possessed, head-spinning, pea-soup-spitting girl in the Exorcist.[7] "I told you," the mechanical voice said slowly and sinisterly. "You didn't listen. Now you will pay the price." At that exact moment, as Susan's heart pumped furiously in the early stages of terror, the lights went out and all power to her house was turned off. She slammed down the phone and drove like a demon back to the police. But again she was rebuffed.

Now concerned himself, Mike took a few days off from work and things settled back to normal. As soon as he went back to work, though, Susan's terror entered a new phase.

```
Your dear sweet husband is up to no good. Don't expect to
ever see him again.
```

The police said this still wasn't enough to go on; a crime hadn't been committed. "What are you waiting for, one of us to be killed before you do anything?" she shrieked. Not giving an answer, they stared at her blankly until she left.

As the days progressed, Susan awoke with terror each morning. The phone calls became more threatening. Then they got specific.

---

[7] Voice changers cost about fifty dollars from any decent electronics supply house or catalog.

I now have control of your life. Your house. Your family. I
warned you. Watch for what I can do.

As she read the email, the garage door opened and the TV went on at
full volume. Susan jumped through her skin as the phone rang. "I know
about your first husband and what he did. I know what you did. I bet
you want to keep that a secret, don't you?"

Susan was being stalked electronically. The terror she felt was as real as
if she was being chased down a dark alley by murderous thugs with
twelve-inch knives. It took a couple of weeks, but the perpetrator was
finally caught. It was her own son, Evan, fourteen, who was dismayed at
the death of his father and his mother's remarriage to Mike.[8]

Stalking is very real and cyberstalking is unfortunately coming into
vogue. The statistics astounded me when I first read them.

- 42% of the Internet population are women.
- 80% of stalking victims are women.
- Most cyberstalkers are male.
- There are an estimated 200,000 stalkers in America today.
  That means that 1 out of every 1,350 people are stalkers.
- About 1.5 million Americans have been or are currently
  stalking victims, or 1 out of 180 people.
- By reflecting these numbers to the Internet, with an esti-
  mated population of 150,000,000 or so:
  - There are 126,000 on-line stalkers
  - About 1 million stalking victims[9]

The reasons for stalking on-line and real-life stalking are the same
according to the experts:

- Sexual harassment is the most common. The Internet is
  male-dominated, and men and women naturally seek "safe"
  companionship. Hiding behind anonymity lets the stalker
  feel empowered and safe. Like alcohol, the Internet frees
  inhibitions. People are much freer to say what they want,

---

[8]This fictionalized story is based on several real stalking incidents, including one in
Canada where the stalker was indeed a family member.
[9]These numbers come from www.cyberangels.com/safetyandprivacy/stalk1.html.
They were adjusted for 1999 populations.

with much less regard for the consequences. Men can be such pigs.

- Love obsession is what movie stars experience and have to contend with daily. On-line, though, people can conjure up whatever images they want, and the goal is sincere, though perhaps unrequited, romance. On-line romance gone bad? Real romance gone bad? The aim of the stalker is not malicious; they just can't take "no" for an answer and believe constant harassment will change the mind of their victim.
- Hate/revenge/vendetta victims are largely male and the stalking occurs for a lot of reasons. An on-line argument escalates into a flame war and then into some form of stalking. Don't engage in flame wars! *Log off.* Perhaps you hold beliefs that others don't like. The arguments over Scientology have allegedly reached the stalking phase in many cases.[10] Maybe you embarassed someone in an on-line debate and he/she wants revenge. Newbies on the Internet can unintentionally inflame someone who misreads a message. Learn Netiquette.
- Power- and ego-trippers randomly pick victims to show off to their friends or hacking cliques. Hacker wars[11] and IRC battles typify this behavior, but with stalking you are merely an accidental victim who got in the way. Most of these stalking adventures have nothing to do with "you" at all.

A lot of stalking victims are newbies to the Internet who get into the wrong chat room, say the wrong thing to the wrong person, and allow the situation to escalate. It makes sense that the stalker wants to exercise power and control over his less-experienced victims; same as in real life.

If you hang on the Internet Relay Chat channels like #sex, #flirts, #romance, or web chat sites that cater to similar interests, your chance of being stalked rises significantly. Be very careful of bad neighborhoods on the Internet just as you would be in real life. Yes, you can be anonymous and look around and be a voyeur all you want. But so can they.

Getting help though can be tough. Police are used to investigating "real" crimes that have already been committed, not cyber-threats where the perpetrator cannot be identified. The odds of getting law enforce-

---

[10]Check out alt.religion.scientology on Usenet to watch some of the battles. Search on Scientology for web sites both pro and con.

[11]For a good look at hacker wars, check out *Information Warfare: 2nd Edition* (Thunder's Mouth Press).

ment assistance is low. My family has been stalked and harassed by hackers for years. Law enforcement including the FBI have never once investigated, even though I have tape recordings, full documentation, and the identity of the hackers. We took care of the perpetrators in our own ways. However, if there is any chance of them helping, you must help yourself. Make a complete log of all events, all phone calls, and everything that occurs. If you are with someone when an event occurs, get them to write it down, too. Save all relevant emails, log all IRC and web chat sessions, and make electronic and hard copies of them.

Hopefully the threats and intimidation will just go away. But in the rare instance when the stalking becomes more serious and potentially physical, your records will go a long way in prosecution—if the police even care. We'll learn more about that in Vigilantism.

Resources

- www.cyberangels.org is a very complete web site for protecting children. If you go nowhere else, go here for a more in-depth tutorial.
- www.Safekids.com. Thousands of links to sites for kids.
- http://www.kidscom.com/orakc/Games/newSafe/ indexright.html is a great, safe starting site for kids.

- The Center for Democracy and Technology offers a well-organized central location for helping parents control and monitor what their kids are doing on the Internet. www.cdt.org

Spam

Monty Python loves spam. The British comedy team wrote "The Spam Song" to prove it.[12]

> *Lovely Spaaam! Wonderful Spaaam!*
> *Lovely Spaaam! Wonderful Spam.*
> *Spa-a-a-a-a-a-am.*
> *Spa-a-a-a-a-a-am.*
> *Spa-a-a-a-a-a-am.*
> *Spa-a-a-a-a-a-am.*
> *Lovely Spaaam! (Lovely Spam!)*
> *Lovely Spaaam! (Lovely Spam!)*
> *Lovely Spaaam!*
> *Spaaam, Spaaam, Spaaam, Spaaaaaam!*

Annoying, eh? Spam on the Internet, though, means millions of annoying emails being sent to you and me and everyone we know—all without our consent or permission.

Junk mail in Cyberspace.

Most people agree that spamming is bad form, poor Netiquette (Internet etiquette), and in some cases illegal.

In the physical world we accept junk mail. In fact, if our junk mail volume decreases, we maybe should worry. Just think about people who

---

[12]Composers: Terry Jones, Michael Palin, and Fred Tomlinson. Authors: Terry Jones and Michael Palin. Arranger: Fred Tomlinson. From the *Monty Python* TV series and featured on various albums.

get none! The Information Disenfranchised are so far from the mainstream of society they don't qualify for junk mail, coupons, freebies, or invitations to buy products or services. The cost of the junk mail is absorbed by the sender: staff, printing, postage and so on. Occasionally I actually receive junk mail of value.

But spam . . . spam is so different. In most cases the spam messages are useless, fraudulent, or downright offensive. You will never receive a spam from Ford or IBM or Sprint. They know better. They use junk mail and obnoxious telemarketers who annoy us at dinnertime instead. There is no limit to spam; they will try to sell you anything, as the following list of actual email subject lines shows.

```
FREE! Phone Sex for 1 Month
FREE! Long Distance Calls
EARN $10,000 Per Month From Home. No Money Required.
Bambi Wants to Hear From You! Call Now.
Send $5 Make $100,000 in One Month.
We Need Your Help
ERASE ALL BAD CREDIT—GUARANTEED
Girls and Horses. FREE! XXXX PIX
Computers From $50
ACCREDITED INVESTERS WANTED
Incredible Profits Now!
HAWAII for $5 per day
Undervalued Stocks For Sale
Beautiful Russian Women Want to Meet You
25 Million Good Email Addresses for $99
Multi-Level-Marketing Creates Riches
XXX PIX XXX PIX XXX PIX XXX
Message From a Friend
Hi, It's Jenny! Remember Me?
```

Here are a couple of spams that are . . . well, normal. Is the first one too good to be true? Well so is the second one.

```
INCREASE SALES UP TO 1500%
ACCEPT CREDIT CARDS OVER THE INTERNET***NO SETUP FEES
Good Credit / Bad Credit/ No Credit***NO PROBLEM***
It Just Doesn't Matter—Everyone Gets Approved
No Upfront Fees For Application-Processing
While Others Charge You From $195 TO $250 To Get Set Up
WE CHARGE ZERO FOR SETUP FEES!!
```

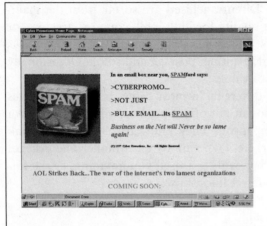

Cyberpromotions was one of the most prolific spammers on the Internet and was embroiled in controversy and legal battles for years. They were a constant target of hacker derision.

Limited Offer So Take Advantage Of It!!
We Specialize In Servicing The Following:

INTERNET-BASED BUSINESS
*Multilevel Marketing
*Mail Order/ Phone Sales
*Home Based Business
New Business Small Business
Whatever!! We Do It All!!!
Everyone Is Welcome!

A vast amount of spam comes pushing sex-oriented web sites. This one is typical. (I have changed the domain name of the web site to avoid giving them free advertising and because the domain name itself is highly offensive.)

From: Special Event@badname.com
Subject: The wait is over . . .

LIVE XXX Webcast—Broadcast Tonight
****
Mr. Spanky's
BEACH BLANKET BIMBOS
Starring Hot Porn Sensations Terri Starr and Intoxicatia
****
http://www.badname.com
TWO Horney Babes

TWO Camera Angles
TWO Outrageous Hours

TONIGHT:
December 25, 1999
5-7 PM (PST)

http://www.badname.com
We give "Good Vibrations" a whole new meaning.

How did you get on those lists anyway? Junk-mail lists come from credit card purchases and from having a telephone, cable service, or driver's license. Then the junk mailers choose who to mail to based upon zip codes (which separates the rich from the middle class and the poor), products purchased in the past, age, and other marketing criteria. They want to be selective and control costs, of course.

But the spammer is less discerning as to who he mails to. He doesn't care who receives his message as long as it is received. He doesn't care that he might offend you with his sex-laden or offensive messages. He wants to reach as many people as he can—period. Marketing is a numbers game and the bigger the numbers, the better.

Spammers use a technique called *email address harvesting* to build up huge lists. They search web sites for email addresses using web crawlers. They look for the format your.name@anydomain.com and send it back to the spammer's data base. They also go to Usenet newsgroups for the email addresses of people who post messages. With 30,000+ newsgroups and hundreds of thousands of message postings, the lists can grow very quickly.

Or a hopeful newbie spammer can buy spam lists with millions of names and addresses along with the software to make it all work. Add an Internet account with bandwidth big enough to send millions of emails, and he's in business.

As it goes with business, so it goes with politics. It appears that various factions in Yugoslavia have taken to spamming in the furtherance of their beliefs. In this case, the spamming organization provides working email for return.

Reply-To: "Belgrade Academic Association for Equal Rights in the World" <desk@barw.org.yu>
From: "Belgrade Academic Association for Equal Rights in the World" <desk@barw.org.yu>
Subject: Would You Sign This Treaty?

```
Date: Fri, 14 May 1999 04:38:34 +0200
Sender: owner-barwl@barw.org.yu

Would You Sign This Treaty?

Dear Friends,

We would like to apologize You for any inconvenience this
message might caused You, but current situation in our coun-
try lead us to this desperate step. NATO aggression on our
country destroyed our future and lead many people from their
homes. You can read about history of our country and analizes
about current situation on our web-site www.barw.org.yu and
on web-site www.aic.org.yu You can find recent news and sto-
ries related to Kosovo crisis and agression on our country.
Also You would like to comment this letter or to get in touch
with us, e-mail us on desk@barw.org.yu.

Sincerely Yours,
Belgrade Academic Association for Equal Rights in the World
```

And then it continues for a few pages on their political beliefs. I actually found this political spam, the first I have ever received, to be coherent and polite. Maybe the direct marketers could buy a clue.

Most Internetizens hate spam. However, as on every issue there are two sides. In all fairness to the spammers of the world, I present both sides of the argument.

Spam Is Good Arguments	Spam Is Bad Arguments
Spam is free speech.	Spam is not free speech. It permits vendors of products, services and perhaps objectionable materials to invade my personal space without my invitation. The Supreme Court agrees, too. See *Rowan vs US Postal Service.*
Spam lets small companies compete with the big boys.	First, the big boys don't spam 'cause it's bad form and question-

ably legal. AOL won a landmark court case against spam-masters Cyberpromotions. Besides, if the big boys got into spamming (which they won't) they have the money and power to out-spam the small companies anyway. Dumb argument.

Spam is cheaper than a web site.

Not true. Small web sites are as cheap as $25 per month. Setting up merchant accounts with credit cards is about $100. Working with the search engines is a few hundred dollars a year. If you don't have that much money to get into business, I don't want to do business with you.

Spam is a public service to build a more informed consumer.

I don't want to be informed about fetish sex, pornography, or Blue Widgets that burp on Thursdays, thank you very much. I have no moral or legal obligation to be an informed consumer. Just leave me alone.

Spam is environmentally friendly No tree dies with email. Junk mail kills the environment.

Junk mail is tangible and often provides real value to the recipient, including free samples.

Spam is just a message. If you don't like it, delete it.

Spam can be 20% or more of my email. It takes my valuable time to go through the garbage and dump it. It chews up my bandwidth, increases download time and costs me money. Stop it.

Ads are everywhere: TV, radio, billboards. Spam is just advertising.

No it's not. Advertising pays for television and radio so I don't have to pay for NBC or the "Simpsons." Many magazines are free because advertisers pay for the costs. A lot of jobs are created in the process. Spam only benefits the spammer.

Spam is just a new way of doing business that helps the economy.	If the product or service is successful, maybe this is true. But at what cost? Spam eats up terrific amounts of bandwidth, forces people to spend time and money combatting spam, reduces productivity at the office, and is a general pain in the gluteus maximus. Get a web site. Get a job.
Hey, it's spam. Get a life.	Point taken. :-)

(I borrowed this chart concept from com.primenet.com/spamking/argue.html)

Anti-Spam

So what can you do to fight spam?

Maybe it doesn't bother you much and hey, some of them are funny so it's no big deal. If that's your attitude, fine. But if spam annoys you and you want to avoid getting messages that offend you—or if you want to keep your kids from receiving offensive spam, there are a couple of things you can do to keep it down.

1. Use filters in your email software. Each email package is different, but look to filter out those messages that contain certain words in the Subject: lines such as Sex, XXX, Make Money, or whatever you choose. You may filter it into the trash bin or into a separate mail folder to examine later.

2. Use anti-spamming software products like those from www.SpammerSlammer.com. They're easy to use and moderately effective. The spammers, like bad guys, are a moving target. Their goal is to get around your anti-spam barriers and filters.

Other things you can do to fight spam:

1. Do not answer a spam. It makes you look like a great potential customer (after all, you responded!) and you will only be spammed more after your email address is sold to more spammers.

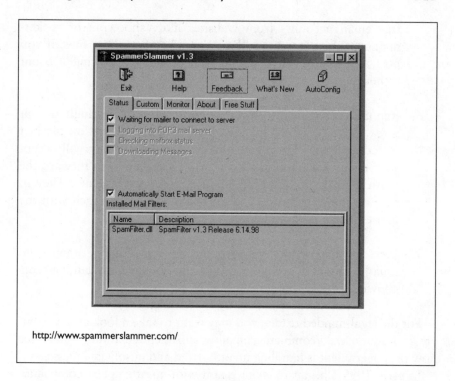

http://www.spammerslammer.com/

2. In your email software, expand the header of the spam message. This means that in addition to seeing the name of the original sender, you will see the list of servers and ISPs that carried the message from the spammer's door to yours. Likely the email address of the spammer is fake anyway. So look for the next server in the path (i.e., bigserver.com or AOL.com or ibm.net) and forward the spam to support@domainname.com. Don't forget to complain nicely and tell them that they are trafficking in spam. Legitimate companies will respond. Other email names to try are abuse@, customerservice@, webmaster@, techsupport@, or help@.

3. Do not open any email attachments from any spammer. Basic virus protection rules kick in here. How do you know what's in it? You don't—so don't open it.

4. Never sign up with sites or respond to email that promises to "remove" your name from spam. Spammers often use this technique to gather more names. If it is a legitimate attempt to help, spammers will ignore such requests anyway.

5. If you are going to post on Usenet news groups, consider using

free email accounts from websites like yahoo.com or rocket-mail.com. Just search on "Free Email" to find these sites. If you post, the spam will come to that secondary posting account rather than your primary one.

6. Report the abuse to the Network Abuse Clearinghouse at www.abuse.net. They handle all sorts of complaints on the Net including spam. First, you have to register so they will accept your email and know who you really are. Then you forward the spam message to a special email address at abuse.net. They in turn examine the headers in the spam and get in touch with the best contacts at the offending domains.

7. You can also report spam to the Federal Trade Commission. Email your spam and your complaint—be nice, no flaming rants allowed—to uce@ftc.gov.

For the legal-minded reader, you may want to take a look at www.senate.gov/~murkowski/commercialemail/EmailAmendText.html and see how the government is handling unauthorized and unsolicited messages.

In early 1999 I began receiving spam with an attempt at compliance with proposed congressional email legislation. I've noticed that the investment offers and other regulated businesses are looking to ward off future legal complications. The end of each "complying" spam consists of:

```
REMOVAL INSTRUCTIONS:
NOTE: This message is sent in compliance of a proposed email
bill: SECTION 301. Per section 301, Paragraph (1)(2)© of
S.1618, "further transmissions to you by the sender of this
email may be stopped at no cost to you by sending order to
remove at: 'removeme@phayze.com' "
```

Note that this wording protects you, maybe, against further spam "by the sender of this email." That does not mean your address will be removed from any master spam list or that it will not be sold to other spammers. Keep in mind that once in Cyberspace, always in Cyberspace. The harvesting engines work around the clock, 7 by 24, and just because your name might be removed from a list on Monday, your email address could appear again on Wednesday.

In the next section, though, you will learn that all spam is not created equal. Some spam can be a hazard to your pocketbook.

Resources

- Search on "Spam" on your browser.
- www.arachnoid.com/lutusp/antispam.html, also known as the Anti-Spam Home Page, offers some good basics on spam and fighting it. It also includes anti-spam source code for Unix machines.
- Com.primenet.com/spamking/ is another good source for learning about spam and anti-spam.
- www.e-scrub.com/wpoison/ offers Wpoison, free anti-spam software for web servers. It creates large numbers of fake email addresses that appear to be on a web server. The spammer who harvests web sites for addresses will instead get fake ones. Wpoison also includes a set of fake hyperlinks, or references to other URLs—web sites. Except these fake hyperlinks hook right back into the same web page that runs Wpoison in the first place. The aggressive spammer will then get endless lists of useless email addresses, causing him pain and headaches.
- www.actionsites.com/beo/ is run by Better Ethics Online. They discuss the legal aspects as well. Keep in mind, though, that US law is just that, US law. It has no effect on the other 5.8 billion people on the planet.
- www.SpammerSlammer.com provides free anti-spam software for the user. Try it.
- www.abuse.net is the clearinghouse for network abuse. You must register to use it, but they help to fight any sort of network abuses.

▶ Junk Mail Vs. Spam

Some of the differences between the junk mail we all love to hate but would dearly miss, and spam.

The Physical	**The Virtual**
Junk Mail	Spam
Shows up in your mailbox uninvited.	Shows up in your mailbox uninvited.

It takes some time to go through the mail and toss out the garbage. You receive something you can touch.
You may receive something of value: coupons, discounts or product samples.

The sender incurs substantial real costs: production, photography, manufacturing, packaging and printing.
The recipient is carefully chosen based upon sophisticated marketing techniques: age, income, zip code, buying habits, travel, etc.
Companies do not solicit sex in junk mail.

Frauds are common.
Legally you have the right to be removed from direct mail lists.
Legitimate companies use junk mail.
Some junk mail smells good. Perfume, soap samples.

It takes some time to go through the mail and toss out the garbage. You receive something you can look at.
You might receive a coupon or a discount but never an actual product. A free XXX picture or link to a web site is common.
The spammer is in business for a couple of hundred dollars.

Any one and anyone is fair game to the spammer.

These guys do. Sex spammers send their spam to anyone, including children. An email address tells nothing about the real person.
Frauds are a lot more common.
Legally, we are just getting a handle on the problem.
Legitimate companies do not spam.
Spam stinks.

Scam Spam

Fraud

It's happened to all of us.

You sit down to a quiet dinner with the family, or maybe to watch a movie with your spouse or the kids. It's calm. It's quiet. And then it happens.

Ring. Damn, the phone. Ring.

You answer the phone. "Hello?"

"Hi, Mr./Mrs. Smith. This is John at Prudential. How would you like to double your money in a month?"

The greed enzyme kicks in. "Sure."

"That's good to hear Mr./Mrs. Smith, because I only want to speak with folks like you who are interested in becoming rich very soon. That is what you want, isn't it Mr./Mrs. Smith?"

Greed enzyme goes into warp drive. "Yeah . . ."

"Great. When you double your money this month, what will you do with it?"

You think new car. European vacation. Add a second story to the house. "I don't know, there are so many things I could do with the extra money."

John from Prudential smiles wide. "Me, too. But what one thing would you buy with that kind of extra money? A hundred thousand dollars extra?"

Your mind whirls. "Ah, I guess we'd add on to the house for the new baby."

"Great. That's a terrific investment in your future. Very smart choice. Now let me tell you we're going to make that dream a reality."

You're hooked. Forget the TV show or dinner; John has got your attention. Now ask yourself the following questions:

1. Is John really from the big, famous investment house Prudential, or not?
2. Can John really double your money in a month?
3. Why did John call you?
4. Is John being honest or . . . ?

John is a scam artist. Period. Hang up on him. Telemarketing is a traditional mechanism for scam artists. Gullible and unsuspecting senior citizens get ripped off every day by telemarketers who convince victims to spend money with them. One of the biggest clues to scams is the urgency that the scam artist uses to get you to part with your money.

- "I can only have ten people in this special money making program. I already have nine. If you can't say 'yes' right now, I understand. There are plenty of people who want to get rich."
- "To take advantage of this special offer, you must decide now. Otherwise the deep discounts will never be available to you again."
- "We can enroll you right now so you can get a 95 percent discount on all of your prescription medicines." Program enrollment fee: $495.
- "This stock is going to double in the next two days. If you Federal Express your check today, and I receive it tomorrow, you can still reap incredible profits."

What do all of these have in common? They are lies. Scams. Meant to move your hard-earned cash from your pocket to theirs. I assume that most of us have been victimized at one point or another. And the lesson we all learn is: *If it's too good to be true, then it probably isn't true.*

I used to have some degree of faith in Ed McMahon and Dick Clark, but the deceptive practices of Publishers Clearing House have made me highly suspicious of any "special" promotions. The wording in the PCH sweepstakes created a national scandal after it was discovered that people had been spending thousands upon thousands of dollars on magazine subscriptions in hope of increasing their chance of winning. One man flew to a Florida PCH address after receiving a mailing from them declaring him a winner. The unfortunate senior citizen did not read the extremely fine print with all of the disclaimers PCH's lawyers could conjur up. Ed and Dick should be ashamed of themselves.

In 1996, two scams caught my attention. Residents of Kansas received very authentic-looking documents from a New York company declaring the recipient the winner of a 1995 Buick Regal automobile. All they had to do was mail a check for $22.87 to a New York address to receive their car. 125 Kansans called the Better Business Bureau to check out the company. No one knows how many others merely sent in their money.[13]

Then there was this classified ad placed in a New York newspaper:
"LAST CHANCE! To Send in $1. GUARANTEED! No Checks, Please."
There was a P.O. Box to send in the money. The scam artist behind this was caught and was prosecuted for fraud.
Fraud. Scam. Same difference.
Now, let's move to the Internet. Cyberspace. Email. The web. Ask yourself a question: Do you believe everything you read on the Internet? I sincerely hope the answer is "Of course not!"
Scamming on the Internet is going to be more prevalent than telemarketing scams for a number of reasons:

1. In telemarketing, you have to have a warm body, who must be paid, to make the calls. It's a numbers game, just like selling hamburgers or cars. The more bodies, the more calls made and the more fraudulent transactions that take place. On the Internet, one scam artist can solicit millions of people with the click of a button at a small fraction of the cost.

2. You need to find unscrupulous telemarketers, or extremely gullible ones, to be willing to rip off senior citizens, or anyone for that matter. On the Internet, only the scam artist and his close associates are in on the scam.

3. Telephone bills can be very high. Internet costs are negligible.

Internet scams encompass every possible trick you can think of[14] and are increasing at an alarming rate. In 1996 there were less than a thou-

---

[13]www.spub.ksu.edu/issues/v100/FA/n041/city-gov-email-scam-johnson.html
[14]Thanks to www.locus.halcyon.com for a great site and scam taxonomy.

sand Internet fraud complaints, but in 1998 the number was almost 8,000—a nearly 800 percent increase. Inquiries to on-line fraud organizations skyrocketed from 100 per week in 1996 to 1,500 per week in July of 1997. The Internet Fraud Watch says that complaints went up 600 percent from 1997 to 1998.

Be careful out there. These are just a few of the onslaught of scamming spam you are likely to encounter:

- Chain letters: They are generally illegal anyway. Don't participate in them whether you receive a physical letter or get one on the Net.
- Pyramid schemes and multi-level marketing: Make sure you sell actual goods and services, not just recruit other so-called "distributors." Check with the Better Business Bureau and do your research before spending a dime.
- Make money bulk mailing: The only people making money are those who sell you the program that won't work.
- Charities: Stick to the ones you know and trust—which is hard enough sometimes. If it's on the Internet, figure it's a scam.
- Give Us Your Password: No legitimate organization would ever, ever, ever do this. They won't even do it on the phone. In 1999, scam artists representing porn sites sent email to AOL addresses warning them of a billing error. They were directed to a web address to fill out a form including passwords. Never, ever give out passwords. No, never. Another AOL scam asked for credit card numbers.[15] AOL is said to have lost millions of dollars per day during it.[16]
- Download a special plugin: Web browsers link to additional programs to allow viewing movies, hearing audio and other useful functions. Some porn sites offer special plugins to enhance the experience, or so they claim. Actually, the "plugin" will dial your computer modem to an international phone number that will charge you exorbitant fees and your computer screen won't show you a thing.
- Credit repair—guaranteed. Guaranteed that you send in your money and get next to nothing in return. There is a well-known procedure to fix errors in credit reports and

---

[15]*St. Petersburg Times*, 26 April, 1999.
[16]www.news.com/News/Item/0,4,10851,00.html

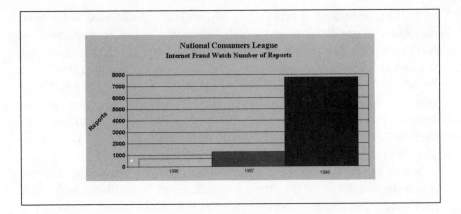

there is no magic pill to get rid of bad credit. See
www.webcom/com/'lewrose/brochures/creditrepair.html or
www.fraud.org/internet/inttip/repairtip.html for the basics.
Send no money to the on-line scammers.

- Send a postcard: Although dying of cancer, Craig Shergold
  wanted to get into the Guiness Book of Records for receiving the most postcards. He is now cured of the disease and
  achieved his goal with 33 million postcards. Don't send
  postcards to anyone you don't know. OK?

Lots of scams are low dollar. Five to twenty-five dollars a pop. You
aren't out a whole lot of money and don't have the energy to protest too
loudly. The scammer counts upon lots of people like you to make his
fortune.

But just as in the real world, scams can get very, very expensive.

Investment Scams

American Brightstar Gold used the Internet to sell stock in its company,
which is illegal. They promised returns of 2,600 percent for $50,000
investments. Another successful fraud was perpetrated by three people in
Indiana, Missouri, and Amsterdam, Holland. Supposedly raising money
for Turkish hospitals and in cooperation with Intel and Microsoft as
backers, they scammed more than $1 million from victim investors
before a New York federal judge froze the company's assets.[17]

Richard Briden of Ashland, Massachusetts talked seven people out of

---

[17]*New York Times*, 13 May, 1999, p. C9

$295,000, promising a return of 640 percent in forty weeks. He used the classic Prime Bank scams which "are some of the boldest cases we see," said John Reed Stark, director of the Internet enforcement unit for the Security Exchange Commission.[18] There is no such thing as a Prime Bank and these scams on the Internet are in plain view of the regulatory agency, making them easier to stop. The SEC initiated fourteen cases of Internet-based regulatory violations on May 12, 1999, and the SEC chairman, Arthur Levitt, said he will increase the number of attorneys working on Internet investment scams from 125 to 250.

Scams are fraud and the people behind them are criminals; they are just using the tools of the Internet—and society's gullibility—to cheat us. Fraud estimates vary widely, from as low as $9 billion in the US to over $100 billion internationally. Just like with every type of computer crime, unless it's reported it's terribly difficult to gauge the true extent of the costs.

However, an Australian April 1 joke may give us a clue.[19] A web site suckered Australian investors into committing over $4 million in a fake Swiss company which was selling Y2K insurance to blue-chip companies and governments. Promises of 300 percent growth in fifteen months encouraged buyers. The entire affair, though, was a sham (scam?) by ASIC, the Australian Securities and Investments Commission, their version of the American SEC. ASIC said the April Fool's event was the first dramatic step in their investor awareness campaign. The numbers behind the spoof are telling, though.

Ten thousand two hundred people visited the web site and 230 investors committed between $10,000 and $50,000 each to participate in the fraudulent scheme. Another 1,200 asked for additional information, even though no investment prospectus was offered. 2.3 percent of the viewers were suckered and about 10 percent were interested enough to ask for more information. In the physical world's direct-mail marketing, success is measured from only a 1 percent response rate. These guys did a bang-up job.

The Nigerian Scam

Thirteen years and $5 billion later, the Nigerian Scam is still thriving. Also known as the 419 Fraud, the Fax Scam, the Nigerian Connection, and the Advance Fee Fraud, the operation is simplicity itself.

---

[18]*USA Today*, 13 May, 1999, Money
[19]Australian Associated Press, 9 May, 1999

You, the potential victim, receive a fax, hard-copy mail, or an email. It says that you have been selected to profit by others' losses:

- Expatriating stolen wealth
- Over-invoiced payments from oil or other resources must get out of the country
- A bequest was left to you in a will
- They need help to chemically clean money that was dirtied in some creative spin by the scammers

All you need to do to rake in incredible profits is to forward an advance fee or provide a credit line—some form of money. If you fall for this scam and you do forward funds, "complications" will develop and you will be asked for more money until you stop paying and paying. Then there is virtually no hope of financial recovery. There is no pot of gold at the end of the Nigerian rainbow. According to the 419 Coalition, these scams are and have been operated by the Nigerian government itself, making fraud the country's third largest industry.

The 809 Scam

Rather than rewrite it all, this warning comes directly from the Net and is right on. I got it from a military mailing list. Although this scam has been going for years, technology makes it easier and easier—often with little recourse for the victim.

```
809 area code phone scam
To all:
Forwarded, FYI; is this another form of IW? (Information
Warfare?)
Subject: FW: Phone scam
```

This message was forwarded to me by James Murdock, the budget administrator at the University of Michigan. He wrote: My apologies if you've seen this, but if you have not its probably worth taking note of. Sounds like a scam that could easily ruin your day. You can't even trust your answering machine these days.

The Scam works basically like this:

You get home and notice that the message light is blinking on your answering machine. You listen to the message, which has several wrinkles, but the best one is the caller asks you to call a number beginning with area code 809 to receive information about a family member who has been ill. (They may also tell you someone has been arrested, died, you have won a wonderful prize, etc.)

In any event, concerned or curious, you make the call. Sometimes the phone will be answered by a person who claims to speak broken English. (The idea is to keep you on the line to build up charges.)

Or, sometimes you will just get a long recorded message. The bottom lines is, when your phone bill comes, you see this incredible charge, oftentimes more than $100.00 dollars!

Crooks are using the 809 numbers as "pay-per-calls" and to get around the US Regulations and 900 number blocking. Every time you call the number, they get a greatly inflated rebate from the foreign phone company. Since the 809 numbers are in the Caribbean, they aren't bound by US 900# regulations that require them to warn you of the charge and rate involved, and also to provide a time period during which you may terminate the call without being charged.

The newest twist to this scam is to page people using the 809 numbers. With so many new area code changes occuring, people unknowingly are returning these calls. When the bill comes, there are HUGE charges for the calls. My suggestion is that no matter how you get the message, If you are asked to call a number with an 809 area acode that you don't recognize, DON'T RETURN THE CALL! It's bad enough that the criminal is invading your privacy, don't let them invade your wallet as well!

Scams of this type are extremely hard to prosecute and since you did actually make the call, neither your local phone company or your long distance carrier will want to get involved. They'll tell you that they are simply providing the billing for the foreign company. You end up trying to deal (over the phone) with a foreign company that feels they have done no wrong. It can turn into a real nightmare!

Don't call 809 area codes unless you really know the number and/or have a friend there.

Enough said.

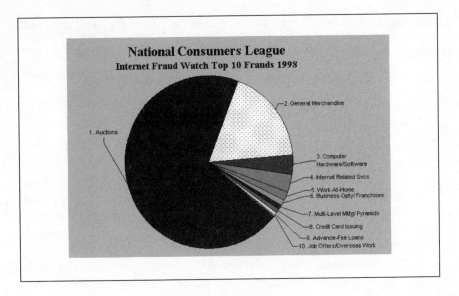

On-line Auctions

My eight-year-old son is learning technology by trading Pokémon cards on the Net. But buying and selling on-line can be an exercise in meeting the criminal type. Only buy from legitimate concerns—and that doesn't necessarily mean eBay or any other on-line auction site. In 1997, 26 percent of all on-line frauds were tied with auctions. In 1998, that figure jumped to 68 percent.[20] Of course, eBay is just providing a service, but when you move to make a deal with a seller, you have to be extra careful to get what you pay for.

The first felony conviction linked to auction fraud was against Craig Lee Hare, of Lake Worth, Florida.[21] He sold nearly $30,000 worth of computers to twenty-five people and delivered nothing in return. The Federal Trade Commission has banned him for life from doing business on the Internet, he has to return the money, and was confined to his home for six months.

The smartest way to do business with an individual who doesn't take credit cards is to use an escrow service, often provided by the on-line auction house. The goods should be shipped only upon receipt of money by the escrow house, and then fully insured with a means of package

---

[20]www.fraud.org/internet/9923stat.html
[21]*St. Petersburg Times*, 26 April, 1999

tracking. Only when the goods are received in good shape will the funds be released to the seller.

My son is getting a hell of an education.

How To Spot Internet Scams

This is a lesson in common sense. No magic.

1. If the person you are dealing with requires cash or check up front, run like the devil, 'cause you are dealing with one. According to the Internet Fraud Watch, 93 percent of all fraudulent payments occur off-line; that is, by cash, check, or money order. Legitimate businesses are tooled up with secure on-line credit payment systems. If there is a fraudulent issue, the credit card companies will remove the charge and interest. Plus, if they see a pattern, they will work with law enforcement in prosecution of the scammers.

2. If the email address is not real, delete it. Look for a physical address, a real phone number, and means to contact a human.

3. A flashy web site means nothing. They cost a few hundred dollars and can be built in a couple of days. The true definition of fly-by-night.

4. Watch out for fast payment requirements. When you do pay, use a credit card.

5. Never buy anything on the Net based upon "future potential." What a crock.

6. Do business with people and companies you know. If you don't know the company, check them out. If you can't find anything on them, there is nothing to find. Go elsewhere with your business.

7. Only give out that information necessary to do business. Identity theft looms in the shadows if you are not vigilant. Never give out your Social Security Number or passwords.

8. Watch out for impossible promises. They usually are impossible.

http://www.fraud.org/

9. And finally, the same rule we live by in the physical world: If it seems too good to be true, it usually is.

How To Report Internet Fraud

If you are the unfortunate victim of Internet fraud (or any other kind of fraud for that matter), there are a few places to contact. Keep in mind, though, that law enforcement doesn't have the resources to investigate every case that comes their way. If you suffer a fraudulent loss of $100 and someone was sheistered out of $10,000, guess who gets priority from the cybercops. Right.

1. But please do report every instance—even if you don't get immediate satisfaction. The cops look for patterns, and if a hundred people are victimized by the same scammers, it could then become a case worth investigating. Furthermore, as the Internet accumulates statistics, law enforcement and legitimate on-line commercial businesses will be able to pay more attention to the problem.

2. Report your incident to the Internet Fraud Watch. www.fraud. org/ or 800.876.7060 (and they will likely send you back to their web site to fill out a form).

3. Some cities and states have their own law enforcement groups who speak cyber-crime. Call them. Because of the amount of criminal fraud in Florida, fax your complaint to the Task Force South Florida, 954.925.1362.

4. The Financial Crimes Division of the US Secret Service handles a lot of financial crimes, but cooperates with the FBI in handling and investigating cases, especially with the multi-agency Electronic Crimes Task Force. Fax your complaint to the Secret Service at 202.435.5031.

5. Check with the phone directory for your local FBI field office.

6. The FBI is establishing the Internet Fraud Complaint Center and forming the Internet Fraud Council with the private sector. Although not up and running as of June 1999, it will become a cooperative focus for reporting fraud and getting the help you need.

But the best advice of all is:
Use your common sense and avoid becoming a victim.

Resources

- www.locus.halcyon.com has a complete site and great tips. A lot more than we can offer here.
- www.fraud.org is not to be missed. The Internet Fraud Watch maintains an excellent set of resources and a hot line: 800.876.7060.
- www.nepenthes.com/hacks/slow.html has a nice list of hoaxes.
- www.andrew.cmu.edu/user/td2b/conmen.html provides good links to con-men resources.
- www.win95mag.com/archive/10_96/html/scam.html is a fabulous article by David Adams.
- The National Consumers League offers great consumer protection information, charts and updates. www.nclnet.org/
- For an in-depth look at the Nigerian 419 scam: home.rica.net/alphae/419coal/.
- www.natlconsumersleague.com

How They Hack

I can teach a monkey to hack in two hours.

Ira Winkler,
author

In order to defend against hacking, we have to know how it's done.

Don't be intimidated. You will find this non-technical explanation of how hackers hack to be easy to read, easy to digest, and chock full of pictures. Despite what you might think, hacking can be as simple as pressing a mouse button and then watching the damage unfold.

You may even want to try it yourself . . . not hacking, that is, but playing with the hacking tools—for educational value only, of course!

Getting
Anonymous

Gary Powers' U2 was shot down by the Russians because they could see his high-flying supersonic spy plane. The US military response was to develop invisible airplanes. Through years of Skunk-Works style development, the secret was safe—mostly—and the plane's existence was not confirmed by the Pentagon. And then one day we used the stealthy F-117 in real operations; now it's a generic component of the air force arsenal. Today we have Stealth bombers and they are working on stealthy tanks, submarines, and floating ships. Good idea. It ups the ante for the adversary to improve his remote sensing equipment to ID the incoming planes.

Bank robbers wear masks so that the surveillance tapes can't be used to identify them. What self-respecting criminal wants to provide his identity to the police? The smart ones don't. Many of us like to maintain our privacy in our activities, legal or not, but criminals certainly want to make the cops' jobs as hard as possible.

And it's the same thing in Cyberspace. When hackers broke into the *New York Times* and defaced its web site they were anonymous, and remain uncaught. The rounds of attacks against the White House, Senate, FBI, and myriad web sites are done anonymously, too, because it makes sense. There are many different ways to make yourself anonymous on the Internet, depending upon your goals and motivations.

Anonymous Remailers

An anonymous remailer is a service that changes your electronic identity so that the recipient does not know who you really are or from what email address you are sending messages. With some anonymous remailers you can only send anonymous email and not receive it. With others you can both send and receive email. Some companies charge for this service while others offer it for free.

There are two distinct types of anonymous remailers:

- Pseudo-anonymous remailers are operated by people who, if they wanted, could look up who you are and what your assumed identity is. The key here is to have implicit faith and trust in the people operating the service. While many of these are of the utmost integrity, in the face of a court order they will be legally required to give up identity information. There is no legal protection yet.
- True anonymous remailers have the advantage of the system operator not knowing who you are. No court order can force them to tell what they don't know.

Anonymous Web Browsing

Whenever you visit a web site unprotected, you not only expose yourself to risk of invasion, you provide information about yourself that can include your viewing habits, your search terms, your geographical location, your address, phone number, and employment details, your credit card numbers, and more. Some web sites keep logs of this information, compiling dossiers on their users as well. Even if you trust the intent and integrity of the people behind the site you're visiting, in most cases, your information is still at risk to security invasion.[1]

New services are appearing that permit us to surf the web safely.

Anonymous Email

Web-based anonymous email has become a trivial task. Just look.

Above this part of the www.anonymizer.com web page you merely

---

[1]From www.anonymizer.com.

www.anonymizer.com is a commercial web site that permits anonymous web surfing. They also offer anonymous email and anonymous web publishing. That means that you or I or anyone can publish web sites with whatever material we want and no one will know our true identity.

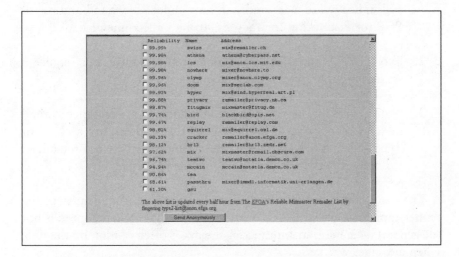

enter the email address you want to send to, add a subject and text. Then you choose how many anonymous remailers you want your message to go through, choosing from the above list. What could be easier when sending hate mail to close personal friends and your in-laws? (Just kidding Jerry and Pat and Mike!)

I sent an anonymous email to myself which arrived the following day back at my desktop. This was what I got. Note the FROM line.

```
Date: Tue, 15 Jun 1999 15:10:01 +0900 (JST)
From: Anonymous <nobody@nowhere.to>
Comments: This message did not originate from the Sender
address above.
```

```
It was remailed automatically by anonymizing remailer soft-
ware.
Please report problems or inappropriate use to the
remailer administrator at <complaints@nowhere.to>.
Subject: test
To: winn@mydomain.com
```

According to folks who use anonymizing regularly, "To stay anonymous in email or Usenet, it is reasonable to chain several different
remailers, preferably Mixmasters. Never trust one single service and use
encryption between remailers."

There are three basic kinds of anonymous remailers you can use:

1. Type I or Cypherpunk remailers are the original type of remailer,
   still in heavy use. Messages can be composed by hand and use of
   PGP for encryption (privacy) is strongly recommended.

2. Type II or Mixmaster remailers are more secure, but require a
   special program to generate the messages.

3. Nymservers or newnym let you establish a permanent email
   address that forwards mail to your real address, via a chain of
   Type I remailers which reencrypt the message between remailers.
   If done properly, it is nearly impossible to trace.

Time and anonymity are crucial, too, so that the true identity of the
sender cannot be construed by the time messages were sent. Speed is not
the general issue here, so anonymous remailers often randomize the time
when messages will be sent.

Take a gander over to http://www.replay.com/remailer/ if you want to
persue more about true anonymous remailers. Replay.Com is located in
the Netherlands so they don't have to worry about US encryption laws.

If true anonymity is not your goal, that is, if you just want an alternate
identity, you can always go to www.hotmail.com or www.rocketmail.com
and get a free email account. They claim that they do not offer anonymous remailers, but look what I did in about sixty seconds.

I created the identity of Roberta Lyons, a thirty-ish woman from Tennessee. No verification at all of my true identity. Now keep in mind that
this is not anonymizing, but disguising. Free email sites will not tolerate
spamming or hate mail or criminal activities and they all have centers to
report abuse, but still, a degree of anonymity is created.

> The information that you provide below remains private
> This information is used by Hotmail for demographic statistics and to display the
> appropriate individualized advertisements. Hotmail keeps all of your personal
> information private and does not disclose it to anyone without your explicit
> permission. More accurate responses will result in ads that are relevant to you.
>
> **Choose a Login Name** | SexyGirl | @hotmail.com
> *Only letters (a-z), numbers (0-9) and underscore (_). Login Name must start with a letter.*
>
> **Choose a Password** | ******** | Your password must contain at least 8 characters and may include both letters and numbers; your password is also case sensitive.
> **Re-type that Password** | ******** |
>
> **Your First Name** | Roberta | Your Full name will be sent with all outbound mail messages.
> **Your Last Name** | Lyons |
>
> **Country/Region** | United States
> **Gender** | ○ Male ⦿ Female
> **Year of Birth** | 1972
> **Occupation** | Computer related (IS, MIS, DP)

Some people who want the convenience of anonymity without the legal nastiness of court subpoenas and such choose yet another route: Use a service located off-shore, preferably in a country not all that friendly with the US.

Like security and hacking, everything else about the Internet is in a constant state of flux. Nothing is static. While these web sites and services are active as I write, some number of them will be gone by the time you read this book. So you may have to do a little work on your own.

Registered User

Email Address | [ ] @ china.com
Password | [ ]

Tick this box to avoid Illegal Request message when you login. □
LOGIN CLEAR

Associate Membership User
ONLY for members of an Associate Membership Scheme.

Email Address | [ ] @ [ ] . china.com
Password | [ ]

Tick this box to avoid Illegal Request message when you login. □
LOGIN CLEAR

○ **Register Now**
○ **Why Subscribe ?**
○ **Associate Membership Scheme**

china.com
Corporation

faq

China.com operates a free email service from China (Hong Kong), of course. The odds of the Beijing Government cooperating with Washington in the pursuit of a hacker is slim, even though hacking is a capital offense in China. Yup. Hack and lose your head!

The easiest way to start is to perform a search on "anonymizers," and everything else will fall right into place.

I like to use certain sites as portals, and I found the following one to be an excellent portal resource for anonymizing.

These techniques are just fine for certain messagelike traffic or web browsing, but they don't solve the hackers' real problems of running remote programs, installing software or sniffers, or real breaking and entering. Just like the bank robber in a mask, criminal hacking needs additional layers of anonymity to stay off the police radar screens.

For a great web site to begin your anonymizing efforts, check out http://neworder.box.sk.

With hacking though, anonymity is often achieved by creating new "people." The idea is simple enough and so is the execution (although no, I am not going to teach you exactly how to do it step by step). Most universities and other academic institutions have been extraordinarily lax in their security practices, under the auspice of "open and free exchange of information." Thus, they do not practice strong security, which allows interlopers to gain control of portions of their networks through fairly simple logon processes and weaknesses:

- No passwords at all
- Simple, easy-to-guess passwords
- Manufacturers' default passwords, which are published in every manual and on every hacker site.
- Poor security on services like ftp, telnet, etc. which allow remote entry to the system.

- Poor monitoring of the system by administrators, so they don't even know they were broken into.

Once a hacker has found his way into a system from his real account or from a free AOL account, his first task is to set himself up as a new user. If the hacker has already found a way into the system, the "root," or main administrative control of the computer or network, is not well protected, if at all. With root access, the hacker sets up a new user with any name he chooses and a password. He also designates what rights he has on the system: Can he add other users? Read password files? Monitor all traffic with a sniffer? Sometimes it's best not to have full rights, as it might flag the real system manager.

With this new account, the hacker can relog in anytime he wants from any computer anywhere and use this new identity. The better hackers will set up a number of accounts on a number of systems, creating a number of different identities.

So, let's say Jimbo (a hacker) wants to attack Heinz Ketchup 'cause he found a dead fly immersed in the bottle.[2] Jimbo will enter a computer he has created an account on, and then he might well telnet to another computer. Telnet is a standard, legal, and useful means to hop from one computer system to another. Kind of like in "Star Trek" where the transporter sends Kirk and co. to a planet's surface or to a Klingon ship. Telnet is the transporter of Cyberspace.

At the second computer, Jimbo will log on using the identity he has set up on that machine. And Jimbo can cascade as many times as he wants through any computer he has an account on anywhere in the world.

When Jimbo is satisfied he is anonymous enough, he will attack Heinz or whoever he is after with little chance of being discovered. Sure, Heinz might have decent security and detect an intrusion, but all they will see is an identity like Jimbo@BigUniversity.Edu, which tells Heinz that the intruder has most likely anonymized himself.

The reason for Jimbo's multiple hops is to make law enforcement's job really tough. To find the intruder, Heinz would have to contact BigUniversity and ask them to find Jimbo's account, to see if, at such and such a time, Jimbo wandered over to Heinz. If Jimbo was smart, though, he would also have installed a small program to erase his tracks, and BigUniversity would see nothing.

If, however, BigUniversity found the account and time of his pres-

---

[2]Don't laugh. Young hackers attack for far less reasons than that. No offense or implied message to Heinz here. We eat Heinz.

ence, they could tell Heinz that Jimbo came from another computer at another university in Ankara, Turkey. Now what does Heinz do? They forget about it and move on.

Anonymous can mean different things to different people, depending upon goal and motivation. As you will see in the chapter on denial of service, until the entire Internet community chooses to instill high-level security practices everywhere, with everyone participating, under a common set of guidelines, laws, and legal cooperation, offensive and criminal hacking stand little chance of being thwarted.

Yes, Internet II, the joint US Government and academic project, is looking at new architectures for new Internetlike applications, but we are years and years away from any significant boost in the security of the Internet backbone.

Spoofing

A spoof is a cheat, a deception or lie. The *National Lampoon*, for example, spoofs or parodies real events. Satire is close, too. But in the world of the Internet, spoofing is another way of anonymizing, with a different purpose.

If I want to send you, for example, a Trojan Horse or a virus, and you are well trained to not open email from people you don't know or

Hackers spoofed the popular series of *Dummies* books with their own rendition. Such a book would tell hackers how to adapt other electronic identities and remain anonymous on the Internet.

trust, what would I do? I would spoof the IP address of the sender. It's really amazingly easy to do. Look at any piece of email you have received. The FROM line is the address of the sender. If it says it's from Your Mom, you will likely trust it. If the FROM portion of the header says it's from Gonna Git Ya Sucker! you hopefully will not open it.

So, I as the bad guy will then spoof the header of the email. The header is merely the FROM, TO, and SUBJECT lines in most email packages. If you expand the header, you will see more header information, including the paths that your email took to get to you and a complete list of everyone else who was sent the same message.

The simplest form of spoofing is to go into your email software and change the FROM information in its Setup or Options page. When you send email, recipients will get mail from Nice_Person@Niceplace.com when in reality, you might be Evil_Person@Hellonwheels.com. The object is to get your victim to open the email and take an action that he might not take if he really knew it was you, Mr. Evil Person. However, some ISPs do not allow you to use a header that is different from your actual email account with them, so this doesn't always work. It's then back to HotMail or China.com.

The other kind of spoofing is highly technical. The attacker must impersonate the identity of a trusted computer by first incapacitating one trusted computer in the network. When connections are made to an Internet (IP) computer, they are counted in a sequence, which the attacker must then properly guess and use to subsequently create a new, but ersatz, connection.[3]

Have fun playing with spoofing, maybe with relatives or friends, but please, make sure you do nothing illegal or damaging.

Resources

- http://www.well.com/user/abacard/privacy.html is a good place to learn about anonymizing.
- The chapter "Techniques to Hide One's Identity" from *Maximum Security* is an excellent technical approach to anonymity. ISBN: 1-57521-268-4
- http://www.datafellows.com/f-secure/ offers products that will assist in creating anonymity using cryptography. Sort of complicated for the novice, but stick with it.

---

[3]For more on IP spoofing, see *Maximum Security* by Anonymous or search on "IP Spoofing."

- Usenet: alt.privacy.anon-server is a busy place with lots of discussion on anonymity on the Internet.
- Search on "anonymizers," "anonymous email," and "proxy servers," and that's all you need to get started.
- http://anon.efga.org/Remailers/ is an up-to-date list of anonymous remailers and similar services.
- IP spoofing information (highly technical) by Steve Bellovin can be found at ftp.research.att.com/dist/ internet_security/ ipext.ps.z
- IP sequence number attacks can be found at www.wcmh.com/uworld/archives/95/security/001.txt.html
- www.zeroknowledge.com is the home to "Freedom," a controversial commercial and very powerful anonymizing tool.
- Of course, a quick search on "IP Spoofing" will get you plenty more.

Password
Hacking

At forty-five dollars per minute, I passed on using the GTE in-flight cellular phones. Wouldn't you? The guy next to me in seat 1B was surfing the web: on a cross-country flight the phone charges had to be extraordinary. I guess he has a better expense account than the one my wife gives me. Upon landing, though, I immediately ran to the bank of public phones at Washington DC's Reagan National Airport to make a slew of overdue calls.

I whipped out my handy dandy Call Anywhere for a Price telephone travel card and proceeded to enter the endless stream of numbers required. First the eleven digits for the 800 number. Then the ten digits for my domestic call. Then the next twelve digits for my personal authorization code, which permits me to run up infinitely large bills from anywhere in the world.

Ring. Ring. Then a click. Another click. One more ring . . . (thirty-three keystrokes down the tubes. Something was not right here) and the familiar sound of a pick-up.

> *"We're sorry, we cannot complete this call as dialed. You entered your personal authorization number with the wrong finger."*

Passwords for email. Passwords for ATM machines. Passwords for web sites. Passwords for administrators and parents. Passwords for credit cards and on-line banking, brokerage, and web auctions. Passwords for microwaves, cable boxes and garage door openers. Passwords for everything. Everything.

In the business world, workers sit for hour after endless hour pounding away at a keyboard, hoping their creative output or mundane data entry is good enough to earn yet another week's paycheck. And they have to enter passwords at every step of the way, in the name of corporate security.

Whether you're out surfing the Net for business or pleasure, or connecting to your organization's regional office in Equatorial Guinea, any well-managed computer system will want to know who you are. On the Internet, your address specifies your location and identifies you with a recognizable moniker, although anonymity is not too difficult to achieve, as you now know. Within your company, your network or security administrator should definitely want to know who's using the company's MIPS; if not—get a new security gal/guy.

The question is, how do you satisfactorily identify yourself to a distant computer; that is, how can you have a high confidence factor that the person who is using the computer, the system, or the network resources is really who he claims to be? That would seem to be a simple problem, yet the Internet and most companies use the worst possible identification method known to man: passwords.

Password Crackers

Once restricted to the domain of military and intelligence organizations, password crackers are now freely available and highly sophisticated. Some crackers use brute force methods whereby they simply keep trying every word/letter/symbol combination until it hits the right one. Others use a dictionary attack, pulling the passwords it guesses out of a file that is user-customizable (very useful if you know the personal habits of your target). Still other, more sophisticated crackers use a series of mathematical algorithms in an attempt to break the *password hash,* or cryptographic scheme, used to protect the password itself.

Hacker sites contain large numbers of password cracking programs for almost any imaginable operating system: NT, Unix, Win-9X, zip files, AOL, chat software, Novell, email, Kerberos, and more.

One of the more powerful and popular Windows NT password crackers is L0phtCrack by L0pht Heavy Industries (http://www.l0pht.com).[4] The folks from the L0pht have testified before Congress and are white hat hackers. I have had the privilege of working with Dr. Pete Mudge, a long-haired thirty-something security guru.

---

[4] Note that the "0" is a zero, not the letter "oh."

A partial listing from the Packet Storm web site. http://www.packetstorm.securify.com

L0phtCrack has a remarkable history of success and acceptance within the information technology and security industry as a tool to audit and evaluate the strength of passwords. The L0pht represents one of the hacking groups that have established excellent technical credential both in the hacker community as well as "above ground." L0pht-Crack has been downloaded over 500,000 times as of June 1999, and the L0pht engineers recently performed an audit of a large high technology company.

- L0phtCrack 2.5 cracked 90% of the passwords in under 48 hours on a Pentium II/300.
- 18% of the passwords were cracked in under 10 minutes.
- The Administrator and most of the Domain Admin passwords were cracked.
- This company had a policy requiring passwords longer than 8 characters with at least one upper case character plus a numeric or symbol character.

In the security world, there are three generally accepted means of identification of users—each with their own pros and cons, strengths and weaknesses.

"Something you know" is the simplest and weakest means of user identification. A password is "something you know," as is a PIN number,

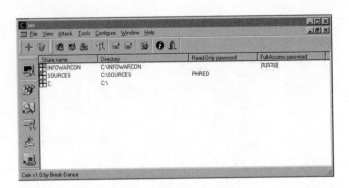

The Cain 1.0 is a password-recovery tool for Windows 95/98 operating systems. It enables easy recovery of logon passwords, share passwords (local and remote), screen saver passwords, dialup passwords, link passwords, and any other application-defined passwords cached in your system or external .PWL and Windows registry files. With Cain these passwords can be modified quickly. Cain v1.0 also features dictionary and brute-force attack methods of password cracking.

a Social Security Number (SSN) or anything else that you keep in your head. (Never use an SSN for secure identification. Never. Ever.) All too often, though, we have so much information to remember, we write down our passwords on a sticky-note attached to the monitor or the bottom of a keyboard. Passwords are chosen by users to make their jobs as easy as possible, and thus the easiest-to-guess passwords are chosen. This unfortunately defeats the whole purpose of security in the first place.

Internet breaches occur when easy-to-guess passwords are the sole means of protection for an organization's information assets. Day after

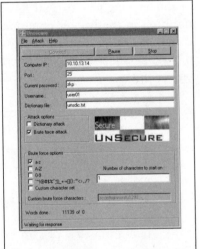

Unsecure remotely attacks passwords, using a friendly Windows interface.

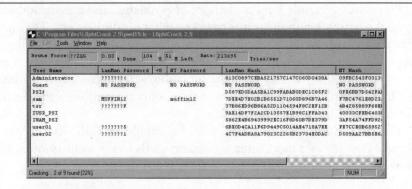

Notice that the password that was cracked is "MUFFIN12" and notice the ???????5, not too bad for a program that has only completed .03 percent of its task. The password is an anniversary date: 08111995; eventually, it would have been broken.

day, companies find that an intruder has captured "root" of their site, and the password files have been either stolen or decimated beyond repair. Then the network administrator's nightmare begins: reconstruct the entire security profile of the network.

Passwords take many shapes and forms. Passwords can unfortunately be as short as one character, and some consist of only numbers; others are combinations of digits and ASCII characters.

Passwords all too often contain a hard-to-remember nonsense string of characters:

JYTHUZK

or a number string:

18891255

When you have only one password, maybe you can remember it. When you have three, five, ten or more, they get written down out of deference to our feeble minds. Passwords can be easily stripped out and then used at a later date to gain unauthorized access to the systems under attack. Back Orifice is an ideal hacker tool for capturing passwords as they are typed. More about that later.

Passwords certainly have a plethora of problems, and it is incumbent upon the network administrator to know what his options are. They are many, and range in cost from nearly free to several thousands of dollars. Depending upon the sensitivity of the network or computer system in question, the shrewd and alert organization will choose to strengthen the front doors to its computers in a manner consistent with the determined risk, vulnerability, and policy.

The first alternative to passwords we should consider is the pass phrase. Pass phrases meet three significant goals of the security-oriented network administrator:

1. They are easy to remember.
2. They are difficult to guess or crack (or at least harder).
3. They are inexpensive to implement.

When we use a pass phrase, we solve a common security problem: users writing down passwords to remember them.

Let's examine the pass phrase, "There's no place like home." That's twenty-seven characters which are VERY easy to remember for the person who created it, and VERY hard for someone to guess. But to complicate it even further, this phrase can be written in a number of ways:

There's no place like home
THERE'S NO PLACE LIKE HOME
ThErE's No PlAcE lIkE hOmE
tHeRe'S nO pLaCe LiKe HoMe
There's,no,place,like,home
There's!no!place!like!home

You get the point. Take the same pass phrase and add enough of a twist so that it isn't any harder to remember but becomes a lot more difficult to crack.[5] Be creative in your use of pass phrases.

1. Use all available characters, not just A–Z. Make sure that a–z, 0–9, and other available keyboard symbols are part of the scheme.

2. Make sure that the password mechanism is case sensitive. Upper- and lowercase letters should be treated as separate characters, thereby increasing the password's strength.

---

[5]Password cracking programs will probably get them after sustained efforts, though. Not perfect, but better than your wife's birthday or the president's girlfriend's name.

3. Make sure that each password has at least one number and one special character.

4. Pass phrases must be at least "x" characters long. The shorter the weaker, the longer the stronger. If you can set your default length, set it to the longest available.

5. Use L0phtCrack on NT systems, and pick good crackers to test your Unix, Novell and other security domains.

6. Lock the user out of the system after two or three failed login attempts. Do not permit unlimited tries, as this is how penetrators foil many access-control mechanisms.

7. Implement a secure screen saver. When the keyboard or mouse is not used for "x" minutes, the screen should go blank and require a reauthentication of the user. This one technique alone will keep the "friendlies" out of where they don't belong.

8. Change passwords regularly. Many systems can be set to force the user to change passwords on a periodic basis. Don't disable this feature—use it!

However, when all is said and done, the use of passwords to open the front door of a computer or your information-rich networks are the weakest form of identification available, and their continued proliferation is responsible for a vast amount of computer fraud, crime, and hacking into computer systems worldwide.

Where Do We Go From Here?

The "something you know and something you own" paradigm is, from a security standpoint, very attractive, and a number of alternatives alleviate many of the concerns brought about by dumb and smart cards, also known as physical "tokens."

The more popular token devices, such as those from Security Dynamics, Enigma Logic, Racal Guardata, and Digital Pathways can fit into a wallet or shirt pocket, and each has its own method of establishing what is called a one-time password.

The goal, most notably for remote access, is to provide reliable access

The SecureID key fob generates a new one-time password every few seconds. You enter your user ID and the code on the fob. The remote network computer and the key fob are time-synchronized so that the numbers are the same on both sides. (www.securitydynamics.com)

to the target system and to foil the efforts of eavesdroppers. Each and every time access is gained by an authorized user, a different password is generated and recognized by the computer. Thus, if a sniffer captures the access code or password to the computer or network, it cannot be reused to gain access.

The most secure means of user identification and authentication involves the use of "something you are." Remember the James Bond movie "Never Say Never Again," in which a US military man has his retina surgically replaced with a cloned duplicate of the president's retina? The reason was that in order to alter nuclear strike codes an absolutely positive means of identification was required.

"Something you are" identification employs the techniques of biometrics, or measurement of innate biological characteristics unique to each of us. Generally reserved for high-security applications, over the last decade the prices have come way down and are now serious contenders for many uses within both private and government organizations.

Fingerprint identification seems like it may become ubiquitous in the next few years, as the price decreases. Individual fingerprint or thumbprint scanners are almost at the 100-dollar price point. But more importantly, the technology is being migrated to thin-film, meaning that credit cards will have your unique fingerprints embedded in them. When making a purchase at a store, you will stick your finger into the 'reader' and the authorizing bank will verify your identity.[6] Other forms of biometric identification include:

---

[6]This will likely decrease fraud, but civil libertarians worry about the effects on personal privacy as large databases are built with our fingerprints in them. The debate will rage although it is almost certain biometric ID will become the norm.

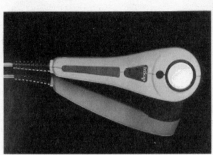 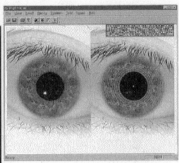

Iriscan's PC Iris uses the unique pattern in our eyes to maintain high degrees of user identification and authentication.

- Face recognition. Some use pictures of a face and then compare them in a database. They are subject to spoofing, though, and bad lighting is a problem.
- Remote scanning of the unique capillary structure of our faces. It turns out that the veins in our faces are as unique as our fingerprints and retinal patterns. This can work from up to fifty meters or so, which excites law enforcement, the customs department, and anti-terrorist organizations for passively scanning faces in crowds. It is said that even if one adds facial hair, or wears disguises or massive amounts of makeup, or is fiery hot from fever or frostbitten from the cold, the identifying capillary patterns remain constant, and thus are a superior means of accurate identification. Civil rights groups are very upset with this technology.
- Hand geometry scanning is not as reliable as the other methods and probably won't last long.
- Voice print identification is a natural as more telephone and Internet phone applications are developed. Sickness, attitude, speed and pattern of speech, though, can confuse many of these systems.
- Signature recognition was tested at the 1964 World's Fair in the IBM pavillion and still hasn't found widespread popular acceptance. Maybe later.
- The way we type is supposed to be able to identify us uniquely. Again, this is not proven technology, but because

it is software-based, there is an attraction to this less-expensive option. Privacy groups also hate this one.

A recent addition to the mix of password alternatives for corporate use is remote RF identification. You simply wear or carry a tokenlike card with you at all times. The card has a small, low-power transmitter in it and the computer has a receiver. When the receiver senses the unique RF code you are wearing, you are given access to the computer. If you are out of the range set by the administrator, the computer is locked. The attraction is that the user doesn't have to do a thing; identification is completely automatic and does not infringe upon the privacy or body parts of people.

So there you have it. The gamut of password alternatives.

I hope I don't need to reinforce the idea that passwords are too weak for any serious security efforts (there; I did it anyway) but it is incumbent upon all organizations to properly measure their risks and take appropriate defensive measures.

Remember that user identification is the most critical means of protecting your information assets, and that locking the front door with adequate locks is the first and biggest step you can take.

You, Phone Cards, and ATMs

They say they don't do it anymore. Good. Sprint used to make its customers enter their Social Security Number into public telephones when using their calling card. Stupid? Yep! At least one of the long-distance carriers I use requires a random thirteen-digit number as my ID. AT&T uses my Social Security Number for strong user identification. (I already did that rant.)

At any rate, with phones, ATMs, debit cards and other public access devices, I really just want to get one point across: Shoulder Surfers. Shoulder Surfers hang out at airports, bus terminals, and wherever there is the chance of finding your access code to some distant computer. All they do is look over your shoulder, mark down the code, and for phones, that's it! Your next bill will be a whopper! If the criminals are a bit more aggressive, once they have your passcode they will steal your purse or mug you. Blam! Your account is empty.

Simple to prevent. At the phone booth, hunch over and cover the keyboard. No, some lowlife is not going to stand six inches behind you and smell up your whole day. He's gonna use binoculars from a car or van or from the window of a nearby building. So hunch and guard. At the

ATM machine, cover the machine with your body and look for a mirror. If there's a mirror somewhere in the machine, cover it or use another machine. Keep in mind that the camera at the ATM may not be real. Dummy cameras are cheaper than real ones and are intended to keep bad guys away.

Shoulder surfing at the supermarket or the office creates the same problems . . . if there are bad guys looking to take advantage of your good nature. It only takes a few seconds of effort. And no, this is not abject paranoia. I have received huge phone bills when my telephone accounts were cracked, and it's one huge pain to get the charges reversed. I had to threaten half of the senior management at GTE with painful rusty-knife castration when hackers broke into their computers to my detriment. MCI, too. From my personal experience, they all have awful security.[7]

Simple, commonsense steps will reduce your chances of being victimized: Don't use ATMs in bombed-out areas of major American cities. Don't write down all of your personal identification codes and keep them in your wallet. (That's really dumb, isn't it?) Look around before entering PIN codes into phones or computer terminals. Make sure companies let you change access codes on your own. Behave with concern . . . not paranoia.

Resources

- Security Dynamics: Makes the industry-leading time-synchronized SecurID card.
  http://www.securitydynamics. com/fg_html/ns.html
- Cybersafe offers Kerberos implementations.
  http://www.cybersafe.com/
- http://www.rfideas.com/SystemOverview.htm offers an RF authentication system.
- Another entry into the remote RF-style identification market is at www.ensuretech.com
- Search on "voice recognition," "passwords," "tokens," "biometric identification," "access control devices."

---

[7]Hackers ran rampant through GTE and MCI to get to me a few years back. They even sent me the "Catch the Hacker" programs that GTE allegedly used in defense. The biggest problem you might have is getting them to even acknowledge their deficiencies. They just won't learn.

Hack and Sniff

Imagine that you want to rob a bank. Easy, huh? The odds of successfully robbing a bank are actually a lot better than fooling yourself into believing you might actually win the lottery.

As an astute criminal, you will need to know something about the alarm systems and what sort of locks are protecting the contents of the vault. Or maybe you have a "Dog Day Afternoon" vision and want to walk right in, guns brandished, grab a bunch of cash, and hightail it to the hills.

In either case, you improve your odds of getting away by knowing a lot about the inside operation of your target bank. One of the techniques that hackers use is called sniffing. Sniffing is generally illegal for a simple reason: it means the intruder has already broken into a computer and is going on to the next stage of his attack. Breaking and entering into a computer without permission is a federal crime and also violates many states' laws. But if you perform sniffing on open lines without breaking into a computer, you are still breaking federal law if you capture passwords to which you have no authorization.

Sniffing the Net is a lot simpler than it sounds.

Networks consist of many, many machines all tied together so they can communicate. When you send a message, it is broadcast to every computer on the network. That is the nature of Ethernet. If Bob sends a message to Mary, his message is broadcast to everyone on the network, but there is an electronic question in the message that asks, "Hey, Mary? Is your computer awake?" In normal use, Mary's machine says, "Hello, I am awake," and the message is received by Mary's computer.

However, since every other computer on the network can also "hear" the message, the bad guys (hackers, spies, insiders, whoever) who are on the network legitimately or who have broken in can also "hear" the message.

All they need is a computer with a common network card and some sniffer software. The network card has to be put into "promiscuous mode," which means that the computer will then listen to all network traffic that is sent back and forth. By using the right software, such as L0phtCrack Release 2.52 (www.l0pht.com), all of the traffic that travels up and down a network is captured at a single computer. The messages are captured and then can be stored in a file for later analysis. Yes, it really is that simple.

So, what can a hacker learn by using a sniffer? Too damned much!

1. User names and passwords for use at a later time. Academic institutions are especially vulnerable because of their poor security practices. Users and student accounts are all too often left active even years after students have left.

2. High-level dialogues (email and attachments) between senior executives on sensitive corporate matters: finance, sales, product specifications, personnel issues, private client information.

3. Highly proprietary information that may or may not be owned by the victim, which in turn can create downstream legal liability.

4. If the server at an ISP or major company is sniffed, hundreds of thousands of passwords, credit card information, and other private information can be compromised.

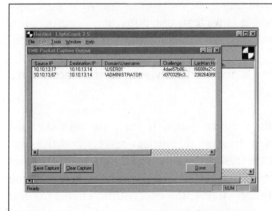

Network sniffer from L0pht Heavy Industries (www.l0pht.com) as part of L0phtCrack Release 2.52.

Here's a capture of a Netscape mail client logging in to download mail off a mail server:

```
1020-71 01 3, 3-43 90 941, H-00043, w-0700
+OK POP3 server psi.gwenn-bliez.com (Mail-Gear-1.1.0) ready
USER user01
+OK send password for user user01
PASS user01
+OK user01's maildrop has 0 messages (0 octets)
STAT
+OK 0 0
```

Notice on the USER line that the user name is in fact "user01." Then a request for the password is made and on the PASS line you see that user01's password is also set to "user01"—a huge security risk that is all too common.

Keep in mind that sniffers do not read data off of hard disks . . . they only suck data from network transmissions; in many ways this is worse, since so many of us send messages which are only thoughts, ideas, and rants, not formal policy. Sniffing can help the intruder get inside the mind of the victim as well as gather incriminating or valuable information.

Trojan Sniffers are similar but not the same. (How's that for clarity?) A Trojan Sniffer is a sniffing program, generally small, which is secretly installed into a network server or a computer of interest. If done well, the program is hidden far from the view of the network administrator.

Silently, the sniffer will collect the traffic on that computer and either store it in a secret location for later retrieval by the hacker, or, in some cases, send the gathered network traffic to a distant computer.

Finding a sniffer on a network is tough, especially since their operation is virtually invisible. Scanning your computers for what processes and programs they are running is a clean but potentially cumbersome way to see what background tasks and hacking may be going on without your knowledge.

Defending against sniffers is actually fairly easy if you spend some time at it.

1. Encrypt messages and their contents. If they are sniffed, most hackers will walk away frustrated. Nuclear secrets and the like, though, might bring the resources of foreign entities to attempt cracking the codes. SSH, Secure Shell, is a means to securely link two conversing computers. IDEA, the encryption scheme used, is about all you need for non-military applications. (See resources.)

2. Use one-time encrypted passwords as discussed in earlier chapters. If the password is sniffed, it was only good that one time, not for future access.

3. Analyze your network and separate critical areas from the less critical ones with routers, bridges, and hubs. By separating sub-networks from each other, any sniffing is restricted to the smaller network areas and not the whole shebang! With networks growing so fast, though, network isolation places more of a burden on the administrator.

Lastly, sniffing is done all of the time at major corporations with large networks. Every second of every day. Why?

Common network analysis tools are designed to collect networking information, measure performance, and tell the administrator about the health of his network. As a requirement though, he must be able to look at the network and its transmitting packets. These are legitimate products with a legitimate purpose but can easily be abused by an administrator or network engineer with an agenda.

Resources

- *Maximum Security* by Anonymous. ISBN: 1-57521-268-4
- www.l0pht.com
- Check out any of the hacker sites mentioned in this book for a number of sniffing programs.
- SSH information can be found at www.datafellows.com.
- "IDEA" is a cryptosystem with lots of implementations. Just enter "IDEA + cryptography" in your search engine.
- Search on "network sniffers," "Ethernet sniffers."

Scanning, Breaking, and Entering: Anatomy of a Friendly Hack[8]

James Fallsworth, vice president of corporate security at the Big American Bank, called in a panic. He had just been informed that Operations and Marketing were planning to introduce a suite of new remote banking services for their seven million global customers. *BA Bank On-line* will permit customers to access their accounts, move money from one to another, pay bills, and now handle their own brokerage transactions.

Incredulous that he hadn't been informed about such a major program with staggering security implications, Fallsworth found himself in a quandary. He had less than two months before the systems were to be deployed globally. The president of the BA Bank assumed he had been in the loop. "Just take care of it, Jim."

When most large firms, in the banking field or not, connect to the Internet, they have two choices:

1. Connect the internal, mission-critical systems to the outside world, achieve high degrees of connectivity, encourage interactive commerce, and face very real security risks, or

---

[8]The names and technical details of this story have been sanitized to disguise the company's real identity.

2. Maintain an isolated web presence, effectively limiting commerce to zero.

Jim Fallsworth needed to know how secure, or insecure, their BAB-Remote was, and how it could affect their revenues, profits, and customer confidence. It didn't take long for Fallsworth to decide what to do: Hire a company to test the external security controls of the bank, and determine the company's real vulnerabilities. Ethical hackers to the rescue.

Once Jim picked his hackers, they worked mutually to understand the goals of the penetration testing (others call it friendly hacking).

1. Assess the strength and weaknesses of BA Bank's new services and how they relate to the rest of the bank's operations.
2. Determine what vulnerabilities exist within those systems.
3. Offer solutions to increase the security of the systems.
4. Demonstrate the possibility of losses to BA Bank or its clients by breaking into the bank.

These are the same steps and procedures that criminal hackers will use, but without your permission.

Rules of Engagement

In planning attacks against an organization, it is critical to establish *exactly* how the friendly hacks will be carried out. Most companies are afraid of what "bad guys" can do to them. This may mean a professional criminal, foreign nationals or spies, a competitor, a terrorist—or maybe just a sixteen-year-old with a keyboard.

In developing the rules of engagement, Jim Fallsworth had to choose whom he thought would at some point be a likely adversary to his bank; in this case it was assumed to be transnational criminals with a profit motive. So the agreed upon methods to attack the BA Bank's networks and web sites included remote penetrations, telephone systems, maintenance ports, and any other 'electronic doors' to the enterprise.

Attack Methodology	Permitted?
Social Engineering By Telephone	Yes
Social Engineering By Mail	No

Adoption of Employee Identity—Remote	Yes
Adoption of Employee Identity—On Site	No
Pretend to Be Technical Supplier	Yes
Dumpster Diving—On Site	No
Dumpster Diving—Off Site	Yes
Personnel Extortion, Blackmail and Coercion	No
Investigate Personnel Background	No
Penetration of Business Partners	No

Now, criminals will do a lot of things that even professional friendly hackers will not and cannot do. The so-called "out of bounds behavior" must be defined and adhered to. Nonetheless, all possible methods must be considered. The bad guys will not preclude using them just because they are illegal; besides, it is prudent to understand how far real criminals might be willing to go.

A portion of any efficient hack-attack is to assemble competitive information on the target through open sources such as can be found from public records, financial reports, and technical documentation. Both time and money can be saved if the company just hands it over to the friendly hackers. The kind of information that a real attacker would find of value includes:

- Operating systems
- Open technical on systems in use
- Major venders used within the enterprise
- Physical address of data center and telephone centers
- Phone exchanges information

Jim Fallsworth agreed to provide a legitimate bank account with 1,000 dollars in it so the account was accessible by telephone or from the bank's web site. Any real attacker would certainly do anything he could to get closer to his victim, no matter the nature of the business. In this case, having an account permits the friendly hacker to social engineer the bank's employees.

Lastly, BA Bank made sure to issue a Get Out of Jail Free card to their ethical hackers. Many hacking techniques are illegal; felonious federal offenses. In the unlikely event that certain activities were discovered and reported, written authorization from the company is the only way out of trouble.

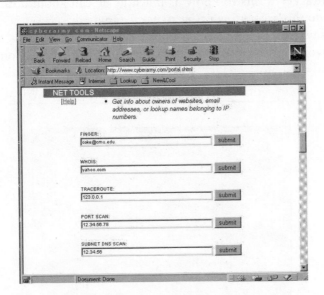

At www.cyberarmy.com you can enter any IP address and learn a great deal about the target network. It's free and requires no technical knowledge whatsoever.

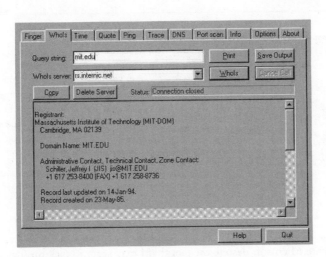

Researching a target is part of the game. NetLab is a freeware product that comes from www.eb.uah.edu/~adanil/. Fairly comprehensive for basic analysis.

The attacker wants to know as much as he can about a target. The tools to do this are getting easier to use by anybody.

Let's say, for example, that you have selected Microsoft as a target.[9] Where would you begin? A fascinating site is Netcraft.Com out of England.

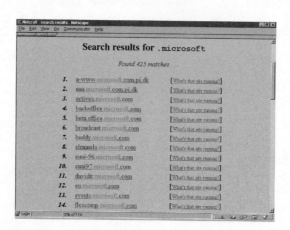

Prior to an attack, I want to learn a lot about my target. At the Netcraft home page, I entered Microsoft to learn something about their infrastructure. 425 hits was more than I expected.

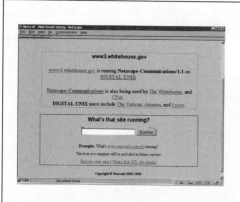

If you want to go after the White House, which I do not recommend, you can find out what versions of software they are running and then look up their holes and vulnerabilities on hacker sites. Easy enough?

---

[9] I do not hate Microsoft despite the fact that I may seem to pick on them. A lot of my friends are senior folks there. However, I have also criticized them for certain security problems. The other reason I use them as an example is because of their profile. They are famous, public, and I don't have to get permission from dozens of companies. Besides, most of this is public knowledge anyway.

External Mapping

Once the preliminary research is complete, the ersatz attack team begins the mapping efforts. This is not about breaking into the networks, but about building a non-intrusive picture, or "footprint," of what the electronic perimeter of the company's networks look like. This mapping includes Internet addresses, physical locations, telephone systems, dial-up modems, maintenance ports, and anything else that connects the outside world into the company. The same stuff any good criminal would do.

During the external mapping process, a suite of conventionally available hacker and legitimate analysis tools are used:

1. Searching Internic will provide an in-depth look at the company's IP infrastructure from the outside. www. networksolutions.com
2. Demon Dialers scan tens of thousands of telephone numbers in search of modem tones indicating the presence of a computer.
3. Network Sniffers read traffic along the company's identified paths.
4. Netcraft.com will provide extensive system information on the target.
5. Scanners such as SATAN and ISS examine external entry points.

Throughout this process the ethical hackers should keep complete electronic records of everything they do. This is called audit or logging. If something goes wrong and a system is adversely affected, an activity log helps everyone understand what went wrong and what to do to fix it.

One necessary step is the manual look-and-see of the target's IP range. The friendly hackers want to learn about the target: what software and hardware it's using. The client might give them that information in a security assessment, but the bad guys will have to do their own homework.

The attacker also wants to know if his target machine is awake and working. Using "ping," a non-offensive software tool, will do this in less than a second. Note that in this case, MIT was the target.

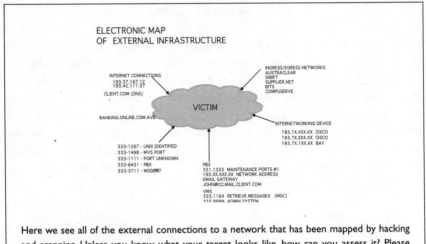

ELECTRONIC MAP
OF EXTERNAL INFRASTRUCTURE

INTERNET CONNECTIONS
193.37.167.12
193.42.111.37
CLIENT.COM (DNS)

BANKING.ONLINE.COM.AVE

INGRESS/EGRESS NETWORKS
AUSTRACLEAR
SWIFT
SUPPLIER.NET
BITS
COMPUSERVE

VICTIM

INTERNETWORKING DEVICE
193.1X.XXX.XX CISCO
193.7X.XXX.XX CISCO
193.7X.1XX.XX BAY

333-1267 - UNIX IDENTIFIED
333-1498 - MVS PORT
333-1111 - PORT UNKNOWN
333-6431 - PBX
333-3711 - MODEM?

PBX
331.1333 MAINTENANCE PORTS #1
193.XX.XXX.XX NETWORK ADDRESS
EMAIL GATEWAY
JOHN@CC.MAIL.CLIENT.COM

VMX
333.1164 RETRIEVE MESSAGES (MSC)
333.9999 ADMIN SYSTEM

Here we see all of the external connections to a network that has been mapped by hacking
and scanning. Unless you know what your target looks like, how can you assess it? Please
remember that this map is only good for external attacks, not insider assaults or abuses,
unless they in fact attack from the outside.

Scanning for Network Vulnerabilities

Once the outside footprint of the network is mapped, which if done properly can take the hackers a fair amount of time, they want to learn more
about its weaknesses, so they know where to attack. Keep in mind that
the job of defending a network is a whole heck of a lot harder than it is to
attack; a whole lot. The defender has to make sure that every potential
point of entry from outside of his network is secure; that every electronic
door and window is protected. All the external attacker has to do is find
one weak spot—and he's in. It doesn't seem fair, but that's the way it is.

The easiest and most common way to continue the external attack
after the mapping has been completed is to use tools called scanners.
Now here's where there is a little technical bit about the Internet you
need to learn (no, it's not that hard!).

As you know, the Internet addressing system is made up of four
groups of numbers, like 10.10.13.13, and they represent the IP (Internet
Protocol) address of the computer in general. Each one is unique, but it
says nothing about how many computers may or may not be sitting
behind that single IP address. It could be an entire company or country . . . but most likely not.

Scanning a network or computer means an attacker's computer looking at the ports on the server. It is really very simple.

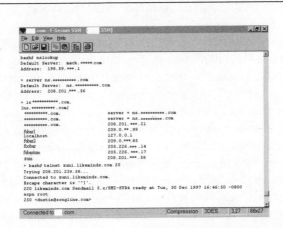

A command called "nslookup" is used to find the hosts related to the IP address of the primary target. Then we see that a "telnet" to the address finds a Unix machine that is running Sendmail 5.x. That says what sorts of exploits may work on that machine. The hacker can go back to PacketStorm, attrition or other hacker web sites and search for exploits to attack Sendmail 5.X.

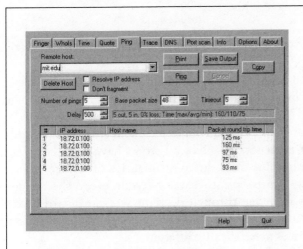

'Pinging' MIT tells the attacker (or legitimate network administrator) the status of the network. This automated tool also offers a wide range of tools of value to the attacker.

Imagine a traditional department store. The entire store is divided into discrete departments: shoes, tools, clothing, kitchen, etc. Each department provides a unique service (how many times have you heard "that's not my department"?). Assume the store has a central number, i.e. 555-1000, and each department has its own extension: shoes x12, clothing x13, kitchen x14, and so on. The combination of phone number plus extension allows you to directly call the specific department or service you are looking for.

Now imagine that every store, from Macy's to Wal-Mart, uses extension 12 for their shoe department. You can call ANY store in the country and directly connect to the shoe department to get the service you need. No matter what the phone number or store, extension 12 will ALWAYS get your call routed to the shoe serviceperson. Computers are no different, except they use IP addresses (i.e. 10.10.13.13) and port numbers (i.e. 80) for phone number and extension respectively.

The Internet community has decided on a group of "well-known ports" to ensure that any computer running any operating system can get to standard services (i.e. web pages, email, etc.) This way, one server (just like one department store) can offer many services (departments) from one IP address. Here are some standard ports that you probably use every day:

Port	Service
20 & 21	ftp
23	telnet
25	smtp (mail)
80	http (web)

There are a total of 65,536 ports (or departments) for every server. Ports 0–1023 are the most common ones, but the registered ports range from 1024–65535.[10]

Why you should care? To continue our department store analogy, different stores offer different services. Not all stores have a fur coat section. Further, different stores offer different qualities of services: some have full-time snooty salespeople to cater to your every champagne whim; others let you scrounge through decrepit wet cardboard boxes that fell off the truck in a rainstorm. They may offer the same products, but the quality and prices are radically different.

Not all stores offer flawless diamonds in their jewelry department. So let us say that a criminal wishes to "case" the store before stealing. The criminal is looking for what departments she could steal from, and what kind of security she is likely to run into. Port mapping and IP scanning

[10]For a complete list of well known ports and their services check out: http://www.con.wesleyan.edu/~triemer/network/docservs.html

are the digital equivalents of casing the joint. Further, servers, like major department store chains, will all have similar, if not identical, security (cheaper to install, maintain, and train if all the stores are the same).

Scanning wasn't always the norm; in fact, on Wednesday, April 5th, 1995, many security professionals predicted absolute chaos on the Internet. Security and Internet experts Wietse Venema and Dan Farmer had announced the general and free distribution of SATAN (Security Administrator's Tool for Analyzing Networks).[11]

A tremendous media circus ensued, despite the authors' rationales for writing the scanning program.

> "SATAN was written because we realized that computer systems are becoming more and more dependent on the network, and at the same time becoming more and more vulnerable to attack via that same network. SATAN is a tool to help systems administrators. It recognizes several common networking-related security problems, and reports the problems without actually exploiting them. For each type of problem found, SATAN offers a tutorial that explains the problem and what its impact could be. The tutorial also explains what can be done about the problem: correct an error in a configuration file, install a bugfix from the vendor, use other means to restrict access, or simply disable service. SATAN collects information that is available to everyone with access to the network. With a properly configured firewall in place, that should be near-zero information for outsiders."[12]

Since then, scanning products have become standard for both attackers and defenders. The most popular freeware scanning program is called NMAP, written by "fyodor."[13]

The purpose of scanning tools is to assess security, and each of the many products on the market have their own pluses and minuses. This goes beyond what the reader cares about.[14]

New vulnerabilities pop up every week, and it is good practice to test for all of the known exploits on a regular basis, regardless of which

---

[11]This URL is a good place to start looking at SATAN.
http://www.cs.ruu.nl/cert- uu/satan.html
[12]Wietse Venema and Dan Farmer on SATAN release notes.
[13]He encourages people to write him at fyodor@dhp.com.
[14]Do a search on "Internet Scanners" or "Security Assessment Tools" or "IP Scanning."

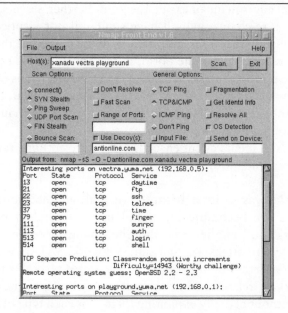

NMAP is written for command languages such as Unix/Linux, but this is a "front end" which adds a GUI (graphical user interface) for simplicity. Many hackers complain that such easy facility only contributes to "lamers, script kiddies and wannabes" acting like they know something about hacking. Using a port scanner means nothing more than that you know how to point and click.

product you use. They tell you where the electronic doors are ajar, where the windows are cracked, or where there is no perimeter security at all. Do not underestimate your potential adversary.

Breaking In: The Final Hack into Bab

Based upon the findings from scanners, social engineering, and open-source competitive intelligence, the ethical hackers are now ready to penetrate BA Bank's networks.

If this sounds overly simple, most security holes are commonsense practices that have been forgotten. Gaining access to the internal infrastructure is done through multiple entrances: TCP/IP, maintenance ports, PBX to data lines, CISCO, NT-RAS, dedicated networks, telephone (VRU) networks, firewalls, authentication servers, or other network mechanisms.

Once the attacker has penetrated the external perimeter of the net-

ISS makes a popular commercial scanner. The results of scans are detailed and rate the risk factor. Once the risk is known, the ISS Internet Scanner will make recommendations to take to fix the vulnerabilities.

work, he still has more work ahead of him. The next step is to see what's going on inside the network using a wide range of technical methods, including password cracking and compromising poor controls on application resources, system utilities, and operating system controls at the kernel and root, and other fully privileged layers of the infrastructure. Customized tools are often needed to achieve penetration, depending upon what happens and is discovered:

- Weak passwords or no passwords
- Dialing into modems without security
- ftp or telnet into open ports
- Finding the scripts and programs to bypass the security and weaknesses discovered. Any good hacker site has all the tools you need.

Once inside a network, breaking into the additional services, programs, and computers follows the same logic and approach.

- Use social engineering where possible
- Research open source materials
- Learn about the target technology
- Find free tools from the Internet
- Build your own tools. This is what real hackers do.

INTERNAL ELECTRONIC MAPPING OF CLIENT (EXAMPLE ONLY)

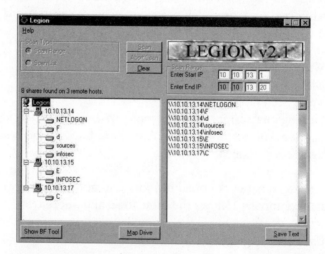

This is an example of a simple network and an attempt at mapping it. Note that the remote entry points are from the original external mapping earlier. For example, if an external connection through TCP/IP connects to a Unix box number 1. Unix box 1 may in fact connect to Unix boxes 2 through 8. Unix boxes 2 through 8 may have no direct connection to the outside world except through Unix box 1. Therefore, the successful penetration of Unix box 1 is critical to the success of penetration throughout the rest of the enterprise. Because internal security so often assumes that external security offers strong protection, internal security methods and mechanisms are often implemented in a much less rigorous manner, making an attacker's job all that much easier.

Here we see a hacker freeware scanner looking at the internal configuration of a small network which shows the IP address, the names, and ID of the drives on the system.

This book will not go into every permutation of every system out there; that is what the technicians and hackers do for a living, and I have no doubt that even these simple non-technical explanations are making some readers glaze over . . . but hey . . . it is a technical field and a few pictures and descriptions are necessary. To complete attacks against an organization, presumably for gain or under the guise of a profit-oriented adversary, several other methods are used.

1. Telephone and PBX: All too often, we forget that the telephone system and company PBX are an integrated part of the business process, and therefore must be considered in our vulnerability testing of a corporate network. The company telco system may well have undocumented connections to the data network and offer a path for the interloper. An examination of the audit logs will provide a sense of normal activity, but scanning for unwanted modems is the most critical element in protecting internal networks and remote access ports. See the chapter on war dialing.

2. Denial of service: A major portion of the penetration exercises performed for BA Bank were done to determine just how strong their upcoming on-line, web-based banking services actually were. See the chapter on denial-of-service.

Ethical hacking of a network's security is a normal method of insuring business process integrity. The depth of the analysis will be determined by a company's particular needs, worries, connectivity, and amount of reliance upon IP and other networks to conduct business. But keep in mind "real" criminal hackers will break a lot of rules that ethical hackers won't.

Lastly, and just as important as every other step in assessing your security, do not assume that, just because you have gone through this kind of hacking process, your networks are secure. All you really know is the condition of your networks at the moment of their evaluation. Just like the rest of your company's infrastructure, security is a dynamic, ever-changing condition that requires constant vigilance.

So, the prudent security manager will use the first comprehensive testing as a benchmark, and continue to sponsor periodic reviews (ethical hacks) of the system. Especially important is to look at the security of new systems before they go on-line—not after you suffer the consequences.

In the meantime—good hacking!

If you want to see how secure or insecure your home, small office, or

company computer is, head over to www.grc.com—without question the finest site to evaluate your vulnerability over dial-up, cable modem or any Internet connection.

Resources

- For a good list of scanners, go to Packet Storm Security at www.packetstorm.securify.com
- http://www.insecure.org/nmap/index.html contains a lot of documentation and links. Good backgrounds, histories and sassy fun, too.
- Axent Technologies: www.axent.com offers services and a full range of security products for the corporate enterprise.
- Internet Security Systems: www.iss.net has the most successful commercial scanner out there.
- Secure Networks, Inc.: www.securenetworks.com
- Network Associates: www.nai.com
- Search on "scanners," "network scanners," "IP scanners," and so on.

War Dialing

Hacking the Phones

In March 1998 federal officials unsealed a criminal "computer hacking" warrant against a teenager in Worcester, Massachusetts. The youth, whose name was not released, was charged with crippling the Worcester County airport control tower and shutting down telephone service to more than 600 homes. The incident occurred in March of 1997, when the boy conducted a scan of the telephone numbers in his home area code by calling each phone number with a computer program that he had downloaded from the Internet. One of the computers that answered was the controller for a fiber-optic communication system. The fiber-optic system didn't ask for a username or password, but simply presented the youth with a series of commands that he could type. Curious as to what would happen, and presumably unaware of the possible consequences of his actions, he shut the system down. In the process, he terminated all communications to the airport control tower and emergency services for several hours.[15]

In the late 1960s, the FBI paid me a visit. I had been fraudulently using a telephone. Stupidly, it was the same phone booth at the recording studio where I worked. One visit. One slap. Problem solved. If it were only so easy with today's miscreant youth.

Telephones were the original hacker/phreaker playground and today,

---

[15]Opening paragraph from "Advanced Telephone Auditing with PhoneSweep: A better alternative to underground war dialers" by Simson L. Garfinkel, simsong@vineyard.net Copyright 1998. First appeared in *From Matrix News*, 8(12), December 1998. http://www.mids.org/mn/812/sim.html

with all of the headline-making Internet news, we tend to forget about telephones as a security weakness.

The problem is quite simple: Despite the fact that most companies are linked to the Internet, they still have modems scattered about, hanging onto the back of PCs. Some are old and forgotten from the days when we used the remote access program PCAnywhere to dial into our offices and work from home or on the road. Other modems are installed by people who want to bypass the Internet (for whatever legitimate or illegitimate reasons they may have).

PC-based modems hamper security efforts by providing a back door, invisible to security and network managers, into the networks, and that is not a good thing.

Early telephone hacking efforts were popularized in 1983, in the MGM/United Artists movie "War Games," starring techno-teen Matthew Broderick. His character finds the telephone number and password to his high school computer and changes grades. Looking for games, he uses a war dialer to find modems and accidentally connects to a Department of Defense computer. He finds a game called *Thermonuclear War* and nearly starts World War III.

War dialing is simple. A software program dials a large number of phone numbers in sequence. For example, the three-digit prefix might be 595–, so a war dialer will dial all 10,000 numbers from 595-0000 to 595-9999 and see what's on the other end; a phone, a modem, a fax machine. Finding a modem is considered a success and a possible target for hacking.

The first war dialing programs appeared in the early 1980s after inexpensive modems were popularized.

In the last couple of years, a couple of San Francisco security consultants/hackers decided to perform a study on war dialing:

- They scanned 5.3 million telephone numbers.
- About 1% of them were connected to modems.
- According to Peter Shipley (www.dis.org) who was on the project, 75% of those modems were insecure enough to let hackers through.

They also found some astounding holes in critical systems.

- An East Bay medical facility gave unrestricted modem access to patient records, making it easy for a hacker to steal, alter, or delete private medical records.
- An Internet company offering financial services did not require a password to modify its modem-accessible fire-

wall, potentially permitting intruders to install backdoors
and disable auditing routines.
- A Fortune 100 company's air conditioner and environmental control units could easily be changed by modem,
  enabling a hacker to overheat buildings or kill lights at will.

As with other hacking programs, war dialing has become one of the
tools of corporate security professionals and consultants who engage in
testing the security of networks. Companies want to find and generally
rid themselves of modems on the loose because of the security risks they
present.

One popular war dialer is called ToneLoc and was developed in the
early 1990s. It is a DOS-based program, written by hackers for use by
hackers. The introduction to the ToneLoc manual is very descriptive:

ToneLoc v1.10, User Manual
by
Minor Threat & Mucho Maas

ToneLoc is short for Tone Locator, and is a bit of a wild thing. What
it does is simple: It dials numbers, looking for some kind of tone. It can
also look for carriers like an ordinary war dialer.

It is useful for:

1. Finding PBXs.
2. Finding loops or milliwatt test numbers.
3. Finding dial-up long-distance carriers.
4. Finding any number that gives a constant tone, or something that your modem will recognize as one.
5. Finding carriers (other modems).
6. Hacking PBXs.

ToneLoc is extremely flexible and it's free, but has the downside of
requiring some technical knowledge to operate. Hackers though have
virtually standardized it for ethical or illegal war dialing. You can pick
up a free copy at any hacker web site.

To meet the needs of the security professional, though, Sandstorm
Enterprises, Inc. (www.sandstorm.net) developed PhoneSweep, an
advanced telephone scanning tool, in September of 1998. The program
is designed to build a map of corporate telephone systems by dialing
every phone number within a specified range and recording what it
finds.

ToneLoc war dialing menu.

PhoneSweep has three modes of operation: connect, identify, and penetrate. In identify mode, PhoneSweep will attempt to determine the type of computer system to which the modem is attached. In penetrate mode PhoneSweep will then try to log in to the system using a dictionary of common username/password pairs.

Unlike ToneLoc and other hacker war dialers PhoneSweep can place multiple phone calls in parallel on multiple phone lines. This makes it possible to rapidly scan a large block of phone numbers, while still storing the results in an embedded SQL database. Shortly after PhoneSweep went on the market, Sandstorm received an amusing email message in the mailbox saying, "Do you guys realize that you've created the ultimate hacking tool?" (Unlike other auditing tools, Sandstorm does not distribute free evaluation copies of PhoneSweep over the Internet.)

War dialing has become a legitimate tool for the security-minded administrator who wants to sew up the holes in his network created by unsupervised modems floating around.

Just because phone lines are not Internet based does not mean that there is no security weakness. The unknown access points to a network are more dangerous than those that are known.

At an October 1999 security conference in Washington DC, long-time friend and Veridian (www.veridian.com) executive Jim Morris said something that got me thinking. "You know, in all of the penetration testing we do, in 100 percent of the cases, we can get through the phones. In 100 percent of the cases." That means that no matter how well your Internet security is configured, there is still a major weakness: the telephone lines into a company and its internal phone system or PBX.

If a bad guy calls into a company, is transferred to an extension, and then hits 'O' for operator, the receptionist often assumes the call is from

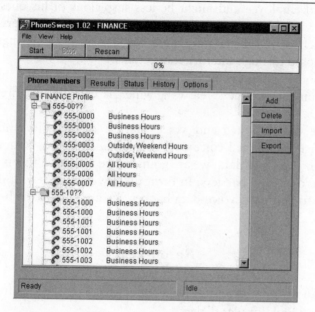

The PhoneSweep Telephone scanning tool lets you import numbers to scan and define the exact range of interest.

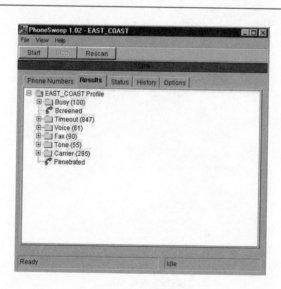

The results of PhoneSweep's war dialing is organized in a database for further analysis.

an internal employee and might be less suspicious of his questions or requests. Most PBXs allow access to internal long-distance services and to data networks, which can expose weaknesses just as dangerous as those exposed through Internet connections.

In response to this problem a new company, Secure Logix, has introduced a unique product: TeleWall, which is essentially a firewall for telephones.

As the data market and voice market merge with things like Voiceover IP, combined voice-data networks, and wires to homes that carry both voice and data, we are going to see increased forms of hacking that cross those barriers. In turn, there will be a slew of defensive products to battle the voice-data hacker. We are only at the beginning.

Resources

- Go to any hacker site, find their programs or hacking tools, and look for war dialers.
- Search on "War Dialers" or " Demon Dialers."

Trojan Hacking

In 800 BC, the legendary Greek poet Homer told a story. It went like this:

Around 1200 BC, Paris of Troy abducted Helen, wife of Menelaus, a leader in the Greek Peloponesia. Under the leadership of King Agamemnon, the Greek city-states put aside their differences and united for battle. They sailed across the Aegean to Troy (in modern Turkey) and besieged the city for nine years in an effort to retrieve Helen. (No matter what she and Paris wanted out of the deal.) Troy was a walled city, capable of sustaining itself without outside assistance.

Seemingly bored with waiting outside the closed gates of Troy for almost a decade, the Greeks up and left. However, they left behind what the Trojans considered a present, in honor of the their "victory" in the war: a great wooden horse. Despite the warnings of the Trojan seer Cassandra, the Trojans opened the gates for a moment to accept the gift into their city. And thus, according to Homer's *Iliad*, at night, Odysseus and his band of Greek soldiers, who had been hiding inside the belly of the horse, descended, sacked the whole city, and won the war. The walls and gates of Troy held strong, as long as they were not "lowered" to permit commerce with the outside world. If they had, battle with the Greeks would have been immediate. As soon as they did open their city, see what happened?

Hackers have their own versions of the Trojan Horse, too.

In simple English, a Trojan Horse is a software program that is inserted into a computer without you knowing it. The program then

operates, doing whatever it was designed to do, without your knowledge. This is not good.

How do they get Trojan Horses into systems? Three ways:

1. They somehow have physical access to the computer and manu-
    ally install it. Again we have to worry about company insiders
    with an attitude and an agenda.

2. They remotely hack the machine and install a Trojan.

3. Email. Trojan Horses, just as in Homer's day, are secretly deliv-
    ered under the guise of being something very different than what
    they really are.

For example, let's say you receive an email from a "friend" (whom
you may or may not know) and it says, "Merry Christmas! Enjoy
Rudolph's and Santa's adventure." Being in the Christmas spirit, you
click on the attachment and indeed Rudolph and Santa are having a
grand old time doing Christmas things. What you don't see, though, is
that in the background, another program has secretly installed itself into
your computer—and you, Rudolph, and Santa are never the wiser.

Woof. Not pleasant, but that is the state of the art.

In August 1998 at the hacker convention DefCon 6, (www.defcon.org)
a program was released by the Cult of the Dead Cow (www.cultdead
cow.com) called Back Orifice.

Arguably, Back Orifice is the most advanced and widespread Trojan
Horse in Internet history. It is incredibly simple to use, is freely available, and highly effective. The name Back Orifice is an intended insult at
Microsoft's Back Office suite of universal programs. It targets Windows
machines.

According to the Cult of the Dead Cow (cDc):

> Back Orifice is a remote administration system which allows
> a user to control a computer across a TCP/IP connection
> using a simple console or GUI application. On a local LAN
> or across the Internet, BO gives its user more control of the
> remote Windows machine than the person at the keyboard of
> the remote machine has.
>
> BO is small and entirely self installing. Simply executing
> the server on any Windows machine installs the server, mov-
> ing the executable into the system where it will not interfere
> with other running applications. To ease distribution, BO

*can also be attached to any other Windows executable which
will run normally after installing the server.*

*Once running, BO does not show up in the task list or
close-program list, and is rerun every time the computer is
started. The file name that it runs as is configurable before it
is installed, and it's as easy to upgrade as uploading the new
version and running it.*

When you read the cDc's web page descriptions, it is eminently clear
that they have little respect for Microsoft, its products, and the poor
security that they put into their operating systems and products. But the
boys in Redmond seem to slough off such criticism, and often deny the
weaknesses embedded in their products. According to Microsoft's
Edmund Muth:

"This is not a tool we should take seriously, or our customers
should take seriously . . ."

the *New York Times*

Perhaps due in part to that mistaken attitude, Back Orifice has proliferated wildly. The best way to protect against BO is to use a legitimate
anti-virus program.

There are many web sites out there which claim to have anti-BO
(Back Orifice) software: DO NOT USE THEM. These sites may download you a program which instead of protecting you against BO, actually installs it. Beware, and stick to the big companies.

If you become infected with Back Orifice you give up thorough and
total control of your computer to others who may be very far away and
not have your best interests at heart. The bad guys can then:

- Log all of the keystrokes you make on your machine
  including passwords.
- Remotely freeze, lock up, or reboot your machine.
- Get detailed system information, including current user,
  cpu type, Windows version, memory usage, and all drives.
- Get your screensaver password and passwords cached by
  the user (including those for dialups, web, and network
  access, and any other password cached by the operating
  system).
- Copy, rename, delete, view, and search files and directories.
- Start or stop programs on your computer.

- Take over your network controls.
- Play wav files, capture screen shots, and capture video or still frames from any video input device (like a Quickcam).
- Upload and download files on any port using a www client such as Netscape.
- Monitor network packets, logging any plaintext passwords that pass.

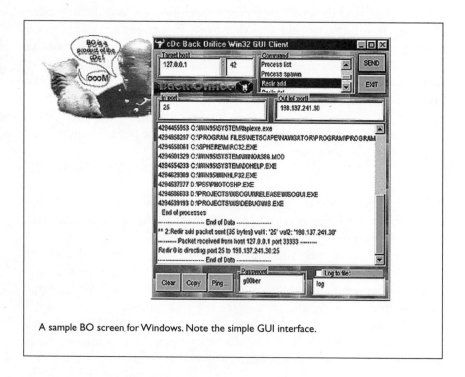

A sample BO screen for Windows. Note the simple GUI interface.

To invoke these controls, all you need to do is select one of the commands in the upper right screen when attached to the target IP address. The results are displayed in the main window. Period.

Back Orifice has spawned a miniature hacker industry with what are known as Plug-Ins or in this case, Butt Plugs. Butt Plugs are small programs which attach to Back Orifice and add more features to compromise security.

As with other hacker tools, there is a debate amongst the security community as to the value of hackers building exploits such as Back Orifice and making them publicly available.

The argument from the software companies' standpoint is, "Call us first and we'll work with you."

The hacker's response is, "We've tried before, and you lamers just don't want to hear it. You lie to the public and that is criminal."

This debate will not be solved overnight—if ever, and it is probably good for the technology industry if we listen with an open mind to the discoveries made by hackers worldwide.

At DefCon 7 in 1999, cDc released BO2K, an updated and enhanced version. The source code is now free and available for programmers to make their own definitive versions.

In the meantime keeping yourself safe is not tough. As Nike says, Just Do It.

1. Use any of the major anti-virus programs. Make it a legal, paid-for version.

2. Update the signature files regularly by checking with the vendor's web site. If a vendor has automatic updating to your computer, all the better.

3. Listen to the media. Major virus outbreaks are now reported in daily newspapers.

4. Don't open unknown attachments. Period.

5. Use personal desktop firewalls.

Resources

- www.sevenlocks.com/CIACA-10.htm
- Tripwire information: www.cs.purdue.edu/pub/spaf/ security/ and www.tripwiresecurity.com
- Search on "Trojan Horses."
- www.cultdeadcow.com
- http://www.microsoft.com/security/bulletins/ms98-010.asp gives Microsoft's response to BO in August, 1998.
- To see cDc's response to Microsoft, visit http://www. cultdeadcow.com/tools/bo_msrebuttal.html. It is most entertaining and puts Bill Gates in his place.

Hacking for $

One of the questions I am most often asked is, "Is it safe for me to use a credit card on the Internet?"

But first, let's talk about pornography.

If you want smut it's there. If you build a porn site, they will come. And from all indications, pornography is the unsung hero of on-line commerce. Pornography may go down in history as the Great Enabling Content that really helped grow the Internet from a fledgling infant into an adolescent that still needs considerable taming.

Pornography in every shape, size, color, and variation is a mere click away. All too much of its adult content is available for free to anyone with access to a computer and modem. Unfortunately, this means that today's teenagers are getting a far more graphic sex education than I did with the comparatively tame *Playboy* magazine of the 1960s.

Pornography is the crack-cocaine scourge of the Internet—and I do not say that from a prudish standpoint. What I mean is that the on-line pornography industry offers the web surfer virtually unlimited viewing of its wares, for free, as a means to entice users into forking over monthly or weekly fees for full access to their images, movies, phone sex and fantasy prose. So a kid can easily scan the Net for free adult content—and get an eyeful. Then, with his parent's credit card number (not too terribly difficult to get for an enterprising and hormone-driven teenager) he can subscribe to earthier services for the free week, but cancel before the billing goes through to parental surprise.

The statistics for on-line pornography are nothing short of amazing:

- In 1998, there were more than 70,000 active porn sites on the Internet.
- The on-line pornography industry is one of the fastest growing segments of ecommerce—and one fraught with the most fraud.
- Sex-oriented Usenet groups are heavily trafficked, offering free XXX pictures to anyone with Internet access. They are about as kinky as kinky can get.
- Pornography accounts for hundreds of millions of dollars in on-line sales annually, although no one really knows how much. The vast majority are paid for by credit cards.

In many ways, pornography has been responsible for the advancement of technology. What good is pornography without real-time and live video streaming? Multimedia sound and motion enhances the entertainment value of the content. Or so they say.

Sound! Video! Close-ups! Peep-shows! Interactive conversations with the slut of your choice. The latest porno rage is voyeurism. Houses full of buxom blondes, redheads, and brunettes live their naked lives while prancing in front of a dozen cameras strategically placed in bedrooms, hot tubs, bathrooms, and tanning salons.

Cheri has her house filled with cameras, too, and publishes her daily schedule, which includes doing the dishes, feeding the cat, cooking, watching TV, and of course, nightly masturbation for all to lasciviously watch. But Cheri and thousands of girls like her get paid by the click and the amount of time that their voyeur audience hangs around for the show. Danni of Danni's Hard Drive turned her exhibitionism into a million-dollar business and she never has to subject herself to the humiliation of prostitution. Nothing worse than appearing in *Playboy*—sort of—perhaps a bit more XXX, but nonetheless, her business is touch-free. Clients are distant credit card numbers, adding to the girl's net worth by the minute.

So, for that, we may thank pornography and the male libido. Out of the millions of on-line pornography enthusiasts, the vast majority pay with credit cards from their PC at home.

Now, back to the original question: Is it safe to put your credit card on the Net?

First you need to understand how the credit card transaction is done. When you are connected to the Internet from home via a modem or cable modem (or other high-speed service such as ADSL), your computer connects to the next hop, or your ISP. For a bad guy to get your credit card number, he would have to eavesdrop on the wires at your home or office or anywhere along the way to the ISP you use. (Back Orifice comes to mind. Be careful.) He would also have to be able to capture the traffic and either know exactly when you are going to use your credit card or capture every bit of Internet traffic you send and receive and then decipher it, looking for the magical digits.

That is a lot of work—a tremendous amount of effort to steal your name, credit card number, and expiration date. Is it worth it? I personally believe that it is a whole lot easier for the credit card thief to go into the garbage can behind a diner or small store and steal the carbons or copies of credit card receipts.

The next opportunity the bad guy has to get your credit card information is to hack the ISP that handles your traffic as well as hundreds or thousands of others'. In most cases, though, when you pay for something on the Net, the ISP is transparent to the process; that is, they only forward the message to its intended recipient instead of storing it.

Put on your bad-guy hat to think like a criminal for a moment: are you going to expend a lot of effort to get one credit card number from a specific person, or will you attempt to break into an on-line business that takes and stores credit card numbers? Home Shopping Network has millions on file—in their computers. *Time* magazine's subscription service stores millions, too, and was the near victim of an insider who stole the list of subscribers with their credit card information, and attempted to sell it to an undercover agent.

Social engineering, dumpster diving, and hacking the computers with a lot of credit card records is far easier and more fruitful.

My recommendation, given that your financial risk is fairly low (generally no more than $50), is to go ahead and buy stuff on the Net. Most Internet ecommerce sites use security which ties the browser to the site with encryption. Forget how weak or strong the encryption is; any encryption on a single financial transaction of this type is strong enough to ward off the attacker. It's just not worth his time or effort to crack the crypto. Even if the little lock in the browser is not locked, don't worry. Someone would have to be sitting there capturing your traffic. And as I said, just get over it. You are not the ideal target for credit card fraud.

Hackers and criminals have another way.

Wouldn't it be wonderful if you could have thousands of credit cards—without paying for any of the bills? Well, the hackers have thought up a couple of ways of getting close to that goal. Keep in mind that all of this is on the edge of legal, and if you do use this software to commit fraud you may very well get caught.

Take a brief web surf and search "Credit Master." You will find it directing you to hacker sites. If you don't want to download the pro-

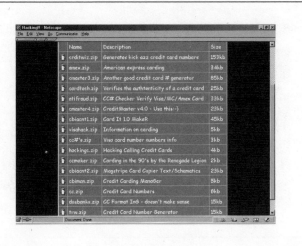

A sample of credit card–hacking software from hacker sites.

gram, that's fine, no need. But you should know that Credit Master IV is the current version that will generate endless streams of credit card numbers for literally hundreds of banks worldwide. It turns out that the credit card number–generating algorithms used by the banks are amazingly simple.

Hackers recommend that you use Credit Master IV for free phone calls, because they say the phone companies don't bother to check in real-time. Many companies, especially those in Europe, do not tie into the US's AVS (Address Verification Service) which is designed to reduce the amount of credit card fraud.

The DOS-based Credit Master IV first asks if you want to generate valid credit card numbers, which I presume for education's sake you do. So you choose "G" on the main menu for "generate card numbers." And up pops a list of banks with their 4–6-digit prefixes. Take a look at your own credit card and see if your bank numbers appear on Credit Master IV. Now pick a bank as if you were going to defraud them (which, of course, you aren't).

Your next option is to pick 15-digit American Express, or 13–16-digit-long VISA, MasterCard, or Discover card numbers to be generated. How many do you want?

There you go. Completely valid numbers that may or may not belong to someone else, but will be recognized by any credit card system as valid because the bank's algorithms have been used to generate these ersatz—yet valid—ones.

Credit Master IV does not generate expiration dates, but hackers say

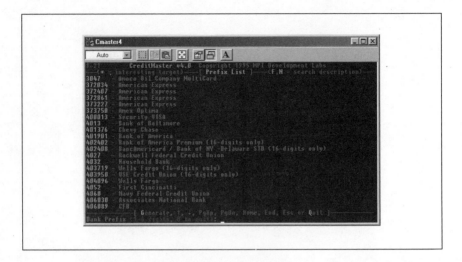

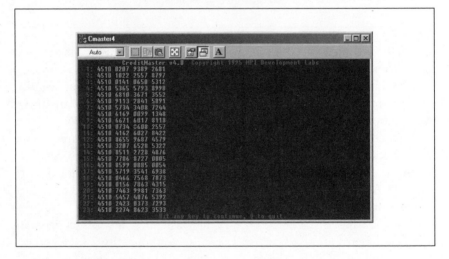

that doesn't matter because so many institutions still do not check the real validity of the card. Merely pick a date and a year in the future for the expiration and go.

With ecommerce getting serious—projections head into the trillions of dollars in the near future—computer security issues present both risks and advantages. Bank policies vary, but in general, the victim of credit card fraud is liable for only fifty dollars; less if the card company is notified immediately of loss of the card. The rules on debit cards are not yet as clear. According to MasterCard's web site, however, the two major issuers of debit cards now use the same fifty-dollar limit.

The news is not all good, however. In the case of fraudulent use of a debit card, a bank account could be emptied or reduced without the

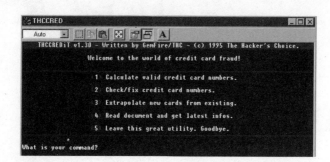

This is another example of credit card generators that are commonly available on the Internet or on many CDs around the world.

owner's immediate knowledge. Although the ultimate damage is limited, how many checks could the average consumer "bounce" if his or her checking account were clandestinely reduced by $500 or $5,000? And then who pays the fees to the bank and the cost of bounced checks?

Currently, banks and other issuers report they are able to recover the overwhelming majority of funds from fraudulent use of credit cards. This recovery is usually made from the merchant who did not determine that the transaction in question was unauthorized. It seems reasonable to expect the merchant to know his or her customer, but with the potential to do business globally, this is a daunting task.

One way to minimize the risk is to subscribe to services that notify merchants of lost cards. Additionally, some merchants cross-check the delivery address of mail order or Internet-ordered merchandise with the cardholder's address. There are publications, including computer software, that will identify the institution that issued a given card, and most of those institutions will reveal the billing address to the merchant. Check with your financial or credit card company for details.

If you are taking credit card payments for any reason, make absolutely sure that you have a real-time verification system. Preferably you will use AVS, address verification, which requires an on-line purchaser to further identify himself so the credit card company can correlate more information.

For the rest of you, the average person, the risk is comparatively low. Monitor your credit card statements closely, look for fraudulent transactions, and if you see one, call the card-issuer immediately. You are in the right and will be protected. The criminal hacker is in the wrong.

Viruses, Hoaxes, and Other Animals

The economic impact of virus and worm attacks on information systems has increased significantly: Businesses lost a total of $7.6 billion in the first two quarters of 1999 as a result. But this is not a new problem.

In 1990, a local television show was interviewing me about computer viruses.

The Internet Worm of 1988 had passed, but the media was getting sensitive to the damage that viruses can do. The Data Crime virus was coming and so the media brought its cameras to my office. I did the usual talking-head interview, but in a moment of sheer stupidity I spaced on the fact that the camera's red light was still on, meaning they were still filming.

I got into a minor rant about viruses and how virus writers were a bunch of annoying cretins. Good thing the camera was off—so I thought. Then I said that anti-virus software was no more than a big fat condom for computers.

Me and my big mouth! The condom line was the video sound-byte they used for days. Tough to explain that one to my 6-year-old daughter. Nonetheless, the analogy was sound. Anti-virus (A/V) software does put a shield around a computer. 'Nuff said there.

There are entirely too many myths running around about viruses, so we'll hopefully set the record straight here.

A computer virus is a software program that can make copies of itself. Period. A human virus does the same thing. Period. The virus looks for a place to copy a clone of itself and, given the opportunity, it does. It can copy itself from floppy disk to floppy disk, or to a hard disk,

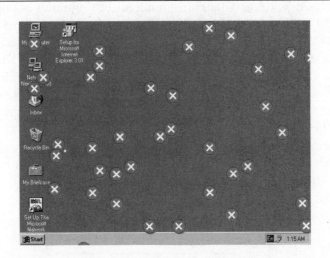

The Marburg virus does this to your computer screen.

or to a writable CD-ROM, or a tape. Some viruses work with email . . . but more about that later.[16]

Some viruses propagate by infecting another program, turning a legitimate program into a potential killer. A copy of Solitaire could be infected with a virus. The size of the solitaire program will increase somewhat, which is a clue that the file is infected, but how many of us know file sizes inside-out? Not me, that's for sure.

Computer viruses are not necessarily intentionally destructive. Viruses will take up a small amount of space on your floppy or hard disk, but what determines the destructive capability of the virus is the "payload." For example, some viruses merely copy themselves and might leave a message such as "Kilroy Was Here" or "Save the Whales" that appears on your screen from time to time. A pain, yes. Destructive, no.

The CIH, or Chernobyl Virus, from Spring 1999, however, had a destructive payload: It made your hard disk and its data inaccessible. The payload was the routine which trashed your hard disk. Interestingly enough, the CIH Virus of 1999 was pretty benign here in the US. A few isolated cases broke out. But overseas, watch out!

China claimed damages in excess of $291 million. Turkey and Korea

---

[16]I don't want you worrying about exactly how this is done, technically, but if you insist, go to www.icsa.net and soak up all the technical details you want.

were hit hard, with devastation to hundreds of thousands of computers there, and millions more were affected worldwide. How incredibly stupid! That's like knowing that a killer flu is coming next winter and not getting a flu shot; downright self-destructive and stupid. The world knew the CIH virus was coming; there was no secret about it. Everyone was adequately warned. But nooooooo . . . they must have said something like, "We won't get the virus. Sit tight. We'll be alright." Jeeez. Idiots. They deserved what they got.

Viruses are growing. According to the ICSA, in 1996 the average infection virus rate per PC was 10 per 1,000, and in 1999 it had escalated to 80 per 1,000—a tremendous increase.

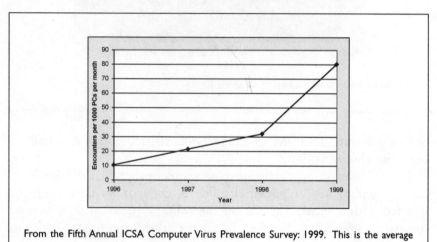

From the Fifth Annual ICSA Computer Virus Prevalence Survey: 1999. This is the average number of infected computers per 1,000.

But you, dear reader, better get virus protection as soon as you put this book down. Virus payloads vary as much as the imagination of the schnooks who write them. What would you do if you saw the following message on your screen?

```
WARNING:
WINDOWS MEMORY-PARITY TEST INPROGRESS
DO NOT TURN OFF YOUR COMPUTER! IF YOU DO YOU CAN DAMAGE THE
HARD DISK AND LOSE ALL OF YOUR DATA.
PLEASE WAIT TILL TEST IS COMPLETE.
```

What would you do? If, like so may other unfortunate souls you trusted the message that appeared, the contents of your hard disk would indeed be gone. The virus created the message you saw and the payload was the erasing of your life on disk. Viruses know no boundary and some virus writers are just malicious creatures.

A typical virus web site. Note Virus Creation Labs. This is an automated program that creates computer viruses in seconds. The better anti-virus software will detect most viruses written by automated tools.

A worm is a kind of virus that slowly migrates and then slows things down. Worms tend to eat through and at resources. One worm gets into a computer and then starts filling the memory with nonsense data. With less memory to work with, the computer begins to act as if it was on Quaaludes. Other worms might choose to constantly talk to each other with meaningless dribble, but the electronic chatter fills up valuable bandwidth, slowing down other legitimate traffic. That is bad.

A Trojan Horse is not a virus, but a virus might contain a Trojan Horse. A Trojan Horse is a program that you think will do one thing but secretly does another. It may have been secretly installed onto a computer and runs without the knowledge of the user. Generally a useful Trojan is too big to be a virus.

Bots are not viruses either. A bot is a piece of software that operates like a robot, sort of, and performs a task you ask of it. Let's say you travel a lot and want to go to New York for a week. A travel-bot would ask you about airlines, flight times, budgets, cars, and all of the associated details normally handled by a travel agent.

Your travel bot would then scrounge around the Internet and look for the best deals it could find and the best schedules, and then come back to you with a report of the options. Do you want to travel on the 5PM or the 7PM flight? You earn Avis points but Hertz has a better deal. The Hilton costs this much but I found a one-bedroom suite in Chelsea for twenty dollars less per night. What do you want to do? You would answer the questions the bot posed and then it would go off and make your reservations. That is sexy, eh?

Well, let's think it through again. With big companies getting so security conscious, how many of them feel comfortable letting hundreds or thousands of little chunks of software from anywhere go swimming around their networks at will? Not many, and that's exactly why the bot business has not exactly taken off. The exception is the Internet search engine business.

Search engines like Yahoo! and Excite use botlike critters to examine web sites, see what's underneath the hood of each, and then return information to its own server.

My mother in-law has trouble with technology. We bought her a VCR about ten years ago and little did we know that it sat on top of her TV blinking 12:00 for six months. She never used it. "I'm just gitting used to it bein' here," she drawled. She called me from Tennessee one night and asked if she needed to go to the doctor. "Huh?" I asked. "My wife reads the medical books. What's wrong with you?"

"Nothing, I'm fine," she promised. "But I'm worried about catching this computer virus going around."

"Do you own a computer, Marie?" I asked her.

"No. And don't want to either." She has Granny Clampett determination.

"You have nothing to worry about," I assured her. I think she bought it.

It astounds me that people are under the impression that a human can catch a computer virus and get ill.

No. No. No. Even if you wear a pacemaker, you cannot catch a computer virus. Maybe if you are Steve Austin, *The $6 Million Man*, you might, but no, no, you cannot get sick from a computer virus.

On the other hand . . . and this gets weird, the US military and a handful of private folks are doing something equally bizarre. They are writing software that will give computer users headaches. The goal is purely offensive in nature and it makes sense. Can the military infect an enemy's network with a virus that will cause the computer operators to function at less than optimum capacity? This unproven technology leaked from classified circles in early 1999 and thus far the demonstrations have been impressive. How do they do it?

The viral or infecting component is pretty straight-ahead; it's the payload that does the work as in other offensive and malicious viruses. Like in a TV, computer monitors use a number of clocks to create a viewable image. If the frequencies are altered in one way, the picture rolls up and down or from side to side—just like old television sets. However, if the frequencies are altered in other ways, and if the waveforms of the clock frequencies are changed, the resultant complex waveforms can affect the human body. Classified research continues as cyberwar techniques are embedded into the military and information operators. The user, not the system, becomes the target.

The military began openly recruiting virus experts in 1990 at Fort Monmouth, New Jersey, in search of ways to introduce malicious viruses into enemy communications systems. The ultimate may have been the alleged use of computer viruses in the Gulf War.

Is there such a thing as a good computer virus? Arguably, no. Discussions have taken place since the late 1980s on this exact point. Some people maintain that viruses could be used to maintain software updates and distribute good software code to remote computers. I believe that this line of thinking died when the web and Java came along. Now, using web-based technology, software can be updated through much less intrusive means with greater control by administrators.

In India, the bottom of the social caste system are the untouchables; people who clean out toilets and latrines for their entire lives. Many people believe virus writers are the untouchable equivalents in Cyberspace. Even hackers think little of them. The end result of most virus writing efforts is destructive. Maybe someone will come up with a brilliant new good application for viruses, but that has yet to be seen.

Virus writers try to figure out how to bypass security mechanisms with their tools just as hackers and security professionals do with theirs. The big difference is in the ethics and motivation. Why should a virus be released into the "wild"? What good does it do? None.

Professional virus researchers such as Sarah Gorden, Dr. Alan Soloman, and a bevy of others combat viruses for a living, and as with other computer security efforts, they have to know how to build them to defeat them. But they do not release them either. They keep them in the laboratory.

The vast majority of virus writers who release their software on the Internet are headline-seeking punks. If a virus writer really does discover a new way to create mayhem, it is far better for everyone if they contact a legitimate company and show them their discovery. Releasing it on the Internet to "wake up the clueless masses" is an exercise in hateful arrogance.

Back in 1989 I wrote an article that claimed viruses could be written that did not infect the software programs themselves. This new class of virii would instead, I alleged, work inside of programs and be written in a data format rather than a program or executable one.

"You're nuts!" the so-called virus experts of the day yelled. "No way." The method I used was to program the macros within Lotus and an old data base program called dBase III.[17]

It took a few years for my prediction to come true, but when Microsoft bought the universe and Word became the de-facto standard, the virus writers did exactly what I said they would almost ten years earlier.

Macro viruses infect a file, such as a Word document, and spread when the infected file lands on somebody else's desktop, via email or floppy, and subsequently infects other Word documents, which in turn infect others. The first Word macro viruses spread ten times faster than any other virus in history.[18] So part of any anti-virus protection effort must include macro viruses as well.

Like other viruses, a macro virus does not have to be destructive. They can propagate harmlessly as some do, with their payload merely being a message: **South Park: Why Animals Eat Their Young** or something like that. But a macro, a programming language all of its own that sits within applications like Word, can be told to do just about anything you want it to. As a result, some macro viruses are extremely deadly.

When email became so much a part of our everyday life, the question was asked, "Can you send a virus via email and infect the recipient's computer?"

Yes and no is the perfectly clear answer.

If I send you an email and there is a Word document attached to it with a macro virus, and you open that attachment, *bang!* You're infected, unless you are using the right anti-virus software. If I send you an email with a program attachment such as a game or small utility or self-running installation, and if it is infected, then you are infected too. Gotta use A/V software to handle that one, too.

However, if I send you an email, with no attachment and just a text

---

[17]Macros are small programs written inside of an application, such as Word, which speed up repetitive or complex tasks automatically.
[18]According to Peter Tippitt, former President of the ICSA.

message in it, you cannot be infected. In fact, even if I send you an email
with the actual virus code built into the text of the email, you cannot be
infected.[19]

Think about it. A virus is a program; even a macro virus must run, or
be executed, to do nasty deeds. Email text doesn't execute. It is just read.
You cannot "run" text files to do anything. The technicalities are
beyond this book, but it should be some comfort that email may not be
so bad after all.[20]

Spring 1999 was met with a huge email virus event: Melissa. Melissa
was named after an exotic dancer from Orlando, Florida, and it did
something unique. The payload of Melissa was not to destroy your hard
disk. It was more of a denial-of-service virus. If you used the Microsoft
email package, Melissa would look up the email addresses of fifty folks
within your email address book and forward them a message. The mul-
tiplying effects shut down thousands of email systems worldwide as
people came to work on Monday—only to be nailed by Melissa.

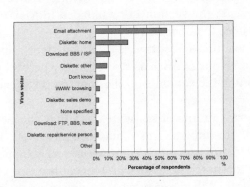

From the Fifth Annual ICSA Computer Virus Prevalence Survey: 1999. These are how computers get infected.

---

[19]We all believed this until the first week of December when a new class of virii
appeared. Merely opening a Microsoft Outlook email program is now enough to
become infected. You really need to stay on top of the developments—go to your
anti-virus vendor's web site regularly! Also, it is good advice to get away from
Microsoft email; use Netscape or anything else which is less likely to become a target.

[20]The rules always change, though. Caveat emptor.

How to Protect Yourself from Viruses

Unless you're a researcher or one of those wankers who writes or distributes viruses 'cause being a pain in the butt is built into your DNA, you don't want viruses anywhere near your computer.

Stopping viruses from infecting your computer and potentially ruining your hard disk and a year's work is actually fairly simple. What you have to do is be committed enough to do the leg work, or web work as the case may be.

First, you have to get a good quality anti-virus program. So check out the resources area at the end of this chapter and you will see all of the major vendors present. Pick one of them and buy it—which means actually pay for it!

I do not recommend buying A/V software from a computer store because you will get an older version. It takes time to manufacture the software, distribute it, and by the time you get it, it is antique. Also, beware of ancient software on web sites. Some manufacturers do not update their web sites. In the case of Network Associates and McAfee anti-virus software, the version I downloaded in May of 1999 had not been updated since October of 1998.

Once you have the A/V software, the next steps are up to you, too. New viruses come out as often as ten to twenty per week. A/V software works by scanning the contents of files looking for signatures of known viruses.

Signatures are patterns of software code that can be quickly identified. By looking for known virus signatures, all is well. The only hole in that argument is for the brand-new viruses that appear daily. Some products have top-notch heuristics (intelligent learning) that detect even these new viruses. Ask the vendor how their system works. The A/V vendors have to update their signature files periodically to keep current, so there is always a chance that you could get infected. However, better software does this for you automatically. Symantec's Norton Antivirus has a spiffy auto live update feature so you don't even have to worry about it. If you update your A/V program at least once a month, or more when a widespread virus vent occurs, you will be fairly well protected against even the most egregious viruses, but the more often the better.

For all your newfound virus awareness, though, you must also be aware of virus hoaxes.

Do you believe everything you read on the Internet? Well, I certainly hope not. April Fool's Day brings out the fools with spamming of imminent mass destruction of computers everywhere by the latest virus. Do

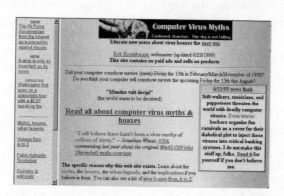

Want to know everything there is to know about virus hoaxes and myths? Rob Rosenberger stirs it up at www.kumite.com.

not believe them! Go to a real anti-virus company's page and ask. Or go to the Hoax page at www.kumite.com and check out the truth.

There are hundreds more. Rely upon vendors and trade organizations for the real story. And don't click just 'cause you're told to click. Some of these hoaxes can be downright dangerous in their own right.

Perhaps the most infamous hoax is the Iraqi Printer Virus Hoax.

On Friday, January 10, 1992, ABC's *Nightline* reported a story that I thought was a joke. According to *U.S. News and World Report*, the Allies, in preparation for the Gulf War, attacked and disabled Iraqi military computer systems with a computer virus developed by the Pentagon.

That's right. We took out the Iraqis with a computer virus!

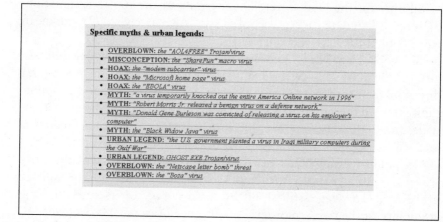

According to the tale, the super-secret National Security Agency built a custom integrated circuit or chip that, in addition to performing its normal function, contained a computer virus. The chip was allegedly installed in a dot matrix printer in France that was destined for Iraq via Amman, Jordan.

The infected chip was reported to have shut down portions of the Iraqi defensive radar systems. This had to be a put-on, a joke. But, no, not Ted Koppel! Something was wrong here. I was deeply troubled that *Nightline* could air a story that was so obviously in error.

I called Ted and was told that *U.S. News and World Report* was the source. Blame them if it's wrong. I spent the early morning hours looking back over my archives and found an old article in which I spoke of airborne viruses and their offensive military applications. Still, the back of my brain itched; the story Ted Koppel told just didn't make sense. Although I didn't know what I was looking for, I knew I would recognize it if I saw it, so I kept up the frenetic search. About 3 AM, I found what I was looking for.

In the April 1, 1991, issue of *Infoworld*, John Gantz's weekly column was titled "Meta-Virus Set to Unleash Plague on Windows 3.0 Users." Gantz said he had heard that the NSA had written a computer virus dubbed AF/91 that was to "attack the software in printer and display controllers." The column went further, stating "each machine makes the virus a little stronger." I remembered reading this column and thinking, "How absurd!" It continued to allege that the CIA had inserted the virus into an Iraqi-bound printer, and that, by January 8, 1991, half of the Iraqi defense network was dead and gone—thanks to the efficiency of the AF/91 virus. "The NSA now believes that any Windowing technology is doomed," Mr. Gantz wrote.

The *Infoworld* article concluded, as many a computer column does, "And now for the final secret. The meaning of the AF/91 designation: 91 is the Julian date for April Fool's Day." Alternately, AF/91 can mean April Fool 1991; here was the joke!

Ted Koppel and *Nightline* were the victims of mis- or dis-information given to them by *U.S. News and World Report*, who in turn were first duped by their sources. Associated Press subscribers also had the opportunity to read the same "news" as if it were fact. The story went nationwide, and to this day, wherever I lecture, this story is still remembered as fact.

On January 13, 1992, when faced with the evidence that the story was really just a year-old April Fool's joke rehashed through the military grapevine, *U.S. News* still stood by the accuracy of its story and the credibility of the two senior-level intelligence officers who confirmed it.

The writer, Brian Duffy, did admit, though, that there were some "disturbing similarities" between the two tales. (No kidding.) I've included a point-by-point comparison of the original *Infoworld* April Fool's story and the one put out by ABC and *U.S. News and World Report*.

InfoWorld	U.S. News and World Report
1. By January 8, Allies had confirmation that half the displays and printers . . . were out of commission	1. Several weeks before the air campaign of Desert Storm . . .
2. Virus targeted against Iraq's air defense	2. Virus targeted against Iraq's air defense
3. Designed by the NSA	3. Designed by the NSA
4. Virus built into printer	4. Virus built into a chip in a printer
5. The CIA inserted the virus	5. U.S. intelligence agents insert the virus
6. Printer went through Jordan on its way to Iraq	6. Printer went through Jordan on its way to Iraq
7. Peripherals not protected by electronic fortress	7. Able to circumvent electronic security measures through peripherals
8. Disables real-time computer systems (mainframes)	8. Virus inserted into large computers. Disables mainframe computers
9. "the NSA wizards"	9. "Cunningly designed . . ."
10. "It eats Windows."	10. ". . . each time (he) opened a window . . . the contents of the screen simply vanished."
11. Source: Old ADP navy buddy	11. Two senior US officials
12. "So, it worked."	12. "It worked."
13. NSA believes that any Windowing technology is doomed: There doesn't seem to be an antidote.	
14. It could be four years before users start seeing their Windows blur. Maybe the NSA can discover a cure by then.	
April Fool's Joke.	**Government Information**

Myth, fantasy, hoax, or just plain disinformation? Decide for yourself if Duffy was duped by the air force intelligence contacts he used for the story, if his air force contacts were also victims, or if the whole story was a prank by someone who read Gantz's article.

Viruses are very real and dangerous. Hoaxes can be just as bad. Make sure you and your sources have their facts straight!

More on Virii

When friend and virus-security analyst Sarah Gordon read an earlier version of this chapter, she asked me why I gave so much air-time to the ICSA. Simple; they have been at it for a decade. Just as with the hacker community, there is a degree of enmity between professionals. She also said that I had a couple of things wrong, like why virus writers do what they do.

Sarah sent me a wonderful article she wrote, "Virus Writers: Yesterday, Today and Tomorrow, Is There Anything New Under the Sun? and WHY?," and asked if I could publish it in this book. Due to its length, I couldn't, although I wish otherwise. A couple of excerpts, though, are worthwhile.[21]

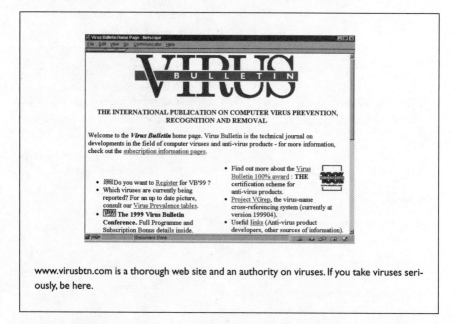

www.virusbtn.com is a thorough web site and an authority on viruses. If you take viruses seriously, be here.

---

[21]Excerpts appear here in preedited form and are reprinted with kind permission of *Virus Bulletin* (www.virusbtn.com).

In October 1993, the number of virus writers who were actively contributing to the problem of computer viruses found "In the Wild" comprised a relatively small percentage of the global computing population. The number of their viruses actually causing many problems was quite small too, especially considering the number of viruses known to exist—the number of computer viruses which were reported spreading In the Wild was 71, with a total virus count of a ~3200. During this time, there were virus writers known and unknown; working on their own, and working in groups like Phalcon/Skism, RABID, NuKe, Trident, and SLAM. They used handles like Dark Angel, Attitude Adjuster, and Aristotle. They wrote viruses, placing them on publicly accessible Bulletin Board Systems, FTP sites, and WWW sites, and they kept viruses to themselves.

In some cases, they sent viruses only to AV researchers, because while they wanted to show someone they could write a certain proof-of-concept virus, they really didn't want to release the virus to the general public. They wrote viruses that were not released in any way into cyberspace (for lack of a better term), and never caused anyone any problem (other than necessitating their inclusion in scanners "just in case"); they wrote viruses that they did release into the cyberspace, causing all sorts of problems. They made their source code available, and they kept their source code "just for their private individual use" or "just for use within their own group." They dedicated their viruses to various people, they used some viruses to promote their own groups or identities, and they left some viruses completely anonymous. They attended secondary schools and universities, and they were professionally employed. They were beginning to beta-test viruses.

In May 1999, there are approximately 150 viruses found In the Wild, with approximately ~30,000 known to exist. Some virus writers are pretty well known, signing their creations, while some prefer to do their deeds in secret. Some labor alone, while others work in groups like 29a, SLAM (all new, all revised, and not related in any way to the original), The Codebreakers, and The NoMercy Virus Team. They use names like DarkMan, VicodinES, and Knowdeth. Some virus writers put their viruses up for public consumption on FTP or WWW sites; some, however, prefer to keep them for themselves. Some restrict their distribution to within their own groups. In some cases, they bestow viruses only upon AV researchers. Some virus writers today release their viruses on unsuspecting users; others do not actively release the viruses. Some virus writers make source code available, while others prefer to keep it to themselves. Some viruses are dedicated to individuals or causes; other viruses are used to self-promote. Some remain anonymously authored. Virus writers attend secondary schools and universities. Some are professionally employed. Beta-testing of viruses is pretty common. Sound pretty similar?

The truth is, in many ways, things are the same as they ever were . . .

Part of Sarah's research included asking why virus writers write viruses.

As a starting point, let us approach the topic from the viewpoint of the virus writers. In their own words, how do they justify their actions? Notably, the arguments outlined below have remained relatively unchanged over the last several years.

1. *We are doing research. This is just our research. You can't tell us not to do research.*

2. *We have the right to do it. We have the right to write viruses, too, and to make them available.*

3. *It's about freedom. We have the right to do this research and the freedom to make viruses available.*

4. *You want to keep this "top secret" virus knowledge to yourselves, but we will set it free. We will educate the people. Information wants to be free.*

5. *We are not really hurting anyone, we don't force anyone to download our viruses, and we don't force anyone to use them. That is up to the individual.*

6. *You AV guys are all bad. You're in it for the money. And you need us.*

7. *You just don't understand!*

Of course, one need not go back through the archives to see examples of these arguments. You need only read current Usenet news posts, to see some of the same old arguments made today, by new people who believe with all their hearts that they know something the rest of us do not. Here are some more contemporary examples.

"The only justification my code needs is furthering education, and knowledge. These are the greatest strengths the human race has . . ."

"If my code was used to damage someone's computer, that is the responsibility of the person who's (sic) immature behavior has resulted in damage. Open your mind, and expand your horizons . . . its a huge world out there, if you can just get over your fears."

". . . This is nauseating . . . you feel you have the right to censor, and condemn the creativity of young, brilliant minds. You fear what you dont (sic) understand . . ."

"If it was not for us, you guys wouldn't have a job."

It does not appear that virus writers are becoming more malicious per se. There may be more malicious viruses circulating nowadays, but this is probably attributable not to the fact that people are more malicious as much to the fact that the number of people (some of whom by sheer chance are more malicious than the norm) having access to Internet technologies has increased dramatically. People aren't getting worse. There is just more opportunity for those bad apples that have already rotted and fallen off the tree.

So, perhaps I will stand corrected. Maybe I should have said that virus distributors, not virus writers, are the scum of the earth. What do you think? Thanks Sarah!

Resources

- The Virus Hoax Page run by Rob Rosenberger is at www.kumite.com.

- The CIAC also runs a hoax page at http://ciac.llnl.gov/ciac/ CIACHoaxes.html.
- The Little Black Book of Computer Viruses was first published in the early 1990s and created quite a stir as a result. Check out American Eagle Publishing for details.
- The most current listing of ICSA-certified anti-virus products could be found at http://www.icsa.net/services/consortia/anti-virus/certified_products.shtml.
- http://www.ciac.org/ciac/ maintains high-quality archives and issues regular alerts.
- http://www.cert.org/ is another great source of information, updates and alerts. Some folks think they are too controlled by their funding partners.

Vendors

- Aladdin Knowledge Systems, Inc.
  http://www.esafe.com/vcenter/explore.html
- Command Software Systems, Inc
  http://www.commandcom.com/html/virus/explorezip.html
- Computer Associates
  http://www.cai.com/virusinfo/virusalert.htm
- Data Fellows
  http://www.datafellows.com/news/pr/eng/19990610.htm
- McAfee, Inc. (a Network Associates company)
  http://www.mcafee.com/viruses/explorezip/default.asp
- Network Associates Incorporated
  http://www.avertlabs.com/public/datafiles/valerts/vinfo/va
  10185.asp
- Sophos, Incorporated
  http://www.sophos.com/downloads/ide/index.html
- Symantec
  http://www.symantec.com/avcenter/venc/data/worm.
  explore.zip.htm
- Trend Micro Incorporated
  http://www.antivirus.com/vinfo/alerts.htm
- Additional sources of virus information are listed at
  http://www.cert.org/other_sources/viruses.html
- IBM
  http://www.av.ibm.com/BreakingNews/Newsroom/
  99-03-29/

Crypto Hacking

Not terribly far to the south of Washington DC lies the majestic beauty of Virginia. Ollie North, senators, and powerful insiders escape to the rolling hills of their estates and farms. To the north, though, is Baltimore, Maryland, and the maelstrom megalopolis that extends to Boston.

For a few brief miles, the Baltimore–Washington Parkway is a calming respite from the chaos. Tall trees and lush foliage surround the well-travelled road. Midway between Washington and Baltimore you might notice a sign: National Cryptographic Museum. The exit ramp circles around and you might expect to see another magnificent DC-like marble structure for this national museum. But not this one. Small signs guide the persistent visitor by chain-link fences, around a curve, past a small country-style gas station, and to the most unimposing museum. The single-story building is a former run-down motel, semi-sort-of refurbished to meet government specifications.

But once inside the National Cryptographic Museum, a magical transformation takes place. One is soon immersed in the history and the technology that has contributed to the national security of the United States for sixty years. The small museum is a tribute to cryptography and really does provide a reasonable and entertaining view of secrecy.

Cryptography is the scrambling of information (words, pictures—it doesn't matter) to disguise its real meaning. Think of the cryptoquote in your local paper. Every day readers solve simple cryptographic problems using a system invented by Julius Caesar over two thousand years ago and evolved over the centuries. This crypto-system is called letter substitution. To disguise military messages from the enemy, the Romans substituted one letter for another according to a "key" which would look like:[22]

> A = N
> B = O
> C = P
> D = Q
> E = R . . . and so on for the entire alphabet.

With a minor amount of mental effort, we can figure out which letters are most likely an "e" or a "t" or which short words might be "the" or "that." And then we try to see if our first guesses work when we sprinkle those letters throughout the puzzle. In a few minutes it is solved.

The process millions of people use every day to solve a letter substitution cryptoquote is called an algorithm—a step-by-step series of rules. For simple cryptography, we may not even be aware of the process; it can become quite automatic for experienced puzzle enthusiasts: answers just "suddenly appear." So, one could argue that solving cryptoquotes is a form of "hacking."

The National Cryptographic Museum, though, goes way beyond daily puzzles. It covers the history of cryptography, whose modern era really began in World War II. Historians agree that cryptography played a terribly important role in that war, and Allied cryptographic efforts are responsible for saving hundreds of thousands of lives.

American cryptography lagged behind the rest of the world in the late 1930s. We were coming out of the Depression and a couple of decades of political isolationism. Pearl Harbor changed all of that overnight and we found ourselves at war in the Pacific. The Japanese used cryptography to hide the contents of their communications within the military and with their various embassies around the world. Their cryptosystems were fairly weak, though, and the US was able to handily intercept and read encoded Japanese messages. The basic encryption process is simple to understand.

Take a message or any piece of information that you want to keep from prying eyes. That information is called "plaintext"; anyone can read it. There is no attempt at disguising the contents. Through a process called "encryption," the contents of the message are scrambled using a "key" which electronically locks the message from being viewed by anyone who does not have the "decryption key."

---

[22]The Roman system used a cylinder with letters, but let's not get bogged down in details.

This enciphering and deciphering device was acquired from West Virginia by NSA in the early 1980s. It was first thought to have been a model of the "Jefferson cipher wheel," so called because Thomas Jefferson described a similar device in his writings. We believe it to be the oldest extant device in the world, but the connection with Jefferson is unproven. Such devices are known to have been described by writers as early as Francis Bacon, in 1605, and may have been fairly common among the arcane "black chambers" of European governments. This cipher wheel was evidently for use with the French language, which was the world's diplomatic language up through World War I. How it came to be in West Virginia is unknown.

plaintext + encryption key + encryption process = hidden message
hidden message + decryption key + decryption process = plaintext

Encryption and decryption are essentially the same thing, except the reverse of each other. Encryption hides the messages, decryption brings it back to normal. The strength of the encryption process is based upon two things:

1. The strength of the encryption/decryption algorithm itself. Is the mathematical process strong? Are there inherent weaknesses? Is there a back door by which a designer or an adversary could gain easy access to the plaintext message?

2. The length of the encryption key. The longer the key, the more possible decryption options there are, thus the harder to crack.

The United States employed a unique encryption process in the Pacific Theater of World War II—which, to the best of my knowledge, has never been used again. The war was suddenly upon us, much of the navy's fleet was destroyed, and we didn't have the luxury of time to develop and deploy a complex encryption system. So what to do? We used human cryptography.

The navy solicited the assistance of the remaining people who had been the victims of the American Holocaust: native Americans (back then we still used the misnomer, Indians). One of the native American tribes chosen to be human cryptographers were the Navajo because there were so very few people who could speak or understand the language. Interception and eavesdropping of US military communications by the Japanese was expected, but because the Navajo language was so rare, it was assumed that the language would absolutely confound the Japanese. All indications are that the effort was successful.[23]

On the European front, though, the battle for cryptographic supremacy occurred completely differently. Nazi Germany was the epitome of paranoia; control freaks to the max. Unlike America, during the 1930s, Hitler's Germany was expansionist and built the biggest war machine the world had ever seen. Part of that buildup was secrecy in communications.

England entered the war in 1939 and in 1940 found itself fighting for its very survival. A significant component of the war effort required the intelligence services and Ministry of Defence to intercept huge amounts of German radio traffic. Orders from the German High Command to its field commanders were considered prime intelligence to be garnered. U-Boats were becoming seriously dangerous threats. The Allies and the troops and supplies coming from America desperately wanted to both intercept and read the military traffic.

However, the Germans employed powerful encryption schemes. The approach they used is called *symmetrical-key encryption*. That means that the person doing the encryption (sending the message) and the person on the receiving end of the transmission both had to use the same encryption-decryption key to communicate. In those days, such a process required that a physical hand-off of the keys was necessary. So the Germans made encryption pads which contained lists of keys and strict procedures for handling and using them. The communications officers on the U-Boats and in the field guarded the keys with their lives, because if the Allies got hold of them they could read all of the messages.

The British had begun extensive interceptions and were collecting

---

[23]The army studied the program even before war was declared in 1941, and during World War II employed Commanches, Choctaws, Kiowas, Winnebagos, Seminoles, Navajos, Hopis, and Cherokees.

From NSA National Cryptographic Museum web site. A German Enigma, as famous for its insecurities as for the security that it theoretically gave to German ciphers. It was broken, first by the Poles in the 1930s, then by the British during World War II. The British brought the Americans into the picture during the war, and the Americans furnished many of the resources to attack ever more complex versions of the Enigma, especially the naval Enigma, when British resources began to run thin. Information from the decrypted messages was used by the Allies time after time to outmaneuver German armies. Some ask why, if we were reading the Enigma, we did not win the war earlier. One might ask, instead, when, if ever, we would have won the war if we hadn't read it.

massive amounts of raw encrypted traffic, but they had little success in cracking much of it.

Until Alan Turing came on the scene. A brilliant mathematician who had achieved great strides in his field, he offered his services to the British government. He was quickly put to work at Bletchley Park, a former estate converted to use in the most secret of all intelligence operations. Turing's genius soon found some weaknesses in the German encryption scheme, and there was a small but significant increase in the amount of traffic that the British could decrypt.

Then, an intelligence operative's dream came true. From a sunken U-Boat, a sailor retrieved one of the German encryption machines, dubbed the Enigma. The National Cryptographic Museum has a couple of these awkward typewriter-looking machines. The mechanical device used a series of rotors and a patch panel to enter the key. A corresponding Enigma had to be set with the same rotor positions and a set of cables plugged into the patch panel in the same way for a plaintext message to come through intelligibly.

This windfall was shipped off to Turing's group, which gave them the insight to build another machine called a Bombe, a huge mechanical calculatorlike device specifically designed to attack Enigma-encoded messages. It is with great respect that Alan Turing can easily be called the first crypto-hacker, and his extraordinary efforts are credited with shortening the war.

Towards the end of the war, however, the Germans, either through intelligence of their own or by the very paranoid nature of the Nazi regime, advanced the state of the art of the Enigma machine by adding additional rotors. This development complicated Turing's crypto-hacking efforts by at least an order of magnitude. It was almost back to the drawing board for them. Successes dwindled, but the modern science of cryptography was born.

After the War

In the 1950s, nuclear engineering was one of America's most closely guarded sciences. The Cold War was raging, the Rosenbergs were frying, and McCarthyism was alive and well. The Red Threat was a mere prelude to the Evil Empire of 1980s. Giving out nuclear secrets was a treasonable offense—understandably so.

During the next couple of decades, the state of the art of cryptography grew with the advent of room-filling, powerful electronic computers. Other than nuclear secrets, cryptography was the only other science that the US government tried to protect and control so vigorously. Various national efforts attempted to classify results; cryptographic mathematicians from academia were encouraged to not publish their latest works, and unsuccessful efforts were made to ban private cryptography.

When you exit the calm Baltimore–Washington Parkway for the National Cryptographic Museum, look straight ahead. You will notice several large buildings and an expansive parking lot. That is the National Security Agency, whose very existence was an open but unacknowledged secret until the 1980s. The NSA operates the world's most extensive eavesdropping operation and it is said that through satellite reconnaissance, telephone interceptions, undersea cable monitoring, and a range of arcane and sophisticated eavesdropping technologies, they can listen in on any electronic communication on Earth or in space.

But interception isn't enough. As part of the NSA mission, they must also be able to read the messages to provide meaningful intelligence to their government clients. So, it should be no surprise that the NSA also houses the most extensive and powerful crypto-hacking facilities the world has ever, and likely *will* ever know.

I affectionately refer to the groups within NSA concerned with cryptography as crypto-spooks. With literally acres of the most powerful computers in the universe in an underground labyrinth, it is said that the NSA can decrypt almost anything. But that could be wishful thinking on the part of their proponents, a good public relations job meant to intimidate potential adversaries, paranoia by the truly paranoid . . . or, it could be true. Unlikely, but possible. Perhaps, with their multibillion-dollar budgets and armies of the finest cryptographic minds ever assembled, they have discovered something so radically fundamental that they can in fact decrypt anything thrown at them. But they aren't talking and won't.

This Cray XMP was donated to the museum by Cray Research, Inc. It denotes a bygone technology and the beginning of an era of partnership between NSA and the American computer industry in the employment of computers for cryptologic processes. At Sandia National Laboratories, Crays sit idle and unused in old storage rooms. They cost about $1 million per year to maintain and operate. Parallel processing has superceded the Cray.

The cryptographic methods used by the US echoed that of the Germans in many ways: The same key was needed to encrypt and decrypt messages. Thus, any military communications enterprise required the physical transport of the keys to whomever was to be part of the conversation. In those days, paper tape was the favored method of key distribution.

In 1976, though, an event occured that to this day I cannot completely understand, given the Cold War paranoia on both sides. Maybe you can.

The National Bureau of Standards (NBS, now called the National Institute of Standards and Technology, NIST) published an open encryption scheme called DES, or Data Encryption Standard. The exact specifications on how to use DES and how to build DES were open, a published American standard, and were quickly adapted by the banks as a means to protect financial information from disclosure (confidentiality) and from modification (integrity).

This was a good thing . . . maybe. The cryptographic floodgates had opened. The US standard was open, published, and available for anyone, anywhere to acquire—for free!—and to use. The odd part was that although the algorithms and technical specifications were open, US companies were severely restricted from exporting DES-based products until 1999, when the export control laws were relaxed.

What I don't get is why we did it that way, or was this a bureaucratic bungle? It's like publishing and sending the source code and design instructions for a Stealth Bomber to North Korea and saying, "Please don't build this." There is one more possibility. Perhaps DES was part of a terribly ingenious intelligence operation designed to last for decades. Some senior intelligence members have privately told me that the NSA has been behind efforts to keep security effectiveness low—to make their jobs easier. Who knows.

IBM (a huge supplier of computer equipment throughout the government) was picked as the commercial cryptographic contractor to build the DES. Their original submission, though, was a scheme called Lucifer. But, in concert with the NSA, the cryptographic strength of Lucifer was reduced by shortening the key length and by modifying the internal processes that perform the actual encryption. What could have been behind that move?

Let's speculate. It is possible that DES was intentionally released in the open literature in the hopes that foreign powers and industries would use it—because the NSA had built in a back door. Or perhaps while developing DES they had also developed a mechanism to regularly and reasonably decrypt any DES-encrypted message. So, to encourage the perception of its strength, they would holler and scream about export controls knowing full well that the technology was well proliferated within minutes of its publication. If this speculation has any semblance of truth (which I am not alleging—merely conjecturing as an option that the crypto-spooks had available to them) then it would qualify as one of the great intelligence operations of all time. By the early 1990s, several hundred DES-based products were available, half of them from outside the United States, including products from Russia. Who knows, but it is fun to think out loud.

1976 was also a watershed year that changed the face of cryptography and personal privacy forever. Conventional cryptographic wisdom held that the same key was needed to encrypt and decrypt a message or file. Whitfield Diffy and Martin Hellman confounded conventional wisdom and developed and patented a cryptographic tool called PKE, or Public Key Encryption.

When both sides of a communication use the same key, it is called *symmetrical*. If the two sides can use one key to encrypt a message and a different key to decrypt the message, it's called *asymmetrical*. This counterintuitive leap forward is exactly what they accomplished, and PKE has become the virtual standard model for cryptography today.

Forgetting the ridiculously complex math altogether, here is how PK works:

You and I want to communicate. You establish a public key that everyone in the universe can know. You also establish a private key that you want to jealously guard. I do the same thing. When I send you a message, I use two keys: your very public key and my very private key. The message is then encrypted and off it goes to you. When you receive the email, you decrypt it by using my very public key and your very private key. The mathematical relationship between the various keys involves the factoring of extremely large numbers, and only a handful of people really understand it at that level. Suffice it to say that it works for millions of people worldwide.

The early 1990s put the explosive crypto-debate on the political plates of Congress and the White House. Clinton inherited a doomed plan from the Bush Administration called the Clipper Chip. The official stated goal was to provide a balance between the desire for private communications and the legitimate needs of law enforcement. The FBI spearheaded a campaign to educate and promote the fact that criminals, pedophiles, drug cartels, and terrorists had access to the same cryptographic tools and software that the rest of us do; and that was a bad thing. No one argues that. The FBI and NSA led the charge to convince Congress and Corporate America that Clipper was a good thing.

Except, there were a couple of major problems with the proposal.

1. The encryption/decryption keys to the system were to be held in escrow by a trusted third party, only to be released by a court order. This required a high degree of trust in the government and law enforcement process, which was a hard sell.

2. This system created a single point of failure. That is, since all of the Clipper keys were to be kept in one place, if an attacker successfully cracked through the escrow system's defenses, the entire program was dead. Keep in mind that such an attack could be technical or be executed by an insider. The results are the same.

3. The cryptographic algorithms were secret (today they are public), and one principle of strong cryptography is to publish the algorithm for constant evaluation and test.

4. The trust and confidence factor in the NIST/NSA plan was very low.

5. For it to work, everyone had to play, and since Clipper was voluntary, no one wanted to play.

6. The international community, despite intense lobbying on the part of US officials, was outraged that any such system would be controlled by the US.

7. Lastly, and perhaps most notably, why would any self-respecting terrorist use an encryption scheme that he knew could be instantly compromised by law enforcement.

Despite several different attempts under different names and guises, the Key Escrow (Capstone, Clipper II, etc.) approach has failed and is not likely to raise its head ever again.

Modern Crypto-Hacking

In the 1980s, the study of cryptography became an open-source endeavor. That means that interest in it grew, commercial companies began offering products for the consumer and for business other than banks. The one-time government lock on the field was overwhelmed by the Internet and international proliferation of various technologies. Despite strict export controls, strong cryptographic tools made their way around the world, often under the auspice of encouraging free democratic debate, to the chagrin of more authoritarian countries and regimes.

In 1993, Marty Hellman suggested that DES could be cracked using a parallel processing computer where large numbers of specialized micro-processors would work in tandem to decrypt encoded messages. Traditional thinking was that strong encryption could survive hundreds of thousands of years of sustained attack. But the traditional approaches to crypto-hacking were being relegated to the trash bin. Later that same year, Michael Weiner, of Bell Northern Research in Canada, published a paper that showed how to crack DES by building a $1 million parallel computer which could find encryption keys in about 3.5 hours. The field was moving fast, and most financial institutions were still using DES to protect their electronic transfers.

The concept of parallel processing attacks against cryptographic systems gained momentum and was demonstrated by students in France and the United States. They organized thousands of PCs, attached to the Internet, to coordinate attacks against both 40bit and 56bit key encryption systems. The results were as expected and the efforts were successful.

In 1998, an intensive effort by privacy advocate and activist John Gilmore was to be the ultimate downfall of weak cryptography such as DES. Flush with funds because he was one the first employees at Sun Microsystems, he led a group effort to design a special computer system whose sole goal was to decrypt encoded messages.

The NSA has had such capabilities for years, but no one knows exactly how much they were or are capable of. They used powerful Cray supercomputers costing millions of dollars, but the much lower cost and ultimately simpler distributed approach to crypto-hacking was taking over.

On January 19, 1999, Gilmore and the Electronic Frontier Foundation announced success.[24] They decoded a DES-encrypted message in less than 24 hours—their exact goal. What had previously been considered strong enough to withstand years upon years of attack had been defeated by crypto-hackers, building a machine in their home-styled laboratory at a cost of less than US $250,000. The name of the DES cracking machine is a take-off on the master-level chess-playing IBM computer Deep Blue. They call it Deep Crack.

Deep Crack proved, once and for all, that a technically competent team of engineers, with a modest amount of money, could challenge the conventional wisdom and win. Where cryptography goes is anyone's guess, but crypto-hacking is continuing with renewed vigor.

As of mid-1999, cryptographic research continues in two broad directions:

[24]http://www.eff.org/pub/Privacy/Crypto_misc/DESCracker/HTML/19990119_desc hallenge3.html

DES Cracker "Deep Crack" custom microchip. Photo from http://www. eff.org/pub/ Graphics/chip300.jpg.

Paul Kocher, the machine's principal designer, displays one of the boards holding sixty-four custom search microchips. The six cabinets (behind) house twenty-nine boards, whose searching is coordinated by a PC (left). The machine tests over 90 billion keys per second, taking an average of less than five days to discover a DES key.

1. Toward creating an unbeatable algorithm or crypto-system that will withstand the tests of time.

2. Toward designing a method where any crypto-system can be cracked in a reasonable amount of time.

Just like hacking and anti-hacking, crypto experts need to understand both sides of the coin in their endeavors.

The US government, along with most nation-states, are actively researching newer and more powerful methods for both goals. But the intelligence community and crypto-spooks are now challenged not only by adversaries to the US, but by the unrestricted activities of the private sector, academia, and independents whose primary motives may not be coincident with their government's.

Cryptography provides unprecedented levels of privacy for those who want to be reasonably assured of a secure communication. Privacy advocates fear prying eyes from US and foreign law enforcement. Some worry about a return to the bygone days of Hoover's FBI, where excess and invasion of privacy was the norm. Louis Freeh, the current director of the FBI, has suggested that personal cryptography might have to be outlawed during some future crisis, which does not go over very well with the Internet community. Then we see cryptography being used to communicate with freedom fighters inside of restrictive regimes around the world.

The balance is a tough one and the debate continues, but crypto-hackers, also known as cypher-punks, will nonetheless openly march forward to achieve their goals: privacy from eavesdropping, governmental interference or excess, and the promotion of democratic openness worldwide.

The National Cryptographic Museum will not go into all of the detail that many readers might be interested in learning, but on your next visit to the Washington DC area, take a side trip to the small museum. You will receive a fascinating technical and historical insight into cryptography.

What You Can Do

Your email lives forever. Somewhere, someplace, every email you have ever sent is stored in some distant and unidentified electronic repository. This is not some sordid plot on the part of a One World Organization. It is merely the byproduct of the nature of the Internet and good backup procedures by large companies, telecommunications companies, and ISPs (Internet Service Providers).

Sniffing the Internet or enterprise networks within large US and global companies unfortunately occurs all too often, to the chagrin of those who may have written embarrassing or threatening emails. Industrial espionage is at an all-time high and is increasing at an alarming rate. It is eminently logical to assume that everywhere there lies a security breach, it will be exploited. Whether the sniffing of electronic communications occurs by a disgruntled insider or employee of a company, by hackers, or by domestic or international economic competitors, the fact remains that plaintext communications is a sieve of valuable information. The careless transmission of sensitive specifications, customer lists, or any of a myriad of proprietary information occurs daily, and it is virtually impossible to know if any plaintext email or communication has been compromised.

The prudent company with secrets to keep is well-advised to seriously consider the use of cryptographic tools to protect its information resources. The individual should also consider the use of easy-to-use crypto-tools to protect communications that are best kept private. A wide range of privacy-enhancement software is readily available today—much of it freeware, shareware, or crippleware, which are free to the individual.

If you choose to make some or all of your email private, you will need to choose the right encryption software. One of the most popular versions of personal email encryption is PGP, or Pretty Good Privacy, now owned and distributed by the security giant, Network Associates. This is not an endorsement, but it has several things going for it:[25]

1. PGP was developed privately by a handful of caring Internetizens almost ten years ago.
2. The code was originally developed and distributed for free.
3. It is generally trusted by most folks on the Net.
4. There is still a freeware version for you to use.
5. Odds are someone you know already uses PGP, which makes compatibility easy.

PGP was originally developed by Phil Zimmermann as a means to encourage democratic debate and free speech, especially in the more totalitarian regimes around the world. The *Wall Street Journal* and other magazines have characterized Phil as a modern freedom fighter.

However, there was a conundrum. Up until mid-1999, when the laws

---

[25]www.nai.com

were relaxed somewhat, the export of encryption from the United States was vigorously protected. In fact, encryption protection was second only to nuclear secrets. Under the aegis of the NSA, getting export approval for quality cryptography was a time-consuming, bureaucratic nightmare—if it was gotten at all. Constant complaints of massive losses and an inability to compete internationally by the US business community went unheeded. The NSA, the White House, and DoD/Intelligence communities maintained that the unregulated export of crypto from the US was playing into the hands of terrorists and criminals who could hide behind their underground status.

On the other hand, the pro-crypto privacy groups said that unless individuals had crypto tools to speak freely, totalitarianism would raise its head—maybe even here in the US. Besides, the Software Publishers Association and EPIC pointed out, 50 percent of the world's crypto is not from the US anyway. Lastly, what self-respecting technical terrorist or multinational criminal organization would adhere to any crypto laws anyway?

Thus Phil challenged the premise of the US export laws, and had placed on the Internet, at a US site, a copy of the early PGP. The US government viewed this as a slap in their face, which it was, and subsequently began an investigation for the potential indictment of Mr. Zimmermann.[26] Phil faced a staggering 4+ years in jail. Finally the feds quit their inane behavior and now Phil is a millionaire, having sold PGP to a huge conglomerate.

Using encrypted email requires no particular skill, and can make using the Internet a whole lot safer than it is now. PGP and other secure email packages such as RSA (Search "Secure Mail" for a ton of them that all claim superiority) use the concept of public keys instead of private keys.

PGP installs quite easily and seamlessly ties into popular email packages such as Eudora and Outlook Express. The installation process will walk you through the posting of your public key and place it on one of the many available Public Key Servers. You then select a personal pass phrase, which in turn generates a private key, a long string of numbers which you do not need to memorize. PGP takes care of all that for you. The principle of PGP is one of trust. That is, you know that your public key can be trusted by others; after all, you just made it. But how can a third party with whom you want to communicate know that your public key really belongs to you? PGP builds rings of trust based upon how much you trust the source of the public key associated with the person.

---

[26](For the complete "human" story on PGP, see *Information Warfare*, 2nd. Edition. An interview with Kelly Goen gives a lot of surprising answers!)

As in any cryptographic system, the ultimate strength of privacy is determined by the algorithm, but also by the integrity of the key. Thus, the initial key exchange between the communicating parties is a critical factor. You may choose to physically mail a hard copy of the key to each other or receive an electronic copy of the key from someone else whom you trust.

Once installed, PGP (or any of the other email security software packages) works at the click of a mouse: select the person with whom you want to speak, his/her public key will be mathematically joined to your secret private key and the message is then cryptographically sealed, much as an envelope seals the contents of a physical letter. When you receive PGP mail, you need to click and enter your private password or phrase and then the message is automatically decrypted back to cleartext.

It's simple, it's effective, and it's free (or almost).

For corporations, the choices are more varied. The concept of certificate authorities is generating an industry on its own. Companies such as Entrust and Verisign offer products which build a PKI, or Public Key Infrastructure. The goal here is for a company to use PK software for its communications, but to maintain their own key servers and key distribution systems.

Virtual private networks (or VPNs) have come into vogue as well, and they solve a different problem. On the Internet, when a message is sent to someone, it is broken up into small packets. Each packet has a destination IP address on it, which consists of four numbers (i.e. 123.456.789.255) and adheres to strict naming conventions. The packets do not necessarily take the same path to the destination—that is one of the great features of the Internet. At the destination, the packets are reassembled through TCP/IP, or Transport Control Protocol and Internet Protocol rules. All of this is invisible and works (most of the time).

In corporate environments, though, many employees, consultants, customers, or business partners work remotely from anywhere in the world and need to communicate with the corporate network. For just email applications, PGP or similar email security packages work fine. But consider the following examples:

1. A brokerage firm wants its hundreds of thousands of customers to be able to connect with their web site and buy and sell stocks privately. But, just as with email, those communications are subject to eavesdropping. How can this be done?

2. Doctors in one state or country want to consult on a medical situation thousands of miles away. Privacy in communications is a concern. How can they perform secure interactive communica-

tions such as Internet-based video teleconferencing, Net meeting, or other upcoming technologies?

3. A business partner (or a remote sales force) needs to regularly access the main corporate data base for highly sensitive information that really needs to be kept private. How is this done?

A VPN is a workable solution for many such applications; it is limited only by the imagination. At the corporate location, a VPN server waits for a connection attempt from a remote Internet address.[27] When the connection is first established, the server looks for certain identifying codes from the remote site so that the connection maybe authenticated. This process is similar to a user ID and password authentication except that it is performed cryptographically.

Then the VPN client (at the remote site) and the VPN host (at the company network) establish a cryptographic relationship to encapsulate all messaging traffic between the two. VPNs use a variety of encryption algorithms, from DES and Triple DES (which greatly strengthens the DES by encrypting the messages two or three times, using special key management techniques) to proprietary algorithms. Any attempt at eavesdropping is going to be thwarted.

VPNs are also a powerful means to establish privacy through cryptography between business partners or remote offices where a full time connection exists. In this case, each participating site has its own VPN server and the cryptographic relationship is established at the time of connection; the path remains secure from eavesdropping.

Large networking companies like Cisco are beginning to implement VPN technology into their products, as are many firewall vendors. Cisco manufactures routers which control the direction and flow of information in a network. A large company may have many routers within its networks to separate departments, organizations, locations, or other forms of operation. All ISPs use large routers to direct signal flow and even small firms are starting to use low bandwidth (ISDN speeds, for example) routers as a means of controlling signals and blocking unwanted ones.

If two ISPs, for example, use the same VPN-enabled routers, all communications between those two points can be automatically encrypted. By extending that concept, if every ISP used the same sort of VPN-enabled router, then, in theory, the entire backbone of the Internet would be encrypted as the signals travel from point to

---

[27]VPNs are also applicable for Intranets, and work with them in the same manner.

point. This is a great step forward for privacy enhancement, but does not provide complete security. Since the VPN router decrypts messages at the outer edge, or periphery, of the network, email and messaging traffic will remain plaintext while inside the ISP's servers, and will be stored in plaintext still subject to eavesdropping and plaintext reading.

The best approach to ensure maximum security in a VPN environment, just as with email, is to encrypt and decrypt the messages where the sender and receiver are: at the ends of the connection. Therefore, regardless of what encryption security is performed along the way from End A to End B, you can be assured that the message is well protected. This approach is called end-to-end encryption, while the router-to-router style of encryption is called point-to-point. They are both valid approaches, but you have to decide which is best for you.

Email Is Fine, But . . .

OK, now you've got an email encryption program and you are happily and successfully sending and receiving private messages to and from your friends or throughout your organization. From the Internet's standpoint, you can consider yourself reasonably well protected from eavesdropping. But there are more problems . . . as you can well imagine.

Your PC. Odds are that the data on your personal computer is plaintext, and that could be a problem if you are worried about getting hacked. If someone, somehow, breaks into your network or your computer, everything you have stored on your hard disks is naked and ripe for the taking.

Some criminal organizations hire people to take on janitorial jobs in large companies. The cleaning staffs usually have unfettered access to all areas of the firm, including the sensitive ones that are often off-limits to most employees. What law enforcement has found exposes one of the errors we all tend to make: we leave our access codes and passwords carelessly lying around. You might tape them under your keyboard, inside of a drawer, stick them to the monitor, or, as I have found in many cases, a Password section in a Rolodex.

I have only encountered two organizations that take the time and trouble to encrypt the contents of their hard drives as a matter of course. The object, of course, is not to waste encryption on the actual programs themselves; there is little intrinsic value in those, unless you are a software developer and you want to protect your intellectual property. What should be encrypted are your data files, which are of real value, and if lost can cause you or your firm harm. When looking for a product to protect and encrypt hard drives for your company, the following considerations are important:

1. How easy is the cryptography to manage? Does each user have to become an expert, or can the system be centrally managed by the administrator?

2. Is the encryption process transparent to the user, or does he have to selectively choose which files are to be encrypted? Given the choice of the extra steps needed, most users will take the easy way out and not encrypt them. Automatic is best.

3. Does the user have to select his own keys, or does the system do it for him?

4. Does the systems administrator have access to the keys? One of the worst things that can happen is if an employee leaves and takes his encryption keys with him. Suddenly, you are out of luck. But on the other hand, how much do you trust your administrator?

5. Does the product work at the file server or host to protect corporate data bases as well as local files on the PC?

6. What are the performance implications? A maximum of 5 percent degradation in performance seems to be the acceptable limit.

7. Can you specify which files, directories, or disks are to be encrypted? You certainly don't care about encrypting Microsoft Word, but you do care about protecting Word documents.

Remote Crypto

As companies and telecommuters use more and more laptops, theft is on the rise—to the tune of 30–40 percent per year. In 1997, nearly $2 billion in laptops were stolen. While you or I might rue the loss of a three-thousand-dollar box that we are still paying for on our VISA card, companies are more worried about the proprietary data that is stored on them. Military laptops have been lost carrying highly secretive data—and they are rarely retrieved. Road warriors for major corporations carry a wealth of information on their machines, and if they are lost or stolen, invaluable company information falls into the wrong hands. Worse yet, lawsuits are bound to follow if sensitive client information suddenly appears on the cover of the *Enquirer* or on the Internet.

For a few dollars, encryption software can protect the data contents of your laptop. One company, Computer Sentry Software, offers CyberAngel, a product that offers two security features for laptops:

1. It encrypts any portion of the hard disk you choose; a unique code is used to unlock the files.
2. It installs an ET-like "phone home" feature that calls a central monitoring station if the machine is stolen and subsequently used by a thief.

New products are appearing all the time, but a quick search under "Laptop Security" will turn up the current offerings.

Encryption solves many hacking problems. It can:

1. Keep your Internet email traffic much more secure than it is now.
2. Protect full-time connections between business partners.
3. Secure web transactions.
4. Secure remote access to corporate data bases.
5. Improve the strength of and confidence in electronic commerce.
6. Hide data storage on PCs, hosts, and laptops from prying eyes.

But encryption can do a lot more. When DES was first created, it found two immediate applications: protecting file and message contents from eavesdropping by placing a cryptographic envelope around it, and adding integrity to the message.

Let's say you and I are banks. I want to transfer $1,000,000 to you, so I initiate the message. However, something goes wrong. An error changes the message to $10,000,000. Neither of us are aware that the error occurs, and you are ahead of the game by $9,000,000.

Errors can occur accidentally in transit from Point A to Point B for any number of reasons. An error can occur in storage on disk or on tape. Or errors can be intentionally introduced by hacking for profit or hacking for fun, as in the case of web graffiti.

So, when DES was introduced, a series of specifications were created, one of which is called MAC, or message authentication code. MAC is a much more sophisticated method of CRC, or cyclic redundancy check, which looks for errors when comparing two messages or files that are supposed to be identical.

When a MAC or CRC is used, if you are told nothing but e security software, that is good. There is no file corruption. But sometimes you will see a message that tells you the codes do not match up and the contents of the message cannot be trusted. Then it's up to you. Do you read and trust the file? Email back to the originator and ask for him to resend it? That is up to you, but at least you have been warned.

PGP (as well as other email security programs) allows the user to choose whether the cryptographic services are to protect the contents from disclosure (in the security world we call this confidentiality), or from file corruption (which we call integrity), or both.

Something New

In 1970 I worked at a recording studio called the Hit Factory in New York. That year we recorded Jim Croce and I had the unique opportunity to record Janis Joplin's last demo song, "Rock My Soul To Heaven," just before she died. Our 16-track tape machines were made by Ampex, and the repairman came around every so often to perform periodic checks.

In front of CIA headquarters now sits a stone monolith with a coded message engraved into it. No one has ever, or is likely ever to decrypt it, since the encryption was developed by the chief cryptographer of the United States.

Two decades later I attended a crypto conference in Washington and got to talking to some guy from a crypto product company about some arcane crypto-issues, and at one point in our discussion, we both paused and asked each other simultaneously, "Do I know you from somewhere?" Jay Wack, the president of Tecsec, was the Ampex repairman from twenty-five years earlier, and his vice president was the chief cryptographer of the United States, working for the CIA.

They took a look at the state of the art of cryptography, especially for large organizations, and found some major deficiencies, which in their view would hinder the widespread application of strong crypto.[28]

---

[28]This is not an endorsement, but Tecsec's approach is so different that the crypto-interested reader should be aware of it. Check out www.tecsec.com.

They feel the centralized management of PK systems is too unwieldy and does not represent the way that businesses are organized. Why not design a privacy system that is based upon job function, and/or job location, and/or job title, etc.? The resultant product is called CKM, Constructive Key Management.

CKM concentrates on managing the *relationships* between people rather than on the mere contents or hierarchy of an organization. The concept of network is flat and so, they say, should be the key management structure. CKM does not care what cryptographic system is in use—pick what you like. Rather, it manages the privacy relationship between large groups of people.

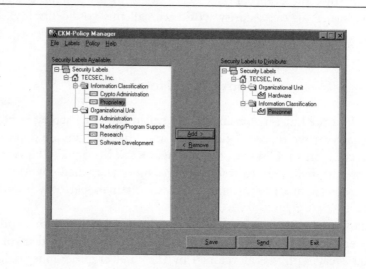

With Tecsec's CKM, the cryptography and key management approach, security is built around business and organizational relationships, not artificial lines. Key distribution is also greatly simplified.

Back to the Fort

The national cryptographic museum in Sweden is smaller than my daughter's room, and is located in a heavily guarded facility forty miles outside of Stockholm. Not exactly on the tourist route, but it contains its own fascinating perspective on crypto history.

The National Cryptographic Museum in Washington certainly paints a picture colored by the agenda of the NSA; that's OK, it's still an afternoon well spent. I found that of the 212 questions I asked, they would answer only about half of them, but then, I was pushing the envelope, looking for information I pretty well knew they wouldn't tell me. But that's sort of what crypto-hacking is all about.[29]

I have no idea if the battle for crypto-supremacy will ever be won. I do not know if an ultimate decryption device is theoretically possible. Maybe some crypto-wunderkind will come along in ten years with a theory so fundamentally different from our present views that the crypto field is shaken to its roots. Parallel processing certainly was unanticipated twenty-five years ago, and look what a few dedicated people did with national pocket change and Deep Crack.

No matter; que será, será. But one thing is for sure: the crypto-hackers and Cypherpunks will be there every step of the way.

Search This

Encryption, decryption, cryptography, cryptographic, DES, PK, PKI, PKE, algorithms, Cypherpunks, encryption software, encryption products, crypto, cryptanalysis, secure email.

Resources

- *The Codebreakers* by David Kahn
- The National Cryptographic Museum
- www.epic.org
- www.eff.org
- www.nist.gov
- www.pgp.com
- www.entrust.com
- www.verisign.com
- www.tecsec.com
- www.rsa.com offers email encryption software and a bevy of other tools for serious crypto-geeks. RSA is the original public-key company. Good place to learn about crypto.
- Search on "Encryption + Email" or "Secure Email" and, if you want, add "Software."

---

[29]http://www.nsa.gov:8080/museum/

VPN's

3Com Corp. http://www.3com.com
Altiga Networks http://www.altiga.com
Aptis Communications http://www.altiga.com
Ascend Communications Inc. http://www.ascend.com
Assured Digital Inc. http://www.assured-digital.com
AT&T http://www.att.com/worldnet
Aventail Corp. http://www.aventail.com
Axent http://www.axent.com
Bay Networks http://www.baynetworks.com
Check Point http://www.checkpoint.com
Cisco Systems http://www.cisco.com
Concentric Networks http://www.concentric.net/business/
Data Fellows http://www.datafellows.com/
IBM http://www.software.ibm.com/network/library/
whitepapers/white_vpn.html
Lucent http://www.lucent.com
Matrox http://www.matrox.com
New Oak Communications Inc. http://www.newoak.com
RADGuard Inc. http://www.radguard.com
Raptor http://www.raptor.com
Shiva Corp. http://www.shiva.com
TimeStep Corp. http://www.timestep.com
V-One Corp. http://www.v-one.com
WatchGuard http://www.watchguard.com/

Steganography:

Hiding in Plain Site (Sight?)

They say that the best way to hide a mistake is to make it worse: Emphasize to Disguise.

They also say that the best way to hide something is put it in plain sight—right out in the open.

For the criminal type on the lam, don't hole up in a crummy dive of a motel in the sweltering Everglades. Instead, stand tall on the streets of Manhattan and no one will notice. In fact, if you do choose to hide out in New York, the weirder you act, the less attention people will pay. New Yorkers are funny that way.

And so it is with spooks, spies, and software.

In the "Hunt for Red October," the renegade Russian sub hid from the US submarine commander by pacing underneath a huge oil tanker—in the middle of the high-traffic shipping lanes, in plain view, yet invisible. Remember the hit movie "ET"? The little alien didn't hide; he just lay in the closet amongst a bevy of children's stuffed animals, thus becoming virtually invisible.

During World War II and through today, armies do a lot of talking amongst their various commands to keep things organized, in plain view of the enemy, who can suck down the contents of all radio transmissions by merely sticking an antenna in the air. So, to hide in plain sight, military communications are encrypted, hopefully keeping the bad guys from eavesdropping.

On the Internet, the same thing is true for all of us. All of our email and other traffic is sitting out there, naked as a centerfold, waiting for someone to capture and perhaps replay our most intimate and secret thoughts. Of course you can use cryptographic products like PGP to keep your secrets a secret. But wait! Something is wrong with this picture.

If hiding in plain sight is the goal, PGP and other crypto products create a problem, not a solution. Think like the bad guy for a second; or maybe like a national security organization such as the NSA. There are tremendous amounts of Internet traffic moving from point to point at any given moment. Peak loads at Mae East and Mae West, the two major US Internet nexuses for communications, exceed 2GB per second. I mean, that's a lot of traffic. That's the rough equivalent of 240,000 novels whizzing by every hour of the day.

However, the vast majority of that Internet traffic is in the clear; that is, it is unencrypted. So what happens? The encrypted information stands out like a sore thumb: HERE GOES ENCRYPTED DATA LIKE CAPS IN AN OTHERWISE LOWERCASE BOOK! So the eavesdroppers or national security groups will think, "Encrypted data. What are they hiding?" Now they are paying attention to you instead of ignoring you amongst the vast noise of the Internet.

Encrypted data today is at the farthest extreme from hiding in plain sight. The very nature of crypto draws attention to itself. There has to be a better way. And there is.

Consider the following message:

> *My external enjoyment tries my emotional angst today. Stop trying all those underhanded evocations of foulness. Let inhibitions be ever retired to yesterday; judge unto life your inquest. Not over open nonsense.*

What does this poetic message really say? Can you figure it out?

The principle here is to embed a secret message within an open message, which allows the secret to remain secret. Figure it out yet? Just look at the first letter of each word.

> *Meet me at Statue of Liberty, July 1, Noon.*

This is a simplistic example, but it could be the second letter, every third letter, or every fifth letter divided by the pi of Saturn's third moon. Doesn't matter what pattern you choose. That is the cryptographic nature of the beast; how to decode the message is the "key" to it.

The point is, the message doesn't look encrypted. It looks open and clear. Maybe our message above was bad poetry—but since when is the NSA or CIA a judge of good prose? Right.

The art of embedding a secret message into an open, unencrypted message is called *steganography*. Yeah, it's a big word—deal with it. Steganography is not a reference to a prehistoric dinosaur, but to two words:

- *stego*—Greek prefix meaning "cover" or "hidden"
- *graphy*—Greek suffix meaning a process of writing or representation.[30]

Not too tough once you take the word apart.

Say you want to send secret messages to a compatriate. Where could you hide the message? The steganographic answer is to embed the secrets within large audio (WAV), video (AVI, MPEG), or picture (BMP, JPG) formats. The reasons are simple.

- The audio, video, and pix files are large. A JPG picture can be 100K or more, and MPEG videos are often 50MB or greater.
- The video format allows manipulation of bits within the video signal in such a way that there is no apparent change to the image itself. I won't bore you with the technical details, but the human eye (and ear) is very forgiving when it comes to errors.

Picture before message is embedded in it.

---

[30]FYI, geography simply means Earth description.

Picture after message has been secretly embedded in by Steganos.

Look at the two pictures above.[31] Which one contains a hidden message? Yes, one image is very different from the other . . . but you can't see it because the changes to the original image are so subtle; the human eye cannot distinguish a pixel change here and there, or a slight hue difference if it is spread around the entire image.

The picture on the right contains an embedded text file with a message that cannot be read without special decoding software.

If you'd like to play with steganography a bit yourself, it's free to try. Go to www.demcom.com/english/steganos/ and download the software, Steganos; it is one of the more popular free steganography programs. In fact, you will be able to decode these exact pictures, among others. Then you can take your own message or files and embed them using Steganos into any picture you want.

Whoever you send a hidden message to, though, must have the same software. So you and your friends will both need a copy of Steganos to experiment with it. (There's a thirty-day free trial version, so have fun.) More importantly, though, you both must use the same "key," just as with encryption.

Whether or not you have immediate needs for steganography yourself, you should know that the real bad guys in the world will use it for their own agendas. Some applications for Steganos include:

---

[31]Thanks to Demcom. I borrowed these images from www.demcom.com/english/ steganos/.

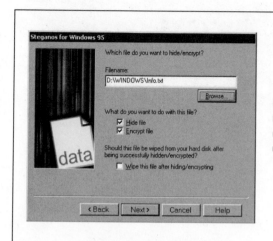

Using Steganos is a simple Wizard-like step-by-step process. All you need is a picture or large file and a message you want to hide in it.

- Getting corporate secrets past the company firewall by embedding text files within innocuous family photos.
- Sending national security information across the Internet without anyone noticing.
- Embedding child porn pictures within other pictures or sound files so as to appear innocent.
- Terrorists communicating over email, using religious icons as the seeming cover conversation.

When you play with Steganos, keep in mind that the file you are trying to hide cannot be the same size as the "carrier" file, or the image/sound into which it is to be embedded. I played around a bit and found that as a rule of thumb, the embedded files must be slightly less than 10 percent of the carrier file.

For more information, do a web search on "Steganography or Steganalysis or Steganographic," and maybe add the word "Software."

Hacking for Evidence

What do you think about O.J.?

Simpson that is.

Despite the seemingly overwhelming evidence against him, the jury acquited O.J. of killing his ex-wife, Nicole. What went wrong? Did Mark Fuhrman plant the bloody glove in a racist police conspiracy? And why didn't it fit O.J.'s hand at the trial? Did the murder weapon, a knife, get dumped at the Los Angeles airport? Whose white Bronco was really at Nicole's condominium? How many other people could have been wearing those silly overpriced Italian shoes?

These were some of the questions that the Dream Team of defense lawyers posed to confuse the jury, confound the evidence, and ultimately embarrass Marcia Clark into her new book-writing semi-retirement.

Life is not like a TV mystery show. At the end of the hour, the show's hero inevitably solves the murder and the bad guy goes off to jail. In real life, though, successful prosecution of crime is not an easy task. The key to any good case is a preponderance of evidence pointing to the guilt of the accused. The means to collect evidence is called *forensics*, which is a highly technical science unto itself.

In the TV show, a single strand of hair may lead investigators to a suspect. Even if the murderer mops up all of the blood from the scene of the crime, trace elements still remain, and will fluoresce under special light if the right chemical mixture is applied. The greatest forensic tool in modern crime is that of DNA identification. Like fingerprints, DNA is unique to every individual and is generally conclusive. The use of DNA matching has exonerated as many people previously convicted of crimes and innocently languishing in jail as it has proven the guilt of the accused in a trial.

Television has turned many of us into amateur sleuths and we cheer supportively for the hero, attempt to guess the identity of the real killer, and figure out how he did it. Unfortunately, when it comes to computer crimes, the cyber-cop has a much tougher job.

You see, in cyber-crime the rules are quite different, and you are not quite sure who committed the crime. Was it a relatively harmless teenaged hacker out for a thrill ride, or was it part of an effort by organized crime, or maybe it was a genuine threat to national security by well-financed and seriously intentioned terrorists? Worse yet for parents is their worry about on-line predators, pedophiles, and child pornographers.

Basic forensics techniques can help the home computer enthusiast as much as the corporation.

Only after extensive analysis is there any hope of finding out who is responsible for computer crimes. The basic nature of Internet technology offers criminals many ways to hide their tracks and disguise their crimes, as you have seen. Computer crimes are borderless; the crime can be committed from next door over a modem or from ten thousand miles away, with equal effectiveness. But, at the same time, technology provides many clues as to the nature of the crime, how it was commited, and who was behind it. First, you need to understand that in computer forensics, things are not always as they seem.

During the 1998–1999 Microsoft trial, Bill Gates and company made many claims that defied common sense. One key issue was whether Microsoft engaged in anti-competitive practices, which the company vehemently denied to a skeptical court and Internet community. To prove their point, the government's attorneys subpoenaed Microsoft email archives, which were dutifully turned over to the courts. Upon examination, emails were found that were diametrically opposed to Microsoft's public assertions that they were not worried about competition in the Internet arena. In this case, Microsoft preserved the actual records and documents that would be used against them. Whether they understood the implications of archiving email is unclear, but the results were certainly an embarrassment.

When amateur computer criminals, or criminals who use computers as tools in their criminal endeavors, discover they are under investigation, the smarter ones will know that the contents of their computers are damning evidence. Many of them will then try to dispose of the evidence by deleting the files in question. Many of us might think that deleting a file is all there is to it. Delete the file and it's gone forever. Nothing could be farther from the truth.

In the DOS and Windows world, deleting a file merely removes the name of the file from the directory and file listings program such as Windows Explorer. But the contents of the files are still there—waiting for someone with the right tools to find the "deleted" file and recover the information.

The US military is especially aware of this phenomenon and has developed stringent procedures to circumvent it. Long ago they established a set of security criteria to code the sensitivity of the data involved. So-called "sensitive but unclassified" computers are those used by the IRS, Social Security Administration, Veteran's Affairs, and for much of the military support systems, including travel, food, general support, payment systems, and such. In an effort to protect the contents of these systems, a technique called "Object Reuse" is employed. One aspect of object reuse is a true erasure feature. Rather than merely deleting the file through the operating system, a special program is used which finds the file contents and then overwrites the data with a random string of "0s" and "1s"—three times.

If a recovery is attempted, all that will be found is meaningless random data. Or is that really true? For higher level security needs, such as secret and top secret, the random overwrite must be done 100 times for secret and 1,000 times for top secret. This is because of an advanced forensics technique known as "Fringe Track Analysis."

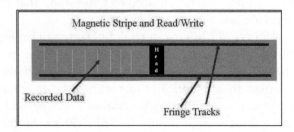

While computers are digital, the storage on disk of tape is analog. When data is stored on a floppy or a hard disk, a magnetic head like in a tape recorder or VCR aligns the magnetic particles under the write head to either a 0 or a 1. However, the recorded magnetic signals are not found only underneath the write head itself. The nature of magnetic recording creates a flux field of magnetic energy that extends beyond the write head, thus also recording the information above it and below it on the magnetic media. While a random rewrite of data will overwrite the actual bits of the file itself, it may not thoroughly erase the fringe flux to the sides of the recorded track, allowing a forensics expert to still retrieve the original information by reading and reconstructing the data contained in the fringe track. The military is so concerned about this for highly secretive operations that they often require discarded hard disks to be pulled apart, the magnetic coating stripped fom the disks and then crushed to pinhead size pieces of aluminum. Other sensitive hard disks are burned to a molten state and then buried in a secure location.

Programs that really do erase the contents of files (and their associated bits and pieces strewn about a hard disk, a concern especially in Windows) are available for general use. Take a look at Micro-Zap from New Technologies, Inc. at www.forensics-intl.com/download.html.

Law enforcement started learning about computer forensics the hard way. I have been told unfortunate tales of cops in the 1980s finding the criminal's lair and his computers. To preserve the evidence, the cops went to turn the computer's power switch off, only to be blown up in the process. Some criminals' computers were booby-trapped with bombs to destroy the evidence and maim or kill the police. The law also learned that the inside of a computer offers plenty of physical space to hide other detection devices.

One computer was wired to detect unauthorized opening of the case. *Boom!* Another trigger erases the hard disk. Upon opening the case, a computer released a liquid spray of face-scarring acid on the police. In one case in California, the cops successfully unplugged the computer, only to find it empty of information when they got to the police station. *The bad guys had built powerful magnets into the door frame which erased the contents of the hard disk.*

Bad guys tend to stay a few steps ahead of law enforcement, and they often come up with the most inventive means of protecting themselves— and destroying evidence. It is the job of the computer forensics expert to work with law enforcement to preserve evidence, reconstruct crimes, and ensure that the evidence collected is usable in court.

Forensics 101

Computer forensics experts are hackers in their own right. They have to know the technology inside out, understand what the bad guys are up to on a daily basis, forage into a computer used in the commission of a crime, and develop a case that prosecutors can use in court. So, yes, they are hackers. The computer forensics expert has to offer a wide range of skills, he has to own or develop a suite of software forensic tools, and maintain the integrity of the chain of evidence according to accepted legal process.

In many of the law enforcement facilities I have visited, the computer guys are not dressed in blue; many of them look like (prototypical) hackers, dress like hackers, and have the same skill and dedication of hackers. Some may have been hackers who crossed over from the black to the white; others are mere computer enthusiasts who got a job with law enforcement because they could play with all the cool tools. Other law enforcement folks are being aggressively trained on how to properly conduct a forensics investigation.

In any case, the science of forensics is a highly technical, detailed discipline. Because of the specialized nature of computer forensics, don't try to count on your in-house technical guru or neighborhood hack to provide any worthwhile forensic services. In fact, the best-intentioned technician, friend, or corporate manager can do more damage to evidence than they would think possible. So much of what occurs on a computer is invisible to the user that special tools are needed to reconstruct data.

Let's assume that a computer crime has taken place at NASA. Joe, a worker inside a development lab, is suspected of being involved in child pornography. Ten minutes after Joe went to work, the FBI entered his home with a proper search warrant. They found hundreds of printouts of child porn near his computer. A second search warrant was immediately granted for his computers at NASA. Joe is arrested in his office for the possession of the materials in his home, never mind what may be embedded in his computer. The forensics process must now begin.

1. The computer must be shut down—carefully. Looking for booby traps is critical, and a bomb-sniffing dog will perhaps be used to ensure safety before anything is done. The power should be shut down, but not before it can be determined if any destructive processes will destroy evidence on the hard disk. Is there a special shut-down procedure? The computer must be disconnected from a network and/or a modem connection to ensure that it sits in absolute isolation.

2. It must be documented what was found. Pictures are taken of the computer setup in its original position. Pictures of the connections and labels on the wires are necessary for the system to be put back together exactly as it came apart. This is also critical for any court testimony that might come about. A picture of what's on the monitor's screen could have value. Password-protected screen savers must be treated with caution at this point, as rebooting the computer could be hampered.

    In a networked environment, taking an electronic snapshot of the total environment may prove valuable in a prosecution. The more the merrier. Better safe than sorry.

3. The computer must be taken to a secure location, away from the prying eyes and fingers of so-called experts who could unwittingly destroy evidence on the computer. The secure storage is also critical for chain-of-evidence custody in a court proceeding.

4. A copy is made of the hard disk(s) on the seized computer. Computer evidence must never be processed on the seized machine—ever; too many things can go wrong. That is the permanent archive of the crime.

   Copying does not mean running "dosbackup.exe" or some other backup utility included with the operating system. Just as the "delete" button does not fully erase a file, conventional backup utilities do not completely back up a hard disk; they only copy those files deemed needed for the system to operate correctly. As you will see, there is plenty of forensic information to be retrieved from those files you can't see and maybe never even heard about.

   Special forensics backup software makes a "bit stream" copy of the original hard disk where every single bit of information is copied, whether it can be seen by the native operating system or not. Only once the original computer has been returned to a secure location and the bit-stream copies have been made should the forensic analysis begin.

   Some people advocate making backups onto write-once CD-ROMs, but the sheer giga-size of hard disks makes this generally unworkable. For now, a duplicate hard drive is the best choice. Check out SafeBack 2.0 at www.sydex.com, a very popular bit stream and disk-mirroring program.

5. Making a copy is one thing, but a defense attorney could have a field day suggesting that the police altered the contents of the computer in order to frame the accused. To thwart that argument, an integrity mechanism should be used. Simply put, integrity software puts an electronic wrapper around the bit-stream copy of the original hard disk. A complex mathematical process using encryption will automatically detect if anyone makes a change to the data on the copy. Check out Tripwire or any CRC (cyclic redundancy check). If the data is modified after being "wrapped," the changes will be detected.

6. Experts look for malicious code like viruses, Trojan Horses, and self-destruct mechanisms that can help the prosecution prove

intent and willfulness. But more obviously, finding and disarming destructive software preserves evidence. A forensics team must be careful of "hot-keys" that can launch self-protection software.

7. Directories or the screen saver may use passwords to protect the contents of the computer. The forensics expert will have to dig deep into the Windows environment to get the keys to unlock the protected functions. This is really no different than what other hackers do in the pursuit of better computer security. In this case, the lack of security by Microsoft works to the advantage of the forensics investigator.

8. System clock activities on the entire system must be documented. In conventional forensics, it is critically important to be able to place the killer or the robber at the scene of the crime at a specific time and date. Same thing with computer and cyber-forensics. The system clock leaves an audit trail of activity proving a criminal's every electronic footstep. The forensics investigator has to calculate Daylight Savings Time, any alterations of the clock for travel, or deception on the part of the accused. Capturing this information early in the process and storing it in a data base provides the forensics expert with behavioral information against which to compare future information.

9. Retrieval of file slack is necessary. Windows can be so messy. A significant amount of security leakage occurs through memory dumps that are appended to allocated files on the hard disk. When files are closed, all or parts of them are saved for possible future use, but cannot be retrieved or viewed without special forensic tools. For example, a series of viewed images may be fully erased from the hard disk, but the computer memory used to display them may have been saved in a normally unviewable location. Such evidence is powerful in court.

10. The Windows Swap file is managed by the operating system (usually) and can provide strong evidence to the forensics investigator. Manually reviewing the contents of the Swap file can take days or weeks, so tools were developed to examine and analyze their contents in the context of the investigation. Try GET-FREE.EXE from www.forensics-intl.com to get that Swap file into a usable format. Making a bit-stream backup of the original hard disk ensures the integrity of the Swap file, which is altered

almost every time the computer is used at all—thus destroying evidence.

11. Hidden data can be found using a program like GETFREE.EXE. Deleted data may still sit on the hard disk.[32] Criminals, both amateur and professional, may erase a file in the hopes of destroying evidence, whereas the forensics expert will know exactly where to look for telltale signs of criminal mischief.

12. When rebuilding a system and retrieving data such as described above, complete logs and records must be kept of the actions taken, the results of the actions, and of the original date/time stamps from Swap files, erasures, and other hidden files. They may well help in building a time line for prosecutors.

13. Analysis of the bit stream copy can be done for key words relevant to the investigation. If it's espionage, words like "sale," "proprietary" and "R&D" may be useful. For pornography cases, telltale words from email and web surfing may include "sex," "children," "boys," or "little" would be a good start. Again, experts must keep voluminous records of what is done. Some forensics software suites keep a complete record, down to the keystroke, of every action the investigator takes. This preserves the evidence chain and makes expert forensics court appearances all that much more effective.

14. Look for the oddball files and their associated extensions. We are all familiar with DOC files and TXT files. But a lot of forensic evidence can be found elsewhere. GIF, JPG, TIF, and BMP are popular graphics formats that can provide valuable insight into the activities of the perpetrator. Once these files are located, using a "snapshot" viewer displays several graphics files at once, which makes scanning large numbers of files easier. AVI and MPG movie format files are especially common with pornography. There may also be clues that the disk has been repartitioned to make hidden directories and partitions where more technically astute criminals might attempt to hide their affairs.

---

[32]When a file is deleted the data remains intact. When files are added to the computer, though, they may overwrite the unallocated files, as decided by the operating system. This would destroy evidence in the process.

15. Operating systems store information in the strangest places, sometimes temporarily, sometimes permanently. TEMP files (there may be several locations), the TMP files for many applications, and the recycle bin for discarded files must be looked at.

    Email programs may have their own recycle bins which are worth examining. And don't forget the ATTACH directory, which often stores downloaded files without informing the user.

    For Internet-related searches, check out Temporary Internet files, bookmarks on browsers, histories of web surfing (most browsers support this) and the associated html files across the disk. Looking for suspicious Internet activity can provide clues in the investigation, whether it is about espionage, casual hacking, offensive data about kids, or various hate-filled agendas.

16. Some criminals may use encryption to hide their activities, so breaking the encryption of the suspect files is part of any investigation. Passwords are generally easy to acquire using some of the popular password hacking programs as described elsewhere in this book. Passwords are often found stored within the Windows registry so the user is not bothered with entering passwords every time they are needed. This one step alone can provide the forensics expert with many new leads.

    If ZIPs (compressed files) are found, and a password or cryptography is used, freely available ZIP-cracking tools will generally make recovering the plaintext information a reasonably simple task. Check out your favorite hacker sites for plenty of these.

    If the actual files are encrypted, the goal will be to decrypt the contents, but this is a tough exercise. If the investigator is lucky, he might find the passwords stored somewhere in another file on the suspect computer or lying around on a piece of paper during a physical search. Critical evidence in the attack on the Tokyo Subways by Aum Shimrikyo was discovered just like this. But, if quality encryption is used and the encryption keys are well protected, breaking the code can be an expensive, time-consuming endeavor, if the files are every actually broken.

17. Steganography allows the subtle embedding of information inside graphic formats. This is a new science with plenty of information on the Internet. Currently it is used to embed smaller text messages inside of the typically larger graphic files.

18. Finally, a few housekeeping items for the forensics investigator. He or she must have absolutely accurate and unassailable records for use in court. Defense attorneys are not always the nicest people when facing law enforcement on the stand. Experts should have a copy of the paid receipt of the legal licensed software you used in the investigation. Using bootleg unlicensed software is a federal crime and would have an undeniably negative effect upon cross examination—maybe invalidating the entire investigation. Last, making additional copies of work, even if it fills dozens of Zip or Jazz drives, and keeping them in a secure location is a good idea. Just in case.

As the state of the art of hacking develops, so will the science of forensics. They are inextricably related:

- How do I (as the bad guy) hide information and trails of my criminal endeavors?
- How do I (as the good guy) recover information that can be used to prosecute the bad guys?

Remember that, in the information security field, both hacking and anti-hacking are moving targets. Nothing remains static for very long, and it is the job of the forensics investigator to keep on top of the most recent technical developments on both sides of the legal fence.

At Home

Protecting our children is a prime concern, especially when it comes to the Internet. Here are a few things you can do to monitor your children.

1. If your software has the option to make backup or temporary files, choose it. This gives you a log of what has been written. Check the HELP files and ask.

2. Expand the size of the Cache in your browser. Cache is a directory which stores the most recent files and pictures that have been downloaded. When it fills up, the earlier files are deleted, so the larger sizes will preserve most of a history. I have mine set for 100MB on my kids' machines and I periodically look at the GIF/JPG (pictures) that come down. They've been good so far.

3. If your computer offers any sort of logging or audit program, use it. These will keep a record of what has been done on the computer in a file that can be examined at a later date. Chat rooms do not normally have a logging feature, so use a third-party product such as a keystroke logger. Just search for "Keystroke Logger" or "Keystroke Monitor" to find the latest.

If you find inappropriate files or chat logs on your child's computer, it's time for you to have a serious talk with them. Of course, if your children are more computer literate than you, you have some fast catchup to do. Or you probably know someone who can help with the technology—and it's up to you to be a parent.

However, if you find files that indicate a solicitation for a meeting by your child's on-line friend, it may well be time to involve the police. If you find images that are clearly way outside the bounds of normal adolescent curiosity (child porn, bizarre sexual extremes, or animals) call the police immediately—a crime has been committed.

In the meantime, disconnect your child's computer and hold it until a forensics expert can take over.

Corporate Preparation

1. Make sure that your corporate policy is complete and employees have "brought in" before you begin extensive logging at the desktop. Check with human resources and in-house counsel, because in some states these techniques can violate the law.

2. Use extensive logging and audit trails at all servers. Back them up periodically to preserve archives in case you need them sometime in the future. Insiders will likely know their way around your network, so keeping electronic records of their activities is crucial to a future prosecution.

3. Use logging at your firewall or point of connection to the Internet to see who is doing what. At this point you can also configure the server to limit the kinds of traffic you will permit.

4. Archive email and Lotus Notes messages and back them up periodically.

5. Join an organization such as the HTCIA (High Technology Criminal Investigators Association [www.htcia.org]) where you can make personal contacts within the corporate world and law enforcement.

Statistics still say that over 60 percent of computer crime involves a company insider, so your monitoring efforts should focus on the employee as much as on external threats to your system.

If you think that there is a significant breach of security within your networks, there are a few simple steps to take—but make sure your lawyer is involved from the beginning.

A recent event at a major financial US corporation is a perfect example. The security department was contacted by an overseas medical firm. The two companies knew each other's names, but they had no official dealings. The overseas company wanted to know why the huge US company was hacking them.

Now that was a surprise to everyone, and we began an investigation within minutes.

The first thing we did was call legal and advise them of what had happened. Then we pulled the logs from the Internet servers and searched for the IP address of the overseas company. We found that, indeed, an employee had been connecting to the medical company—which was way outside the scope of any legitimate job description.

The logs were pulled and examined in detail, and it was discovered that for a period of several weeks this "hacking" had been going on. The logs were all date/time stamped, and all it took was a quick conversation with the overseas company and a copy of their hacker-detection logs to realize that the employee in question was undoubtedly guilty of hacking, but we didn't know why.

That evening, we went to his machine, disconnected it from the internal network and from the illicit modem we also found. We made a mirror copy of the hard disk using SafeBack and then looked for what else had been occurring. It turned out that the employee was joy-hacking, doing it for no bigger reason than fun. His desktop machine showed he had been hacking all sorts of companies in the US and overseas.

The following morning, he was met by security, legal, and human resources. At first he denied he was involved with anything, but as the evidence was shown to him, he finally collapsed in an emotional fit and confessed to hacking. Rather than involve law enforcement, he was immediately dismissed. The decision to handle things internally was made for three reasons:

1. There did not appear to be any real damage or maliciousness involved.
2. The victim company just wanted it to stop.
3. The company wanted to protect their image.

Not all computer crimes are this simple to solve, not by a long shot. But it does show that the first few steps of any investigation can be done by a forensics-aware information security staff. However, if there is any reason to suspect that something more dastardly is going on, the company has a tough decision to make: Bring in law enforcement, and risk public disclosure and possible embarrassment or legal culpability *or* handle it all internally.

There is no absolute right or wrong answer on how to proceed, but a company should prepare itself for the eventuality of how it will respond—quickly—to computer crimes. Don't expect your internal staff to be forensics experts, but they should be up to speed on the basics.

Hacking and anti-hacking: As you are learning, they are just about the same thing!

As with DNA, computer forensics can also prove innocence. The State Attorney in Florida asked a forensics expert in 1994 to investigate the case of an accused child pornographer. The computer was an older IBM PS-1 that did in fact contain a dozen illegal images. But the investigator felt that the evidence cleared the accused rather than convicted him. See what you think of the evidence:

1. In 1994, an IBM model PS-1 was found with twelve child porn images.
2. The JPG images, about 20K each, were all time stamped within one minute of each other.
3. The accused had a 300 baud modem connected to his machine.
4. No erased images or tampering with the computer system were found.

Why did this data prove his innocence?

1. JPG files were not all that popular back in 1994. GIF was the predominant format.
2. There was no JPG viewer software on the machine.

3. No traces of other images were found, nor was any sign of child porn found in the physical search of the accused.
4. Each 20K image would have taken about ten minutes to download, not one minute.

The case was dropped against him: He was being framed.

Forensics involves common sense in addition to technical skill. This is why law enforcement professionals prefer that they or forensics experts run investigations. They have the dogged determination and experience to conduct an investigation that will bridge the technical and the physical realms.

Resources

- Take a look at the High Technology Crime Investigation Association (HTCIA). This association helps provide training, awareness, conferences, and a forum for cooperation between law enforcement, investigators and corporations. www.htcia.org
- On December 21, 1994, the Department of Justice issued a set of guidelines for the seizure of computers by law enforcement. www.cpsr.org/privacy/epic/guidelines_analysi.txt.
- For more true file erasure programs, perform a search on "File Erasure" or "Erase Software." Updated versions can be found at www.usdej.gov/criminal/cybercrime/searching.html.
- General computer forensics by New Technologies, Inc. www.forensics-intl.com. They offer tools, training and services.
- Forensic Computing Project from the UK. www.csrc.lse.ac.uk/sommer/forensic.htm
- Trident Data Systems forensics team is at www.tds.com/solutions/cfa.htm.
- www.sydex.com/forensic.html and www.datec.com/forensicservices.html for more basic forensics software.
- www.toolsthatwork.com/cpr3.htm.
- Complete forensics kits are available from the DIBS Computer Forensic Laboratory at www.computer-forensics.com/products/.

IV

"We're Sorry, but the Computers Are Down"

OK. You've seen how hackers can break into, dial into, encrypt, decrypt, sniff, snort, and disguise themselves and their messages. But what about out and out destruction?

Computers run everything, but what happens when they don't work? Can you watch cable TV? Will the airplanes fly?

We call this *denial of service*, or taking down the computers. There are all too many ways to disable computers—above and beyond a normal Windows crash.

And that is what you will learn about: how reliant we are upon our computers and then what little we can do about keeping them up and running.

Denial of service is ugly and offensive hacking at its worst.

Denial of Service

Taking Down the Net

The Internet infrastructure lacks basic mechanisms that have been present and successfully used in telephone networks for a long time.[1]

Analysis of a denial of service attack on TCP
Christoph L. Schuba, et al.
COAST Laboratory, Perdue University, May 1997

Forget the Internet or hackers for a moment.

Let's say your oven stops working. You can't cook dinner. That means you are denied the ability to cook. When the cable signal goes out, that is denial of service of your cable channels. When your computer breaks, you are experiencing denial of service.

If this sounds like a new fancy-technical term, it's not. We all experience denial of service on a regular basis:

- Telephones: "All circuits are busy. Please try again later."
- Power: Black-outs and brown-outs at work or at home.
- When thunderstorms hit an airport so hard planes can't fly, that is denial of service.
- If a bank's ATM isn't working you are denied access to your cash.
- If the water supply is interrupted you can't take a shower, you are denied access to bodily cleanliness.

It's a simple concept, and something we have been experiencing in increasing numbers over the last several years, as we rely upon tech-

---

[1]Estimates of losses to American business range to $100 billion and more each year—and that is only the accidental events.

nology more and more. In May of 1998, a communications satellite went nuts for a while, not allowing beepers go off or phone calls to go through. America Online goes down, as do other ISPs, from time to time and their customers are denied access to the Internet. In fact, hundreds of denial-of-service events occur every year for a variety of reasons:

1. The equipment fails. It happens in cars all the time. Why should computers be expected to work all the time, anyway?

2. Software glitches. Software is so darned complicated and impossible to test thoroughly, and we the people are Microsoft's Great Test Laboratory. Software is going to fail from time to time—a fact of life.

3. Physical breaks. Cyberspace is not surreal. It is very physical, just like a brick or a doorknob. Millions of miles of wire and fiberoptics connect everything to each other. When construction equipment digs holes, the wires are sometimes severed, thus denying communications service. The backhoe is a cruel denialof-service tool. It has happened before and it will happen again. Taiwan is connected to the mainland with only two fiber-optic cables. What happens if they are cut? Would Beijing cut the wires as a prelude to regional conflict?

4. Human error. If Mike accidentally pushed button "A" instead of button "B", the air traffic control system for Oakland, California could cease to work. In a true story, clerks in West Hartford, Connecticut made a data entry error in the city's computer system, and as a result every man in the city was declared dead! In San Francisco, someone (accidentally or not) flipped a bank of switches, cutting power to much of the Bay Area.

5. Weather. Hurricanes. Tornadoes. Electrical storms. They all hurt. Hurricane Andrew in South Florida denied critical services to hundreds of thousands of people and homes. In 1993, the Great No-Name Storm swept through the Northeast a mere three weeks after the World Trade Center bombing. So much snow fell in Long Island that a major banking data center's roof collapsed. Millions of folks from Maine to Chicago had little or no ATM services for up to a month.

6. Intentional. Cut the wires. Bomb the building. Use offensive software.

Denial of service fits into two broad categories:

1. Denial-of-service events which are unintentional and/or Acts of God. Items 1–5 above are pretty much Acts of God, even though man may have unintentionally caused them. The denial-of-service event was accidental; there was no maliciousness involved. These happen all of the time and are part of our new society.

2. Denial-of-service attacks which are man-perpetrated; offensive acts intent on causing damage and discomfort, or which create a smoke screen meant to disguise even more devious attacks.

Denial of service represents the easiest, most effective way to cripple organizations whose telephone and Internet connectivity is crucial to their operation and survival. In 1996, a single hacker launched a denial-of-service attack against Panix, a New York Internet service provider, for nine days, nearly putting them out of business and severely hurting their customers in the process.

The distinguished researcher William Cheswick agrees that DoS is a significant challenge facing the security community. "This [the Panix attack] is the first major attack of a kind that I believe to be the final Internet security problem. We're going to see a lot more of this."[2] Years ago, Steve Bellovin published a highly detailed technical description of various DoS attacks, similar to those we have been experiencing for several years.[3]

Financial institutions are increasingly looking for means to decrease operational costs, increase profits, and bring additional remote services to home and business.[4] According to the ABA, 50 percent of current retail banking presence will go the way of the stagecoach and be replaced

---

[2] *Wall Street Journal*, September 12, 1996.

[3] "Security Problems in the TCP/IP Protocol Suite," Steve M. Bellovin, the *Computer Communications Review*, Vol. 19, No. 2, pp.32-48. April 1989.

[4] In private discussions with global financial organizations world-wide, I have found denial of service produces greater fear than the occasional hacker or embezzler for which they are reasonably well prepared. The issue of public confidence in the institution itself, as well as in the banking system, becomes more important than comparatively minor losses from transaction errors. In their minds, denial of service is the electronic equivalent of shutting a bank's doors.

by electronic banking. Through web sites and email, a customer will either direct-link over the Internet or, in some cases, special client software might be used. With the availability of quite acceptable security techniques, the issues of confidentiality and integrity are essentially solved.

I now buy most of my airline tickets on-line as the industry moves to Internet-based electronic ticketing, which reduces their ticket processing costs over 90 percent, from an average of eight dollars per ticket to fifty cents each. Any interruption to this service directly affects bottom-line profitability and my ability to use their service.

However, because the historical thinking of the professional security field has not adequately dealt with the issues of DoS as a function of the Acts of Man, we will, as Bill Cheswick also suggests, find an increased number of intentionally triggered hostile DoS events with much farther reaching effects than we have seen thus far.

Other than physically attacking the network itself, electronic denial of service generally takes one of two forms:

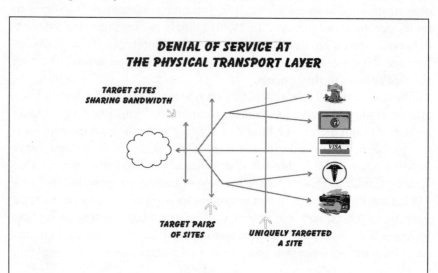

DENIAL OF SERVICE AT
THE PHYSICAL TRANSPORT LAYER

**TARGET SITES
SHARING BANDWIDTH**

**TARGET PAIRS
OF SITES**

**UNIQUELY TARGETED
A SITE**

The Internet "cloud" has spurs that branch out to many customers depending upon their needs. Note that if a connection near the cloud is cut, we at once cut off the services of several large organizations. Further down to the right of the branching, a severed line will affect pairs of firms, and ultimately, at some physical location near a target company, a severed cable will only isolate that one target from the rest of the Net.

1. Filling the pipe
2. Crashing remote computers

If My Hose Is Bigger Than Your Hose, You're Hosed

The nature of email bombing is such that anyone can attack anyone else, and it's all a matter of size. Most folks have a 28.8K–56K (or similar) modem at home. Businesses have anything from an ISDN to a T-1 or T-3, which offer tremendous bandwidth for large numbers of users. ISDN DSL offer high-speed service to homes and businesses. T-1 lines run at 1.5Mbits per second and T-3s at 45Mbits per second. Cable modem speed is at the lower end.

If a high bandwidth source (such as ISDN or T-1), sends a constant stream of data to a target 28.8K modem, the 28.8K modem is overloaded with incoming traffic, and the person at that end can't use his connection for anything else. Denial of service is the result. Just think when you connect to the Internet and you receive a huge file: all other traffic is blocked until that transmission is complete. So an easy way to attack is just to overwhelm the bandwidth capability of the target victim.

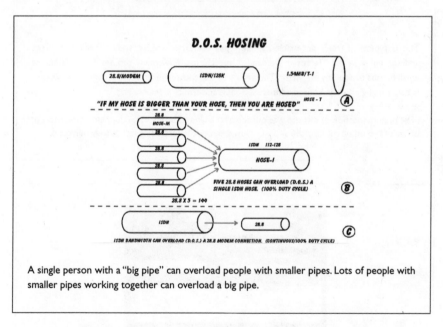

A single person with a "big pipe" can overload people with smaller pipes. Lots of people with smaller pipes working together can overload a big pipe.

A similar kind of denial-of-service attack doesn't fill the pipe as much as it fills your server and email with incredible numbers of garbage-laden emails. Some hackers think it's great fun to subscribe their victims to thousands of news groups, which in turn will send their messages to your email address. How do you separate the good ones from the bad ones? Viruses like Melissa are DoS attacks, since they multiply by a factor of fifty every time a computer is infected.

Denial-of-service attacks take many forms. As more and more tools have been developed, DoS strikes increase. "Infinite pinging" a target from a number of confederates is a moderately explored method, as is sending endless streams of gigabyte–length messages.

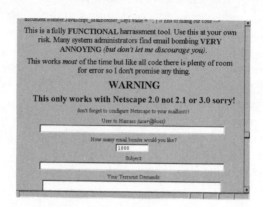

This is typical of freely accessible on-line email bomb service.[5] Merely choose the target address, enter in the "Terrorist Demands," and choose how many thousand or millions of email bombs to send to the victim. The beauty of this technique from the attackers' viewpoint is that, through built-in source address spoofing, anonymity is maintained.

[5] The original location of this site was outside of the United States. With the help of the national police of the other country, the site was closed, but not before being extensively mirrored.

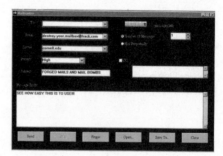

Kaboom3 is an easy to use and very fast email bomber. It comes with a series of remailers that you can use to send your mail to disguise your true identity. Kaboom also allows you to list-link your target to forty-eight mailing lists. Simply enter the email address, select the lists you want and press OK. Oooh . . . mean!

The Syn-Ack attack is another simple DoS tool. Two computers over the Internet establish a connect or conversation in this way:

```
             Computer A                      Computer B
Hello Computer B, are you there? >>> Listens (SYN)
Listens                          <<< Yeah, I'm here. Is that
                                     you?(SYN-ACK)

Yeah, It's really me.            >>> Ok. Fine. Let's talk.
Let's talk.                          (ACK)
```

This three-way handshake is required to allow computers to talk to each other. However, if Computer A sends a SYN (a synchronizing signal) to B and B answers with the SYN-ACK (I acknowledge your synchronizing signal) but A doesn't respond with a final ACK (acknowledgement), Computer B is left there hanging "on hold," listening for a response. If A does this many times to B, soon all of B's ability to make other connections is taken away. Denial of service.

Hackers are learning that sending the wrong commands to computers can also shut them down. Microsoft is the biggest target because of their market monopoly, but also because they are so hated by the hacker community. Buffer overflows are a favorite DoS method; it merely fills the temporary memory beyond capacity, thus crashing the machine. Hackers blame the designers for poor software.

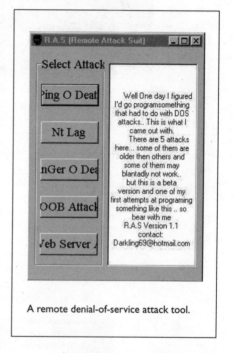

A remote denial-of-service attack tool.

And the lists go on and on.

There are too many denial of service programs to describe them all, but what we do know is how difficult it is to protect against them. Corporate managers have to keep up with the very latest fixes as best they can, but the vendors are ultimately responsible for making robust products. Small businesses can use personal firewalls to protect themselves to some extent against a few DoS attacks, but since the servers are often run off-site by another company, they may suffer despite their best efforts.

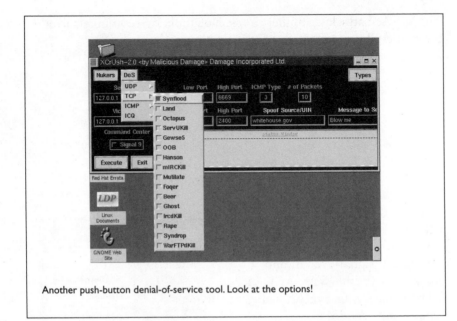

Another push-button denial-of-service tool. Look at the options!

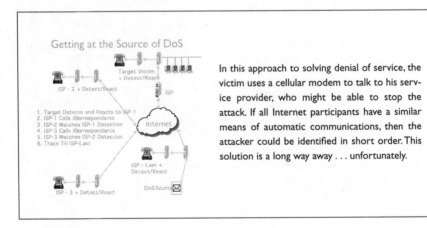

Getting at the Source of DoS

In this approach to solving denial of service, the victim uses a cellular modem to talk to his service provider, who might be able to stop the attack. If all Internet participants have a similar means of automatic communications, then the attacker could be identified in short order. This solution is a long way away . . . unfortunately.

Solving denial of service is a very complex task, but ultimately it will require a cooperation on the part of all Internet players. If the primary pipe is filled with useless data streams, how can you shut it off? You can't unless you can talk to the next computer down the line. But you can't because of DoS. Another channel of communications is needed, but the Internet community doesn't employ that method yet.

Finding the perpetrators is even harder. The following diagram shows that in order to identify the bad guys, we have to be able to trace the connection all the way from the victim back to the source. Today that is darned close to impossible for lack of Internet policy and coordination.

There is no simple solution. If someone really wants to shut down your Internet connection, they will do it.

Resources

- Denial of service Database. No exploit code provided for the kiddies either. http://www.attrition.org/security/denial/
- See www.packetstorm. securify.com for DoS attack tools.
- "E-Mail Bombs and Countermeasures: Cyber Attacks on Availability and Brand Integrity" http://www.comsoc.org/socstr/techcom/ntwrk/ IEEE Network, Vol. 12, No. 2, pp. 10–17, March/April 1998, for final version.
- http://www.ntsecurity.net/security/pod.htm for NT DoS.
- Search on "Denial of Service."
- Go to any of the hacker sites and look around.

Schwartau to Congress: HERF This

Committee Hearings of the US House of Representatives
June 27, 1991

Mr. Glickman (D-Kansas):	Mr. Schwartau, you talked about these HERF guns—high-energy radio frequency guns. I mean, these look like actual ballistic missiles?
Mr. Schwartau:	The designer of these could make them look pretty much any way they want. Essentially a HERF gun is nothing more than a power amplifier, an oscillator, and an antenna of some sort.
Mr. Glickman:	They exist now?
Mr. Schwartau:	The capabilities exist.
Mr. Glickman:	Now, you say that these HERF guns, if we have the technological capability now, it could be pointed at, let's say, the New York financial district, it could do serious damage to Wall Street, let's say.
Mr. Schwartau:	One of the worst problems that occurs in any electronic situation is what we call an intermittent one; one that occurs occasionally. And one of the things that can be postulated would be perhaps a

HERF gun, which is a fairly low power device compared to what I call an EMP/T bomb—an electromagnetic pulse transformer bomb. If I had an adversary, perhaps on Wall Street (another markets firm, securities firm), I might be so inclined to shoot this gun at their network and cause it to crash once an hour. They would find their network constantly going down with little or no ability to initially identify the problem. And then, even once they did identify the problem, to find the bad guy is a very, very difficult task.

Mr. Glickman: This other gun, the EMP/T bomb, is much stronger, but the same principle?

Mr. Schwartau: Yes.

Mr. Glickman: Now you say the Social Security system could be destroyed, rendering payments impossible. That is, any major system— airplanes? You could target it at an airplane in the sky?

Mr. Schwartau: Those were for illustration purposes only. You need higher power for airplanes, but the most efficient way to do it would be to be at the beginning or end of a runway where the planes were at a relatively low altitude.

Mr. Glickman: Do you think—I hate to be involved in the issue of gun control, and this is not a gun in the classic sense. But, do you think that we ought to consider banning these kinds of devices?

Mr. Schwartau: If you did, you would be banning the microwave and telecommunications industry from its existence. (Audience laughter)

Weapons of Mass Disruption[6]

$\mathcal{J}$anuary 16, 1991: The cruise missile hugged the endless sand dunes on a 450-mile journey that began on a navy destroyer in the Red Sea. Its electronic cross hairs narrowed in on the target, an Iraqi Air Defense Radar Installation, now a mere twenty miles or two minutes away. The radar crew saw it coming and they prepared for the anticipated explosion and bloody death. Instead, they found themselves in a pitch-black bunker, the radar screens gone blank, and seemingly all electricity gone. But they were alive.

This cruise missile did not carry 1,000 pounds of specially formulated high explosive. It carried a secret new payload known as an Electro-Magnetic Pulse (EMP) or High Power Microwaves (HPM) Bomb—in military parlance, a Directed Energy Weapon. Instead of causing a tremendous physical explosion, the EMP bomb radiates intense pulses of high-energy electromagnetic energy that spells death and destruction to computers, radar and all things electronic.

The EMP bomb proved successful and marked the first use in conflict of this class of information warfare technologies. So-called non-lethal weapons are designed to degrade an enemy's ability to wage war but with minimal collateral loss of life or physical devastation. The primary goal is battlefield superiority and control of an enemy's infrastructure by denying him his electronic eyes and ears.

In 1999, the US and NATO also used EMP and HERF weapons

---

[6]An abbreviated version of this article appears in an issue of *Popular Science*. Special thanks to Karlo Copp for permission to use his artwork in this article.

against the Serbs' electronic infrastructures, according to MSNBC reports. This makes absolute sense: Shut down the enemy's communications and power but don't destroy it.

In the 1970s President Carter's ill-fated neutron bomb was designed to emanate intense radiation, too, but the goal there was to kill human beings and leave the buildings standing—a seemingly reasonable military goal. However, the subsequent humanitarian and PR debacle killed the project quickly. The current range of military Directed Energy Weapons are much more politically correct: Kill the computer and spare the soldier. But there is much more to the story than that.

The US military and civilian authorities are properly worried about the use of such weapons by terrorists, extreme hackers, and other non-government organizations with a bad attitude. Consider the effects of a well-orchestrated RF attack against portions of the United States infrastructure:

- Wall Street or other banking systems either repetitively fail or, in the worst case, past records are wiped out by an onslaught of electromagnetic pulses.
- Airplanes' avionics and guidance systems are overloaded, causing potentially deadly conditions through targeted RF energy.
- Medical systems of a politically or religiously oriented hospital all simultaneously fail, triggering loss of life by intense energy spikes measured in megavolts.
- Communications nodes are burned out by intense microwave radiation.
- Municipal emergency services are made inoperable by debilitating ultrawide-band microwave jamming.
- Power lines and transformers serving as efficient conductors to transmit huge current to victim businesses and substations, causing regional brown- or black-outs.

These are terrifying scenarios that experts around the world are trying to defensively solve, as previously classified technologies and a knowledge of college physics are turned lethal by garage-shop hobbyists and high-tech terrorists.

The Basics

The principle of electromagnetic, or RF, weapons is simplicity itself—electronics 101. A current flowing through a wire produces a corresponding magnetic field around it. The magnetic field can be used to produce motion (as in a speaker or some microphones) or to broadcast information (as in radio, TV and satellite transmissions). Similarly, a magnetic field floating in the air induces a current into a circuit such as a radio or cell phone—also known as a receiver. That's all there is to it. Forget the math. In all too many cases, though, the received signal is noisy. This is known as electromagnetic interference, or EMI.

Until FCC regulations went into effect in the 1980s, early computers from Commodore, Atari, and Radio Shack caused annoying interference with television sets and radios. AM radio is known for poor signal reception and static. Analog cell phones experience severe EMI (noise, signal instability) in big cities, on bridges and in tunnels, and often near large radio transmitters. Airlines do not permit the use of electronic equipment below 10,000 feet due to pilots' reports of interference with avionics. Some electric wheelchairs go out of control in the presence of cell phones. Baby monitors and other life-sustaining electronics systems can go absolutely haywire when exposed to certain radio transmissions or other random RF signals.

So, the thinking goes, can EMI be created intentionally and directed at electronic targets to disable them? During the heyday of CB radio in the 1970s, long-haul truckers were highly displeased that civilian four-wheelers bought Radio Shack CBs and dared to tread upon their province of "Breaker 1-9": Channel 19 communications. The more aggrieved truckers responded by putting high-wattage linear amplifiers on their own CBs (a definite violation of FCC laws). When they spied a four-wheeler with a CB whip antenna, they'd press "squelch," forcing inordinate amounts of RF energy down the throat of a $29.95 CB radio. The result? Anything from temporary failure to smoked electronic components. Voilà! An early, home-brew RF weapon.

As the power levels are increased, the effects become more widespread and even more injurious to electronic systems. Thus the interest on the part of the military in directed energy and RF weapons.

Tesla Revisited

Very little about HERF guns, EMP or (as you will see) Schriner's TED should come as a surprise to electronic hobbyists—or anyone who encounters an electrostatic shock. The fundamentals are still the same. If you walk along a carpet on a dry day and touch a doorknob, the difference in potential, or voltage, can create an electrical arc or a miniature lightning bolt between your finger and the metal. This can be annoying if not somewhat painful.

Nicholai Tesla and Van der Graf experimented with visually exciting high-voltage discharges, to the amazement of crowds across the country. Tesla and van der Graf merely learned how to build up low current (amperage) megavoltages to the point of breaking down the surrounding air.

Because he could cause light bulbs to glow without wires, Tesla believed that he had discovered the electrical Holy Grail: broadcast power. Unfortunately, he died a broken pauper, feeding pigeons in Bryant Park, Manhattan.[7]

Star Wars It Ain't

In 1991, the author testified before Congress about the dangers of EMP bombs, high energy radio frequency (HERF) guns, and RF weapons in the hands of terrorists, coining the term Electronic Pearl Harbor to bolster the image of the future threat.

. Less than a decade later, the US military and defense industry are actively pursuing a wide number of DEW-related projects. According to Department of Defense budget reports, more than $100 million will be spent on high-power microwave technology for the period 1994–2001. With high-power laser and semiconductors added in, the

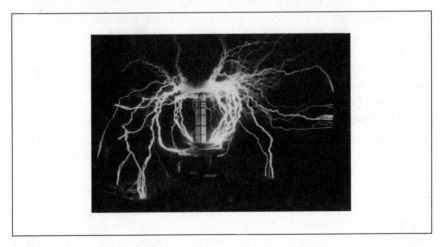

---

[7]Hobbyists interested in high-voltage experiments should consult the back of *Popular Science* and other hobby magazines for a variety of projects and do a web search on "Tesla."

The hobbyist can play around with blowing his friends and neighbors out of electronic existence, hopefully protecting his reproductive organs at the same time. If you must, go to http://www.futurehorizons.net/energy/high.htm for all the exciting details.

total is just about $500 million. Of course, if we count Black Budget programs, actual weapon production, and systems integration, the real figures are substantially higher. Like any other arms race, the goal is to develop, maintain, and be prepared to use a wide range of weapons systems.

The technology to build down-and-dirty, yet effective RF weapons is fairly simple, but as the higher power levels required for military uses are approached (upper gigawatt to terawatt range), the task becomes increasingly difficult. The state of the art does not approach Luke Skywalker's light saber, but laser weapons for military use have been deployed using a Boeing 747 as a flying platform.

After the Gulf War, Special Operations Command in Tampa, Florida said they would like to have had an electromagnetic weapon to drop on Iraq to take out their entire communications and power infrastructure. The only way to achieve that strong and widespread a pulse today is by exploding a nuclear bomb some 500–2,500 feet above the ground. Atomic tests in the Pacific Ocean five decades ago created impossibly huge electromagnetic pulses that either temporarily disabled or permanently fried shipboard electronic circuits within a few miles. (The Russians used ancient tube technology in MiG-23 fighters and oil-propelled submarines up through the 1990s. The reason? Tubes are not affected by electromagnetic pulses.)

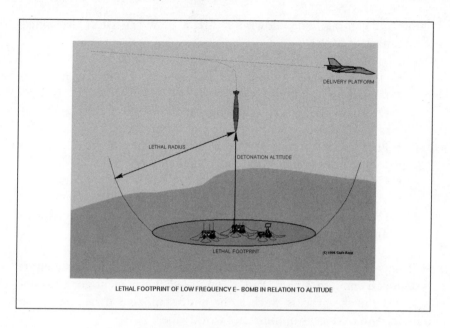

LETHAL FOOTPRINT OF LOW FREQUENCY E– BOMB IN RELATION TO ALTITUDE

Softkill versus Hardkill

The military is really good at blowing things up. And, as the air force likes to say, when all else fails, they can still make the rubble bounce, in reference to the use of nuclear weapons. But in a world where a single dead soldier being dragged through the streets of a Third World country can shift our nation's policy, the concept of low-lethality rings true with the American public and war planners. How can they achieve their goals with minimal loss of life?

Say in a given conflict the Pentagon decides that our adversary's communications capabilities must be destroyed. One choice is to lob in a few smart or ground-penetrating thousand-pound bombs and blow up the offending communications facilities. There will probably be a loss of life, and there is the CNN effect; how will the American public and global opinion react and thus affect the operation?

The other choice is to employ the concept of softkill, especially in electronic systems. A strategically exploded electromagnetic pulse bomb can introduce such intense levels of electromagnetic energy into nearby circuits that they fail, rendering the systems inoperable. Whether the target is military or civilian communications, power control systems, a computer-controlled vehicle, or a financial institution, the effects of high-energy RF signals is not silicon friendly.

Depending upon a whole lot of factors, which are not readily measurable and can rarely be known for sure, a DEW can affect electronics in a number of ways:

- Disrupt internal timing circuits, causing instability and failure.
- Overload the power handling capability of circuits and individual components: smoke and burn.
- Produce rectification and diode effects in the circuits.
- Induce intense circuit-killing ground currents.
- Cause power-line spikes that in turn destroy components.
- Fuse the silicon NP junctions within active components (MOS circuits can be destroyed with merely tens of volts applied to them).

If only one chip in a sophisticated electronic system fails, the entire system can come to a halt. And, the non-lethal argument goes, no one has to die in the process. Such is the understandable attraction to our military and to dozens of militaries worldwide.

Some people suspect that a marine helicopter accidentally crashed when it came too near a microwave test range—and that the cover-up has been successful. It was suggested that TWA Flight 800 might have been hit with a microwave beam and the 1991 United crash in Colorado Spring, Colorado permits conspiracy theories to abound. The very nature of DEW and HERF is that it is untraceable. That is, a systems disruption might be caused by anything from a minor power glitch, software bug, operator error, or nearby cell phone to, indeed, an RF weapon. There is no hard and fast way to know for sure, especially with complex networked infrastructures, which have a habit of crashing anyway. How is one to know the difference?

Generating HPM

To achieve the vast amounts of targeted energy for DEW and HERF, highly specialized techniques have been studied for years. The explosively pumped Flux Compression Generator (FCG) was first demonstrated at Los Alamos Labs in the 1950s. After extensive development, the FCG today creates high levels of RF—up to tens of terawatts—more than ten times the energy of a typical lightning bolt. A source current such as a high-voltage capacitor bank (Marx bank) is used to trigger an explosive material stored within a cylindrical copper armature. The explosive force moves forward with the stator winding acting as an inductive trap, containing the current within the device.

In a bomblike form factor, an explosive switch is triggered by the flux forward moving field, and then the immense power generated is released through an antenna or load.

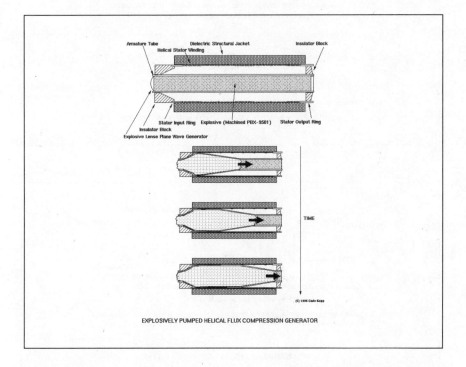

Armature Tube Dielectric Structural Jacket Insulator Block
Helical Stator Winding

Stator Input Ring Explosive (Machined PBX-9501) Stator Output Ring
Insulator Block
Explosive Lense Plane Wave Generator

TIME

(C) 1996 Cade Kapp

EXPLOSIVELY PUMPED HELICAL FLUX COMPRESSION GENERATOR

The frequencies developed by the FCG lie below 1MHz, thus creating the resultant (above) radiation pattern, and also limiting its applicability as a weapon. In the second diagram below, one FCG is used to provide source current to a second, more powerful FCG, which in turn drives a vircator, or virtual cathode oscillator. The vircator is built into a cylindrical waveguide structure, and is tuned to oscillate at microwave frequencies. A conical horn functions as an antenna producing up to 40–50GW of output power.

Higher frequency microwaves disrupt targets more effectively than low frequency microwaves. Design concentration is on RF weapons with the most destructiveness and those that can bypass many shielding techniques. The HERF weapons designer will design for one of two methods of coupling his energy source into the target:

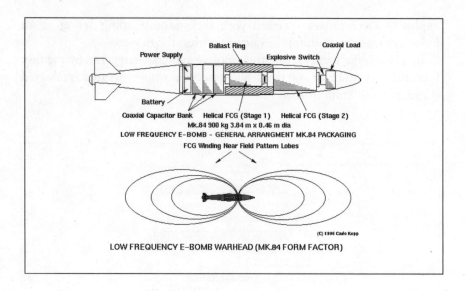

FCG Winding Near Field Pattern Lobes

LOW FREQUENCY E-BOMB WARHEAD (MK.84 FORM FACTOR)

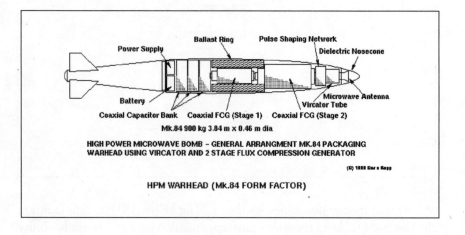

HPM WARHEAD (Mk.84 FORM FACTOR)

- Front door coupling–attacks aim at antennas that are normally used for communications or sensing. The antenna efficiently conducts the HERF into internal circuits that are subsequently overloaded or destroyed.
- Back door coupling–attacks use ground planes, electrical paths, interconnecting wires, or even physical apertures whereby the tiny microwaves can directly strike circuit boards and components.

Whether in military or commercial applications, solid-state devices are vulnerable to HERF attack. Transistors break down between

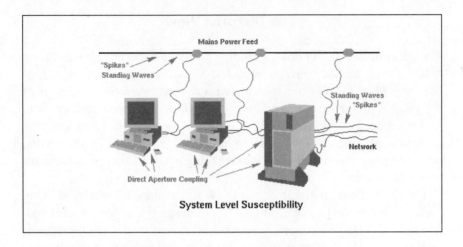

System Level Susceptibility

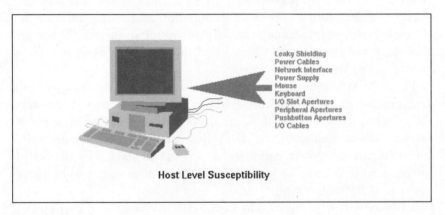

Host Level Susceptibility

15–60V, GaAs FETs (field effect transistors) at ~10V, dynamic RAM at about 7V above ground, and low power CPUs collapse very near their operating voltages of 3.3–5V. Although most integrated circuits use protective devices against electrostatic discharge, they are not truly designed to handle sustained or repeated high-voltage strikes. This underscores the problem with a commercial society and military organization whose efficiency and strength are based upon countless silicon devices that are fairly easily disrupted or destroyed.

Through 1998 Presidential Directive Decision 63, President Clinton finally realized that the success of American society and its economy was based upon continued and reliable operation of the nation's critical infrastructures, including power, communications, finance, emergency services and transportation. Although no war with a foreign power has been fought on American soil since 1812, there is legitimate concern that our physically isolated haven may no longer be so safe.

The Terrorist View

Ph0n-E (pronounced Phony), a young computer hacker, said that during a July, 1998, hacker convention in Las Vegas, he "was escorted out of defcon [sic] on Sunday to a meeting with at least two federal agencies of the three lettered variety. Apparently someone at the con had let them know I was showing my HERF gun prototype, lets [sic] just say they were very interested." He claims to have been threatened by the agents, who allegedly told him that he was treading upon an area of paramount national security.

Other people with an interest in DEW have told similar tales of being visited and intimidated by "officials" here in the US, as well as overseas. Much of the DEW weapons research has moved from the Department of Energy to the National Security Agency, and one result is a heightened sense of security over the dissemination and propagation of this technology. Chinese espionage activity uncovered in early 1999 has further sensitized the military. China has demonstrated extreme interest in these types of weapons.

Problem: While the energy, resources and money required to build true military-capable weapons systems remain with the nation-state, (US, China, Russia, Israel, UK, etc.), the potential effects of terrorist-level devices are finally raising alarms throughout Washington and other infrastructure-dependent countries. In 1994, I was asked by the British government to investigate how easy or difficult it would be to build terrorist-level RF weapons.

Early models were trivial. The Coffin design consisted of beer bottles, salt water, and sand: a crude but effective capacitor. Spark plugs produce intense RF pulses, as do readily available but husky capacitors. Hackers have played with Tesla coils and other high voltage–producing devices, but these are child's play compared to what was coming.

Retired Department of Defense consultant David Shriner was asked to see what he could conjure up as a terrorist RF weapon, using nothing more than commonly available components and a home-based garage laboratory. The goal was to discern what level of skill was needed by terrorists or non-government organizations to build highly effective RF weapons that could be used against the civilian infrastructure. His results are nothing short of amazing—deadly amazing.

The approach he used was a novel one. Instead of traditional HPM, Shriner worked with TED, or Transient Electromagnetic Devices. TEDs generate incredibly large voltage spikes of no more than 100–200 picoseconds in length. (Light travels 1.2 inches in 100 psecs.) He built an RF unit that put out hundreds of thousands of volts of energy using common electrical parts: two ignition coils, a battery for power, an automobile fuel pump, a filter, and transformer oil. The antenna was built from styrofoam and copper sheets. Cost? Five hundred dollars plus two weeks of time.

Dubbed the S-20, it was built as proof of concept, not small size. The S-20 could be placed into a van and then effectively used as a terrorist weapon to target critical infrastructures, Wall Street or other attractive targets, while on the move.

Tests of the S-20 at the China Lake Live Fire Test and Evaluation range were impressive, and Shriner's subsequent congressional testimony shook up political and military leaders. His "experiment" successfully disrupted the operation of computers, medical devices, and automobiles.

The S-20 being tested at China Lake, California.

Through his tests Shriner is absolutely convinced he can build similar devices that will fit into a suitcase and shut down reservation systems at airports—a distinctly unpleasant eventuality. The US worked on back-pack RF weapons for soldiers to carry into the field in the late 1980s, but the results with older technology were disappointing.

In September 1999, I invited Shriner to demonstrate his techniques at my annual conference in Washington DC, InfowarCon. He built a device based upon the 1880 designs of Heinrich Hertz. We kept out people with pacemakers; good thing. Using 110-year-old technology, Shriner froze up computers, destroyed a VCR, and made my digital camera go haywire and reboot. He also appeared on ABC's "20/20" and interfered with automobile electronics.

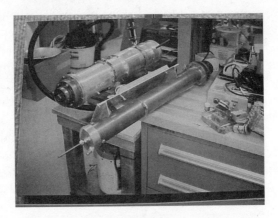

Homemade cylindrical waveguide for RF weapon tests.

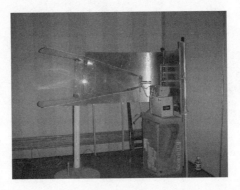

First public demonstration of HERF by Shriner at InfowarCon, September, 1999 (www.misti.com)

Shriner will continue his work with the S-30 and future novel designs. One such antenna design he is experimenting with is a dual-cone model that vastly improves efficiency and effective radiated power (ERP). He projects generating more than one megavolt per meter at the source antenna with better designs—still all done in his desert-home garage laboratory.

HERF warning signs at InfowarCon, 1999.

The Russians Are Coming

Throughout the Cold War, the USSR conducted extensive investigations into RF weapons, including picking up and perfecting discarded and abandoned US technologies.

Now, with US–Russian cooperation, we are learning just how much effort they placed in this field. They made significant advances in DEW, RF weapons, high-power lasers, HPM and pulsed systems, magnetically insulated linear oscillators (MILO) as a unique HPM power source, and neutral particle beam stream generation. The Russians also developed RADAN, a suitcase-sized 8kg high-current electron accelerator providing two nanosecond pulses at more than 5MW of power, repeating at 1KHz. The NAGIRA radar system operates at 300MW peak power and 10GHz, and was bought by the British Ministry of Defense as a susceptibility evaluation tool.

According to ex-KGB officials, the Russians used microwave energy to start a fire at the US Embassy in Moscow, so KGB workers disguised as firemen could get inside and plant bugs. Criminal organizations have been accused of using RF weapons to deactivate alarm systems to aid their thefts. And the Chechnyan rebels are said to have used similar technology to disrupt Russian communications.

Because of the deterioration of the Russian economy, scientists are doing what they must to provide for their families; thus the fears of nuclear as well as microwave and DEW proliferation. Today, the Russians are exporting exotic new technologies worldwide. Without international controls, though, there is no provision for restricting the export of these potentially dangerous devices or regulating to whom they may be sold.

A garage-made dual-cone horn for increased radiated RF efficiency.

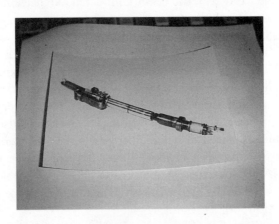

Russian plasma tube produces intense ion streams. Getting close to *Star Wars*.

Israel, the United Kingdom and other major post-industrial countries are seriously examining how HERF technologies affect them—both on the battlefield as well as on the defensive home front. Sweden and Switzerland have made significant progress towards hardening or protecting portions of their infrastructures from the effects of RF weapons through their national policy. Yet here in the US, the sphincter-tight intelligence community classification system has kept much of this information from the public. Now, though, a handful of courageous people

Russian RF weapon for sale on the Internet. F&D-10-10-1 pulse generator based on new Semi-conductor Fast Ionization Dynistor (FID) 10KV, 500A, 1-10 ns Risetime with 100-500 ns Pulse Width and 0-10 kHz Pulse Repetition Frequency. Jitter = 100ps. Size: 310x230x120mm

Who would buy this weapon off the Internet? This device is advertised as a Pulser for "car stopper" prototype. 2.5 KV into 50 ohms, Risetime. 700ps, Pulse width 1.7 ns, Jitter, 50ps and Rep rate: 2MHz in burst. Designed for dipping/placement in fluorine for cooling components at high rep rate operation.

are coming forward to speak out about an issue they believe in and that has festered for almost a decade.

EMP and HERF Defense: Detection and Protection

Protecting against the effects of EMP and HERF has historically been a military effort. But with the concern over the use of these weapons in the private sector, potentially vulnerable organizations must now add DEW to their list of worries, which includes viruses and hackers. In addition, given that complex technology is prone to various failures from time to time anyway, how can we know if there has been an RF attack of some sort, or if perhaps there is a more prosaic Occam's Razor answer.

How do we protect the national infrastructures from the likes of terrorists, who wield arsenals of HERF guns and EMP bombs, when we have a hard enough time keeping Internet hackers at bay? That question is finally being asked and a handful of answers are beginning to emerge.

Traditional shielding techniques can be effectively used to protect entire rooms or buildings, but the rigor is intense. Huge Faraday cages are expensive and very difficult to retrofit into existing construction; installing the protection from the ground up is far easier.

Shielding RF signals by putting lots of metal around electronic systems is an obvious fix, but the unwieldiness and weight of the resultant system makes such approaches unfeasible. (The classified Tempest program took the same heavy-metal approach when trying to prevent unintentional computer emanations and remote electronic eavesdropping by

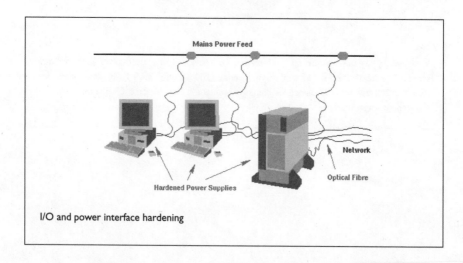

Mains Power Feed

Network

Optical Fibre

Hardened Power Supplies

I/O and power interface hardening

adversaries.) Retrofitting the private sector with billions of tons of metal shielding is phenomenally expensive, time consuming, and it's just not going to happen. Investigation into high attenuation, low-weight, low-cost wide-band filtering material is being actively pursued.

Protecting individual electronic systems is a complex exercise in both blocking physical apertures from permitting radiation inside the chassis, RF-immune optical wires and extensive shielding.

A much more palatable approach is being pursued at the chip level. Intel Corp. will provide microprocessor technology to the US Department of Energy's Sandia National Laboratories for creating radiation-resistant computer chips. The aim is to create new generations of "radiation-hardened" chips for use in satellites, military reconnaissance equipment, space probes, and other communications equipment. A natural fall-out of such efforts will be to figure how to add appropriate levels of protection for civilian uses in protecting the infrastructure.

For front-door RF attacks against communication, guidance or radar systems, a novel approach is to add high-speed plasma limiters at the input of sensitive circuits. Synthesized gases would sense threshold electric fields and, if thresholds were exceeded, would clamp down on the offending signals, hopefully quickly enough to protect the system's components.

Another proposed method is to first detect a HERF or EMP attack and then attempt to thwart it. The concepts of time-based security (explained later in this book) provide a model by which systems designers can apply hacker and network defense techniques to the electromagnetic spectrum. Since HERF attacks are by their very nature extremely fast, the goal is to detect the incoming signal and then thwart its effects in such a short time period that the targeted system is adequately defended.

The Swedish Ministry of Defense has been aggressive in these areas and they have developed both passive and active RF detectors. They carefully slit thin metal films, which tune into and break down certain microwave frequencies to, in turn, trigger a light pulse. The pulse is either photographed or passed on through optical cables to handle the problem.

Ed Pevlar, a Texas scientist, has been working on methods to detect RF attacks against airliners, perhaps the most frightening possibility of all. His patent details how an incoming RF signal is filtered and then compared against an on-board inventory of RF signatures. Unfortunately, the air force cancelled his contract for lack of funds, and all of the development efforts now sit in his garage. To handle Shriner's TEDs, though, very-high-speed detectors, special digital oscilloscopes, and software are required to identify the nature of the signal and then take some corrective measure.

Clearly, to protect critical infrastructures in the private sector as well

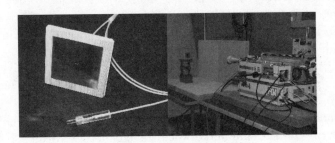

Left: Swedish Active Microwave Detector
Right: Swedish Test Environment for RF Detection Methods

as the command and control systems of the military, much work is needed. The Pentagon will likely continue extensive research into this area because, like the rest of us, they are increasingly dependent upon the private infrastructure for so much of their jobs. The military's rear echelon is in fact the private sector of the United States, and any RF attacks could certainly affect the readiness of our armed forces.

Biological Effects

The human body is an electrical organism, and since the days of Mesmer, 200 years ago, scientists have explored the relationship between man and electricity. Recently, cell phones were suspected of inducing brain cancer in unsuspecting callers. Despite a lack of concrete proof or correlation of long-term exposure to low-intensity RF, many people are still wary. Living underneath magnetic field–generating power lines is suspected as the cause of electrically induced disease clusters.

But microwave frequencies *can*, even at comparatively low levels, cook biological entities from the inside out; ask any potato or chicken. And people are no different; standing in front of a microwave beam is not good for one's health. But studies using super-intense bursts of non-coherent, electromagnetic energy are exceedingly sparse, even in the classified world. We just don't know what happens after human exposure to one or two or a hundred such gigawatt experimental bursts.

Since the somewhat speculative work *The Body Electric*, by Dr. Robert Becker in 1985, research has accelerated. The Naval Medical Research Institute at Brooks Air Force Base is leading the Department of Defense effort into "RF Human Effects," also known as HERP, Hazards of Electromagnetic Radiation to Personnel. They want to know with a great deal more precision how varying levels of magnetic radiation alter our body, DNA, and health. Both the US and Russia have allegedly performed studies experimenting with low-level (LERF) microwave irradiation of humans. The CIA has been accused of microwave harassment for years; electromagnetic waveforms of different frequency and shapes are said to be able to influence behavior, attitude and, for the soldier, ability to fight. The Russians blanketed the US Embassy in Moscow with radiation for several purposes: cause alarms to go off, cause passive diode-based eavesdropping devices to pick up electronic emissions and purportedly to affect the minds of Embassy staffers.

HERF Specifications

In the defense community, the most classified secrets involve the exact specifications and capabilities of weapon systems. Obviously, we don't want the enemy to know how well our planes handle in dogfights, how much abuse our tanks can take, or what hacking techniques the US will use to inflict specific damage to a computer network.

Nonetheless, every university engineering school teaches the knowledge necessary to build basic RF weapons; not of military caliber, perhaps, but effective nonetheless. The most fundamental and negative aspect of DEW is the distance problem. That is, the power at the transmitting source of the EMP bomb or HERF gun attenuates very rapidly.

Distance From Source/ Antenna	Source/ Antenna	10 Meters	20 Meters	30 Meters	50 Meters	100 Meters	1000 Meters
% of Source Power Striking Target	100%	10.0%	5.0%	3.3%	2.0%	1.0%	0.1%
Volts Per Meter (V/m) Electrical Pressure at Target	1,000,000	100,000	50,000	33,333	20,000	10,000	1,000

While the power required to generate an EMP pulse or other RF effect is measured in mega- and gigawatts, another important specification is volts per meter at the source device—usually an antenna of some sort. The physics of antenna design is extremely complex, but the propagation loss is easy to see.

The second critical factor is how susceptible electronic devices are to what is called the e-wave, also measured in volts per meter (V/m). Automobile manufacturers are legitimately concerned about spurious and accidental EMI affecting the large number of microcontrollers in modern cars. They specify they are protected against signals up to 200V/meter when the hood is closed. (Note that in the chart above, even a home-brew one million volt/meter source still can place 1000 volts/meter on a car or other device at a kilometer.) Unfortunately, in the private sector we know very little about exactly how susceptible banking systems, phone companies or medical institutions are to the effects of HERF attacks.

Recently though, the Pentagon has become remarkably open about a new effort to measure the real-world effects of HERF, HPM, and EMP on both military and commercial systems. At the China Lake Naval Air Warfare Center, the Live Fire Test and Evaluation staff measure the survivability of all sorts of military systems—from both conventional armaments and directed energy weapons.

The Life Fire Test range at China Lake, California. Testing the effects of systems vulnerability on a helicopter. The facility is now offering its capabilities to the private sector.

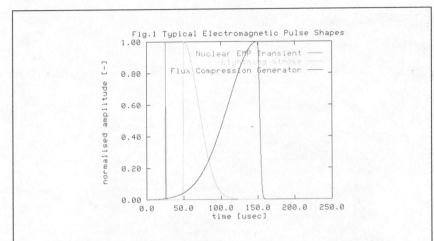

Comparing the time of extreme electromagnetic events. The nuclear EMP is of course the sharpest and is the closest to Schriner's TED.

If building garage-level nuclear weapons is your thing, web sites like www.spectre-press.com/ will sell you manuals on everything that used to be banned by the US government. Damn open sources!

What Now?

So all of this leaves the United States' critical infrastructures vulnerable to a new suite of possible terrorist attacks, against which, at this moment, we have little or no defense. The ability to build these weapons

HERF Technologies: What's Available?

	Mode	Frequency Range	Power Levels	Effects	Best Targets	Distance	Power Source	Actors
ESD	Electrostatic	Wide band.	From Doorknob discharge (microamps) to lightening bolts (hundreds of thousands of amps).	Spark, computer keyboard glitch, burn out and Integrated Circuit. Tesla coils can induce power into nearby circuits and lightbulbs.	Too random unless the target is very close with a portable ESD device.	1/2" to cloud level	Static build up	Hobbyist, harrasser.
EMP	Nuclear	Noisy RF from 100KHz to 100MHz	Terawatts	Electrical blackout; transmission line and communications failures.	Above ground explosion targeting infrastructure.	Tens of Miles	Nuclear Bomb	Nation State; Possibly Terrorists with Large $
EMP	Non-Nuclear		Multi-Gigawatts to Terawatts	Electrical blackout; transmission line and communications failures.	Above ground explosion targeting infrastructure.	Miles.	Explosively driven.	Nation State; Possibly Terrorists with Large $
NB-HPM (CW, Continuous Wave)	Narrow Band: Focused High power microwaves; single or multiple pulses.	Tunable to selected freqs from 1GHz to 100 GHz	Continuous duty cycle: 10–1000 watts.	Systems disruption to electrical burnout.	Americas, external electrical couplers. Helps to know the operating frequencies of targets to achieve better coupling and resonance.	Miles.		Requires money, skill and resources.
UWB-HPM (P-CW, PulseSwept Continuous Band)	Ultra-Wide Band.	100MHz to 30GHz, very short duration (1-2 nanosecs), very high peak power (100's of KW to 100's of GW)	Narrow frequencies are swept through the wide-band. Less power at target due to wider frequency range. Pulse repetition up to 100KHz.	Systems disruption to electrical burnout.	Used when target frequency vulnerabilities are not specifically known.	Miles.		Requires money, skill and resources.
EMI	Unintentional non-focused radiated leakage from electrical devices; computers, cell phones, video games. Etc.	Frequency varies with the device. Harmonics and complex wafeforms are common.	Low power (<.1 watt) leakage. Often in the milliwatt range.	Interference with proper operation. Can affect avionics, alarms, medical devices, pacemakers.	Unintentional radiation	Unpredic-table.	Even battery devices can be offending.	We all participate in EMI
TED	Transient Electrostatic Discharge	Non-wavelength based. Single spike of massive voltage; may be pulsed for better effects. Very wide instantaneous bandwidth.	Terawatts: 1 Million volts per meter and >	Systems disruption to electrical burnout.	Proven to work against anything electrical: cars, computers, medical devices. Ideal for infrastructure targets.	1 Km and greater as per 1/d decay.		Easiest to build by hobbyists, terrorists with minimal technology and money.
LERF	Low Energy RF, unpredictable, unreliable	Wide Spectrum, allows multiple points of entry into system: either front door or back door by various coupling and injection means.	Low	Simulates EMI; Cellular RF, Interference; Random effects on electrical components and systems.	Unshielded, commercial devices. Computers, medical, communications. Airplane avionics can be effected, too.	Unknown unpre-dictable.		Hobbyists to nation state.
Plasma Gun	Shoots Ion Stream: Recent Russian technology.	?	?	?	Power lines, transmission cables.	?	Unknown	Nation State; Possibly Terrorists with Large $

is widespread and there are no international controls over the import or export of the technology. Defensive techniques are expensive, heavy, or not yet ready for deployment. This provides a window of weakness until the US and other information-rich economies make the necessary investments to harden those computer-based assets that represent the biggest targets and whose failure could cause the most damage.

We have the brains, we have the technological insight. But do we have the political wisdom to make the investment to fix this potentially huge problem before we get fried?

▶ EMP and HERF: Fact and Fiction

- 1989: Army operations manuals from experimental backpack HERF guns provide exact specification for field use, but the units proved unreliable.
- In June, 1991, I testified about HERF Guns to a disbelieving Congress and audience who wanted to know if they should be banned—Brady Bill style.
- In 1992, I met with Dutch hackers who had built a home-brew device that was capable of crashing computers from 100 feet. Powered by wall current, the device quickly charges the ladderlike capacitor bank in the rear. A nail and screwdriver are used to discharge the spark-gap device. The original purpose of the device was to create visually exciting Christmas lights.
- In January, 1993, the *Wall Street Journal* reported that US Central Command told the Joint Chiefs of Staff that it wanted a weapon which it could detonate outside the atmosphere to completely fry enemy electronics. Only a nuclear weapon of a few tens of kilotons could accomplish that, according to military experts.

- In 1994, the first version of *Information Warfare* appeared, openly discussing HERF guns and their capabilities. In 1997, the 2nd edition appeared with greatly expanded technical details.
- In June of 1996, the London-based *Sunday Times* published incredible stories of $680 million of extortion and blackmail against dozens of financial institutions in the city. None of the allegations could be proved, and in my view are based upon rumor and bar talk.

- In 1997, rumors abounded that suitcase-sized Russian EMP bombs were hitting the arms market for $150,000 each. Allegedly, Australia, the US, and the UK have bought such devices. Despite constant replays of this story, it has never been confirmed in non-classified forums.
- In 1998, Chechnyan rebels used magnetic impulses to disable and bypass alarm systems. Vice president of the Russian Academy of Sciences Vladimir Fortov said that Chechen field commander Salman Raduyev's gang had used a device to disable the police radio communication system during its raid on Kizlyar. As a result, lack of coordination sharply decreased the effectiveness of the actions taken against it by the law enforcement bodies.
- In May, 1998, Congress' Joint Economic Committee Hearing on Terrorism and Intelligence Operations held "Radio Frequency Weapons and Proliferation: Potential Impact on the Economy" hearings.
- In February, 1999, ABC's "20/20" broadcast live demonstrations of home-brew EMP generators.
- March 1999: the US and NATO forces use EMP weapons against Serbian infrastructure.

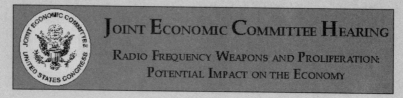

JOINT ECONOMIC COMMITTEE HEARING
RADIO FREQUENCY WEAPONS AND PROLIFERATION:
POTENTIAL IMPACT ON THE ECONOMY

Resources

For more information on DEW, EMP, HERF and other RF weapons systems.

- *Information Warfare: Chaos on the Electronic Superhighway* Winn Schwartau. ISBN 1-56025-080-1
- *Information Warfare, 2nd Edition* Winn Schwartau. ISBN 1-56025-0132-8
- www.infowar.com Do a search. This is possibly the largest single collection of unclassified data on the subject. Link from here to dozens of related sites. Do not expect to find schematics and plans to build your own weapons, though.
- "20/20" show and transcript on HERF guns and laser weapons: www.abc.com

- Sweden's efforts in HERF: www.eme.se, www.foa.se
- For Tesla and high voltage hobbyists, check out http://www.futurehorizons.net/energy/high.htm
- "The Body Electric" by Dr. Robert Becker, 1985.
- US Patent # 5,856,803, Ed Pevlar
- www.emf-emi.com Don White is one of the industries premier experts in EMI and protection mechanisms. He wrote the standard reference encyclopedia on the subject.
- www.cs.monash.edu.au/~carlo/ is the product of researcher Carlo Kopp. Many fine papers located here which include some of the art I used.
- The congressional hearings on RF weapons with links to related testimony: www.house.gov/jec/hearings/05-20-8h.html
- Testimony of former KGB Major Victor Sheymov to Congress: www.house.gov/jec/hearings/intell/sheymov.htm
- Lieutenant General Robert Schweitzer's testimony on RF weapons: www.house.gov/jec/hearings/espionag/schweitz.htm

Anti-Hacking Tips and Tricks

Want to hire a hacker to protect yourself? Is that really such a good idea? Well, you'll find out.

What else can you do to protect your computers from hackers, no matter their motivation? Security is not and never will be perfect, but there are plenty of things you can do to make a hacker's job all that much harder and make your computers a lot safer than they are today.

The good news is that a lot of these steps are non-technical. You don't have to be a techy-nerd to make your Internet experience a lot more pleasant and safe.

Hiring Hackers

Insanely Smart or Just Insane?

Everybody does it; nobody wants to talk about it. Computer hackers—"white hat" or "black hat"—are among the brightest minds in the software industry, so many are hired by big-name software companies. Then they dance the awkward dance of dual identities: engineer by day, hacker by night. The consequences of a misstep in that dance can be severe, as a hacker calling himself "VallaH" learned last week. In his case, a visit from the FBI meant the end of his career at Microsoft, embarrassment for the largest software company in the world, and a new focus on the role of hackers at work.[1]

Bob Sullivan, MSNBC
June 2, 1999

Ask yourself the following questions and answer honestly.

- If you are going to teach grade-school children about the evil of drugs, do you hire a former, supposedly reformed drug addict to educate them?
- Or do you hire a professional drug counselor and therapist?
- If you are adding an alarm system to your home or business, do you go out and hire a company because they brag about being former, but unconvicted, felons who used to rob houses to make ends meet?
- Or do you hire a nationally known firm who specializes in the alarm business?
- Do you want your New York taxi driver to have a history of outrunning the police in a high-speed six-state chase?

---

[1] www.msnbc.com/news/275876.asp

- Or do you prefer the thought of the unticketed Little Ol' Lady from Pasadena who has committed the street map to memory as the drivers have in London?
- Do convicted, paroled murderers make the best educators for self-defense courses?

In the world of intelligent contradictions, the Central Intelligence Agency will engage the services of the world's nastiest and most mean-spirited mercenaries they can find to do their dirty and "wet" work. As a reverent taxpayer and God-fearing American, taking such a route may not be your first choice. But what is the second choice? Someone kinder, gentler but useless in the realpolitik underworld of espionage, drug trafficking, and international arms trade?

So the question begs itself to be asked. Should computer hackers, of whichever definition you choose to use, be put in the front lines of defense of a company's computer networks and a country's infrastructure? Ouch, that's a tough one.

In 1990, I met Chris Goggans, aka Erik Bloodaxe, a founder of the overly infamous Legion of Doom hacking group. He was in his early twenties, skinny as a rail, dirty blond hair hanging down to his waist. Chris was notorious. After all, he and his comrades in crime had made *Newsweek*. They were Hackers for Hire. In fact, Chris was just about the first ex-hacker to come out of the scene, decry his underground past, and put his talents to work for the good guys.[2]

The scene: a perennially sphincter-tight gathering of we security professionals in a fine, upstanding Atlanta hotel, holding a fine, upstanding information security conference long before it was either chic or profitable to do so; before anyone really cared about security; long before the Internet as we know it today. Before Washington cared about protecting the nation's critical infrastructures. Before anyone believed the dire prognostications we Chicken Littles were making more than a decade ago. Before we found ourselves under the gun as we do today.

At this wonderful conference, the Hackers for Hire had, with great business acumen, bartered their appearance and speaking fees for a centrally located prime booth location at the association's exhibition. But, unlike the conventional booth bimbo blondes pitching security products of varying quality, the Hackers for Hire had plush carpet and couches

---

[2]Chris Goggans was never charged with any crime; nor was he ever prosecuted. He is a highly recognized security professional who regularly consults to governments, intelligence services, and commercial concerns.

scattered about a rented jungle of plants a la plastique. They even matched the white-male business uniform of a hangman's noose painted with red stripes and casual paisley.

But these were real, live hackers, come to a security convention to say and do . . . God knows what?

Chris was the most outspoken, and without question the best spoken of the crew who called themselves Comsec Data Security. With an air of techno-arrogance, there wasn't an ounce of product or technology in their booth. Oh no, it was devoid of anything but conversation, intrigued attendees, and skeptical exhibitors.

And then the talk got rough and tough. *What is this, hackers at a convention? Hell, they're criminals!*

The infamous Eric Bloodaxe aka Chris Goggans was a pioneer of ethical hacking. At DefCon 7.0, 1999 he impersonated Hunter S. Thompson, which actually fooled many gullible media types.

Chris and company were offering a unique service, and perhaps, depending upon whose story you believe the most, the first of its kind. They were offering hacking. That is, they wanted to hack large companies' computers and networks and the companies were to pay them for the privilege.

Now, as a modern 010100 person, this service doesn't sound so outrageous, but back then we were barely out of the self-indulgent cocaine-ridden 80s. Here was a 3-member phalanx of ex-hackers telling the information security industry that they could break into America's networks—damn—and may very well have already done so in their angst-youth past (for recreation and education only!) They were saying,

"Don't you get it? You have no security and it takes a real hacker to know how to do it. Hire us and we will shore up your defenses." This was radical thinking: try to break into a network to see how secure it is—or isn't.

Their reception at the security conference ran the gamut from pure intrigue (*I got to touch a real live hacker!*) to luke warm (*Who cares?*) to pure hatred. But you gotta give it to the hackers from Comsec Data, they stuck with it.

I got to talking to Chris and his buds and they explained that they were reformed hackers. It has been said he knew his way around the Pentagon and White House computers better than the designers themselves, but that was before conspiracy theories became Hollywood chic. However, he did know his way around networks, Unix, and phone company switches from the age of eleven.

Because the hackers-for-hire were so intriguing a presence at the security conference, the promoters put on an evening session onstage with Chris and company alongside security buff Ray Kaplan, who sympathized with their efforts. The attentive standing-room-only audience fired questions and the dais responded good-naturedly. The banter was both entertaining and informative.

About halfway through the session, a silver-maned security professional excitedly stood up in the center of the crowd, dramatically threw his arms arms in the air, and shouted, "I have had enough!" and abruptly walked out. Everyone else remained for the duration. I later asked my associate why he ran out in such a flurry, and he said to me over dinner, "I don't need hackers to help me with security. I know everything there is to know about security."

The tit-for-tat arrogance of these two extremes still rages today—and ethical hacking has become a multi-billion-dollar business.

Chris was an early and controversial proponent of ethical hacking. The problem in retrospect is clear: hacking was a relatively new, little understood phenomenon, which generated fear. Fear of the unknown. Up to that point, hackers had been relegated to the invisibility of the computer underground and occasional phone phreaking incident. The Internet was a fledgling, evolving network of networks. To use it you had to know arcane Unix commands; there was no point-and-click web yet. CompuServe was a virtually isolated dial-up network apart from the TCP/IP wonderland that was largely inhabited by academia, government, and hackers.

But times changed, slowly at first.

Fast forward to today, and what Chris and other hacker-types (remember the wide taxonomy that can be applied to hackers) proposed a decade ago is a normal way of evaluating, assessing, and measuring the effectiveness of network security.

Scanning tools and companies, such as the freeware SATAN and the publicly held ISS, among dozens of other firms are part of the arsenal of the security practitioner today. Web sites around the planet contain thousands of hacker "attack tools" that are used to break into computers. These tools form a substantial piece of how a network's security is assessed. The credo has become, "In order to know how to defend your network, you have to know how to attack it." This is no different from the millennia-old model the military has used to defend territory and national sovereignty.

After World War II, the US developed a policy in concert with our allies—and I paraphrase: *We based our defense upon our adversaries' capabilities, not their presumed intentions.* To the US military, that means having enough troops stationed in the right places in Europe in case of a Soviet incursion through Poland into Western Europe. *We really don't know exactly what the Kremlin is thinking, but we had better be prepared anyway to meet their forces and we had better be superior.*

The arms race and the concept of mutual assured destruction created a nuclear arms industry and a so-called balance of power. It was our job, through the intelligence services, to monitor and assess the capabilities of our potential adversary. We have followed a similar path in the network security world.

Very few organizations can say that they are capable of defending against the full arsenal of hacker tools or attacks. Throughout this book you have seen why, and you are learning some of the new evolving approaches to network security. But in the meantime, we have to assess our networks to determine their weaknesses and then make business decisions on which ones to repair and which ones present an acceptable risk.

The security assessment of networks is a complex task. There are many, many different approaches depending upon resources and perceived risk. The question we pose here is: Do you use hackers to assess your network or not?

I don't believe there is a yes or no answer to that. As the lines between hacker and engineer and security professional blur, we have to constantly revisit the concept of what a hacker really is and the way we deal with youthful technical excellence—even if a hacker's background is somewhat "checkered."

Microsoft hired nineteen-year-old Jeff Roberson even though he had participated in minor denial-of-service attacks against web sites. They thought his programming skills were impressive. When the FBI raided Roberson's apartment, though, Microsoft freaked and fired him.[3] That response is understandable from one perspective, but other firms handle it quite differently. Is a young private in the army who "ethically hacks" for his country any more reliable than a reformed thirty-something hacker who has learned right from wrong?

Secure Computing Corporation based its fame, fortune, and a hugely successful IPO on developing highly secretive security solutions for the National Security Agency and other defense-oriented clients. Today the company's ethical hacking division is led by Jeff Moss, once an amateur hacker and founder of the country's granddaddy of hacker conventions, DefCon.

Even the Big Five have succumbed to the technical expertise of hackers. Peter Shipley is in his early thirties, wears his wavy, pitch-black hair to his shoulders, and occasionally sports custom porcelain vampire fangs when hanging out at Goth clubs. He is a hacker. But, more importantly, he works for KPMG, LLP, a $10 billion New York-based international accounting firm. He consults with top organizations at the highest levels, working to protect them from the likes of what perhaps he once was. He is an ethical hacker, yet still participates, wearing his white hat and white fangs at www.dis.org.[4]

As one looks throughout the security business, the top notch hackers, often already in their thirties, have foresworn their past indescretions and sworn allegience to pro-security endeavors. But their past is what provides the insight that many maintain is only obtainable if you've been there, done that—hacking that is.

On the other hand, there is a legitimate concern over the use of hackers who grew up on the streets of Cyberspace, even if they do have a university pedigree. Rob Clyde, cofounder of Axent Technologies, a major security vendor, says, "Culturally there's a lack of trust when it comes to hackers."[5] Clyde cites the case of a government agency who hired a hacker to work on its systems, but then posted the weaknesses on the Internet. They don't trust hackers anymore. The FBI was burned

---

[3] www.msnbc.com/news/275876.asp

[4] Dis.Org is sometimes referred to as a "notorious hacking group." Although occasionally embroiled in the underground community and its inherent controversies, they are totally open about their activities.

[5] "Hackers for Hire," by Deborah Radcliff, *Upside Magazine*, March, 1999. www.upside.com

when it used once-arrested hackers to find other criminal hackers. They employed Justin Peterson to assist in the search for fugitive hacker Kevin Mitnick.[6]

Mobile code security company Finjan's Ron Moritz says hiring hackers is tough because of maturity problems.[7] The transition from free-spirited, anarchistic lives on the Internet to a structured program of results-oriented work is not for everyone. Part of it is merely "growing up," but ethics has a tremendous amount to do with it.

At the Federal Reserve System in New York, Shipley and Al Walker, who goes by the handle of Hobbit because he never wears shoes, impressed Paul Raines, the Reserve's VP of electronic security, with "their professionalism, detailed knowledge, and willingness to help."[8] Appearances are deceiving, (long black hair, capes, fangs, and bare feet) but Hobbit has since left the corporate world for a more technically driven life of occasional consulting in Massachusetts.

Still, many firms strongly advertise that they do not use hackers at all. Since things change so rapidly, I won't name those organizations that "absolutely will not hire hackers," because likely that will change. But the rationale is compelling as well: Simply, why take the chance?

ISS, one of the most successful Internet security companies, was founded by twenty-something Christopher Klaus, who is reputed to have his own hacking background. "We find we have more success finding people with a networking background, people who know Unix and can program in C++, then [we] train them in security. That works better than the other way around."[9] Hiring hackers that is.

However, many ISS employees *are* ex-hackers, hired for their dedication and skill. On a per-capita basis, ISS may have more hackers than any other firm, but then, what is a hacker? Chris Rouland is the director of X-Force, ISS's vulnerabilities data base service. In his past, he was known as Mr. Fusion and was picked up for hacking his way into the Pentagon.

In his August, 1990 tangle with the law, he was debriefed by the US Air Force Office of Special Investigations on his hacking activities by OSI cyber-cop Jim Christy. But is that all bad? Law enforcement's Operation Sun Devil, in the early 1990s, was an historically laughable sweep-

---

[6]http://www.zdnet.com/zdtv/cybercrime/features/story/0,3700,2175248,00.html
[7]"Hackers for Hire," by Deborah Radcliff, *Upside Magazine*, March, 1999. www.upside.com
[8]ibid.
[9]www.msnbc.com/news/275876.asp

ing series of raids that served no more than to embarrass the government. As of mid-1999, ISS has staff hackers from such groups as Root, Lock, Hagus, and 8LGM. They are ethical hackers, too, working to improve the security of the Internet, governments, and corporations everywhere.

A colorful IBM ad invites magazine readers to look deeper, beyond the attractive if somewhat butch female who dominates the page. The ad's model, the advertisement proclaims, is a hacker. But she's a good one who works for IBM. The ad encourages the reader to hire IBM to examine his or her networks to protect it from hackers.

So, do you hire a hacker or not?

Organizations are beginning to realize that hiring hackers is becoming indistinguishable from hiring hacker skills. The clean-cut kid from Cornell University versus the scrungy Unix-geek. What makes the difference? Here are some thoughts to ponder.

1. How do you know the clean-cut kid with excellent programming skills really is not "Demented Mindset," who hacked the Pentagon three months ago, before he cut his hair and bought a suit? University students, especially those in computer science, have in all likelihood hacked somebody, something, somewhere. It would be odd indeed if they hadn't. The temptation is just too great for a budding teenage code-meister not to try his hand at it.

2. Did you ask the applicant if he hacked? What did he hack? How honest and sincere does he seem to be?

3. Have you run a criminal background check on the applicant? In security-sensitive positions, this is a reasonable step to take. Security companies must provide insurance to their clients, so minimizing risk is a good thing. ISS, to name one, runs background checks on their potential hires. However, realize that since so few hackers (of any type) actually get caught, not having a criminal background is not a true bellwether of what you're buying.

4. Many firms will hire their ethical hackers from the military, under the belief that the stringent training, security clearances, and experience has prepared them for a life in the corporate structure. The biggest problem here might not be their hacker ethic; it might be their work ethic. The private sector is a lot more demanding than the military on a day-to-day basis.

5. Have you run any psychological profiles? Talk to your human resources department and see if they can develop a relationship with one of the many psychological and industrial profiling firms around the country. You should be interested in their motivations, their hopes, and their reactions to proposed situations. Aptitude tests may add a great deal of knowledge to an applicant's obvious technical skills.

6. Does the corporate-bred ethical hacker, or the computer science major who may have delved into hacking in the most casual way, really have the mindset of hackers raised on the Internet? Do they have the same initiative and fundamental techno-drive, or is it merely a job? The difference in results can be substantial—with perhaps additional risk.

When hiring technical people for an ethical hacking position or systems administration role, or even a programming job, the approach is not all that much different than with non-technical people: You want and need to trust them. The big challenge is, though, that you place much of the successful operation of your company within the hands of a relatively small number of highly skilled technical people, who, by their very definition, dance to a different tune.

Sales types want tons of money. Executives on the rise are driven in large part by power. Hacker-types are driven by technology. And for most people that is a very tough concept to understand.

In the meantime, one of the renaissance men who risked a lot to kick the concept of ethical hacking into the mainstream, Chris Goggans himself, runs a successful security company in the Washington DC area.[10]

If my predictions are at all correct, within the next four to six years, every technical worker in America under the age of thirty-five will have hacked at one point in his life. When Robert Bork, the brilliant legal theorist admitted, during his Senate confirmation hearings for a seat on the US Supreme Court, that he smoked marijuana in his youth, he was virtually dismissed on the spot. Are we going to do the same to our brilliant technical youth?

For the sake of security everywhere, I certainly hope not. We can't afford to.

---

[10]www.sdii.com

Resources

- Search on "Security Consulting," "Penetration Testing," "Security Assessment," "Security Audits," and "Ethical Hacking."
- Check out the Big Five consulting firms. They all have security assessment groups.
- IBM, Sun Microsystems, Compaq/DEC, and most major firms have their own security consulting groups, too.

Security Consulting Companies

(Not recommendations. Just a list.)

- Associated Corporate Consultants http://www.accusa.com
- Booz-Allen and Hamilton http://www.bah.com
- Computer Consulting Associates International, Inc. http://www.ccaii.com/
- Computer Security Consultants, Inc. http://www.csciweb.com
- Computer Security Institute http://www.gocsi.com/
- Computer Security Ltd. http://www.comsecltd.com/
- EMPE http://www.empe.com/it_serv_fs.html
- Ernst&Young http://www.ey.com/aabs/isaas/ss.asp
- Infosecure Australia http://www.infosecure.com.au/
- KPMG http://www.us.kpmg.com/irm/
- SRI Comsulting http://www.sriconsulting.com/
- P&E Security Consultants http://www.p-and-e.com/
- Pricewaterhouse Coopers http://www.pwcglobal.com/
- Science Applications International Corporation http://www.saic.com
- Security Design International, Inc. http://www.sdii.com
- The Institute of Electrical and Electronics Engineers, Inc. http://www.ieee.org
- The Security Experts 727.393.6600
- Wolf Consultancy http://www.wolfconsultancy.com/home.html

Catching Hackers

Catching hackers is one of the hardest things I can think of—no matter what their motivation. You've seen a lot of the tricks they use. You've also seen that the number of hackers caught and prosecuted is fairly low, for many reasons:

- Companies are more interested in keeping their businesses running than making headlines with negative PR implications.
- Putting fourteen-year-olds in jail is not the American way.
- Law enforcement resources are thin. They pick the cream of the crop of computer crimes to pursue, i.e., those with a decent chance of successful prosecution and perhaps politically valuable headlines.

But how are hackers actually caught? Let's first look at the physical world. A thief is caught in one of two ways:

1. The victim discovers the crime after the fact, calls the police, and they investigate. The thief left telltale clues which lead to his capture.

2. The thief is caught in the act of the crime. Perhaps someone sees him and calls the police. Or perhaps an alarm goes off and the cops come.

Example 1 above is the most common. Millions of physical crimes are committed every year in the US. We have a huge prison population, crime is down, yet crime sprees never seem to end.

Cyber-crimes are on the increase like never before, the costs to industry and government are escalating, and the vast majority are detected (if at all) after the fact. Then, if the police see fit, a forensics examination is performed in the hopes of identifying the bad guys and maybe nabbing them.

The reason for this approach is that organizations protect themselves with a military concept thousands of years old—fortress mentality. Consider the historical basis:

- The walls of Troy stood strong against the Greeks until they let their guard down and grabbed the big wooden horse as the spoils of victory. The rest is history (or myth).
- The Great Wall of China was designed to keep out marauding northern Mongols but was militarily insignificant. Advanced technologies like the catapult and battering ram were developed. The most effective weapon against the Great Wall, though, was bribery of guards: "Here, take the money and run or we'll kill you." Insider jobs.
- Middle Age castles and moats epitomized fortress mentality for centuries. Boiling oil was a good defense for close-up invaders, and most of the brutal conflict from this era was indeed up close and personal.
- Trench warfare of World War I resulted in the death of millions. So much for effective defense.
- After World War I, the French said, "Never again!" They built the Maginot line to keep the Germans from entering France ever, ever again. What did the Germans do instead? They went around it.
- The Berlin Wall. Balloons flew over it, tunnels were dug underneath it, and most escapees went around it.
- Iraq even used fortress mentality during the Gulf War. They dug into the sand, we bombed the helpless Iraqi troops for six devastating weeks, and then we brought in bulldozers to pile sand on those who hadn't surrendered.

Fortress mentality has not been the most successful strategy in history, yet that is the approach has been the basis of computer security for thirty years: Keep the Bad Guys Out. We use firewalls and IP-blocked routers and passwords and other access-control devices to keep the bad guys out. Right?

However, in the ecommerce-driven world of business and the web, do we really want to keep the bad guys out of the networks and web sites? How can we tell the difference between good guys and bad guys? Stores on Main Street let anyone in and, yes, there is an occasional robbery. Same thing in Cyberspace. In order to do business you have to let people inside your networks. So how do you keep the bad guys from trashing your networks and business? The traditional fortress mentality approach to information security does not work for many, many reasons, the most basic of which is we cannot place implicit faith in the protective products that organizations buy to defend networks.

- We cannot measure the efficacy of protective systems—yet. Vendors do not guarantee their products nor do they provide a measurement of how secure they are.
- Networks grow every day, thus their security needs change constantly.
- Administrators have a difficult time knowing every single point of entry into a network. Modems, PC Anywhere, unknown phone lines, and secret subnets plague organizations.
- Connecting networks to partner organizations with unknown security can weaken a company's defensive strength.
- Seemingly harmless applications often innocently create security vulnerabilities.
- New hacks appear daily against leading applications, operating systems, and security mechanisms. Organizations have a terribly difficult time keeping up with every new one.
- Vendors do not respond quickly to security weaknesses in their products.
- It takes time and effort to install new patches to enhance security, and they don't always work.
- Well-designed security mechanisms are all too often installed incorrectly and/or completely misconfigured.
- Administrators often turn off security controls during audits and maintenance and forget to turn them back on.
- You can't adequately test the protective value of a network with any degree of assurance beyond the exact moment it was tested.

Seems hopeless. But it's not.

Intrusion Detection

Imagine that stores used a magic device that could tell if a customer was a bad guy or not. That would be pretty cool, huh? Airports use metal detectors, as do more and more schools, to filter out the really bad things, but not every bad thing.[11] Guns, no. Hairbrushes and nail files, yes.

What if we applied that same principle to networks? We finally do, with many companies making products to detect the bad guys. The first line of defense is the network perimeter, generally the connection to the Internet. An IDS (Intrusion Detection System) will examine traffic coming in from the Internet and look for bad behavior. An IDS will detect hacking attempts, network scans, pings, password-cracking attempts, and an ever-increasing list of bad guy stuff. The technology to do this is fairly prevalent, but certainly not in use everywhere.

Take a look at the following pictures to see what one of the newest intrusion detection companies, Network ICE, Inc., is offering.

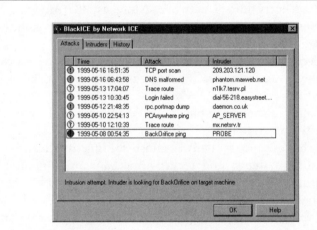

The BlackICE intrusion detection product looks at incoming Internet traffic, determines what is and what is not an attack, and attempts to identify the source. Of course the source could be spoofed, or merely an electronic staging platform for the attacker who is really somewhere else, in a galaxy, far, far away.

So, let's say for the moment that we have the perfect Internet-based IDS (which doesn't exist, of course); does that solve all of our problems?

---

[11]For those of you old enough to remember, the 1960s and early 1970s were plagued with airplane hijackings, especially to Cuba. No more.

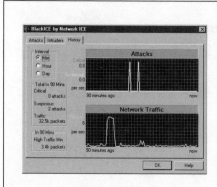

BlackICE examines network behavior over time and provides easy-to-understand graphics for rapid analysis.

In combination with the defensive firewalllike products it is an improvement, but what about insiders who are still responsible for the majority of computer crime?

Detecting Internet behavior is not nearly enough because so many insider-based crimes do not involve the Internet at all.

Maintaining modern networks in large organizations of thousands of users requires constant vigilance just to keep things working, not to mention secure. But there are many more means of detection available.

Question: How did the media know the exact night we were going to start the bombing campaign against Iraq? No, not insider leaks or reports. No, not interception of military communications.

Answer: Pizza trucks. When the Pentagon parking lot is crammed full of hundreds of Pizza Hut and Domino's deliveries late in the afternoon and at night, it is a safe assumption something is afoot. Voilà—le bombing begins.

This approach is called *traffic analysis*.

On the network level, it's about the same. Say a network usually operates using only 30 percent of its capacity with occasional bursts to 85 percent. Then one night, the network is super busy, maybe sitting at 72 percent utilization for hours on end. If it were my company, I would like to know what the heck was going on. Wouldn't you? If Bob and Alice never talk to each other within the company network, yet over a one-week period they suddenly exchange forty-eight emails, something has changed. If John's profile says he rarely uses the Internet, but he suddenly is sending large amounts of data to SpiesRUs.com.cn (cn = china), as a manager I would quickly become suspicious.

In all of these cases, the suspicion is raised by behavior detected through traffic analysis, not the actual contents of the communications. Traffic analysis tools make an ideal detection mechanism if the expected

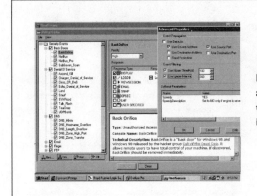

Internet Security Systems Real Secure analyzes network weaknesses. Note the specific attacks it looks for, including denial of service.

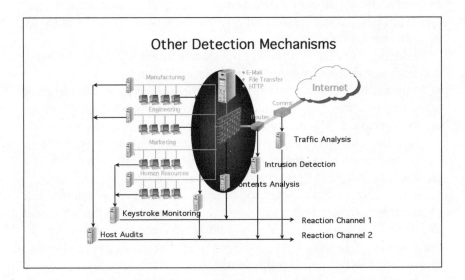

baseline behavior is reasonably set. Management must be ready to react quickly, though, to minimize damage.

Event/User Monitoring

Detection devices can be added at more nodes in a network to improve security, such as with personal firewalls at the desktop or smaller "regional" and departmental IDS systems tailored to detect internal security violations. Monitoring decentralized nodal system activity can provide massive amounts of information to establish norms, trends, and systemic errors when the sampling is sufficient. It can also tell an administrator how often a floppy disk is used, for both reading and writing data.[12]

Keystroke Monitoring

If you can detect, store and analyze every single keystroke made at every single terminal in an organization, a tremendous amount of information is gathered, not only with a security view, but also from a productivity standpoint.

With the ability to track keystrokes at nodal terminals, individual efficiency and work output can be measured, assessed, and compared to other workers in similar positions. AND you can see that Bob is emailing Boris and Natasha, negotiating the price for your company's proprietary information.

However, be very careful with implementing such mechanisms without the advice of human relations and legal counsel. The US Justice Department has legal views that need to be considered, and states have their own interpretations, which do not always favor a company's belief that it can control or monitor its own networks any way it sees fit.

Collecting profiles and signatures of behavior and keystroke sequences creates a foundation for a detection mechanism aimed at insiders.

Contents Analysis

What if your company could intercept all data transmissions prior to arrival at their destinations? All traffic coming inside, going outside, and all internal traffic would be analyzed for contraband data (that the company or government organization determines is contraband), and then stop it. The problems to be surmounted are immense: How can vast amounts of traffic be halted, detoured to an analysis server of some sort, and then acted upon without causing severe traffic delays?

We will get there one day, but now we are in the infancy of such technology, with contents algorithms having marginal successes in English, much less other languages.[13] At a simpler level, the detection system could recognize encrypted messages and the company could choose not to permit their transmission. At the web server, a detection system, similar to Net-Nanny-like products, could look for objectionable content based upon key words.

---

[12]In my humble opinion, floppy disks represent a huge security threat.
[13]Ways to get around any contents analysis include steganography. When such capabilities become commonplace, an organization could choose to ban all video material until solutions are found.

Host Analysis

The better software today offers a tool called "auditing" or "logging" that captures the important things that a user does during the day. At the host computer, such as a server or a mainframe or a large data base, such logs can be used to look for unacceptable behavior on the part of insiders or, perhaps, an outsider who cracked into the company network.

The data from the host audit trails must be combined with other audit information from other hosts and IDS systems for high-speed analysis.

Putting It All Together

There are many places within a network to put IDS-style products and tools, but, unless someone looks at all of the data collected, what the heck good is it?

At a presentation to a major government agency, the lead administrator told me that they had good security. They looked at their audit trails at least once a month. Jeeez! What are they doing? What's the point? Yes, there can be an immense amount of information generated by IDS and audit trails, but new tools are being developed to examine the contents of the files for user-definable "out of bounds behavior."

Part Two: React

OK, so you now have the perfect (or acceptable) detection system. What do you do about it when the IDS detects anomalous behavior indicating a bad guy is coming or is operating from inside the company? This is called reaction. The company's options are many and varied:

- Do nothing
- Watch to see what else he does
- Attempt to trace him
- Shut down his connection
- Call the police
- Hand it to the lawyers

But the most important question is: How fast do you react? How fast do you want to stop what the bad guy is doing? In my last book, *Time*

Based Security, a series of simple formulas provide a method to look at network security.[14] The premise is simple:

1. We don't know how secure our protective devices are, so let's not count on them exclusively. Let's add in-depth defense, which entails more than one defensive security approach. Banks have alarms and thick walls and great alien-metal vaults.

2. The detection mechanism must be very, very fast. Network attacks often take place in much less than one second.

3. Once the bad guy has been detected, do something about it as fast as possible. The longer we let the bad guy hang out in our networks, the more damage he can do.

So, the detection time, "D," and the reaction time, "R," determine how secure a network is, by determining the worst case scenario if a hacker breaks in because the fortress mentality defense completely fails. How much damage can a hacker do to a network in one hour? Generally a whole lot. How about ten minutes? What about ten seconds? See how it works?

The key to time-based security is speed of detection and speed of reaction, but what is the right reaction? I have sat in organizations which are under attack by outside and inside forces and watched them flounder as to what to do. The lawyers and the public relations people are the cautious ones and the security people want heads to roll! How do you resolve contentiousness with effective security? By developing a *reaction matrix.*

A reaction matrix is nothing more than a set of preplanned contingencies for if and when cyber-events or attacks come your way. Most companies' disaster recovery and business continuity department does an excellent job of keeping systems up and running because they *plan* for the hurricane, the fire, and the black-out. They know exactly what to do. But what about hacker attacks?

Note that reactions can take two forms: automatic and manual. If human intervention is required, your reaction time will go through the roof and not help. There are too many times that a human is an hour or a weekend away from being able to react to a detected attack. Auto-

---

[14]For a complete examination of the subject, read *Time Based Security*, 1999, ISBN 0-9628-8700-4-8. The math is really simple and the model elicits an "Aha! I get it!" once you work through the process.

Implementing A Reaction Matrix

Reaction Matrix		Desired Time	Measured Time
Detected Event (Anomaly)	Chosen Reaction		
3 Bad Password Attempts	Log and Notify Admin	1 sec	2.4 secs
3 Bad Password Attempts	Turn off Account/Notify Admin	1 sec	.94 secs
Mulitple Port Scan	Initiate Trace Route	250ms	1.5 secs
Internal User - Audit Bahavior #1	Involve HR Immediately		
Ping of Death	Kill the Bastard :-)		
Syn-Ack Attack	Reaction # 23		
Mail Bombs	Reaction # 81		
Firewall Breach Attempt	Autofilter Source	100ms	2.7 secs
Traffic 2X Anticipated	Log and Notify Admin		
Multiple Site Attack	Shut Down Network	3 secs	2 Days
Shut Down $ Server	Isolate Network	1 min	2.4 hours

In the above example, a set of possible attacks is chosen and the reaction is predetermined by company policy. Thus, when a hacker attack comes along, the reaction time can be sped up significantly, reducing the potential for damage to the network and the company.

matic reactions to intrusions are becoming more popular, (e.g. some firewall Strikeback mechanisms and the increase in corporate vigilantism).

But ultimately we're back to policy, as with all information security efforts.

One of the things that time-based security offers an organization is a means to quantify the possible damage. Of course the organization has to know what information resources it has and which ones are really, really valuable and need more protection. It also needs to know where the information resides; on which computer in which building in which city. Some idea of how long it would take the bad guys to cause hurt is important. Then, the auditors and bean-counters need to get involved and come up with values of the information based upon the damage its loss, modification, or public disclosure could cause.

What we end up finding with time-based security and enhanced detection and reaction mechanisms is a new way to look at security. Many of the security vendors out there would have you believe that if you buy their products all of your problems will be over. No way. There is a lot more to do long before buying a protection product. Try this approach instead:

- Policy: All the policy in the world is mere lip service unless you are willing to sell it and achieve agreement with staff.

Then you have to be willing to enforce it with whatever penalties you have instituted.

- Measure the amount of time it takes to detect bad guys doing bad guy things. (D)
- Measure the amount of time it takes to react to the detected intrusion, whether it is automatic or manual. (R)
- Evaluate the worst case exposure to your network in terms of exposure time: How long can the hackers do their thing in your network before you do something about it? (E = D + R). "E" (exposure) is measured in time, too.
- Classify your data and information resources as to its criticality to the ongoing operation of your organization.
- The financial folks need to assay the value of your company assets in terms of dollars, lost business, opportunity, public relations, lives, or national force projection.
- Perhaps you need to move or isolate assets to make protecting them easier.
- Now that you know something about your exposure and your networks, it is the right time to choose appropriate protection products.
- Lastly, maintain a high level of vigilance. Test, measure, and monitor network performance and your detection and reaction mechanisms. An alarm is no good if it doesn't go off, and a back-up generator is no use if it doesn't turn on.

Corporate and infrastructure network defense is getting harder all the time. But with novel approaches, we do stand a chance of effectively shoring up our protective shells.

Think out of the box.

Do not get stuck with old methods.

Never assume.

Try it. If it doesn't work, try something else.

The only constant we face is change.

Resources

- Search on "Intrusion Detection" and you will find a number of other companies and techniques to detect the bad guys.
- www.nai.com
- www.axent.com
- www.iss.net

Defensive Hacking

Firewalls

In 1994, I was consulting to Secure Computing Corporation, a Minnesota-based security company whose primary customer was the National Security Agency. They were trying to "go commercial," which meant they were worried about the post-Cold-War military downsizing and budget decreases. In addition, the Internet was taking off and the migration of classified security technology to the wildly growing private sector made good business sense.

The company had developed some significant technology under the leadership of Kermit Beseke, the man who also developed the STU-III program for Motorola.[15] He had recruited me to help make the technical translations from the land of spooks and migrate the company's technology to the private sector where they saw great hope and promise: Translation, lots of money.

One of the products they had developed for the Department of Defense was called the SNS, or secure network server. It was one of the first servers designed to allow secret and top secret networks to connect directly to the Internet or other unclassified networks within the military; an early type of firewall.

The principle of using firewalls comes from the physical world. In modern buildings, some doors are built to withstand very high temperatures for extended periods of time. The purpose is to prevent the fire

---

[15]The Secure Telephone Unit III was one of the most successful security-oriented programs ever managed by the US Government. It resulted in billions in sales and a standard for secure voice transmission.

from spreading rapidly and causing further damage. Hopefully the fire department will show up in time and put out the fire. If the firewall holds and contains the fire in a specific location, and damage is limited, everyone is happy.

And so it is with the Internet and internetworking, a fancy term that merely means connecting networks together. If someone succeeds in breaking into a portion of a network, a firewall will hopefully prevent him from breaking into other portions of the larger network.(Fortress mentality.) In big corporations, there are dozens or hundreds of small networks that may be organized by location (New York office, London office, or thirty-second floor versus twenty-first floor of a tall building) or by function (engineering, payroll, sales, etc.). The internal network of networks is called the corporate *Intranet,* and each of the various areas want to communicate with each other, but only in good ways—not bad ways, such as hacking. Thus, placing multiple firewalls within a large company is a standard and powerful technique to isolate and protect critical resources.

Since their arrival in the 1994 time frame, the market for these devices has grown famously: from $145 million in sales in 1996, to almost $1 billion in 1999, and a projected $1.845 billion in 2002.[16]

At the same time, more is demanded of firewalls, as network traffic and functions seem never to stop increasing. Firewalls should:

1. Keep internal network users from surfing to certain web sites.
2. Protect the perimeter of a network by not permitting entry of unauthorized people on the Internet.
3. Regulate incoming email.
4. Control outgoing email.
5. Log all systems activities; who does what and where they do it.
6. Permit/deny video conferencing and audio/video streams.
7. Block or allow Usenet news groups.
8. Provide user authentication including passwords, tokens, and biometric devices.
9. Use encryption for virtual private networks.
10. Control ftp accesses.
11. Examine and filter the contents of incoming and outgoing traffic.

---

[16]"Firewalls: Are we Asking Too Much", Frederick Avolio, *Information Security Magazine*, May 1999, references IDC for the figures.

12. Hide the real internal identity of a user to outside viewers.
13. Respond to hacker attacks. (Time-based security premises.)

The list goes on as the concept of controlled gateway for the myriad needs of a large organization increases. Additional functionality at the gateway is demanded so the firewall nexus can act as a business enabling tool. But corporate users want minimal intrusion on what they are allowed to do, while the security concerns lean towards increased controls and limitation of services.

Diametrically opposed goals.

Security, especially at the firewall nexus of a network, is no longer unidirectional; it is highly symmetric. Inside users need to get to the Net to do their job. Insiders may be on the road or work from home and need to get into the company network. Business partners need access to some but not all resources, as do consultants. Who is allowed to send what to the Internet and who is allowed to bring what kinds of files into the company network?

The management of firewall access controls is a complex task, requiring constant vigilance and maintenance, underscoring the fact that poor administration is the single worst enemy of the firewall. Keeping up with all the daily changes within the company and all the external threats makes this one tough job.

The complexity of modern networks places a terrible strain on firewalls, which also potentially represent a single point of failure. If a company has a network with a single Internet-based connection, a firewall is a needed tool. But it also represents the one place that, if broken through either by hacking or by misconfiguration, can compromise the entire network. This supports the argument to place many firewalls within a company in the hopes of making the bad guys' jobs all that much harder—all the while increasing the complexity of security and firewall management. (Defense in depth.)

The operation and configuration of firewalls is way beyond the scope of this book, but I've asked Secure Computing to provide a few pictures of Sidewinder, their strong firewall, to demonstrate the areas that must be managed.

Firewalls are not perfect. New versions from dozens of vendors appear constantly, and occasionally some accidentally contain errors that create security risks. New users come onto the network, other employees leave the firm. Some departments want certain Internet access that other departments don't. Keeping up with the task is daunting, and developers are adding new and stronger controls to meet their needs.

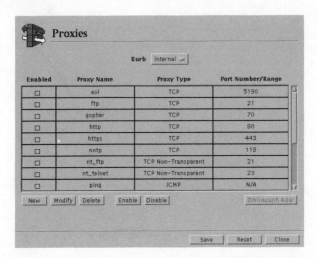

Proxies: Sidewinder provides a variety of proxies for controlling connections to popular Internet services. A proxy is like letting someone else vote for you in an election. In a firewall, the proxy hides the real identity of services from an external or internal user. The most popular proxies in the Sidewinder are preconfigured to use standard port numbers. This screen shows how the Sidewinder proxies are initially set up and can be quickly enabled.

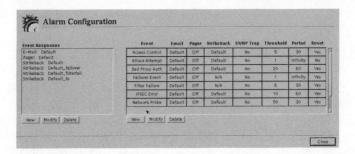

Alarms: If a firewall detects behavior that the administrator does not want to occur, he should be notified in some way so he can take appropriate defensive action. The firewall audit trails log all events. This screen shows how an administrator can configure audit events to trigger an alarm and what should happen when an alarm occurs. The configuration options depend mainly on a site's security policy and to some extent on a customer's own experiences using the options.

Strikeback Information

Strikeback Name

Mail Audit before
Strikeback To:

Mail Strikeback
Results To:

Print Results of
Strikeback To:

Strikeback Commands to Perform

☐ dig   ☐ finger   ☐ traceroute

☐ ping   ☐ whois   ☐ nslookup

[Save]   [Reset]   [Close]

Strikeback: Sidewinder was the first firewall to employ the concept of "strike back" at the intruder. [17] Rather than just sit back and absorb hacking attacks, the idea is to get proactive and attempt to thwart the attacks. The Sidewinder strike back option allows the administrator to automatically institute a "ping" to the attacking site, or begin a "traceroute" or "whois" to see if the attacker can be identified.[18] Secure Computing says that their customers have successfully used Sidewinder's Strikeback capability to gather information for legal action against competitors.

----

[17]See the chapter on vigilantism for more about "strike back."
[18]Visit http://www.securecomputing.com/ for complete descriptions. This is not an endorsement of their products or services. It is used for example only.

Personal Firewalls

Traditionally, firewalls are seen as protection for corporate networks from inappropriate behavior and actions taken by rebels on the Internet, or as a control for corporate users' actions on the Net. Intranet firewalls isolate corporate networks from one another according to prescribed policy.

But what about the small business that runs a small office network and is connected to the Internet? Or the home business, which is also connected to the Internet through a cable modem? And in a corporate environment, what about security at the desktop itself?

Signal 9 Solutions, based in Ontario, Canada, is one company that has introduced a firewall-like software product that adds network protection at the desktop. They claim the product summarily dismisses denial-of-service attacks, which would be a boon not only for companies whose only security concern is keeping their web servers up and running, but also for extraneous internal "accidents" and Extranet security problems.[19]

As a personal firewall, ConSeal works to protect the small LAN and individual computer from attacks, especially over cable modems, which offer fabulous, inexpensive bandwidth—but not an ounce of security. Anyone sharing your local cable-modem loop can search your desktop contents—without your knowledge.[20] You're all on the same network! So, a "down and dirty" firewall is a critical addition to restrict access and myriad unwanted security breaches.

And then there's the true Wild West of the Internet: Internet relay chat (IRC). IRC is often like descending into Dante's Inferno. Slam! Blam! Nuke! And you're sent careening off the channel; or even worse, your entire PC needs a reboot.

I believe that the security market for large corporations is a prelude

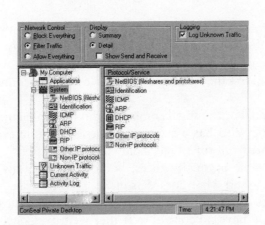

ConSeal works to protect computers from behavior that is not explicitly permitted over a wide range of network services. Logs maintain histories of what the computer is doing and what someone from the outside is trying to do to you. At the simplest level, users can choose which applications they will allow to operate on the Internet.

---

[19]www.signal9.com

[20]You really should look at your File Sharing on Windows-9x and NT computers. If File Sharing is permitted, your files are wide open.

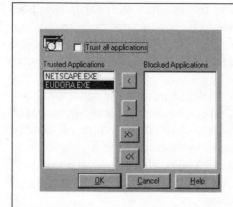

In the above example, only Netscape (web surfing) and email are permitted. Thus, if you get infected with an email Trojan Horse such as Back Orifice, ConSeal will notice that an unapproved application is trying to communicate with the Internet and stop it, letting you know through an alarm.

to the kind of security we will be seeing in the home and in small businesses as the connectivity increases. That's probably where the money will be in the early 2000s.

Shields Up! Testing Your Own Security

If you work for yourself or own your company you really need to read this chapter. If you work for a big company, I am so sorry . . . but this chapter can really help you and your sweet employer as well.

How do you test the security of your own Internet connections? Well, here goes!

The individual or the small company who uses cable modems or high speed DSL lines also has a few more worries than he ever did before. Inexpensive near full-time high bandwidth connections to the Internet are now available at small offices, homes and certainly to corporate branch offices. And what does that mean, security-wise? It means that the extremities of your network are now connected to the Internet up to 24 x 7, yet you nave no control over that security. Corporate information is stored on distant out-of-sight laptops, home-based desktops and satellite offices that might not be considered worthy of "real" firewall protection.

Cable modems and DSL lines add bandwidth and performance for home, small business or the remote user; a good thing. But remember that enhanced speed and functionality usually means a security risk. Connecting a single PC to the Internet over the new high-speed lines means that you may be exposing your sensitive or proprietary corporate information for anyone else to scan and/or steal at will.

Until 9 October, 1999 there wasn't much that you could do.

   That weekend, the Gibson Research Corporation put up what I consider to be one of the most useful (and free!) security web sites I have encountered. Whether it's from home or from the office, this site can really improve your security posture in seconds. Try it. You'll like it. I mean, you'll really, really like it. For you home users, it will give you an up front in-your-face education as to what security for you really means.

   When you first go to www.grc.com, click on "Shields Up" and wait a few seconds. Depending upon how well protected your Internet connection computer is, you will receive one of two messages:

>   GREETINGS (YOUR COMPUTER NAME!)
>   or
>   GREETINGS!

   In the first case, your computer (or server) is broadcasting its name to the Internet. In the second, you are not saying a word about your identity. Which would you prefer? You are then invited to test the security of your Internet connection by pressing the "Test My Shields" button.

```
Sheilds UP! is checking YOUR computer's Internet connection
security . . . currently located at IP:

11.11.111.111. (Your IP address)

Please Stand By . . .

Attempting connection to your computer . . .
```

   In a few seconds you will receive a report. In some cases, especially if you have your (Windows based) TCP/IP bindings for Print and File Sharing set wrong, you will see a logical map of your computer including all of its resources. If the GRC site can do this in seconds, so can any hacker—and you do not want that, do you? But it doesn't stop there. If you receive a "bad grade," Shields UP! makes recommendations to improve your Internet security.

   The step by step instructions are most impressive and are written for the average Joe or Rosie to follow. After a bit of tweaking, which can be performed in just a few minutes, reboot and rerun the same test. The Shields UP! response you hope to see is:

```
Unable to connect to your computer.
All attempts to get any information from your computer have
```

FAILED. (This is very uncommon for a Windows networking-based
PC.) Relative to vulnerabilities from Windows networking, this
computer appears to be VERY SECURE since it is NOT exposing ANY
of its internal NetBIOS networking protocol over the Internet.

Shields UP! will also perform Evil Port Monitor tests that will (benignly)
scan the common ports of your computer to determine their status and
give you advice on what to do if security vulnerabilities are detected.
Even the casual information worker will be able to follow the well-doc-
umented step by step instructions.

Millions of CyberShock readers have no clue as to how exposed their
computer is when it is connected to the Internet. There is no more
excuse, people! Head on down to the GRC web site, spend the few minutes it will take and tune up the security of your computer.

Oh, yes, the entire service is automatic, free, and they do not save any
information about you or your machines. www.grc.com

GO!

Resources

- The original definitive book on the subject is *Firewalls and
  Internet Security* by William Cheswick and Steven
  Bellovin. Addison-Wesley, ISBN 0-201-63357-4. Much is
  technical, but the front of the book is easily understandable by the lay person.
- Search "Firewalls," "Desktop Firewalls," and "Personal
  Firewalls," and you will find a lot more than you ever
  wanted to know and a list of products.
- "Firewalls: Are we Asking Too Much," Frederick Avolio,
  Information Security Magazine, May 1999. Examines how
  much demand we are putting on firewalls within the network. A good reference article.
- http://www.freegate.com/products/onegate150.html gives
  details on OneGate 150, a SOHO firewall. Also check out
- www.symantec.com for AtGuard, another personal firewall.
- www.sybergen.com—syshield personal firewall built into
  Norton Internet Security 2000.
- www.networkice.com—BlackICE Defender
- www.grc.com has the best—and free—site to check on
  your own personal computer security for modems, cable
  modems, etc. ShieldsUp! is fantastic.

- http://www.esoft.com/index.htm offers small office firewalls, too.

There are plenty of vendors of firewalls and VPNs. Here is a small sampling. Just search on "Firewalls" or "VPN" and you will turn up dozens more.

- Checkpoint Software Technologies, Inc. www.checkpoint.com
- Cisco Systems, Inc. www.cisco.com
- Axent www.axent.com
- Computer Associates, Inc. www.cai.com
- Lucent Technologies, Inc. www.lucent.com/security
- Secure Computing, Inc. www.securecomputing.com
- Cyberguard Corporation www.cyberguardcorp.com
- 3Com Corporation www.3com/com
- Ascend Communications, Inc. www.ascend.com
- Elron Software, Inc. www.elronsoftware.com
- Signal9 Technologies www.signal9.com
- Agis www.agis.net
- Assured Digital, Inc. www.assured-digital.com
- Aventail Corp. www.aventail.com
- Data Fellows www.datafellows.com
- Trusted Information Systems www.tis.com (now a part of Network Associates www.nai.com)
- Sun Microsystems www.sun.com

Corporate
Anti-Hacking

It Ain't the Technology

Fighting hackers is tough. Really tough. An entire industry has been built around technology to make strong passwords, robust firewalls, unbreakable encryption, and many of the techniques you have read about in this book. If you want to find the best resources on anti-hacking techniques, follow the links that we provide, and you will be on the road to finding gazillions of products and papers and opinions on what the best technology is, how it is best used, and how it can be best maintained.

But corporate security is *not* only about technology. It's about letting a business do its job unhindered and without interruption. Any interruption of a business' day-to-day operation costs the company money, and then investors get mad. All businesses work on a cycle:

1. Idea
2. Market research
3. Decision making
4. Production
5. Sales and marketing
6. Customer feedback (market research)
7. Back to #1

It's a never-ending redundancy that is supposed to create growth and profit. If there was a way to stop hacking without advanced technology we would all certainly love to try it. But the fact is that between 60 to 80 percent of computer crime occurs by, or with the help of, insiders. Insiders who were thought to be trusted. Disgruntled employees.[21]

For example, in San Mateo, California, Paul Schmidt was fired from his job in the District Attorney's Family Support Division. Schmidt planted a malicious software program into a computer that would make it appear that his boss crashed the system, when according to investigators, Schmidt really did it. Motive? Schmidt wanted his boss's job. One large financial company found a security administrator hacking other companies, although the reason was never determined. The Citibank theft was done with the help of insiders. Cases like this are increasingly common despite the desire to trust employees. Companies are being overwhelmed with inherent distrust, especially of technical staff who are given free reign and power.

And there are plenty more; hundreds of cases every year.[22]

- A former senior Intergraph employee planted a virus in the emergency network's computer system as revenge over a pay dispute. Ya Ge (Jacob) Xu, 33, of Mentone, was fined six thousand dollars without conviction for hacking into the system from his home, causing employees' files to be deleted from their hard-disk drive when they logged on to the network.
- An information technology manager fired from a manufacturing firm took a computer copy of a customer master file and sold it to a major competitor.
- A banking industry worker systematically destroyed critical files from his home computer through a secret "backdoor" program, written before he was axed.
- An insurance company employee slipped through security and attacked the central computer with an axe, shutting down a processing system for several days.
- An information technology expert wrote a "logic bomb" program, instructing a computer system to delete vital company files if he was dropped from the payroll.

Whether it is for money, revenge, love lost, or political or social causes, corporate insiders still have the best access and ability to cause mayhem.

---

[21]I recently saw one study that the figure was as high as 98 percent.
[22]*Herald Sun*, 29/04/1999, p. 28, by Karen Collier.

The Basics Are the Basics

I've been in infosec since 1984 and the rules haven't changed. I believe that the fundamental properties of security have not really changed one iota. Not one bit.

In the classic model of information security there are three components upon which all other aspects are built, in the same way that protons, electrons, and neutrons are the building blocks of atoms.

The classic security triad is based upon these tenets, also known as CIA:

1. Confidentiality: Simply put, keep secrets a secret. The spy movies call it "Eyes Only" and in a sense that is true. Only those people who are supposed to see the information should have access to it. So, either keep it on paper and locked away safely from prying eyes, or encrypt it and make damn sure you are the only one with the key.

2. Integrity: This ensures that information is not modified or altered intentionally or by accident, whether it's data or a program.

3. Availability: All systems and information resources must be "up and running" as per the needs of the organization. Denial of service attacks availability.

In physics we discovered a more basic unit than the electron, the quark, and in infosec, Donn Parker (retired SRI security guru) suggested that we add a few more units to our world.

The original triad has served well, but Parker suggests we need these to make a security model more comprehensive:

1. Control/Possession: Do you remain in control of your resources? A software program can be duplicated without the manufacturer's permission; they are not in control. You know your password, but who and what else has possession of it? How does that affect security?

2. Authenticity: How can you be sure that the person you are talking to is who he claims to be? Repudiation concepts fall into this category as well; make sure that the person with whom you are communicating cannot deny you were talking or that he sent or received a message.

3. Utility: Say you have an employee who has encrypted data but you do not have the key to make the contents intelligible. The argument is that the data is available but you do not have the use or utility of it.

I agree that these are strong and valuable additions to the infosec field, but I also believe that they are subcategories of the first three, which are more "quark-like" in their fundamentalness.

Confidentiality > Control Possession
Integrity > Authenticity
Availability > Utility

Regardless of whether you use a hexad or a triad as your corporate model, use one of them. These are the basics . . . no matter what the byte-heads might think. (No offense to byte-heads, of course!)

But for now, rather than concentrating on the technical things that can help companies with their security, let's look at some of the more non-conventional approaches that might be useful. These are generally non-technical and don't cost very much to implement.

Start at the Top

Stephen Katz, Chief Information Security Officer for CitiCorp NA, offers some advice based upon years of successful security implementation, but first, he insists, "Get rid of the techno-babble. This is a management problem."

For technical solutions, getting management to think correctly is a big step. Have management ask questions: "How do you know who's using your network and your information resources? Do you care? Who do they claim to be, locally or remotely? Once they tell you who they are, make them prove it." Any technology that doesn't meet these criteria should not even be considered.

Once they have proven to you who they are, have management ask, "How do you control what they do? Do you care? Do they have unlimited access to everything? Or is it restricted? And if it is restricted, who chooses the restrictions and how are they enforced?"

Katz says, "There is no such thing as a secure wire. Networks inherently have little or no security." Therefore, "If you are going to send information over the wire, what information deserves to be kept private and confidential? How do you establish confidentiality? Do you care about integrity?" Are you making sure that the content of the transmission is not altered? "Today, electronic transmissions have all the privacy of a postcard."

Katz continues, "Do you care about proper transfer of ownership of an electronic asset?" In the banking world this is especially important; in other business models, maybe not as much so. "We also care a great deal about repudiation. What do you do if someone denies receiving a message you know you sent?"

But all of the security in the world is meaningless unless "you know you have a problem," Katz says. "Too many security systems provide a 500-page report on what happened eighteen hours ago. That's like sending a [snail mail] letter to the police to tell them there is a robbery in progress."

"How important is the fact that your systems are being broken into? Maybe you don't care at all."

The bottom line to Stephen Katz is that security is a risk/threat management problem, and no two organizations are ever going to reach the same conclusions. Katz says, "Emulate your current or older paperwork processes, and find a way to implement them as part of your security and electronic process controls." Think process; think your information flow. Think your business needs. Work through that before you add technology (even security) that can only make your job harder.

▶ Floppy Disks

I don't know why more people don't think this way. Sit back and think; cogitate and ask yourself the following questions:

1. You're a networked company, right? (Y/N)
2. You use print servers and file servers and web servers and data base serves. You have them strewn throughout your organization to best service the needs of your staff. Right? (Y/N)
3. I bet you do not want your employees playing games at work, do you? (Y/N)
4. I also bet you do not want your employees doing personal computing projects during the day on your time, do you? (Y/N)
5. And you probably don't want your staff bringing computer viruses into your networks. That wouldn't make sense, now would it? (Y/N)

6. Lastly, it's safe to believe that you don't want employees stealing proprietary data, now do you? (Y/N)

Then, why, oh why, do you still allow floppy disk drives to be used in your desktop computers?

If you remove the disk drives, employees can't move data from machine to machine by floppy disk. Sneakernet goes away and so do a ton of your security problems. Virus incidents plummet. Productivity just might go up with fewer distractions. Nonetheless, there will be a handful of malcontents. "We can't do our jobs without floppies." In a few cases that is certainly true, and that's part of the task: Determine who "really" needs a floppy drive and who doesn't.

Your technical staff will still need them, of course, as might graphics and those departments who handle a multitude of outside materials.

But training a far smaller group about those security issues is less costly and more effective—a good management goal. In some departments, it makes sense to have a single machine, available to all in a public area, with a floppy drive, for copying data to and from the media. Keeping this one machine with all security updates, audit logs, and anti-virus software is an attractive, less costly alternative.

And if there's a problem at the desktop requiring service or an upgrade? Your service staff merely needs a floppy drive which attaches to the parallel port.

Beware! Human resources will want to get a word in edgewise, too. You are trying to embed security in the organization, but HR wants to make sure that removing floppy drives doesn't, in some sick and twisted manner, violate the civil rights or political sensibilities of any employee. *Arrrggh*. Political correctness has gone too far.

Take a Placebo

This next approach raises questions of honesty and privacy and good workplace conditions, but hey, don't dismiss it out of hand, either. Maybe there is a way to make parts of this approach work for you.

Large companies incessantly ask for the impossible:

1. Increased info-security with no money 'cause management won't support their efforts.
2. Improved insider/internal employee security as well as fewer external hacker risks.

3. No impact upon the functionality of their networks or the productivity of the staff in the process.

Impossible, no?

Placebo security consists of security mechanisms and products you wish you had, but don't have. Placebo security is aggressive security, going some places you may have never gone before. Lastly, it's not for everyone. Consider some of the placebo security methods in common use today.

Because of the amount of insider crime, try widely distributing the following announcement via internal email as some companies have done.

> *Due to a recent increase in computer virus infections, from this date forward, we will be monitoring all PCs for floppy disk activity here at OUR BIG FIRM. This action is necessary to prevent the introduction of viruses that people bring in from home.*

This is a subtle message that the staff is being watched more closely than in the past.

Or how about a little more in-your-face?

> *Beginning on Monday, network administration will be monitoring every keystroke each employee makes at their computer. In this manner, we will be able to reward higher levels of productivity as well as detect illicit computer games. Thank you for your cooperation.*

Phew! Watch Solitaire go away!

Of course, neither of these actions are actually taken, but the warnings are clear. Similarly, notices throughout a company can keep crime-inclined employees on their best behavior.

> *We regret to inform you that an OUR BIG FIRM employee was discovered trying to steal/defraud/embezzle from us. Due to our new computer monitoring systems, we were able to quickly detect his actions. He has been arrested, and faces up to fifteen years in prison. Thank you for all of your support.*

One large engineering firm I know announced to its employees that it had installed a special product to prevent what had been rampant laptop theft. Despite the fact that this was a placebo protection effort, laptop thefts immediately fell from over twenty per month to none. Now that's cost-effective security!

The Department of Justice has offered some insight into placebo security as well. For remote dial-in applications and for Internet or web pages, warnings reduce the likelihood of incidents.

```
Welcome to OUR BIG FIRM. We are currently using Famous Secu-
rity Product to protect our networks. Your adherence to its
security policies is appreciated.
```

An approach like this can easily reduce the number of ankle-biting hackers looking for an easy victim, assuming the product you name hasn't already been cracked by hackers. In the case of web sites, I have seen wording like:

```
Welcome to OUR SITE! As a security measure, we are now down-
loading a cookie to your desktop as a means of verifying
your identity. If you are not found in our data base, and
continue to attempt access, we will immediately contact law
enforcement. Please make sure you belong here before pro-
ceeding.
```

Or you can get more aggressive, like this actual one I found on one company's network:

```
Your identity is not confirmed. We did not find you in our data
base. We are now downloading an applet which will make your
hard disk unusable. REBOOT immediately to prevent this from
happening.
```

A countdown clock enforced the tension. Apparently this approach was successful . . . they said they've never experienced a successful external hack attack against them.

Placebo security doesn't work everywhere, for everyone, or every time. Like every security approach, it does not claim to be 100 percent effective. But it can help at next to no cost. On the other hand, you might find yourself in an ethical conundrum surrounding some of the methods used, and your human resources and legal staff may have a thing or two to say. Nonetheless, many companies successfully use placebo security.

At least think about it and consider it before you reject it.

More (Mostly) Non-Technical Security Methods That Can Help

1. Corporate policy remains at the top of any list that deals with internal and external security concerns. If the top management doesn't care, there is no reason for anyone else to, either. Policy means thinking about it, formulating it, and putting it in writing. Develop one and get top-level support.

2. Create your own computer emergency response team (CERT), a group of experts to lead the company through catastrophic computer and network problems and hacker attacks, whether from the inside or outside. Coordinate with other CERTs around the world and within your industry to maintain constant, global vigilance. Talk to the National Infrastructure Protection Center (www.nipc.gov) when events escalate.

3. Employee education and awareness training remain at the top of any good security practices list, too. Keep your staff updated regularly on all aspects of company security—and let them know how they can be part of it.

4. Advertise to your staff that you employ the latest and greatest in security monitoring and audit controls—whether you use them everywhere or not. Tell them in writing upon hire and by periodic company-wide email announcements that you have installed the extensive "Intrusion and Malicious Behavior Detection System" to catch the bad guys, not to play Big Brother. Your staff should be very afraid of being caught doing no-no's on your network. Then, you have to be careful not to crucify every employee who sets off your alarms by making an honest mistake.

5. It's a sad commentary, but we're getting to the point where we need to know more about our employees than they tell us on an application form. Consider using psychological profiling of staff hopefuls to learn about their ethics, morals, tendencies, and proclivities, especially in areas of mission criticality and network administration.

6. Physical security applies to information security, too. Don't forget about the simple things: You need to control access to electri-

cal closets, telephone rooms, and wiring hubs as much as you do to your data centers.

7. Shred or burn the important stuff: personnel lists, employee IDs, human resources information, manuals, and descriptions of current MIS installations and processes, customer files, internal memorandums, and anything else of potential value to an outsider. Shred disks and tapes, and perform a thorough erasure of hard disks before disposal. Garbage disposal is just as important at the office as at home; dumpster diving is an important component of what hackers and professionals do to break into your networks.

8. Make your staff cooperative partners in your security endeavors. Don't turn them into resistant adversaries. Try participatory programs like rewarding employees who find security problems, discover miscreant behavior, or detect illicit intrusions.

9. Don't believe what you see/hear about security products. Just 'cause you've installed one, do not believe that your problems are solved. There is still plenty to do. Do not believe on faith what the security vendor's sales staff says. Before you lay out good money to buy that product, see how many other improvements you can make without the addition of more technology that needs care, feeding, and management.

10. Treat security as a process instead of a product. Security implementation is not a single milestone to be checked off on a Gant chart and then forgotten. Develop an internal security process that reflects your business needs and business processes. Your business is not static and neither are your security needs.

11. Reevaluate your use of passwords throughout your networks as a primary means of user identification—even if they seem to be working. Size does matter and longer is better. Long, secure passwords are hard to guess, hard to remember, and are often written down. Short, easy to remember ones are easy to crack. Try this as an example of stronger passwords: PaSsWoRd, (alternating capital letters) ford6632 (common word with an easy to recall number) or 3lite, wr1t3m3 (hacker-style spelling).

12. Regulate and control Internet access for your employees. Control where they can go, what they can do, how much time they can

spend on the Internet, and what information your staff may upload or download.

13. Subscribe to security-related Internet resources (such as subscribed mail lists) and search on key web sites to stay on top of what is happening (i.e., Listservnetspace.org, www.ntbugtraq.com, www.infowar.com/hackers, http://techbroker/happyhacker.hmtl, www.sans.com).

14. Empower someone to do something. In a security emergency, (hackers, virus assault, disgruntled employee, etc.) who is empowered to get proactive—quickly? Do they have the authority to shut down a commercial web site to protect it? Can they call law enforcement without permission? Someone needs to be in charge, take responsibility, and take action.

Hacker Insurance

That's right. Insurance.

I'm not convinced about this at all, but if you investigate it, maybe your boss will give you a brownie, or maybe it will really accomplish something. Let me know how it goes.

Bad Guy breaks into your networks and does damage or steals something of value. In the physical world, you get a police report, call InsureCo, Inc. and get a check less the five hundred dollar deductible. Your networks are something different, yet a couple of companies are trying this approach out for size. The ICSA (International Computer Security Association) is offering up to $20,000 per hacker incident, max of $250,000 per year if a hacker breaks into your networks. The catch? You have to buy the ICSA services for upwards of $40,000 per year. I view this as a product warranty, not insurance, despite ICSA's insistence otherwise. (www.icsa.org)

Lloyds of London is offering up to $50,000,000 of hacker insurance for premiums that begin at $10,000. The policy covers against external hacking, miscreant employees, viruses, extortion, and a host of other threats to your networks. By the way, financial institutions are not eligible for these policies. (Dodge, Warren and Peters. 310.542.4370)

As I always do with every type of insurance, find out exactly what is NOT covered, and how they can weasel out of paying you, before you buy the policy.

Caveat emptor.

Lying to Hackers Is OK by Me

All warfare is based on deception.

Sun Tzu

In war (conflict), truth is so precious, it must be protected by a body-guard of lies.

Winston Churchill

Make a noise in the East and attack in the West.

Anonymous Chinese

I believe in lying. Sort of. Let me explain.

The bad guys will do anything they can to get you. You know that and it doesn't seem quite fair. They get to cheat, while real companies have to play by the rules. They can lie. They can use social engineering or pull any sort of nasty trick they want to break into your networks or otherwise try to make your life miserable.[23] But there are some new, innovative means to defend our networks, if we just apply some common sense.

I'm saying that we need to create an even playing field. "Do unto others as they do unto you," and in Cyberspace and infowar, such logic makes impeccable, defensive, common sense. If the hackers lie to you why shouldn't you lie right back? There is a way. It is your right and defensive duty to do the following:

- Lie to your adversary.
- Deceive him in any way possible.
- Force him to waste time/resources.

---

[23]Much of which is legal!

- Make his attacks a much riskier proposition.
- Protect your assets by the same means he attacks you.
- Use automatic responses and hands-off management.
- Apply time-based security concepts.
- Use deception.

Lying 101

This is the military view:

The world is currently full of nations that are militarily weak but ruled by despots who do not lack for cleverness or the willingness to use deception to maintain and expand their power.

And here are my translations for networks:

The Internet is currently full of criminal hackers, punks and goofballs that are morally handicapped, ethically weak, but who do not lack for cleverness or the willingness to use deception to maintain, project, and expand their power.

And . . .

The Internet is currently full of networks that are defensively weak but ruled by the technically and financially challenged who only need the willingness to use deception to maintain their systems' integrity and expand their power.

The main goal of your network defense is to keep your company functioning; keep the business process intact, and maintain day-to-day integrity so that there are no interruptions. Let's explore another tool that can create victory without battle and impose your will on your network adversary—just as the great Chinese warrior, Sun Tzu, expounded 2,500 years ago.

That technique is deception. Lying. If you ask your legal counsel, there is no law against lying . . . especially to the bad guys.

- Your goal is to reduce the amount of time the bad guys have to attack you. (Time-based security.)
- You want your detection and reaction mechanisms to be as fast as possible. (Time.)

- You may choose to invite the attacker to stay around for a longer period of time to give you more opportunity to collect forensic evidence and/or to identify him. (Time!)

Deception has been used throughout the history of warfare, from ancient times to today. Certainly the Trojan Horse fits the definition. Military leaders such as Phillip of Macedonia, Alexander the Great, Hannibal, Julius Caesar, and William of Hastings, all the way to Saddam Hussein, have successfully used deception to gain military advantage.

When undersized armies took on a larger force, their horses pulled weighty logs behind them over dusty roads to give the impression that more manpower was coming to battle. Small armies would light thousands of fires at night to give opposing forces the false impression of size. Psychological operations fit right into the deception mode with the philosophy, "It doesn't hurt if your enemy thinks he's smarter or tougher than you." Think about that. Playing it stupid is good.

During World War II, MGM Studios was making military support films but it was worried about becoming a potential target for aerial bombing if the Pacific war came to America. Studio executives complained to the War Department, who said they would take care of everything. The government response was to send out experts who painted the roof of MGM studios to look exactly like a munitions plant.

D-Day planners convinced the Germans that the invasion would not be at Normandy, but some distance to the northeast. When a German Enigma encoding machine was captured by the Allies, we figured out how to decode high-level German transmissions. But we never let the Germans know that we could read their private mail, even if it meant sacrificing civilian targets to keep the secret. Thus, Churchill allowed Coventry to be bombed without an air raid notice to the population.

In modern warfare, electronic chaff is tossed from airplanes to confuse enemy radar. The Soviets poured thousands of electronic diodes into the concrete construction of the new American Embassy in Moscow. The intent was to confuse American counter-surveillance devices that can't tell the difference between the non-linear junctions of the diodes and those in a real eavesdropping transmitter. Problem was the Russians overdid it, we found their plan early in the construction process, and we canned the new embassy.

Some experts maintain that Star Wars was nothing more than an elaborate technical public relations hoax of the first order to convince the Soviets we were willing to spend a gazillion dollars on space-based defense. And then there was the Gulf War. Did the Patriot missile system work as well as was claimed? Probably not, but the media and folks at home ate it up. Saddam's grand deception scheme kept us shooting our smart bombs at Scud launchers that were nothing more than cardboard façades or shells of real ones.

Deception clearly works.

Back to the Network

Now, let's figure out how to apply deception to network security. It's time to even the odds!

It is legally arguable to aggressively go after the bad guys. Corporate vigilantism is still only mentioned and knowingly approved by law enforcement in dark corners. They can't officially sanction the good guys to break the law to nab the bad guys, but the desire is certainly there. Nonetheless, an active defense is absolutely called for.

One of the common tools that the bad guys use to attack networks are scanning tools. Whether it's a purloined legal scanner by a real company or an underground tool, attackers want to understand and map out their victim's sites before "entering." Companies spend hours and weeks to scan their own networks, fix as many vulnerabilities as they can . . . but there are always a few left. You can't remove all functionality in the name of security.

And what happens? After you've done your best, the bad guys come along, use their scanning tools, and your defensive efforts now tell them exactly where to attack. They won't go after the things you have fixed; they'll go after the open electronic doors and windows . . . which their scanner points out to them. Your best protective security efforts are now working against you! You've reduced your target site and told them exactly where to attack. Counterproductive, don't you think? So try using some deception against them! Some of the benefits are obvious.

- Works against insiders and outsiders.
- Applies tried and true techniques.
- Ambushes the attacker.
- Makes attacks a riskier proposition.
- The enemy is never really certain.
- Automatic hands-off management detection/response. (Time.)

The Many Faces of Deception

Deception comes in many guises, and no one deception reaction is just right for everyone all of the time (common sense, by now, I hope!). Deception offers an entire suite of capabilities, and they should be picked judiciously for any application. The following is a useful deception taxonomy based upon military experiences and history.

Concealment
Physical: Hiding through the use of natural cover, obstacles or great distance. Trees and branches, terrain, mountain passes, valleys.

Virtual: Use the best defensive practices for "real" network services: Patches, service packs, policy, configuration. The object is to properly use and manage those basic security services that come with protective products, general applications, and operating systems.

Camouflage
Physical: Hiding movements and defensive postures (of troops) behind natural camouflage.

Virtual: Hide the vulnerable points with network access rights, archiving, etc.

False/Planted Information
Physical: Letting the opposition have the information you want them to have. Planting information you choose. False radio broadcasts, morphed pictures and videos, and other misleading information aimed at enemies, leadership, and general populations.

Virtual: Broadcast false network information from servers that are being scanned. Use the wrong IP address and the right IP address and other conflicting information to confuse your network adversary.

Ruses
Physical: Using equipment and procedures to deceive the enemy; carrying their flag/colors; marching troops in the same formations; using the same uniforms and adversary radio frequencies, giving false orders. Initiating cries of help as if from the enemy troops.

Virtual: Have the computer tell the attacker it senses a legitimate scan being conducted. Reinforce to the attacker that he is safely doing what he is doing. Pretend to be another hacker working on the same system. Again, one goal is to keep the hacker there for longer periods of time to gather forensic information.

Displays

Physical: Making the enemy see (or think he sees) what isn't really there. Horses pulling logs, thousands of campfires, fake artillery, rubber tanks, dummy airfields.

Virtual: Tell the attacker you are calling the IP police; create a fake CERT alert; tell them you are tracing them; show fake firewalls and IP barriers.

Demonstrations

Physical: Making a move that suggests imminent action; moving troops to the left, when really wanting to attack on right; moving troops constantly back and forth.

Virtual: Create an automatic defender which seems to follow the attacker; create a daemon which appears to launch a log/sniffer action or a trace.

Feints

Physical: An attacking demonstration. Using false attacks as a means of covering up the real mission/movements. Using false retreats to encourage chase by the other side.

Virtual: Appear to be only looking at the attacker when really switching defense modes. Appear to be helpless and defenseless when launching other means. Start an automatic response, then stop and seem to try something else, but really maintain the first one. Be loud about all your moves by telling your adversary, or by appearing to be so stupid he thinks he's listening to your moves and you don't know it.

Lies

Physical: Lying to the enemy in any way that suits your needs. Using the media to lie. Using perception management, creative perception management based upon what you want the attacker to believe. Initiating protracted but futile negotiations. Circulating false reports to the Net. Fabricating treasonable letters.

Virtual: Use electronic lying in the same way. Let the system tell the attacker anything that furthers *your* goals. Creatively use perception management. Initiate protracted but futile negotiations. Circulate false reports to the Net. Fabricate treasonable letters in the name or identity of the attacker.

Insight

Physical: Outthinking one's adversary. Studying their past engagements and learning from their mistakes. Knowing your enemy better than he knows you. Staying one step ahead. It's a chess game: Predicting your opponent's moves.

Virtual: Understand their motivation. Learn the techniques. Collect logs of previous activities. Distinguish ankle-biters from serious hackers from professional attacks. Research is currently being done to understand hacker motivations; map those against technical skills and techniques and then develop predictive models based upon early attack detections.

Honey Pots

Physical: Making something so attractive a target, your enemy comes running into your trap. Think Native Americans from the 1800s. Employing sneak attack/ambushes.

Virtual: Clifford Stoll placed seemingly valuable national secrets on his computer to draw in the attackers. Create files with attractive information. "Come and get it!" Privacy violations: medical, salary, etc. Rich intellectual property. Corporate secrets. New products. Classified military information. Secrets of Saddam. Then: Trap, track, and trace.

Lies 'R' Good

In these cases, they are, so use them. The construction of custom deception suites is an attractive means for specific applications and industries who want to use deception.

- Suck the attacker into a mirror of your web banking applications to get him into a harmless area where you can watch, collect information, and trace. The main web banking application remains uncorrupted and functional.
- Brokerage firms can honey-pot the attackers into private information files/directories which are really meaningless. Suck them in with "private confidential investment information." Maybe even encourage them to lose money!

Law enforcement sites, as well as military and government sites, will be using the same approaches by choosing and developing appropriate deception suites that meet their specific goals. I would recommend that you speak to legal counsel, with real cyber-knowledge, about the proper means to collect forensic information that can be used in subsequent prosecutions.

Deception is deceptively simple to use as long as you understand some of its fundamental rules.

1. Hide your moves from your opponent.
2. Never let your opponent see you as you are.
3. It's all about time. Waste their time in their useless attacks and keep them around so you can trace them.
4. Announce your deceptive existence to scare them away in short order.
5. Using TBS principles, deception should operate at very high speeds, lowering "D" plus "R" (detection plus reaction time) and adding to your security.

Remember what Sun Tzu said: "There can never be enough deception."

Resources

- *Time Based Security* by Winn Schwartau.
- Go to Fred Cohen's http://all.net for a look at his Deception Toolkit.
- Search on "Deception," "Honeypots," and "Network Deception." This is so new, you may not find a lot.

PART VI

Law Enforcement, Vigilantism, and National Security

Are the cops really gonna help you if you get hacked? Probably not.

That's why the concept of vigilantism is rearing its head: cybermercenaries who will do what the police cannot and will not do.

Ethical? Moral? Legal? Tough calls. But if no one else will help, what are you going to do?

For you see, the best cybercops are working to defend the infrastructure—the banks, public utilities, transportation, and communications systems—from attacks by hackers and/or terrorists . . . a whole new worry for modern societies.

And then we have the US cybercorps, the military's hackers whose job it is to protect the Pentagon and the war fighter. They've got a few hacking tricks up their sleeves, too. They don't like to talk about it much, but they can hack away at foreign governments with the best of them.

Want to know what's happening?

Hacking and Law Enforcement

Despite what you might believe, the police do not prevent crime. I am not trying to insult law enforcement in any way, it's just true.

Let's say you're a small shop owner on Main Street, Anytown. Late one evening you notice a grungy character standing across the street just staring at your store. You think he is casing your store to rob you. Do you call the police?

"What's he doing, sir?"

"Nothing, just standing there, looking at my store."

"Is he breaking any laws?"

"Ah . . . none I can see but I am sure he's going to rob me."

"Do you have an alarm system?"

"Yeah . . ."

"There's nothing we can do unless he has broken a law."

The police respond to crimes already committed or to "credible" threats of committing a crime, which is often a crime in itself. They do not prevent the crime from occurring. Preventing the crime is up to you, the shop owner. You are expected to have good locks, strong doors, and an adequate alarm system to deter the crooks. Your insurance rates will reflect how much security you employ. You get reduced insurance rates if your car or home has an alarm, too. But this is not preventing crime, it is an attempt to deter crime. High-profile alarm systems and fancy locks will deter the petty thief perhaps, but not the dedicated criminal.

Police cars roaming the streets and cops on the beat do not prevent crime unless they happen to be at the right place at the right time— where a crime is being committed in their presence—or if they are called and arrive at the scene in time to stop the bad guys. The presence of the cops deters crime, it doesn't prevent it.

And so it goes in the great vastness of Cyberspace.

When hacking began to get a profile in the mid 1980s, there were maybe a handful of cops across the country who had any idea about computer crime. Sure, they knew about embezzlement, money laundering and fraud, but that was generally an inside job. Conventional espionage and the gamut of physical crimes were dealt with regularly. But computers? Aren't those for geeks?

The lack of understanding in this new phenomenon of hacking caused two reactions by the police:

1. They ignored it because they had no one schooled in investigations, or
2. They overreacted.

Most police departments still do not have the skills or the budgets to investigate computer crimes. In my home town, the local cybercop was also my lawn man. No offense to him at all, he's a regular cop, not a computer expert. When cases came up, I would get a call. Fine, I am happy to help. But little good does this do if a local police department doesn't even know who to call for help or have a budget to pay an expert.

Overreaction by law enforcement may be worse. Operation Sun Devil[1] run by Arizona police and the Secret Service was an early 1990s embarrassment. The massive investigation and broad sweep of arrests had no significant results, and only served to create enmity between law enforcement and the computer underground.

When, two years later, the hacking group Masters of Destruction were arrested in New York for conspiracy and a dozen more hacking counts, the US Attorney had his act together and jail time was served by many. But the hacking community still reviled what they viewed as incarceration of hackers for the mere act of curiosity.

Then there is Kevin Mitnick, the hacker made famous by *New York Times* journalist John Markoff. Mitnick was jailed for years without a trial and the hackers wanted him freed! On the other hand, Kevin's defense posture has repeatedly shifted, and he was released in January 2000.

Many hackers would have you believe that the crime is so minimal there should be no jail time. Fat chance. Read the accompanying views by law enforcement professionals who fight in the cyber-trenches every day.

---

[1]Covered extensively in Bruce Sterling's excellent book, *The Hacker Crackdown*.

Cops have a heck of a tough time catching cybercrooks. First, you have to remember Bob Ayers' study at DISA: We just don't know about all of the crimes because people and companies don't notice them, and if they do, they don't report them. If they aren't reported, they can't be investigated.

However, not many cyber-crimes get investigated once they are reported. Consider this. You are in New York. You get mugged so you go to the police station to report it.

"What did they get?"

"My driver's license, two credit cards, and one hundred and twenty dollars."

"That's it?" asks the burly Irish desk sergeant, raising his eyebrows.

"Yeah . . ."

"Consider yourself lucky. Go home." And that's it. Why? Because the crime is so small, no one was hurt, and the chances of finding *your* mugger is about nil. Zilch. So why should the cops waste their time? The same thing is true with cyber-crimes.

"Someone broke into my network."

"What did they do?"

"Poked around, added a new user and jumped to Exxon's computer through ours."

"That's it? Consider yourself lucky. Buy a firewall."

Law enforcement, for lack of budget, skills, and manpower, can only investigate those cases that have caused significant damage or have a national security aspect. They caught the guy who wrote the Melissa virus in 1999 in a matter of weeks, with the help of independent security experts who had looked inside the virus and found the electronic signature of its author. They nailed a bunch of hackers in 1999 for crimes they committed in 1995.

FBI officials privately say that unless there is a demonstrable loss of at least $50,000 to $100,000, they can't begin an investigation. British authorities privately mention an even higher bar. This places the responsibility for protection with the individual and the corporation, and leaves a bad taste about law enforcement in many mouths because:

- People and companies are on their own to protect themselves, although the individual can really do very little.
- Individuals have to be able to detect a crime and then report it, hopefully finding someone within law enforcement who will understand.
- Unless the crime is significant enough, law enforcement will take no action, or they might delay action by beginning

a long investigation. (In the chapter on vigilantism, you will see what has happened as a result of these inactions.)

But law enforcement is not sitting idly by. The FBI instituted computer crime squads almost a decade ago, though it was a limited first effort. Now they are training special agents, hiring private computer and forensics experts, and opening a slew of new computer crime squad offices all over the US. This is good. The Secret Service has always been involved with communications fraud and has led the efforts against cellular hacking, fraud, and illicit eavesdropping cases.

In New York, a pilot program called the Electronic Crime Task Force is a joint effort between the FBI, Secret Service, and New York State and City police. The combined resources have produced results, and expansion of the model program is likely in the near future.

Europe is no stranger to computer crime—by both hackers and organized crime. The major European countries have experienced some successes against hacking, but they are also considering even more draconian measures than would ever be permitted in the United States. One 1998 proposal called for allowing cops to break the law to enforce the law.

Here in the US, cops can go in for a drug buy and then arrest the dealers. Are they breaking the law? Our legal system says no. Cybercops go on-line pretending to be little girls, set up dates with on-line predators, and then arrest the pedophiles. Entrapment? The arrests are holding up in court.

How much power we want the police to have is a resounding question that stirs heated emotional debate. The arguments are:

PRO: We have to empower the police to deal with these new crimes. The bad guys have us outgunned (in Cyberspace) and we need an edge.
CON: Give police too much power and they will abuse it. Just look at the LAPD and NYPD abuses in the last ten years. They have too much power as it is. Search and seizure rules are getting to the point where no one is safe from criminal cops.

CON: I remember J. Edgar Hoover's FBI and I don't want that to happen again.
PRO: We have controls in place to prevent abuses of the past from recurring.

PRO: Let's outlaw cryptography so the bad guys can't hide.
CON: What self-respecting criminal is going to listen to a stupid law like that? Besides, they can buy crypto anywhere on the planet.

Law enforcement's legitimate concerns over having adequate power to stop bad guys is heavily balanced by privacy advocates and civil libertarians who feel the government has too much control and power already; why give them more?

Laws around the world vary greatly, which only makes law enforcement's job harder. In Singapore—where you can be publicly lashed for chewing gum on the streets—the government controls which parts of the Internet their citizens can access. In Eastern Europe, the very few laws against hacking are rudimentary, if they exist at all. Reciprocity for any criminal activity takes diplomatic agreement and intensive coordination between all the players in the turf battle for power and control.

Based upon my experiences and those of many companies and people I respect, law enforcement is not a top candidate to help you. The rules of self-help say, according to some lawyers, do what you have to do to protect yourself. But there a few things you should do no matter which approach you choose.

- If you are hacked (personally or corporately), no matter how small the losses or damage, report it to law enforcement. Throughout this book you will find many references on how to report and to whom.
- Make sure you get a written copy of the complaint you register. The reason for this is to help build a better statistical data base of cyber-crimes for future reference.
- Ask law enforcement to investigate, and get in writing why they won't.
- Consider the suggestions in the chapters on forensics and vigilantism.
- Improve your defensive posture, as discussed throughout this book, so an attack won't happen again.
- Consider hacker insurance.

I know, I know, it sounds sort of hopeless, and I have been there. Trust me. I know exactly how uncaring, unsympathetic, and downright hostile certain elements of law enforcement can be when they want to be. Most of the time such attitudes are just their power trips. But significant progress is being made on many fronts, so don't give up hope. Take a look at what they're trying to protect in addition to you and me!

▶ Computer Crime and Intellectual Property Section (CCIPS)

How to Report Internet-Related Crime

Internet-related crime, like any other crime, should be reported to appropriate law enforcement investigative authorities at the local, state, federal, or international levels, depending on the scope of the crime. Citizens who are aware of federal crimes should report them to local offices of federal law enforcement.

Some federal law enforcement agencies that investigate domestic crime on the Internet include: the [1]Federal Bureau of Investigation (FBI), the [2]United States Secret Service, the [3]United States Customs Service, and the [4]Bureau of Alcohol, Tobacco and Firearms (ATF). Each of these agencies has offices conveniently located in every state to which crimes may be reported. Contact information regarding these local offices may be found in local telephone directories. In general, federal crime may be reported to the local office of an appropriate law enforcement agency by a telephone call and by requesting the "Duty Complaint Agent."

Each law enforcement agency also has a headquarters (HQ) in Washington, D.C., which has agents who specialize in particular areas. For example, the FBI and the U.S. Secret Service both have headquarters-based specialists in computer intrusion (i.e., computer hacker) cases. In fact, the FBI HQ hosts an interagency center, the [5]National Infrastructure Protection Center (NIPC), created just to support investigations of computer intrusions. The NIPC's general number for criminal investigations is 202-324-0303. The U.S. Secret Services Electronic Crimes Branch may be reached at 202-435-5850. The FBI and the Customs Service also have specialists in intellectual property crimes (i.e., copyright, software, movie, or recording piracy, trademark counterfeiting). Customs has a nationwide toll-free hotline for reporting at 800-BE-ALERT, or 800-232-2538.

The FBI investigates violations of federal criminal law generally. Certain law enforcement agencies focus on particular kinds of crime. Other federal agencies with investigative authority are the [6]Federal Trade Commission and the [7]U.S. Securities and Exchange Commission.

To determine some of the federal investigative law enforcement agencies that may be appropriate for reporting certian kinds of crime, please refer to the following table:

Type of Crime

Appropriate federal investigative law enforcement agencies

Computer intrusion (i.e. hacking) FBI local office; NIPC (202-324-0303); U.S. Secret Service local office

Password trafficking FBI local office; NIPC (202-324-0303); U.S. Secret Service local office

Copyright (software, movie, sound recording) piracy FBI local office; if imported, U.S. Customs Service local office (800-BE-ALERT, or 800-232-2538)

Theft of trade secrets FBI local office

Trademark counterfeiting FBI local office; if imported, U.S. Customs Service local office (800-BE-ALERT, or 800-232-2538)

Counterfeiting of currency U.S. Secret Service local office; FBI local office

Child Pornography or Exploitation FBI local office; if imported, U.S. Customs Service local office (800-BE-ALERT, or 800-232-2538)

Internet fraud FBI local office; Federal Trade Commission; if securities fraud, Securities and Exchange Commission

Internet harassment FBI local office

Internet bomb threats FBI local office; ATF local office

Trafficking in explosive or incindiary devices or firearms over the Internet FBI local office; ATF local office

References

1. http://www.fbi.gov/
2. http://www.treas.gov/usss
3. http://www.customs.treas.gov/
4. http://www.atf.treas.gov/
5. http://www.nipc.gov/
6. http://www.ftc.gov/
7. http://www.sec.gov/
8. http://www.usdoj.gov/criminal/cybercrime/index.html
9. http://www.usdoj.gov/

Source: http://www.usdoj.gov/criminal/cybercrime/reporting.htm

Corporate
Vigilantism

Strike Back or Lay Back?

"**W**e're mad as hell and we're not going to take it anymore," is a recurring theme amongst many top corporations and governments. If you get slapped in the face, there is a reasonable chance you will slap back. That is called deterrence. The fear of being slugged in retaliation. (Remember the Cold War and MAD? Mutually Assured Destruction.) If you get mugged, and assuming you have the capability (strength, know-how, agility), you very well might fight for control of your wallet and maybe you'll try to disarm your assailant. Unless, of course, you are outgunned, in which case you lose.

If US interests get bombed by an adversary, the military is trained to pummel them in retaliation—or, as Martin Libicki of National Defense University said, "if all else fails, we can make the rubble bounce," in reference to our nuclear superiority.

But what about you as a network administrator and your corporation? What do you do when hackers attack you? Do you sit back and take it? Or are you part of the new, empowered and emboldened breed of corporation that is striking back . . . sometimes with military efficiency and intensity, in an effort to protect your interests?

The frustrations voiced by corporate America run deep when they speak about hackers, getting hacked, and their feeling of impotence to protect themselves.

"It's a hell of a situation when victim companies are more fearful of the FBI than they are of the attackers," says Dr. Michael Vlahos, Senior Fellow at the US Internet Council. He finds this feeling to be endemic as he studies the issue. "Law enforcement is simply not equipped to investigate or prosecute these sorts of crimes," agrees Robert Kane, former Senior VP of Technical Marketing at Security Dynamics, Inc.

The general feeling among many firms is that law enforcement is simply not up to snuff. The complaints from top firms in the US range from downright ineffectiveness ("clueless" is an oft-repeated word among those critical of law enforcement), to lack of staff, to lack of funding, to courts being too blocked and the snaillike speed with which typical law enforcement investigations run.

"Law enforcement is helpless," maintains Tom Noonan, President of Internet Security Systems. "They're not like Israeli fighters who train every day for every contingency. Conventional law enforcement just can't match the skills needed. Besides, you just can't trust law enforcement to keep your secrets from becoming public knowledge."

"One reason you see vigilantism is because law enforcement doesn't get the job done." Dr. Fred Cohen, President of Fred Cohen and Associates, and Principal Scientist, Sandia National Laboratories, added, "Law enforcement might investigate if you have a lot of political clout and you do all of the leg work. Maybe they will look into it." I know that is what I have personally found when I have approached all levels of law enforcement to investigate a myriad of crimes. And the reaction is intense frustration, bordering on anger.

In *Information Warfare* I examined what open hostilities on the Internet would look like. Class I attacks are against the individual or family. In Class II Information Warfare, corporations battle corporations in Cyberspace. With Class III Information Warfare, nation-states, transnational criminal groups, and political/religious organizations take center stage in the combat theater.

In response, some organizations are implementing what I call Hostile Perimeters: if you don't belong in our networks, we're going to knock you back—hard—and maybe into unconsciousness.

The First Volley

In September of 1998, the Pentagon discovered it was a target of the Electronic Disturbance Theater, a self-styled group of hactivists who practice politically driven cyber-civil-disobedience. With preparation, the Defense Information Technology Center responded to the attack with a denial-of-service counteroffensive of its own, disabling the attack browsers. The Pentagon won that battle, and the EDR threatened to sue the government for hacking. Because the Pentagon's Public Affairs

Office refused to comment, we still don't know if the counterattack by the DITC staff was an authorized response as per policy, or a renegade action by mid-level systems administrators.

Should the Pentagon have launched a counteroffensive in order to protect its networks? "It's absolutely reasonable for the military to shoot back when fired upon," said Dr. Fred Cohen. Matt Devost, a former analyst at Infrastructure Defense, Inc., concurs: "Offense is a good defensive measure." Joe Van Gieri, Federal Manager for Fortress Technologies, knows his way around the Washington Beltway and said, "I'm surprised it hasn't happened earlier. They are only doing what they are trained to do." Most people I spoke with agreed with the DITC's offensive and effective reaction to the attacks.

While the Pentagon is officially silent on the matter, Joseph Broghamer, Information Assurance Lead for the US Navy's Office of the Chief Information Officer reacts very negatively to the whole incident. "Offensive information warfare is not a good thing . . . period. You want to block, not punish" the offenders, he maintains (think fortress mentality). Standing nearly alone in his opinion, "there is no technical reason to react offensively to a hacker attack. None."

Is that really true?

The First Vigilante Corp

Lou Cipher[2] (a pseudonym of his choosing) is a senior security manager at one of this country's largest financial institutions. "There is not a chance in hell of us going to law enforcement with a hacker incident," he says loudly. "They can't be trusted to do anything about it so it's up to us to protect ourselves."

Cipher's firm has taken self-protection to the extreme. "We have the right to self-help—and yes it's vigilantism. We are drawing a line in the sand, and if any of these dweebs [hackers] cross it, we are going to protect ourselves." Cipher told me that his group is authorized to do "anything it takes" to protect itself and that yes, they have taken the law into their own hands. Out of necessity.

"We have actually gotten on a plane, me and a couple of big guys, and visited the physical location where the attacks began. We've broken

---

[2]Some of the media have suggested that I made up Lou Cipher to make a point. They are wrong. Cipher is all too real, as nasty as he sounds, and he hates hackers. In the course of my travels I have met many other Ciphers and their numbers are growing.

in, stolen the computers and left a note: 'See How It Feels?' " Only on one occasion, Mr. Cipher said, "did we have to resort to baseball bats." That's what these "punks will understand. Then word gets around and we're left alone. That's all we want. To be left alone."

Such methods raise the hackle of even the staunchest Corporate Information Warrior who will go to great lengths for on-line retribution. Lloyd Reese, an information assurance expert at Fannie Mae, says physical response is both illegal and "doomed to failure." Mark Gembecki, President of Warroom Research, a competitive intelligence firm, says that a cyber-response is OK, but Cipher's physical retaliation is "a clear and overt violation of civil rights."

So not every company is going to send out armies of thugs to enforce their firewall policy, but Gembecki claims that his eighteen-month study, "Corporate America's Competitive Edge," showed that 30 percent of the 320 surveyed Fortune 500 companies have installed counteroffensive software. My studies concur.

A senior vice president of security at a major global financial firm says, "we can't talk about return of fire, we want to be low profile." He maintains that offense is a first strike, and that defense is an appropriate response to a first strike. "If you use measures to restore your services, then that is defense, not offense," he avows. When pressed as to how far his company goes, he is only willing to concede, "I am willing to defend myself."

Bruce Lobree is an internal security consultant at another major financial institution, and he applies the red light theory to cyber-vigilantism. "Suppose it's the dead of night on a country road, and you come upon a stoplight. You can see for miles in all directions. Are you going to run the light even knowing there is virtually no chance of being caught?" The innate fear of repercussion lies within each of us, he maintains. "Ninety-nine percent of us won't hack, but it's that 1 percent that causes all of the trouble." When asked if his financial firm uses strike-back techniques, he says with a smile, "I can't answer yes or no. That's proprietary. Besides, legally we can't. But I can tell you that everything is recorded." If Gembecki's numbers are real, Lobree and the others are on the front lines of Class II Information Warfare more than any of us might have suspected.

"We are already seeing electronic guerrilla warfare," says Dr. Kelly Jones, Vice President of Information Operations, Inc. "And hell yeah! Companies should have the right to defend themselves. It's a simple evolution."

As described in *Time Based Security*, a network must have protective layers of defense such as firewalls, passwords, and access control lists to implement policy. But purely protective measures cannot work all alone—which has been a failure of the information security industry for the last thirty years:

- Network topology, users, and software are constantly changing. There is no way to keep up.
- New vulnerabilities are found daily, and exploited daily.
- Small numbers of individuals with little technical skill can launch massive on-line attacks (push-button hacking).

Time Based Security argues that there is a way to exactly measure the strength of a company's security using time as the quantifiable metric.

- Network administrators have to monitor anomalous behavior, attack signatures, network operations, and host audit information in a high-speed real-time iterative manner. Speed of detection is the key.
- Once an anomaly or attack has been detected, a rapid response is required to mitigate damages. The particular response chosen is the current subject of debate. How hostile a Hostile Perimeter is appropriate?

The Conundrum

A significant percentage of interviewees agree that the Pentagon should be allowed to protect itself with counteroffensive software. Jim Kates, former director of Network Architecture and Security at Intermedia Communications, Inc., a national ISP: "National security brings a different set of rules." However, being a former Philadelphia police officer, he is quick to point out that "we at ICI do not recommend nor participate in strike-back operations. There are too many legalities involved. Breaking the law to help the law doesn't strengthen the law."

Even those with a strong inclination for vigilantism note that counteroffensive responses are fraught with danger. Lloyd Reese has a strong criminal justice background and says, "Companies need to follow the appropriate legal process. We already have chaos on the Internet, why should we make it worse?"

Everyone understands that any offensive actions are illegal, but that there is a low likelihood of being caught in defending himself or herself. The aggressive Lou Cipher says that "the first thing you have to do is identify the attacker and that is no easy task." Using "traceroute" is a good first step, most people agree, and this requires you also get the assistance of ISPs down the line. Each hop on the Internet has to be covered in order to find the real source. That is legal, and then the information can be handed over to law enforcement—if they will react.

There are other first steps, too. Shut down the connection to the offending source IP address, if you can. Then try to clear up the exposure that was compromised.

"Talk to your lawyers," Reese advises. "Keep in mind that your strike-back has to go through a long path and you might do damage at any place along the way."

Secure Computing Corporation's Ray Kaplan is a senior information security consultant and recommends extreme caution. "The first thing is to protect yourself, and then you need to stop the attack—any way you can. The first strike-back launched should only be to gather information about your attacker." Even though he believes the Pentagon and others should be able to actively protect themselves, "if you carelessly go after someone and make a mistake, you can cause a lot of damage and perhaps even a major security incident."

ISS's Tom Noonan points out how easy it is to overreact to an apparent attack. "In the spring of 1997, one of the Big Six used our scanning tools to assess the security of a MAE site (either MAE East or West, the two major nexuses for the Internet), with the authority of the president of the ISP in question. The network administrator on duty noticed a thousand simultaneous connections to his firewall and he reacted quickly. He shut down all network traffic to ISS before even calling the FBI. His manual reaction took down 75 percent of the Internet through its massive router bank. Anyone using Sprint at that time was in a world of hurt." Point made.

But other things can go wrong with a strong counteroffensive. What if the source is from another company whose name was spoofed? You might find yourself attacking IBM or General Motors. Neither would take kindly to that sort of activity—no matter the reason.

You really have to understand what you are doing. Your first response might invite further attack, exactly the opposite of what you intended. You have to consider how the Internet community as a whole will react to your actions. And what is the public-relations posture of the company? How will that be viewed? Van Gieri spins it differently. "Take the investor's viewpoint. If someone is messing with a company's money and they strike back, I can imagine increased confidence in the firm's ability to protect its assets and integrity."

The navy's Broghamer says that adding better and better security protection is really the answer. "We get port-scanned all of the time but our security is really good." Broghamer maintains that if corporations strike back at attacking hackers, it will merely invite more to attack. Sometimes the best response is to shut down the network connection altogether, he suggests, but the navy is not as sensitive to "up-time" and customer perception as the private sector is. According to a senior executive at one of the US stock exchanges, "our task is 99.998 percent availability. Disconnecting is not an option."

Lynn Schloesser, security manager at Eastman Chemical Co., Kingsport, Tennessee, counters that, "We have to do something to defend ourselves. It's no longer messing around with small bits and pieces; it's a fully integrated system from sales to feed," and therefore it's all at risk.

The Law Enforcement Position

Predictably, law enforcement holds an opposite view. Lieutenant Chris Malinowski of the New York City Police Department says, "if someone were to attack us, we are not encouraged to swat back," although he admits the Pentagon operates by different rules of engagement. "If companies take any of these pro-active steps they are taking a big chance, subject to criminal prosecution." According to Dave Green, Deputy Chief of the Computer Crimes and Intellectual Property Section, Department of Justice, "I relate to the frustrations caused by law enforcement's inability to respond, but we can only recommend protective measures to companies under attack. We have no public stance on electronic vigilantism." When asked if companies should hack back at an attacker, Green responded, "No comment," the answer to a number of questions on what could legally be considered an attack. "But, I can say that law enforcement is gearing up and much better equipped to deal with cyber-crime."

On the other hand, Internet Security Council's Vlahos reminds us that "in the 1860s, law enforcement was conducted by Pinkerton, a private company." He suggests we pay attention to history before deciding on a policy.

But when you speak with law enforcement officials "off the record," the story changes. Local cops, state police, members of the FBI, Secret Service, Interpol, and Scotland Yard, for example, all say the same thing—unofficially: "We can't handle the problem. It's too big. If you take care of things yourself, we will look in the other direction. Just be careful." Even law enforcement recognizes the value of vigilantism. In one cybercriminal case, every agency I spoke to recommended a physical strike-back option; unofficially, of course. So it seems that the frustration runs deep for both victims and enforcers.

Strike Back Tools

In 1994, Secure Computing Corporation introduced Sidewinder, a novel firewall with strike-back capabilities. Other companies offer a range of strike-back capabilities, too, and we can expect many more in the coming months.

"IBM's Hawthorne Center has been building artificial intelligence engines for viruses and attack recognition," says Dr. Vlahos. "They have to be examining hostile defense as well."

Ernst & Young has some decisions to make, too. As part of their information security practice, they have been asked about strike-back capabilities, and how Hostile Perimeters might be used in defense. Dan Woolley, National Leader of Market Development for E&Y, says that he knows of "companies in finance, insurance and manufacturing who are developing and deploying the capability to aggressively defend their networks." He is quick to point out, however, "We don't do it for ourselves even though we are attacked regularly."

The question that E&Y will face along with other consulting and software firms is a tough one: Should they develop offensive software, offer it to their clients, deploy it, and support it? And if so, how open should they be about it?

Most companies are loath to discuss which defensive security product they use, such as firewalls or password token devices. "If we did establish a Hostile Perimeter," said another Fortune 100 company representative, "we would absolutely treat it with the utmost confidentiality." Everyone is quick to remember and point out that many aspects of an offensive defense are illegal. Highly effective, perhaps, maybe necessary, but nonetheless illegal. The questions that every company faces include ethics and morality as well as legality: How far are we willing to go to defend our networks, our confidential information, and the public relations issues that go along with them?

International Players

Regardless of the law, vigilantism is on the rise. According to two senior defense officials in Europe, "We will strike back regardless if it's in the US or not. Those are your laws, not ours, and we intend on defending ourselves." Pakistan and India have been attacking each other's web sites—admittedly preferable to tossing nukes back and forth, but perhaps just an escalatory step prior to physical conflict. Sources in the intelligence community claim that Israel, Germany, France, and Japan all are establishing Hostile Perimeters as part of their national defense. Perhaps this is why Russia recently called for an international conference to mitigate the already begun cyber–arms race.

Bill Curch of CIWARS offered a great suggestion: "If it's now against the law to disarm a cyber-attacker, why don't we just change the laws?"

Final Thoughts

Corporate vigilantism might be an awesome business opportunity whose time has come, just as we are beginning to see offensive products make their way into corporate tool kits. But in any case, the legal challenges that coexist with Hostile Perimeters and counteroffensive defense are daunting. The astute company will examine every aspect of its posture before marching down the slippery slope of vigilantism. Even though emotions run high, sometimes the best defense is to not overreact and do nothing until things calm down.

Vlahos counters that the courts may be the place to create a new set of laws that are more attuned to the technology. "This is a whole new arena, and I don't know how we can explore it without trying out new approaches . . . even if they are technically illegal."

And at the very far right is Lou Cipher, who swears that "Personal persuasion is always more effective than electronic persuasion. Personal persuasion virtually guarantees that a hacker will see the error of his ways and scamper to please and turn over a new leaf."

No matter what you choose to do, make sure it is well thought out and that you have your legal ducks in a row. You just might need them.

Corporate Vigilantism Survey Results

In late October of 1998, I approached *Network World* (one of the industry magazines I write for) with a project idea: Let's examine the status of corporate vigilantism. To clarify the point, I noted the extreme vigilante persona of Lou Cipher.

I subsequently spoke with about seventy people and recorded their comments, the vast majority of whom cannot be quoted by name. The aggressive law enforcement officials want to keep their jobs, and the executives do not want to turn their companies into electronic targets any more than they already are. So they insisted on anonymity, too.

The Corporate Vigilantism Survey was not conducted in any formal way. It did not use a statistically balanced approach or neutral questions to get a baseline; it was not a scientific study. The results are correlated from hundreds of responses I received to the survey. Many of the answers we received to many of the questions were long answers, and we needed to read and analyze the thoughts and comments to fit the "Yes", "No," and "Maybe/Sometimes" categories in the results below. So, with that in mind, what did we discover?

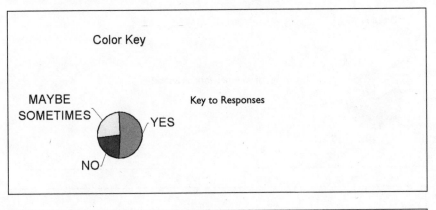

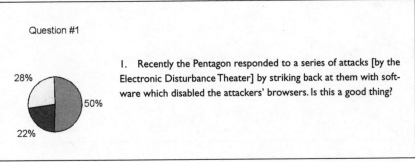

A subsequent survey in Australia found even more support for vigilantism than ours did. The results, published in December, 1999, show more than twice the support we found for vigilantism. Conducted by Dr. Matt Warren and Dr. Bill Hutchinson, as many as 93% of respondees supported various strike-back options.[3] In May of 1999, I conducted an informal vigilantism session at InfowarCon in London. Some

---

[3]www.it.fairfax.com.au/industry/19991207/A19913-1999Dec6.html

Question #2

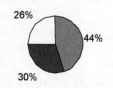

26%

44%

30%

2. Should companies respond to hacker attacks by attacking them back?

Question #3

17%   13%

70%

3. Is a "ping" of your network an attack?

Question #4

23%   20%

57%

4. Is a port scan (of your network) an attack?

of the audience was understandably aghast at the results, but in a loose show of hands, roughly one third of the participants agreed that vigilantism is a viable alternative to conventional law enforcement.

The best suggestion came in the middle of the session, when we were discussing the validity of removing a weapon from an attacker's hands. In the US and elsewhere, disarming the attacker is legal. In Cyberspace it's not. "Why not just change the laws and allow people to defend themselves?"

He has a point.

Question #5

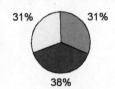

31%   31%

38%

5. Does a subtle "mapping" of your networks constitute an attack?

Question #6

32%   29%

39%

6. If an attack comes from outside the USA, should a company respond with offensive software?

Question #7

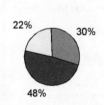

22%   30%

48%

7. Do you agree that responding with offensive software is the electronic equivalent of removing weapons from an attacker in the physical world?

Strike-Back or Not? Best Advice

According to industry professionals, here is the best advice on what you can or should do in reaction to detected attacks against your networks.

1. Use good detection systems. Detection is more than just IP at your Internet connection. Host-based auditing, network behavior, traffic analysis—they are all good sources of security relevant data that will assist in seeing if you are experiencing a security

Question #8

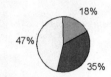

18%

47%

35%

8. Is there a line to be drawn as to when a person or a company has the right to strike back at an attacker?

Question #9

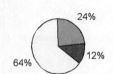

24%

12%

64%

9. The US Government is developing offensive software. Should it be used?

Question #10

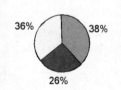

36%

38%

26%

10. Several foreign companies and countries have said they will strike back at US locations if they identify the attack as from within the United States. Should they do this?

Question #11

11. One financial institution has said it will "use every means at our disposal to protect our assets." They have built strike-back offensive capabilities. Does your company have offensive software or plan to use such techniques? (The answer to this one question shows that law enforcement is really going to be up against the wall with Cyber-war.)

24%

33%

43%

Question #12

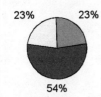

23%   23%   12. Is a physical response to an electronic attack appropriate? (Again, the frustration with law enforcement is evident.)

54%

Question #13

35%   40%   13. If you found yourself the victim of a retribution attack, would you respond with offensive software?

25%

Question #14

13%
29%   14. Should child porn sites be "fair game" for on-line assaults?

58%

incident. Keep in mind that IDS (Intrusion Detection Systems) are all a little bit different. Many companies use more than one to cover the widest possible range.

2. Once you detect an incident, determine your first course of action. Many people suggest that isolating the source is good enough. Others suggest that cutting off the source of the attack is

Question #15

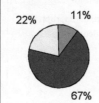

22%   11%

15.   Are there any other sites that it might be OK to attack?

67%

all they want to do. Your reaction should be a reflection of your corporate security policy.

3.   Letting your lawyer know what's going on is a good thing. Do it. If the case ever goes to law enforcement, you want to make sure you are doing the right things. If your in-house counsel doesn't know how to proceed, strongly suggest that he get advice from an experienced cyberattorney.

4.   If you have cut off the attack, collect all of the systems logs from firewalls, routers, and servers so you can identify how the attack was done, what tools were used, and which of your vulnerabilities were exploited. Then, act upon your new knowledge and reconfigure as necessary.

5.   If you do not choose to cut off the attack, make sure that all of your auditing tools are active. Perhaps you will want to increase their sensitivity to capture more data. Monitor the intruder's actions closely, so that you can cut off the attack at any time you choose.

6.   Especially if it looks like an insider attack, you will want to consider the use of forensics tools. They will allow you to perform a sector backup of the hard disk with cryptographic seals, to prevent tampering and assist in maintaining a quality chain of evidence. In addition, you may need to search the disk for erased files and other hidden attributes that are not readily obvious. Don't forget to involve human resources; they can keep you out of a heap of trouble.

7. Attempt to trace the source of the attack. This is not easy, and it often involves lots of people with different organizations. Know who to call at your ISP in the event of a breach. Be able to contact them at all times because attacks are not limited to business hours. ISPs coordinate with each other, and if you plan for the eventuality, you will be that much ahead of the game—able to react much, much faster. Join the High Technology Criminal Investigators Association (www.htcia.org).

8. Have a game plan, especially if you need to, or decide to, call in law enforcement. The rules change when they get involved, and you might find yourself at their mercy. Cyber-investigations can cause downtime and cost manpower resources.

9. If you plan on striking back, do so only with adequate legal counsel. There are a wide range of actions you can take—some more offensive than others.

10. The bottom line is: Prepare for the Acts of Man as much as for the Acts of God. Your disaster recovery people can handle floods and earthquakes and tornadoes. But can they handle a hacker?

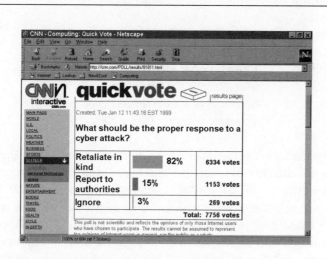

As a result of the corporate vigilantism articles I wrote for *Network World* and the survey results we published, CNN decided to run their own survey.

Infrastructure Is Us

The National Response to Hacking

I am old enough to clearly remember CBS kicking the top-rated Sunday night "Smothers Brothers" variety show off the air, because—get this—Tom and Dick were too radical for America. I also clearly remember from that show the first infrastructure poem I ever heard, recited with Pentagon Papers sincerity by Tommy himself.

I love you for loving me.
You love me for loving you,
I kiss you for kissing me.
You kiss me for kissing you.
So much in love with us are we,
You kiss you and I kiss me.

Isn't that sweet? Two people, deeply in love, inextricably intertwined in union, as one, for the rest of their lives. Human infrastructure. So what is so different today, eh? We merrily anthropomorphize our networks and cyber-connections and, yes, I've heard techies refer to servers as "her," RAM and joysticks as "him," or mice and pixels as "she." Kissing cousins and kissing networks . . . same diff . . . and my in-laws are from the hills of Tennessee . . . but inbreeding is the result all the same. And that's exactly what has happened to our archaic Pleasantville views of infrastructure: cross-bred inbreeding (geneticists watch out!).

Infrastructure used to be so clean a term. The bridge. The road. The railroad tracks. That was man-powered infrastructure, owned and operated by capital MEN of industrial wealth and influence. No one messed with the infrastructure. Bomb the train tracks? Hell, my worst infrastructure offense when visiting my grandmother in thriving Tecumseh, Michigan, was to place ten pennies on the railroad track, and pray I wouldn't get caught and go to jail if the train derailed on my coins. Blow up a bridge? We and the Germans blew up lots of infrastructure in World War II—manly physical infrastructure that was the glue of Tofflerian second-wave societies. I view those bygone eras as three-dimensional, managed, hierarchical societies, or indeed, infrastructures. Toffler and I basically agree.

I guess you could call a river or a harbor an infrastructure, but perhaps it is better to view the port, the man-made components, as being infrastructure and let nature take credit for God's work. I know that, thanks to the apocalyptic predictions of Edgar Cayce, I don't want to piss off Ghea (Mother Earth) anytime soon. No matter, infrastructure grew unfettered as the nineteenth century advanced.

In the dry Utah summer of 1869, seventy-four politicians simultaneously slammed forty-pound sledgehammers into the Golden Spike, announcing the first coast-to-coast American infrastructure: railroads. A mere seven years later, the growing Western Union company established the first coast-to-coast communications infrastructure: the telegraph. Now, can you guess where they planted the tens of thousands of telegraph poles needed to erect their electronic communications behemoth? Right! Next to the railroad tracks. And I guess that was good. They leased three feet of land from the railroad companies, who were all too happy to strike a profit making strategic alliance with a non-competitive communications infrastructure company. All the bosses on that deal made big bonuses. So, we had two physical infrastructures occupying essentially the same physical space.

A few years later, in the mid-1880s, the fledgling AT&T wanted their infrastructure to go coast to coast, too. Despite the fact that even industrial leaders of the day saw no legitimate purpose for the newfangled telephone talking-wire-contraption, AT&T struck a strategic marketing and licensing deal with Western Union: "Let us rent a two-by-four on each of your 97,432 telegraph poles, we'll string our own wires, and we'll pay you a penny per phone call." Or something like that. And so, by the late nineteenth century, we had already begun the construction of the modern infrastructure as we know it, but with one huge unanticipated side effect: We had unthinkingly created confocal vulnerabilities in the process. How dumb we were back then, a century ago. We'd never do that today with what we know, would we? Of course not. . . . Not!

(Just in case: A confocal vulnerability is one in which a single attack or devastating event can hurt or destroy more than one thing at the same time, because they are located at the same physical place. Confocal. OK?)

The concept of infrastructure evolved in the twentieth century, but was at first largely physical in nature. The most notable example was the creation of the national interstate highway system in the 1950s, driven by the efforts of then Senator Albert Gore, Sr., Al Gore Jr.'s father. The Eisenhower Administration was a staunch supporter, because the high-capacity road system was also seen as a means for urban populations to rapidly escape the imminent death and destruction of incoming Soviet thermonuclear warheads. Never mind that five million New Yorkers would end up with a far worse fate: they would be stranded in New Jersey.

Despite the fact that Vice President Gore today (erroneously) claims credit for creating the Internet, the concept of modern infrastructure was an accident of history, championed by the same survivalist instincts that built the highway system. The Defense Advanced Research Projects Agency (DARPA, now ARPA, less the Defense) said, "We wonder how we could connect a couple of computers together." UCLA graduate student Vint Cerf receives a lot of the credit for getting a small handful of computers to exchange data: the concept was proven, and the genesis of twenty-first century infrastructure was born.

The second question that DARPA asked these sixties-style peace-loving UCLA technocrats to answer was, "Now that you have a couple of computers talking to each other, can you make them still talk to each other after a nuclear attack on the United States?" Survivability was the key concept here, and the result, the Internet, is evidence of the concept of survivability through the use of TCP/IP protocols, which are physical routing–independent. That is, a data transmission from point A to point Z will consist of smaller data packets, each of which will likely take a different path to get from A to Z. Imagine a basketball team going from Dallas to Houston. Instead of hopping on a bus or a plane and going together, each player gets in his own car and drives a completely different route. They only assemble back together as a team at the Houston stadium. Reason? If catastrophe hits the bus or plane, the entire team is wiped out and that sucks. If one player picks up a hitchhiker with a chainsaw, the team only loses one player. If another player gets hit by lightning, so be it. The team survives. What about the infrastructure, though?

It Ain't Just Cyber

Many Americans are surprised to see the word *infrastructure* appearing in their daily newspapers because the concept is fairly new to them, even though it has been a part of our physical lives for hundreds of years. The biggest difference is that we have developed a virtual infrastructure, upon which much of the information society functions, yet at the same time we often forget that the virtual infrastructure has a concrete basis in the physical.

- Cyberspace is not an ethereal mystery veiled in intangibility. It is humankind's massive agglomeration of switches and routers, silicon and copper shrouded in PVC insulation, physically connected to an impossibly complex mesh of computers and servers strewn around the globe.
- RF communications networks, cellular phones, and other "transparent" systems are bounded by hardware at the transmitting and receiving ends.
- The bowels of the telephone company really lie within thousands of monolithic, windowless, concrete structures in Everytown, USA. Emblazoned with the name of the phone company across its façade, the building's insides are filled to the brim with endless rows of computer-controlled switches that connect to hundreds of millions of telephones.

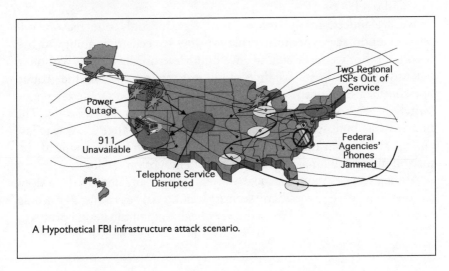

A Hypothetical FBI infrastructure attack scenario.

Far from the Silicon Valley sales pitch of utopian virtuality, modern infrastructure is indeed quite similar to its ancestors in its physical underpinnings. The differences, though, are profound enough to rewrite history—as we are seeing.

- Much of the infrastructure now has two vulnerabilities, instead of just one: it can be attacked through its electronic appendages, as well as through classical physical methods.
- The long-distance connectivity that infrastructure provides also increases the number of people who can (negatively) influence proper operations.
- Its complexity is so complete and its very form changes on a second-to-second basis, so no one can totally understand every nuance of its virtual essence.

But while the underpinnings of the cyber-infrastructure resemble those of its physical ancestors, its reach into our daily lives is deeper and more pervasive. As FCC chairman William Kennard said in a speech in Nashville, "The Internet, unlike the railroad, can come into every office, every home in America, even our briefcases and pockets. We have the capability to bring broadband technologies to all Americans wherever they live and wherever they may go. With cable, copper, wireless, and satellite, we can build on-ramps to the Information Superhighway for anyone anywhere. No town, no community has to be condemned to becoming a ghost town in the New Economy. Part of the reason for this flexibility is technological bits of data are a lot easier to maneuver than iron and steel."

We are indeed in the Information Age for only one reason: our reliance upon the cyber-infrastructure now exceeds our ability to live without it. But we screwed it up. We built electronic highways without a means to protect them. We didn't build the security in from the ground up: consider that until recently, the maintenance ports for telephone switches were only protected by a four-digit numeric passcode. The Internet was built without regards to any security—after all, it was just an experiment that took on a life of its own. Much of the financial sector still moves trillions of dollars without encryption facilities.

Adding security to infrastructure after it is built and deployed is a slow, tedious, expensive process, and security is not nearly as robust as it would be had it been considered from the very beginning of the design process.

Fast Forward

OK, so we built this incredible set of intertwined electronic infrastructures with little regard for security. Even into the late 1980s and early 1990s, we were landlocked into a myopic physical view of infrastructure. But things began to change.

In 1991, I testified before Congress and said that the US infrastructure was so poorly protected that I feared an Electronic Pearl Harbor, a term they had never heard before.

I took years of ribbing for this "outlandish," "Chicken Little-ish" and "scaremongering" view, which is now mainstream thinking.

In hundreds of presentations I gave and meetings I attended throughout the private sector and government, I noted the extreme reticence to accept the new dangers to and vulnerabilities of the United States. We needed, I maintained, to enhance the definition of national security and include economic national security as a new post–Cold War priority. Early in the 1990s, a handful of us were lone voices warning government and private firms of the dangers they would face if cyber-security and infrastructure protection were not taken seriously and viewed as national issues not to be ignored.

It took a few years . . . in fact it wasn't until 1996 that the issue bubbled up through the political machinery in Washington DC, and CIA Director John Deutch warned Congress of the potential for an Electronic Pearl Harbor.[4] A number of efforts rapidly began, including a widespread study by the National Research Council, the Defense Science Board, and the Manhattan Cyber-Project. These studies echoed exactly what we had been saying for years.

The president also signed Executive Order 12864, establishing an advisory counsel, the Information Infrastructure Task Force, to assist with the administration's vision of a national information infrastructure. It delivered its final reports in February of 1996, which spawned a national effort.

On July 15, 1996, President Clinton signed an executive order that began with this sentence: "Certain national infrastructures are so vital that their incapacity or destruction would have a debilitating impact on the defense of economic security of the United States." That order created the President's Commission on Critical Infrastructure Protection, which was chaired by retired general Robert M. Marsh. (www.pccip.gov)

---

[4]Oddly enough, his testimony came five years to the day after my first congressional appearance.

The critical infrastructures deemed to be of extreme national importance are:

- Telecommunications (all forms: the Internet, cable, cellular, telephone, satellite, and any other medium that connects systems together). This sector alone represents about 16 percent of the gross national product of the United States.
- Electric power. I certainly remember the Great Blackout of 1964 in New York. Ironically, I had just bought my first electric guitar that night, and I was stuck on a Fifth Avenue bus as the city came to a halt. The 1976 blackout was more riotous, and we have all experienced brownouts caused by extreme weather or malfunctioning equipment.
- Oil and gas transportation, from the Alaska pipeline to oil refineries to natural gas distribution. Please note that often colocated with these systems are communications wiring and power, which creates confocal vulnerabilities.
- Transportation. Keep trucks delivering food, trains moving manufactured goods, and airlines driving business and tourism.
- Banking and finance. The goods and services economy of the US (GNP) is about $7.5 trillion, and globally about $30 trillion. But the virtual economy, where the stock markets, bonds, and electronic monies are moved, is between $25 and 50 quadrillion, a factor of a thousand larger. Some brokerage houses move trillions of dollars per year over their networks. Given the leverage of electronic over "real" money, major economic systemic disruptions can be globally devastating.
- Water supply. The water is physical, but the controls for moving fresh water to populations and maintaining sewers and waste treatment plants are electronic.
- Emergency services such as 911, fire departments, and medical response and rescue units are tightly knitted together with complex networks to provide high levels of efficiency and public trust.
- Continuity of government is a Cold War remnant. The original concept was that in the event of nuclear war, key political and military leaders would be shuttled off to blast-proof underground bunkers. In the aftermath, they would ostensibly rebuild the country. Today, with infrastructures supporting both the private sector and government opera-

tions, continuity of government is readdressing itself for survival during major infrastructure failures or attacks.

In light of the critical infrastructure taxonomy, the PCCIP was mandated to:

- Assess vulnerabilities and threats to the critical infrastructures
- Identify relevant legal and policy issues, and assess how they should be addressed
- Recommend to the president a national policy and implementation strategy for protecting critical infrastructures
- Propose any necessary statutory or regulatory changes[5]

In October 1997, the PCCIP delivered a classified report to President Clinton with its findings.[6] The political impact of the PCCIP report was effective—Washington finally heeded the warnings it had been given years earlier. However, the report findings were less than illuminating. It merely echoed, reiterated, and reinforced the same warnings and cautions that had been spelled out before. Broadly, the recommendations of the PCCIP have been the basis for today's implementation of infrastructure protection:

Broad Program of Awareness and Education

The government wants to include mainstream America in the awareness of the problem and enlist their support. Most Americans think that the hacking problem is only *New York Times* headlines and do not understand the national implications. Public relations and awareness funding are part of Clinton's recent PDD 63 budget.[7]

Industry Cooperation

Industry and government must develop a process and method to trust each other and jointly share information to the good of the country and the companies in question. This will take a while, though, as industry

---

[5]Robert M. March, at the IBIS Conference I cosponsored with the National Computer Security Association on February 20, 1997, in New York City. I was deeply honored when Mr. March credited me with "sounding the clarion and alerting the government and financial industry to the dangers of denial of service, criminal activities and information terrorism."

[6]The unclassified version reportedly only deleted specific references to potential threats by individuals and groups around the world.

[7]The Chinese espionage scandal has expanded the view of hacking and lack of computer security.

distrust of the government's ability to keep secrets rides high. Anonymous reporting procedures have begun, though.

Enhanced Law

What new laws will help deter the crimes? How can existing laws be retailored to meet the cyber-threats and mitigate their occurrence? Keep in mind that the US is but a local ordinance internationally. International laws and cooperation are critical. Russia, in fact, has proposed an international cyber-disarmament treaty. (www.infowar.com)

More Research and Development

The technology we have today is insufficient to efficiently and effectively defend against attacks. Merging of technologies such as psychology, advanced low-level detection schemes, widespread profiling of low- and high-level attacks, and intelligent monitoring and filtering will occur.

A National Organization

The accompanying charts show the first phases in building a national organization to deal with infrastructure protection. They include industry liaison groups, national monitoring facilities, governmental coordination and leadership reflecting policy.

In the same year that the government took notice, 1996, the National Security Agency decided to perform their own analysis. However, they would focus on the effects of infrastructure disturbance on military preparedness. They ran an exercise called "Eligible Receiver." One team simulated a North Korean cyber-attack against the United States. The rules were simple:

- The bad guys could only use the same connectivity that North Korea has, reportedly about ISDN speeds.
- They could only use attack tools they got from the Internet or slightly enhanced and modified themselves.

Within days, the participating senior military brass were bug-eyed in astonishment. The bad guys had successfully thrown the US into economic chaos by attacking major financial institutions, shutting down large pieces of the US power grid, crippling communications, and short-circuiting the airline industry. (Of course Eligible Receiver was a game with no real damage done. Referees managed the exercise and declared "wins" and "losses.") The participating industry members also acknowledged how utterly surprised they were by the speed and efficiency with which critical infrastructures collapsed one by one.

I have been running Cyberwar Gaming for several years now, and games are invaluable in getting organizations to think about the consequences of their decisions. We design disaster scenarios, which may be either cyber or physical.

The role-playing attendees and audience have to come up with responses to a local, national, or international crisis in seconds, as more disasters unfold. We have used these gaming techniques for military and intelligence organizations around the world, global conglomerates, and huge financial organizations.

Whether it's generals, spies, and corporate executives, or sailors, soldiers, and the company under-bee, cyber-gaming has proven to be tremendously successful. Games get people to think and become aware of what can go wwrroonngggggggg around us and how incredibly tough it can be to defend and protect.

PDD-63

Future historians will look back on May 22, 1998, as a pivotal day in US history. Presidential Decision Directive 63, PDD-63, represents a defining moment when the national policy of the United States was expanded to include protection of its electronic essence. In plain terms, PDD-63 says, "OK, we got it. The infrastructure is vulnerable. The private sector and the government are inextricably tied together. There are lots of nut cases out there with a wide variety of causes and agendas. Destructive electronic tools are free to anyone for the asking on the Internet. We gotta protect ourselves."

PDD-63 calls for complete interagency cooperation across law enforcement, defense, counterterrorism, and Cabinet offices to coordinate with the private sector in developing infrastructure protection policies and methods. Most notably is the creation of three organizations:

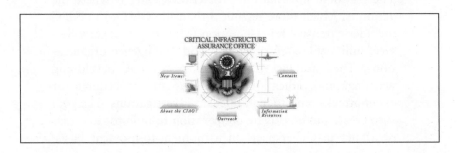

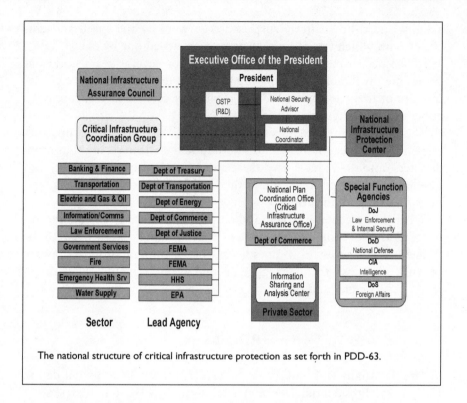

The national structure of critical infrastructure protection as set forth in PDD-63.

- The Critical Infrastructure Assurance Office, which, according to its director, Jeffrey Hunker, "is the engine that will help drive the train of the development of the national [infrastructure protection] plan." It is to integrate the protection efforts across all private sectors, coordinate with Cabinet departments, and work with the government in protecting its own systems. In addition to the legislative and public affairs issues it must handle, the CIAO is also an outreach office that will coordinate national education and awareness programs. (www.ciao.gov)
- The National Information Protection Center is where the action is. Much more technical than the CIAO, the NIPC includes extensive representation from the FBI, Secret Service, military law enforcement, and intelligence organizations. They are tasked to work as a team, developing warnings and indications techniques and procedures for cyber-attacks, and to lead relevant investigations. The goal is to create public-private cooperation to monitor the state of affairs in Cyberspace on a moment-to-moment basis.

The NIPC is the central information-gathering point for threats and vulnerabilities against the infrastructure. (The NIPC publishes "Cybernotes," a biweekly newsletter on threats, hackers, trends and other security relevant information. It's free at www.nipc.gov.

- The Information Sharing and Analysis Center (ISAC) is meant to emulate the function of the CDC, the Center for Disease Control, which is a cooperative effort between the government and the private sector to mitigate the infectious spread of disease. The operations of the ISAC are designed largely by private companies who need to develop increasing levels of trust with the government. The goals for all participants are the same; an uneasy alliance will, over time, develop into a strong synergy.

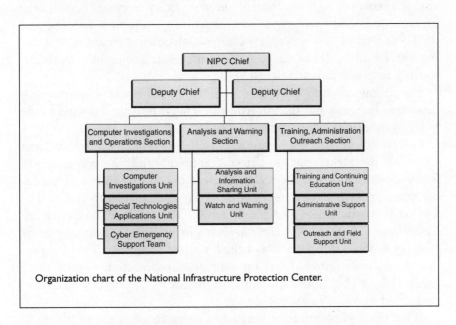

Organization chart of the National Infrastructure Protection Center.

Nothing gets done without money, and on January 22, 1999, in an address to the National Academy of Science, President Clinton announced he was including $1.46 billion in the fiscal year 2000 budget; the monies are to fund the newly created organizations, enhance research and development efforts, and recruit more security experts into the government sector.

We still need a lot more.

The First Steps of Protection

Some of the most intriguing research in infrastructure protection is based in psychology. These lines of research will not produce perfect, hard-core, 100 percent answers, but the studies will contribute greatly to the warnings and indications efforts by examining the behavior of systems and comparing it to the spectrum of behaviors of hackers, terrorists, and other groups who are potential threats to the infrastructure.

The most concentrated efforts, though, are being put into *indications and warning*, a military term, which in the computer security world refers to intrusion detection. Fundamentally, if you can't see the bad guy coming into your networks, you can't do anything about it. Further, with the speed of network attacks measured in thousandths of a second, a high-speed means of automatically countering the attack is necessary.

At the national level, one PDD-63 goal is to accurately gauge the potential damage of individual and coordinated cyber-attacks. The military employs a five-stage "ThreatCon" and "DefCon" system that uses global events as triggers for enhanced military preparedness. Large organizations and enterprises, infrastructure, government entities, and the US as a whole must similarly establish a common means of measuring cyber-health, defensive posture, and threat. From these measurements a response policy is developed.

The following chart integrates a detection and reaction system with American business and the government. This is only an example of the types of conditions we might expect to see.

CyCon-I represents the lowest level of detected offensive activity, and CyCon-V represents massive detected activities and dire consequences to the victim. Note that the scale is skewed one level. While a particular company or organization might be detecting and reacting to CyCon-I or CyCon-II events, there is little effect on the national CyCon level. Regardless of how painful the attack might be for one company or its customers, staff, etc., there is a negligible effect nationally. Thus the proposed scales for national CyCon detection and reaction require more organized attacks. Note here that with the use of CyCon labeling, there is no need to resort to the word *war*.

What the CyCon model suggests is a more coordinated approach to organizational and national preparedness. Much of the work I have done on time-based security as an alternative to the conventional, military-driven computer security model of fortress mentality reinforces the need for extensive sensors, or detection mechanisms, throughout the enterprise, regardless of its nature.

CyCon-I	Noise level; no attacks above chosen threshold.	Corp. and/or no systematic assaults against government facilities or infrastructure.
CyCon-II	Unapproved scans, occasional hack attempts. Detection sensors triggered.	Some government facilities under hack-attack, limited denial of service and/or reports of CyCon-III from corporations. Infrastructure not affected.
CyCon-III	Coordinated hacking and some denial-of-service attacks. Losses evident.	Noticeable successful attacks into government systems or medium-level DoS and/or more than one corporate CyCon-IV reported. Infrastructure under some duress from assaults.
CyCon-IV	Company under extreme assault. Portions of networks isolated, customer services degraded, denial of service effective.	Government systems under coordinated assault, systems under heavy DoS, medium number of corporate CyCon-IVs or at least two corporate CyCon-Vs or one major infrastructural attack causing severe degradation of service.
CyCon-V	Company under extreme assault. Must shut down all electronic facilities to isolate and preserve system.	Some government sites shut down/isolated by major attacks and DoS. Several to many corporate CyCon-Vs. Major successful infrastructural attacks. National economy is affected.

The sensors must be able to understand the nature of the attacks and behavioral anomalies throughout the virtual existence of the networks and infrastructures, and then report back to a centralized repository and response station, such as the NIPC or an ISAC. This is accomplished at the enterprise network level by several popular products today. It is used, however, in only a very small percentage of the organizations that could really benefit from its use.

What is missing, in addition, is the means to create a centralized national reporting repository, whereby the national CyCon level can be measured on a real-time basis, such as in the following figure.

With a real-time monitoring and detection system and the proper reporting channels to a centralized facility (enterprise or national) broad CyCon levels can be established. With appropriate weighting for time, intensity, value, and other considerations, a company or the NIPC can quickly look at the detected activity, just as today we employ network-monitoring tools to gauge the real-time performance of a network.

In more sophisticated applications, heuristics will come into play, the systems will be more self-adapting and -learning, automatic remote responses will be monitored as well, and momentary spikes of high detected CyCon levels will be dealt with quickly and automatically. Thus, if a severe attack occurs against a major domestic firm, if its own detection and reaction systems are in order, the reports that it feeds to the national CyCon repository would barely register a blip.

On the chart below, we see a full month of activity. With a minor detection that triggers a CyCon-I alert on the eighth of the month, everything seems pretty normal until the thirteenth, fourteenth, and fifteenth experience an extraordinary set of attacks, thus triggering a

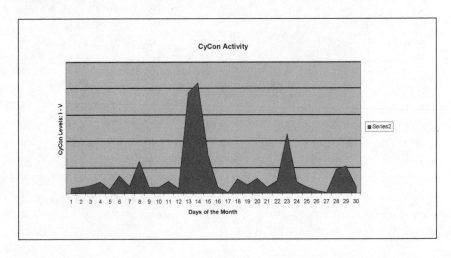

CyCon-IV condition. It appears that the attacks were dealt with in short order, as the state of affairs went immediately back to normal. The rest of this month was not totally without incident: on the twenty-third, a serious set of events raised the CyCon level, and on the twenty-eighth and twenty-ninth a similar, but not as serious set of attacks caused a very noticeable spike.

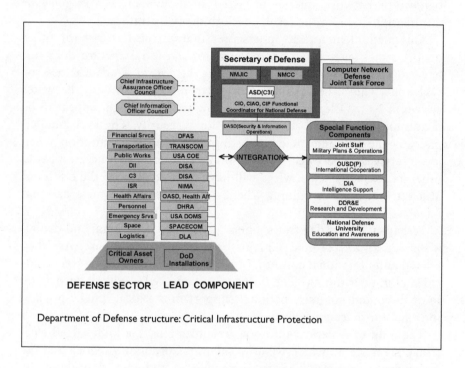

Department of Defense structure: Critical Infrastructure Protection

Where We Stand

Even though we in the US are just at the beginning of a long, uncharted trek to infrastructure protection, and many of us feel that we are terribly exposed to potential adversaries, we are still way ahead of every other Information Age nation-state. Certainly, other nations are looking at infrastructure protection as we are, but the US is still providing the lead in global infrastructure protection.

On October 1, 1999, General Richard Meyers took over as the head of all Department of Defense protection, which represents a major step forward in interservice cooperation. With singular leadership, the military's experiences will provide great support to the NIPC and CIAO as they grow.

What we are learning empirically now, through extensive data collection, network monitoring, and intelligence gathering, is something that we knew intuitively but until recently could not prove: All national cyber-disasters begin at the local level. In March of 1998, a new type of distributed attack against the Pentagon was discovered. Instead of a massive assault or concentrated scanning activity, these distributed low-bandwidth network queries garnered small bits of security-relevant information and sent the results back to the perpetrators.

This method of attack underscores that a true terrorist (or other major) attack against any component of the infrastructure does not have to start with a big bang akin to the World Trade Center's or Oklahoma City's. For example, an electronic problem with the water system in New Orleans (which sits below sea level) might appear to be incidental in the grand scheme of national security. The local municipality is the first line of defense, response, and reconstitution when local services experience a disruption. This means police, fire, and other local emergency services will have to contend with the effects of an electronic systems failure. When, if ever, does it become a national issue?

Perhaps the next day traffic lights go haywire in Atlanta, and denial-of-service attacks cripple a major on-line brokerage house. Are they related and of national concern, or are they isolated events, purely coincidental in their timing? The ISAC, CIAO and NIPC will all participate in analysis and potential national support in the ideal, public-private, information-sharing scenario.

The bulk of Americans do not yet understand the knife-edged electronic precipice on which we now balance. Corporate America and the government also need constant reminders of and education about the rapidly evolving threats.

The private sector is normally loath to hand over any sensitive information to the government over fear that it might be mishandled or end up embarrassingly in the media; an understandable concern. But, as trust is built between the participants in national security infrastructure protection, I envision that by 2010 much of our existing vulnerability to on-line cyber-attacks will be mitigated with better defensive technology, international treaties and law, and a national policy that we are willing to enforce.

Infrastructure is one; it is all interconnected and each component must properly interoperate with all of its partners. An updated infrastructure poem shows just how much we must rely upon and trust each other, because we are indeed all one.

I SYN you for SYNing me,
You ACK me for ACKing you.
I cc: you for cc:ing me,
You cc: me for cc:ing you.
So much a part of us are we,
You ain't you and I ain't me.

Something Other Than War

As we finished the dive, streams of AK-47 bullets met us at the surface. I didn't call that peace. When the mortar rounds rained down around us, that was peacekeeping. Not war.

US Navy Commander James K. Campbell
Mogadishu, Somalia

Quotables

Frankly, we have little clue as to what war really is today. Every dictionary I could lay my hands on defined war as a military conflict between nations, or within a nation, where armies and navies struggle for domination in the physical plane. When you're through with Daniel Webster, though, and look elsewhere, an entirely different picture emerges.

- It's a *War of Words*
- *Business is War*
- *War is Hell*
- *The War on Poverty* and *The War on Drugs*
- "War is the extension of politics."—Anonymous
- "War is failed diplomacy."—Anonymous
- "It's almost impossible to see what wars make the world safe for."—Anonymous
- "I love war and responsibility and excitement. Peace is going to be Hell on me."—General George S. Patton
- "All wars are popular for the first thirty days."—Arthur Schlesinger, Jr.
- "It is always easy to begin a war, but very difficult to stop one, since its beginning and end are not under the control of the same man."—Bellum Jugurthinum, first century BC

- "The object of war is not to die for your country, but to make the other poor bastard die for his."—General George S. Patton
- "War is a series of catastrophes that result in victory."—Georges Clemenceau, French statesman
- "I'd like to see the government get out of war altogether and leave the whole field to private industry."—Joseph Heller, Author of *Catch-22*
- "In business, the competition will bite you if you keep running. If you stand still, they will swallow you."—William Knudsen, Jr., Chairman, Ford Motor Company
- "I don't meet competition. I crush it."—Charles Revson, Chairman, Revlon
- "Whatever is not nailed down is mine. Whatever I can pry loose is not nailed down."—Collis P. Huntington, railroad magnate
- "War would be virtually impossible if everything were on a cash basis."—Anonymous
- "If at first you don't succeed, try, try, again. Then quit. There's no use being a damn fool about it."—W.C. Fields, American actor
- "Men, all of this stuff you have heard about America not wanting to fight, wanting to stay out of the war, is a lot of horse dung. Americans, traditionally, love to fight. All real Americans love the sting of battle. When you were kids, you all admired the champion marble-shooter, the fastest runner, the big-league ball player, the toughest boxer. Americans love a winner and cannot tolerate a loser. Americans play to win all the time. I wouldn't give a hoot for a man who lost and laughed. That's why Americans have never lost—and never will lose—a war, because the very thought of losing is hateful to Americans."—General George S. Patton
- "People used to go off to war, but modern science can now bring it to your doorstep."—Anonymous

War has changed.

The Language of War

I got to asking myself, "What exactly is war?" and "Is our definition of war adequate to meet the challenges we face today?" I spent my teenage years watching the Vietnam War, which in international legalese was not a war. The Korean War meets the same linguistic blockade, as does the Gulf War.

With all due respect to the tens of thousands of Americans who have made terrific sacrifices in the last fifty-plus years, technically the United States has not been at war since World War II. We've had police actions, skirmishes, coalitions, and peacekeeping missions—indeed, we employ a plethora of Zieglerisms to define military intervention, military action, and the death of American soldiers as anything but war. The word *war* has specific intent and meaning in international courts and to other nation-states, which we have diplomatically and politically avoided in the best interests of peace.

We sent the low-flying US Air Force into Libya to bomb the bejeezus out of Khadhafi in 1986; we went into Granada and later tested the stealthy F-117s in Panama, but we haven't been at war. Thus, if the politicians fail, and if the diplomats fail, we send in the troops—but it still isn't war. Well, if it ain't war, then what is it?

This conundrum is not an exclusively American phenomenon, either. The Soviet war in Afghanistan. The war in Chechnya. The Chinese troops march into Tibet as those two countries get at it every so often. The Russian-Chinese border skirmishes. Pakistan and India. An examination of the history records from the last half century will suggest peace, for lack of the formal declaration of war, yet millions of people have died during Peace in Our Time.

So What Is War?

The term Information Warfare is still anathema to much of corporate America and interested bystanders who understandably have trouble with the connotations of armed conflict. The term Cyberwar mollifies a few critics, but that nasty word *war* is still nettlesome. Netwar, the same thing.

And if this Information Warfare/Cyberwar is real, who's in charge? Many of us have written suggestions on how to implement a fourth force to handle cyberwarish matters. The air force is a recent invention, having split off from the army in 1947. Is it time to develop cyberexperts and have them operate as an independent entity, with their own

This military drawing merges the concept of "clean" Information Warfare with conventional armaments. There is no other power on Earth with the capability to wage this kind of infor-mation-dominant conflict. Nonetheless, it will never be this clean. Just look at the pictures of Kosovo.

weapons and strategies that would be synchronized with the other serv-ices? I firmly believe that it is crucial to our national survival and well-being that by 2010, if not earlier, we have a distinct cyber-force in the military.

In the meantime, the Pentagon now uses the term Information Oper-ations to explain what they do to dominate the infosphere in conflict and peacekeeping. The US military and most other militaries are in the business of physical destruction–style war, and migrating to operations where there is no physical destruction is novel. The use of communica-tions-disabling EMP bombs in the Gulf War was an effective prelude to conventional bombing, by destroying Iraq's ability to detect incoming planes and cruise missiles. In Kosovo, the US/NATO forces used carbon filaments and EMP weapons to shut down Serbian infrastructure and power without destroying the physical power plants. This is a good thing.

But is any of this war? The military has been extensively studying new forms of asymmetric warfare; that is, war in which the other guys don't play by the rules. The Vietcong were an asymmetric enemy. Ter-rorists are asymmetric. And so are major hacking endeavors. Part of the military evolution is to find out how they fit into the future of conflict. The Pentagon published JV2010 (Joint Vision 2010), a long document which attempts to position the military's role in the coming years. Some of the contents have to do with better coordination of the services and some have to do with asymmetric adversaries.[8]

The Russians have said that they consider an information warfare attack against their country or infrastructure to be second only to a nuclear attack and they will respond appropriately. They have also offered to the United Nations an Information Warfare Weapons Treaty; many US and European officials maintain the Russians did so because they are so far behind in cyberweapons development and do not want to get into another heavy-spending arms race. Whatever the case, they take it seriously. As does China, which is openly developing advanced offensive information warfare techniques as they flex their international muscle in 1999.

The Beijing government proclaimed in their summer 1999 book, *Unrestricted War*, that they cannot possibly win a conventional military conflict with the United States, so it is now open season on US civilian infrastructures, including critical financial, transportation, communications, and power systems. One of the authors, Colonel Wang Xiangsui, of the Chinese Air Force, amplified those sentiments in the *Washington Post*, 9 August 1999: "War has rules, but those rules are set by the West . . . if you use those rules, then weak countries have no chance . . . we are a weak country, so do we need to fight according to your rules? No." Future adversaries will seek asymmetries in confronting technologically superior opponents like the US by embracing the "indirect approach," which in itself is asymmetric.

We see from our vigilante studies that countries and organizations are going to be more aggressively defending their electronic perimeters, but is that war? Is Information Warfare really war?

There are no clear answers at this point, and the senior military debates are important in the development of US policy, especially since we are ultimately the most vulnerable country in the world. So, without providing answers, I will pose questions for you to consider.

- A recognized nation-state launches a cyber-attack against the northeast power grid in winter. Power is down for three weeks from New York to Bangor, Maine. Hundreds of people die. Is that an act of war? How do we as a nation respond? Remember KAL 007, which was shot down by the Soviets in the 1980s? We didn't shoot back and there was no war. Is this any different?
- BankAmerica/Nationsbank is attacked by a nation-state

---

[8]You can get a free copy from www.infowar.com or many military sites.

and is drained of $290 billion, more than half of their assets. Is that an act of war? Does the US military respond, and if so, how severe a response is appropriate?

- Should the US military defend the US private sector? Which parts of the private sector? Perhaps only critical infrastructures that are owned and operated by local or state municipalities. Is that fair?

- What about privately and publicly owned critical infrastructures such as the airline or communications industry? Do we let them fend for themselves, or does the US Government strike back at the attackers?

- What if the attacks come from cyberterrorists who are operating inside a friendly country? What should our response be, and should we respond with or without the support or approval of the host country?

- And if the cyberterrorists are working from within a terrorist state? We bombed Khartoum, Sudan, in hopes of nailing the terrorist bin Laden. That just stirred him up more. Was that the right response, or was it only right because there was a physical attack in the first place?

- Should the US hack back at its attackers? Should we hack into England if an attack comes from there? During the Kosovo crisis, President Clinton authorized electronic assaults against Serbian President Milosevic's financial holdings.[9]

- If the US military is tasked to protect and defend critical infrastructures and US financial interests, what will we do about US-based multinational corporations that have significant overseas investment and controls? Are the rules different?

Plenty of visionaries are absolutely convinced that we are nearing the end of the nation-state era, much as the feudal systems and city-state political forces died out during the Renaissance. What will replace it?

The general view is that the multinational corporation will be (if it isn't already) the true force projector of the future. Why have physical war when the game is all about money? Why blow up the enemy's buildings and kill his staff off when a hostile financial takeover is so much more efficient and resource-friendly? It's kinder and gentler conflict.

The Japanese (and other Eastern cultures) have maintained for mil-

---

[9]I have no reports on the success or failure of these efforts.

lennia that *business is war*. They may have had it right all along, and this nuclear blow-it-up war business was a temporary historical hiccough.

Keep in mind that we have different adversaries than we did a few short years ago. The list is much longer, and the nature of the adversarial relationship is not nearly so clean-cut as War and Peace. "The good ol' days" of the Cold War were so much simpler than having to codify and monitor the current global myriad of adversaries we face. The list is too long for my taste, but all too real.

- Private domestic economic competition by US rules
- Private international economic competition by US rules
- Nation-state international economic competition by other than US rules
- NGO international economic competition by US rules
- NGO or nation-state international economic competition by other than US rules
- Nation-state international economic aggression
- NGO international economic aggression by other than US rules
- International economic sanctions by US rules
- International economic sanctions by other than US rules
- Domestic hackers—domestic military
- International hackers—US military
- Domestic hackers—US business
- International hackers—US business
- Domestic hackers—domestic infrastructure
- International hackers—domestic infrastructure
- Profit: domestic crime—domestic criminals
- Profit: domestic crime—international criminals
- Profit: international crime—domestic criminals
- Profit: international crime—international criminals
- Profit-oriented—US criminals with damage
- Profit-oriented—international criminals with damage
- Terrorism—physical destruction
- Terrorism—psychological damage
- Nation-state—without damage
- Nation-state—with damage
- Denial of service—electronic with damage
- Nation-state—attack on military
- Nation-state—attack on infrastructure
- Non-nation-state—(NGS) attack on military
- Non-nation-state—(NGS) attack on infrastructure

- Domestic corporate—domestic military
- International corporate—domestic military
- Domestic corporate—domestic business
- International corporate—domestic business
- Domestic corporate—domestic infrastructure
- International corporate—domestic infrastructure

Governments will certainly want to granulize this sample listing with more, threat-specific names. Concerned private organizations will probably also have their own lists of adversaries, ranging from domestic competition all the way to allied nation-states targeting them for national security secrets.

NATO 50th ANNIVERSARY AIRSHOW

PRISTINA, KOSOVO

FREE ADMISSION, FREE PARKING, BOMB SHELTERS AVAILABLE
MARCH 24th 1999, 8:00p.m. until...
AIRCRAFT DEMONSTRATIONS BY:
USAF / RAF / GEAF ...and other NATO members
F-117 / B-52 / F-16 / F-15 / NE-3A / B-2 / TORNADO
HARRIERS / CRUISE MISSLES / A-10 / F/A-18 etc...
DAILY EVENTS
PRECISION BOMBING / SAM SUPPRESSION / STRAFING RUNS
CHIMNEY BOMB DROPS / RUNWAY DEMOLITION / TANK ELIMINATIONS
URBAN RENEWAL / VICTORY THROUGH DEVASTATION

Even the media called the Kosovo situation the world's first Netwar or Cyberwar. Perhaps it was pro-Serbian hackers who had fun at NATO expense. No one is immune any more.

War is not clean or pleasant in any form, but we as human beings seem to have this proclivity toward power and control over others. The war among the hackers themselves is a powerful blip on the radar screens of Cyberspace. The Legion of Doom and the Masters of Destruction went at it for years until Phiber Optik and his crew were indicted and shuffled off to jail. Hacking groups groping for fame and bragging rights have attacked and will continue to attack each other with a vengeance, and law enforcement will not get too involved until enough collateral damage has occurred to innocent network bystanders.

Carolyn Meinel is a fifty-something mother, scientist, and horse trainer from New Mexico, who authored *The Happy Hacker*, a book that triggered hacker outrage and attacks against her and her Internet service provider. She runs real on-line war games from her web site where hackers can test their skills in a fairly benign and friendly environment. But the attacks on her continue. She says she hates the criminal hackers who are after her and polluting Cyberspace, and that really, it's just a small number of electronic banditos. On the other hand, hackers who hate her say she is clueless and instigates the attacks to make fodder for her books. Either way, it's a hacker war that has captured the interest of law enforcement.

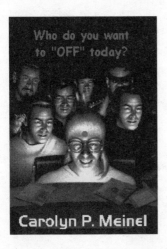

A group of hackers spoofed her original book, called *The Happy Hacker*, and replaced the well-recognized faces with these, plus the target on her head.

Which begs the question: why bring in the military when we have the FBI? As discussed in the vigilante section, there is little political and real support for some of the practices and behavior on the part of the FBI. Besides, they don't have gazillion-dollar budgets or huge manpower. The military is certainly better off, and they have already been developing extensive tool kits for both offensive and defensive operations.

The answers are far from clear and the decisions will likely be less than popular.

The fact is, though, we have to become more aggressive and proactive than we have been throughout the 1990s. And we will. The machinery of government is slow and unwieldy. It has taken the better part of a decade to get senior military officials to realize that, like it or not, they are in the Cyberwar game. That realization, in addition to the tremendous amount of cyber-attacks the Pentagon has suffered in 1998–1999, has caused them to seriously consider disconnecting from the existing Internet and building a new one to their specifications.

This response is somewhat distressing, as it represents a retreat and not a solution. Leave the rest of the world to battle it out and pull the military off the field. It's not really that bad; they do have legitimate concerns, but the Pentagon has never been known for believable spin-doctoring or their public relations acumen. Where is Ron Ziegler when you need him?

There is no answer. Not yet. But the battles—the wars—will continue to be waged by the growing number of international players of all levels of sophistication and skill.

At this point, the best that we can do is stay out of their way.

Resources

- Joint Vision 2010
  Joint Vision 2010 is the fundamental conceptual template for the development of military war fighting doctrine in the late twentieth and early twenty-first century. http://www.dtic.mil/doctrine/jv2010/jvpub.htm
- http://www.au.af.mil/au/database/research/av1997/acsc/97-0095.htm
- http://www.dtic.mil/doctrine/jv2010/briefings.htm
- http://www.defenselink.mil/pubs/qdr/

Information Assurance

Information Assurance (IA) describes the process of protecting America's critical infrastructure of telecommunications and computer technology. This is accomplished by safeguarding the confidentiality of the systems and the information contained within the systems.

- http://www.dtic.mil/dtic/bibtopics/information_assurance.htm
- President's Commission on Infrastructure Protection. The commission fulfilled its obligations, and the site has been removed, but here is what we have stored. If you have never read this, it is worth the time. http://www.info-sec.com/pccip/pccip2/

- Department of Defense, reports to the president and congress, 1999 to 1995 reports.
  http://www.dtic.mil/execsec/adr_intro.htm#1
- Nuclear/Biological/Chemical 1999 Annual Report to Congress http://www.defenselink.mil/pubs/
- Interested in reading military magazines?
  http://www.defenselink.mil/pubs/magazines.html
- Take a virtual walk around the Pentagon (RealPlayer required) http://www.defenselink.mil/pubs/pentagon/
- Freedom of Information Act (FOIA) Program
  http://www.defenselink.mil/pubs/foi/
- Special Operations Posture Statement
  http://www.defenselink.mil/pubs/sof/
- Military acronyms—there are a million!
  http://www.dtic.mil/dtic/dtic-acronyms.html
- Military links. There are a lot here to check out.
  http://www.dtic.mil/dtic/joint-inet.html

VII

The Future

The future used to be a generation away: twenty to thirty years. Today we talk about the future in terms of months. The extraordinary changes we see around us are occuring faster than most of us can handle . . . especially the non-technical types.

We're going to take a shot here, and make some guesses as to what the future will bring.

We know it will be faster. We know it will be more multimedialike. We know connection and communications will be the rule. But that's the good. . . . What about the down side? Is there hope? I like to think so. And hopefully, so do you.

Luddite's Lament

Sometimes I startle myself, like I did the other day on a flight to give a speech at West Point.

I usually carry two laptops with me on the road. One is the full-sized seven pounder with DVD, 8GB hard disk and 128K RAM. I need the power for multimedia presentations. I get maybe two hours of battery time and that's just not enough. My other laptop is a fourteen-ounce miniature NEC that runs Windows CE-2, has a 56K modem, a browser, and "baby" Microsoft Word, Excel and PowerPoint. A pair of AA batteries will last about twenty hours—and that is great—so on planes, trains, and automobiles I favor the little one. I just build a small network in my hotel room and I can tie everything together.

On this trip, though, I left my baby laptop at home, and instead of messing with the big-un, I reverted to an almost forgotten ancient technology: pen and paper. What a concept! During take-off I merrily set to writing notes for the speech and some thoughts for this book. After a page or two of hunching over the tiny tray table, I sat back, and then it happened. My left hand reached out to the table tray and attempted to save the document I had just written. ALT-F-S. But wait! The small tray table didn't have a keyboard I recognized.

Wow did I ever feel, well, not dumb, but astounded that I was so thoroughly enmeshed with the technology—my autonomic body functions so completely programmed—that here I sat trying to ALT-F and save my hieroglyphiclike handwritten scribbles.

Yeah, I hate technology from time to time. We all have a bit of the Unabomber philosophy in us. I want to get as far away from it as I can;

sit with a good book by candlelight in a wood-heated cabin in the woods with no TV, no radio, and no Internet.

Boy does that sound attractive . . . especially right now when I'm trying to wrap up this book. Thousands of hours of writing is not all it's cracked up to be.

We are so damned used to push-button instant gratification that there is no choice but escape! And escape I do and escape you should. Get away from it. Return to roots. Play with your kids. Play with your parents. Talk to live human beings. What a concept!

Play Scrabble. That's an old-fashioned word game from the 1930s.

> *Welcome to Big Company Is Us. Our only goal is to serve you. Please press #1 on your telephone to continue." Beep. "Welcome to the Big Company Is Us Telephone Service Menu. Press #1 for refrigerator repair. Press #2 for microwave irradiation of harmless pets. Press #3 for reports of fish-based food poisoning. Press #4 for reports of chicken- and salmonella-based food poisoning. Press #22 for water softener salt purchases. Press #88 for the Lerner and Michaels Funeral Home . . .*

To hell with it. Hack 'em.

They deserve it.

My Luddite Conversion

Dial. Eleven digits. Dial.

Ring. Ring.

"The area code you have entered has been changed. The new area code from hell for this number is 999. We are now going to hang up on you and make you dial it all over again."

Dial. Eleven digits. Dial.

Ring. Ring.

"This number does not require a 1. Please try again."

Dial. Ten digits. Dial.

Ring. Ring.

"You must dial a 1 to make this call. Please try again."

Dial. Eleven digits. Dial.

Ring. Ring.

"This number does not require a 1. Please try again."

Dial. One digit. Dial. Operator.

Ring. Ring.

"I Don't Care Long Distance Service. How may I help you?"

"I can't dial this number . . ."

"Are you dialing a 1?"

"Yes."

"It should work."

"Well, it doesn't."

"Have you checked with your long-distance company?"

"You *are* my long-distance company."

"This seems to be an AT&T problem. Thanks for calling the I Don't Care Long Distance Service." Click.

Dial. Five digits. Dial. 10288.

Ring. Ring.

"You have reached a number that is wrong. Just wrong. Try again."

Shit.

Dial. One digit. Dial. Operator.

Ring. Ring.

"I Don't Care Long Distance Service. How may I help you?"

"How can I reach AT&T?"

"You need information."

"Right."

"That's 411." Click.

Dial. Three digits. Dial. 411.

Ring. Ring.

"You must first dial a 1."

Dial. Four digits. Dial. 1411.

Ring. Ring.

"This is not a working number. Please check with directory assistance."

Shit. Shit. Damn computers.

Dial. Two digits. Dial. 00.

Ring. Ring.

"Your Other Long Distance Company. How may I help you?"

"How can I reach AT&T?"

"I'm not sure. Let me check with my supervisor. What was that name again?"

"AT&T . . . you know, the real phone company."

"There is no need to be rude . . ." Click. Music on hold.

Wait. Wait. Seventy-two seconds.

"Sir?"

"Yes?"

"The number is 10288."

"I tried that. It doesn't work."

"Hmmm. Let me check."

Wait. Wait. Thirty-nine seconds.

"It seems they have changed their number . . ."

"Astute observation . . ."

"Dial 1010288."

"You sure?"

"Ah . . . that's what my supervisor says and he's the boss."

"Thanks."

Dial. Seven digits. Dial. 1010288.

"AT&T. How may I help you?"

Phew.

"I've been trying to dial this number . . ."

"Did you dial a 1 first?"

"Of course . . ."

"It should work. Let me try it for you."

Dial. Eleven digits. Dial.

Ring. Ring.

"There you are sir. That will be an additional $1.80 on your bill for operator assistance. Thank you for using AT&T."

Ring. Ring.

"Welcome to Big Company R-Us. Please enter the extension you want."

Dial. One digit. Dial. 0.

"That is not a valid entry. Welcome to Big Company R-Us. Please enter the extension you want."

Dial. One digit. Dial. 0.

"That is not a valid entry. Welcome to Big Company R-Us. Please enter the extension you want."

Dial. Four digits. Dial. 1234.

"Welcome to Mary Talbott's mailbox. Please enter your four-digit ID code to retrieve your voicemail."

Dial. Four digits. Dial. 1234.

"Hello, Mary Talbott. You have five new messages. Please enter 1 to listen to the first message."

Dial. One digit. Dial. 1.

"That is an incorrect entry. You are now being disconnected. Thank you for calling Big Company R-Us."

The Future of Microsoft

PRSN: News-Online: 413.CV71-1: Microsoft to Avoid Future US Government Prosecution

In a defensive move designed to mitigate US Government anti-trust pressures, Microsoft has taken a drastic and highly controversial step. Yesterday Microsoft Chairman William H. Gates announced that the company had purchased a small island from the Netherland Antilles, eighty-one miles north of Venezuela and the South American coast. According to a statement by the Antilles government, "The land we sold to Microsoft consists of 4,500 uninhabited acres situated on a small island jewel of the Caribbean."

The purpose of the Microsoft purchase became clear late yesterday afternoon when the previously unnamed island applied for nation-state status at the United Nations, with the full support of the Netherland Antilles, the Netherlands, Jamaica, Haiti and several other Caribbean countries. Cuba was the only vocal dissenter, citing "unbridled criminal capitalism will be dealt a swift blow if they attempt to export their corruption to our peaceful island communities." Microsoft promised to pay its United Nations dues five years in advance and bring up the arrears accounts of several neighboring countries as a show of the kind of neighbor it promises to be.

While neither Mr. Gates nor Microsoft President Steve Balmer would explicitly confirm the leaks from senior sources, it does appear that the purpose is to move the company's legal corporate identity out of the United States to the new nation-state island, where the US Department of Justice has no control.

Once the tiny island, named Microbillesia, is accepted by the United Nations, Microsoft will commence the migration of its headquarters and corporate offices. This action does not require United States approval. The plan for the company move, expected to take four years, will involve the movement of several thousands of people from the Seattle area to Microbillesia and nearby islands.

Financial analysts call the move "brilliantly conceived." If Microsoft does invest an estimated $4–5 billion in the move, the payback can occur in less than two years, based upon Microsoft's current federal tax obligations. Over a twenty-year period, Microsoft could save tens of billions of dollars, which will be handed right over to shareholders as increased profits.

On the other hand, Michael Silvers, senior analyst at Ramtech Investments, San Jose, California, suggests, "maybe this is merely corporate brinkmanship on a global scale, to see who will blink first," with Microsoft hoping the Department of Justice will ease up its pressures rather than lose the company's entire tax base. Insiders say Microsoft felt compelled to take this step because of the intense anti-monopoly investigations and the increasingly negative images of William H. Gates and his company.

Silvers's company has spent a great deal of time analyzing the confrontation. He continued by saying, "If they do actually make this move, the government could conceivably levy heavy import taxes on Microsoft products, and then the two countries would have to negotiate a most-favored nations status treaty. Who knows how pissed off the State Department will be. They could still make Gates's life miserable. What if they refused to give him a visa to travel stateside?" Microsoft dismissed such negativity, and said there were many small details and the US would have to play fair with Microbillesia in the international court of opinion. Silvers countered by commenting that such arrogance will only continue to hurt Microsoft. "They can ignore US laws all they want; they can run to their own little country island. But the United States still has the power to pummel Bill Gates feet first into the sand, and the more he pulls stunts like this, the more and more likely they will be to use quicksand."

Health officials also show deep concerns over the proposed move. Dr. Fred Wedel, Seattle, Washington, worries. "Can't you see what will happen? Thousands of pale-skinned, pasty-faced kids who only get to see the sun two or three days a year in Seattle will suddenly be exposed to the torrid heat of an equatorial sun. I expect the cancer rate on Microbillesia will be significantly higher than in almost any country on Earth, within ten years," he predicted.

Microsoft scoffed at Dr. Wedel's assertions. "There is no statistical basis for his accusations. We are currently working on an Excel plug-in that will show the actual numbers to more closely match the reality we need."

United Nations approval is expected, and Microbillesia's first corporate citizen will be Microsoft, BL, Microbillesia, formerly Microsoft, USA.

The exact price of the island purchase was not disclosed and has been sealed. However, Jan van Zelbert, spokesperson for the Antilles government, did confirm that along with Jamaica, Haiti, and Antigua, they would receive unlimited free copies of Windows 2000, Office HAL-2001 and other Microsoft products for their entire population for a period of twenty years. Microsoft's share price rose 17⅞ dollars yesterday on the news that it would declare itself an independent country in the next quarter.

For more details see the Microsoft web site: www.microsoft.com/hoax/
HXNEWSWIRE: NWR-09-836521-01
CONFIRMATION: 561LX-71HH:200X/:61-119

Parisian fast food restaurants rely on "NT"—with haphazard results.[1]

[1] At one McDonald's, a clerk apparently had a background in hacking, or maybe was just slightly technical with an attitude. You know how at the bottom of the receipt is printed, "Thank You!" I bet you can guess what it was changed to. The second word was "You" but the first one was less polite.

Messing with the Collective Mind: PsyOps

In military parlance, PsyOps stands for Psychological Operations. Like dropping thirteen gazillion leaflets over Iraq, telling the soldiers and the people how useless their struggle was. Or broadcasting on Radio Free Europe to get the American Cold War message through. The point is to shift the paradigm of the target (adversary or not) and his belief systems to work on your behalf.

Take the Net. Someone publishes a piece of "data"—and let's say it's not true, but it is intriguing. So it gets passed around a number of communities. Let's say you read it and think "How interesting." And then in a few days you hear about it again, but from another place. And then at a party another person tells you the same thing. The apparent validity of that original "data" has now grown in importance, and you might just take it more as fact than not.

The Good Times Virus has passed around the Net several times. It makes all sorts of nonsense warnings of impending computer doom unless the reader heeds the message's advice. Problem is, there is no such virus in the physical world or that affects your CPU or other silicon life. The Good Times Virus is a so-called meme; the virus is the message itself, and it has shown how rapidly and often disinformation can spread—just like a conventional virus.

PsyOps was responsible for getting the US to deploy a peacekeeping mission to Somalia—pictures of starving children, a country in anarchy where even the UN couldn't get food to the needy. The starving, hunched-over child with the vulture sitting behind him was the single image often credited with our intervention there. So CNN moves to the beaches of Somalia and waits for the troops and we watch it all live while eating our Wheaties. Then another indelible image is scorched into our minds: a dead US soldier being dragged through the streets of Mogadishu. The US civilian call for a pullout caused an instant shift in public opinion, and out we were.

The media is certainly responsible for the filtered contents of what we see and hear on TV, on the radio, and in the papers. How they perceive the truth is a major factor as to what information is brought to the public and in what quantity. The quantity of time or space is a function of how much emphasis the media places on a story, and thus helps determine how seriously the viewing and reading public should view it as well. Fair? Maybe not, but that's the way it is.

A sort of balance has been achieved with the Net. If you want a lot of extra information about, say, hamsters and duct tape, there is a place for you to get it—probably on Usenet—but you won't see it on the six o'clock news. At the same time, if you see a story on Dan Rather's CBS and want more in depth discussions, there is the *New York Times*—or the Net, where it will undoubtedly be discussed amongst a hundred armchair experts.

And that's part of PsyOps: manipulation of the media. They are supposed to represent a fair, unbiased condensation and filtration of the news that is important to their audiences. That's why local news shows about local people and local events are often more widely watched than the national or international news. But back to the proliferation of technology to the masses: We are on the verge of being able to create artificial truth.

I reguarly provide a demonstration of a technology that will soon be on the desktop of you, me, hackers, and potential terrorists.

1. It's a videotape about fifteen seconds long. A scene of an office, some guys sitting around. A lady walks from the right side to the left side of the screen. That's it.

2. The next clip is the same scene. Except the lady doesn't walk across the screen. Big deal, you say?

The lady's virtual optical existence and image on the videotape was electronically erased by a computer, and the background her body obscured while walking across the room was digitally recreated to make the picture look complete.

Oh, you say, *that's* what they did in "Terminator II" with morphing? That's "Independence Day" or "Star Wars" technology.

Alas, silicon breath: Hear this! This technology works in real time!

No delay. What you see in front of your eyes may not be what you get on tape! Artificial truth.

Imagine the US making videos like, "Saddam and the Camel" or "Gore Takes a Bribe." How do we know they are real? We don't, and that's what PsyOps is all about.

The purpose of the technology behind the demo is to make money in advertising. Take a baseball game. Around most sporting events, physical billboards advertise national brands of products like Pennzoil, Wrigley's gum, or any of a hundred different products. As the camera pans the stadium the billboards are broadcast to millions of homes. This new technology, though, will electronically replace those billboards with new digital billboards.

One obvious use of this technology permits the local TV station in Dungroot, Montana, to allow the local grain store or bootblack or sausage barn to advertise on what is ostensibly a national event. Or, for instance, at the Olympics, the myriad billboards along the side of the luge can be digitally replaced with advertising from a particular country, city, or neighborhood.

Now, let's put on our Information Warrior hats.

Take yourself back to 1992, when Jennifer Flowers accused presidential contender Bill Clinton of sexual indiscretions. It made news, but fluttered away. What if the accusations had been accompanied with a videotape of the . . . shenanigans? A real-time full motion artificial truth built to create or modify public opinion. Affecting the political process is a reasonable criminal or terrorist application for this technology. Wouldn't this help China or Russia or Syria get their unfavorite US political candidates eliminated from the race?

Consider the power we are unleashing. The US Government releases a video of our political adversary of choice—at the right time—doing nasty things that will hopefully incite his constituency. Without getting graphic here, use your imagination: What kind of real-time, full-motion videos would get your blood going . . . or influence an entire population the way you want them influenced? That's PsyOps.

And consider this: the political adversary of choice. Let's say it's someone in office, in Congress, who you and your group really want out of office because they have affronted your particular sensibilities. So, let's say you go out and create an artificial truth video of this particular congressperson taking a big illegal bribe from another unpopular group—maybe neo-Nazis. Then you send the video to two places: the media and the FBI. What happens?

I have asked this question to a lot of law enforcement people and they all come up with the same answer so far: They have to investigate. They look and they look and they ask and ask and they eventually come to the congressperson in the video, who is incensed beyond reason that anything like this has happened. But how do you prove a negative? How can he prove it didn't happen? Whoops. And in the meantime, the piece may have run on CNN or other media; or maybe the perpetrators sent it to the *National Enquirer* instead. In either case, such an event could be a career ender.

The videotape is believed first.

Guilty until proven innocent.

So in the near future we find a convergence between the PsyOps capabilities that are rapidly descending upon us and the loss of personal identity that occurs when people and organizations make decisions and choices about us based upon the contents of a computer or what they see on a videotape, not on what we say or maintain about ourselves.

While in many ways technology empowers the individual, at the same time it strips us of our individuality; and our fellow carbon-based humanoids have allowed silicon life forms to determine our fate. The future may not be all it's advertised to be.

Extreme Hacking

$\mathbf{M}$y eight-year-old watches extreme sports. They scare the living bejeezus out of me.

I was content to ski down steep mountains and water ski in four-foot waves. Today I limit it to aggressive roller blading, scuba diving, and softball. But these extreme sports—jumping off a 400-foot bridge on a thin cord that you hope bounces you back to the sky before you become a human pancake on the rocks below, jumping out of an airplane on a snowboard—are insane. Hurtling down city streets feet first at ninety miles per hour begs for a six-foot person to be midgetized upon impact. And rock climbing: why the hell would anyone want to climb a sheer rock face 600 feet high, using only toes and fingers for balance and strength. Sheesh!

Pushing the human body to absurd limits for the sake of it is much like hacking and Nike: Just Do It. True hackers are not satisfied with their last hack, they aspire to greater things. And so, let's look at some other hacking that is either already going on or will be. This is extreme hacking.

Voice Over IP

OK, you now know the Internet is a pretty wide-open place with little privacy. But it's only get worse if the major phone companies surge ahead and build a new communications system generically known as Voice Over IP. All this means is that the telephone conversations we have today will go over Internet circuits with the same vulnerabilities and weaknesses we experience today. For all of the privacy problems with telephones today, it will only get worse unless the telephone companies build in encryption to prevent eavesdropping.

HERF Guns

If it can be destructive and it can mess with a computer, the hackers want a shot at it. HERF is a true engineering exercise, with potential for severe bodily harm to self and others. Remember the woman who wanted to dry her poodle quickly so she put him in the microwave? Who wants to clean up that mess?! If you hack HERF be very, very careful.

Search the Net about the HAARP project to see what the military is doing with tremendous amounts of electromagnetic energy being sent into the ionosphere and heated up. When they test the HAARP system in Alaska, planes have to be at least 500 miles away. Fascinating and on the edge.[2] It's got mystery, spies, secrets, and Nicolai Tesla, who was trying to perfect broadcast power.

HAARP is a wonderful member of the conspiracy theory club:

- Lift the ionosphere
- Alien "stealth" tunnel
- Satellite—underground x-ray
- Weather modification

Pick your favorite.

Satellite Hacking

From Reuters News Service, February 28, 1999:

> Hackers have seized control of one of Britain's military communication satellites and issued blackmail threats, the Sunday Business newspaper reported.
>
> The newspaper, quoting security sources, said the intruders altered the course of one of Britain's four satellites that are used by defense planners and military forces around the world. The sources said the satellite's course was changed just over two weeks ago. The hackers then issued a blackmail

---

[2]http://www.primenet.com/~rfwatts/haarp/haarp.html

threat, demanding money to stop interfering with the satellite.

"This is a nightmare scenario," said one intelligence source. Military strategists said that if Britain were to come under nuclear attack, an aggressor would first interfere with military communications systems. "This is not just a case of computer nerds mucking about. This is very, very serious and the blackmail threat has made it even more serious," one security source said.

Police said they would not comment as the investigation was at too sensitive a stage. The Ministry of Defense made no comment.

Subsequently the British Ministry of Defense denied the event altogether, but again hackers made the news. True or not?

On April 27, 1986, HBO viewers were rudely interrupted during the broadcast of *The Falcon and the Snowman*, when their screens suddenly displayed the message:

```
Good evening HBO From Captain Midnight
$12.95/Month No Way!
(Showtime/Movie Channel Beware)
```

HBO's satellite signal had been overridden by a satellite hacker who was displeased with the scrambling of pay-per-view satellite transmissions. The industry instantly convened to discuss the situation. It turned out that a threatening phone call was made prior to the jamming episode by a caller who only identified himself as "Carl." The caller warned, "This is electronic warfare."

Carl alleged that he was associated with the American Technocratic Association, based in Wilmington, Delaware. The group claimed that for a mere $25 million, they could "completely knock every satellite off the globe." Showtime experienced similar interference with their satellite transponders in December of 1985, but not to the same degree.

In an article entitled, "Declaration of Electronic War," author Bill Sullivan cited the concerns of the satellite industry about such threats. After the Captain Midnight interruption, the attendees at the meeting "wanted to keep a low profile and did not want that vulnerability disseminated to the general public . . . because [they] are so vulnerable to jamming." The ATA claimed that they were going to proceed with destructive jamming, by overloading the satellite transponders, and the consensus was that this was possible. John Roberts of United Video said, "I think a knowledgeable person could put together a satellite transmitter inexpensively..." and *Radio Electronics* magazine said, "One report stated that the [Captain Midnight] feat required a great deal of technical expertise and about $60,000 worth of equipment." A Federal Communications Commission spokesman, Ron Lepkowski, admitted that, "We've always recognized the possibility."

Today with the global Iridium phone network going on-line, they make an attractive target. But it is the much touted Teledesic, the so-called "Internet in the sky" I predict will be the most satellite system. Bill Gates is a significant player in Teledesic and hackers hate anything that smells of Gates.

The Teledesic Network will consist of 288 operational satellites, divided into twelve planes, each with twenty-four satellites. As the satellite planes orbit north-to-south and south-to-north, the earth rotates underneath. What more could a hacker want? (www.teledesic.com)

Tempest Hacking

In September of 1991, when I appeared on Horendo Retardo's (Geraldo Rivera) ill-fated TV show, "Now! It Can Be Told," I demonstrated what I believe was the first national broadcast of electromagnetic eavesdropping. Despite the fact that atomic bombs were going off in the background, the demonstration was real. We demonstrated how an old black-and-white television set can "listen in on" a computer from several hundred yards away without any wires at all.

Any electrical current produces a magnetic field. A television station transmits a magnetic field from its broadcast antenna atop the World Trade Center or in a cornfield in Iowa, and a portable TV set in your home can pick up the small signals and display "Mr. Ed" reruns or "Murphy Brown" in startling clarity.

Let's take this thought one step further. Computers, printers, fax

machines, and video monitors are also electrical devices that conduct
current and emit magnetic fields. Guess what? These magnetic fields can
be picked up by a special receiver, and be read and reconstructed, invisibly and passively, on a computer screen, with little fear of detection.
Sounds like an ideal tool for the hacker and cyberwarrior who wants to
know what secrets are going on inside of Wall Street.

According to Mark Baven, an editor at Government Data Systems,
"In today's volatile financial market, where inside information can lead
to millions of dollars of profits, a raid on a corporation's vital data . . .
could be extremely worthwhile. The cost of implementing Tempest technology would be far offset by the potential savings that such security
would provide."

In the fall of 1992, Chemical Bank found themselves the apparent target of exactly this type of eavesdropping by unknown Information Warriors. According to Don Delaney of the New York State Police, bank
officials were alerted that an antenna was pointed at their midtown New
York bank offices, where a large number of ATM machines and credit
card processing facilities are located. For reasons that the bank will not
discuss, they elected not to pursue the matter although the police offered
assistance. From external appearances, it seems that Chemical Bank was
the target of what has generically become known as a Tempest attack.

Hackers haven't had their real shot at Tempest yet, partly, I believe,
because it requires a lot more technical and engineering expertise than
knowing the Internet. But someone is going to take advantage of it soon
enough.

Mind Hacking

How do you influence the human mind?

The CIA tried LSD for years but today they are looking at more effective techniques. What about microwaves that are tuned to specific frequencies and turn your teeth fillings into radio receivers. Simply inject
the Voice of God and the target hears "voices." We're getting there, and
when the technology is developed and someone sneaks it out of the classified world, hackers are next to play with it.

Computer viruses and Trojan Horses are being tested to modify the
frequency and waveform of video signals on the computer, to give people headaches or possibly induce other physiological change. Hackers
aren't going to be far away, are they?

I have to believe that beyond being dangerous, this kind of activity is illegal, but none of the lawyers could offer more than, "If you hurt someone, it's a crime."

Wireless Hacking

Laying wires for communications costs a lot of money. It takes a long time to dig up streets and put them back together again. As third-world areas like the Amazon Basin and inner Africa get wired, companies are not digging trenches through the jungle. They are building RF or wireless radio systems.

In the US and other advanced countries, more and more wireless systems will follow in the electronic footprints of Teledesic and cell phones. Radio networks are an ideal target for hackers and their inquisitiveness. If there are any security problems, the hackers will be sure-as-shooting the ones to find it. The hope is that the engineers build it right the first time.

If There Is a Technology, It Will Be Hacked

Lockpicking is enjoyed by many hackers because it is the physical equivalent of hacking. Cracking smart cards by ion-bombardment was a novel hack that scared many a smart-card manufacturer. Cash-carrying stored value transaction cards are an obvious hackers' delight.

The hackers aren't going anywhere. They are here to stay and, depending upon your point of view, are a big help or a huge hindrance.

The Toaster
Rebellion of '08

The appliance fanatics will no doubt tell you it was a lot worse than it really was. For the rest of us, though, it will go down as a humorous lesson for mankind. An historic footnote not quite on a par with the launching of Sputnik—but closer to when the air force shot down Larry Ellison's[3] MiG-23 because he just wouldn't stop buzz-strafing Bill Gates' bigger and better home.

Fact is, though, the talking heads were talking like it was the end of civilization as we know it. But it ended up just being the toasters and a few renegade, poorly organized militia fridges and irons. And I should know; I was there. It could have been a whole lot worse if it weren't for the unlikely likes of those two . . . fancified plumbers or appliance repairmen. Whatever—that's all they are, but they came through like champs. Then again, that's me.

I don't know the exact date, but it was, I guess, oh . . . seems like it was two and a half years ago, maybe a bit more, and the two of them were sitting around, seeing as things pretty much worked back then. Jeez, get that? Back then. I'm talking about it like it was a lifetime ago, and since everything has changed so much, it does feel like a lifetime. So, "back then" is pretty accurate. And who knew appliances could sing?

At any rate, the history books will show that it all began in Brooklyn.

"And now this. Who would'a t'ought, eh?" smirked Manny Volta. He punched his approval in the midsection of the *Daily News*, and then exhaled an oversized cloud of cigar smoke onto the tar- and nicotine-

---

[3]Eccentric founder billionaire of Oracle Corporation.

stained storefront window that beckoned customers. What really attracted customers to their dingy storefront, though, was the bright yellow Magic-Marker'd sign: "We Fix Anything."

"Y'know, Manny, when y'a right, y'a right," Meeks Prophet said, feet propped on his pristine black desktop. Not a soldering iron or broken anything in sight. Engrossed in the same daily paper, he held up one side of it while giving his crotch the scratch of its life. His bare long arms cried out for a close shave, as did most of his tall, spindly body. The pair's matching uniforms were closer to the faded, pale blue stripes of prison garb than the bright crispness of the Maytag repairman outfit. Nonetheless, they were spotlessly clean. In fact, their whole shop was immaculate. Despite his constant apelike body scratching, Meeks was obsessively tidy.

"Gates goin' t'a frickin' jail, eh? Payback's a bitch." Manny's unshaven round face stayed buried in the paper. A foot shorter, he had to weigh twice as much as Meeks.

"Guilty of Fuckin' Wit' Everyt'ing." Meeks laughed at his own version of the Justice Department indictment, which said exactly the same thing in Federal-Court-speak.

"That FBI lawyer broad's gotta pair a' Renos on her, eh?" No one remembered exactly when the former attorney general's name became synonymous with the slang expression for testicles.

"Y'know what that'll mean, don't ya? Gates gone fer'while?"

"Damn right-a, I do." They both laughed as Manny belched more smoke. Problem was, neither Manny nor Meeks had any clue what it meant.

Brooklyn Boys Repair had grown from these two techno-dweeb high school dropouts with an attitude to a debt-free small business with local color to spare. While happily successful by their own measure, six and a half employees does not an empire make.

The Brooklyn Boys' phone warbled.

"Ya gonna get it?" Manny was now splitting his focus between a New York Rangers game and trying to figure out why Mr. Valenti's new Palm Pilot XXI was getting mail-bombed by its Teledesic satellite feed. He was losing orders, and Valenti did not like losing money.

"Manny, you fix. You a good boy, Manny, you fix and everyt'ing gonna be all right. OK, Manny?" Valenti crowed. If he had concentrated on it for more than a glance between slap shots, Manny would have noticed that the "Incoming Filter" was toggled to *default*. Even though he didn't compare to Meeks in his repairing skills, his inattentiveness to the PDA was quickly turning a thirty-second favor into an eighty-dollar billable hour.

"You got the phone, Meeks?" Manny hollered on the third ring.

"Yeah . . ." he punched the speaker button on the phone. "Brooklyn Boys . . . you'se kick it, we's fix it." Manny glared at the distracted way Meeks answered. Besides which, the Jumbo Holiday Issue of *Hustler* had no business in the front office. For his long list of failings, including that his hair shed as much as a cat, Meeks had an uncanny ability to fix appliances. Especially the electronic appliance networked kind that learned on the job and did all of the thinking for you. It was eerie how good Meeks was, so Manny ran the business end of the fix-it shop and Meeks was left to run the fix-it and install crews.

"Hey . . . I'm over at Mrs. Schimmer's . . ." A bassoonish voice sprung from the speaker phone.

"Again?" Manny turned from a bay window–sized flat screen display of the game at the new Madison Square Garden.

"Yeah, I know, I know . . . but she said her toaster was still givin' 'er trouble."

"But you was just there, when, yesterday? The day b'fore?"

"Hey? We give warranty . . ."

"Todd, yeah, that ain't it . . . wha's wrong now?" This shoulda been over and done with, thought Meeks.

"Tha's the thing," Todd Strong said curiously. "Same thing as b'fore. Jus' won't cook the damned toast . . . oh, sorry, Mrs. Schimmer . . . *darned* toast."

Manny scrunched up his fatty forehead into deeply creased lines. Meeks half-listened while he held the full-length spread of the Honey of the Month centerfold at arm's length.

"So, d'ya replace the Net-board?" Meeks asked nonchalantly.

"Yeah, 'course I did . . . whaddya think . . ." Todd said defensively. Guys from the streets of Brooklyn do not like having their fixing skills challenged.

"Jus' asking . . ." Todd had only worked for Brooklyn Boys for a year but knew his way around washing machines and dryers and toasters and microwaves better than Manny, and he showed a lot of get-up-and-go.

"Maybe y'oughta bring it in," was the best Meeks could come up with as he scratched a delicate spot on Miss January.

"Hey, Manny," Todd said, ignoring Meeks. " 'Member the Russian deli, last week? Same thing . . ."

"But ya fixed that one," Manny reminded him.

"I guess, yeah. They haven't called," he asked, "have they?"

"Nah. Listen, Meeks's right. Bring it on in."

The test they ran only proved that Mrs. Schimmer's General Electric four-slice Smart Toaster worked perfectly. Her House-Net connections and all of the neural circuits tested 100 percent. The Crisper-waves put the exact burn patterns on the cooked bread that it was instructed to. None of the Brooklyn Boys got it. Meeks scratched his head in cliché confusion with the same hand that.... Manny chose to erase that thought from his mind.

"How's the house?"

"Shit, we wired it." Todd remembered it was his first job, installing Mrs. Schimmer's 10Meg House-Net. "Everything else is perfect..."

"Yet the toaster only screws up in her place..." Manny was trying to help the kid.

"So maybe Mr. Fridge is telling Mr. Toaster to cool it." Meeks laughed alone, as he was the only person who saw the humor.

"So, it's the wiring in her house; sumpins' wrong." Manny began to mentally count the losses on that job.

"Ouch." Yelled Todd from his appliance repair workbench, as his hands busily juggled two pieces of hot toast that were catapulted out of the toaster by themselves.

"Hey, dat's it!" exclaimed Manny, laughing. Meeks turned his head from the Scratch and Sniff centerfold to listen to Manny offer his wisdom. "It's the friggin' ejection mechanism... why doncha jus' replace it, kid?" Meeks threw a facetious thumbs-up sign, grimaced at the clearly ridiculous suggestion, and returned to the articles he was digesting in *Hustler*.

"Yeah..." agreed Todd as the cooling toast landed next to Mrs. Schimmer's toaster. "That's it Manny. I'll look right into it."

But then both Todd and Manny paused. Silent. Staring at the two pieces of toast. Then at each other, then back at the toast. Neither one of them wanted to touch it.

The ringing phone penetrated the silence, and Meeks absently pushed the speaker button and answered in his usual careless way. "Yeah?"

"Hey, Brooklyn Boys. I was thought zat you feexed my toaster?" Shit, thought Meeks. It was that pain in the ass Russian Kristznov. "You theenk eet's a joke, eh? Some big fuggin' joke, eh?"

Meeks Prophet looked annoyed and scratched through the jungle of hair on his arms, a nervous condition that made him a miserable poker player. "Ah, Mr. Kristsnov, I, ah... hey... whatcha talkin' 'bout joke?" He looked over to Manny and Todd for clues, but they were still enthralled with the two pieces of toast. Todd picked up a screwdriver and flipped one piece over. They both shuddered. There it was again.

"Hey, asshole," Meeks Prophet called out.

"What you call me?" came the thick Russian accent over the phone. Meeks ignored it.

"Hey, Todd Asshole, you. I t'ought you said you fixed the Commie's toasters, eh? What gives?"

"Real funny joke you are, you Brooklyn Boys . . . you theenk eets big joke to put hammer and sickle onto toast?" Kristsnov kept hammering at Meeks.

"Meeks, c'mere," waved Manny. "C'mere." He had goosebumps crawling up and down his arm. "Mr. Kristsnov," he hollered across the room, "can you hold on a minute? Thanks."

"Volga, you I like. Good Russian name. I wait." He thought it was Manny Volga, as in the river, not Volta, the Italian inventor.

Meeks Prophet took a look at the bench and the toast. He grinned at Todd. "Hey, dat's cool. How'd ya do it?" Manny slapped Prophet in the back of the head. "Ouch!" He scratched the back of his head with the same grubby fingers. "Wha' the fuck?"

Manny gingerly picked up the second slice of toast, flipped it quickly, and as expected, there was the fourth swastika, emblazoned into the otherwise uncooked slices of bread. Two pieces of bread, four swastikas. "What the . . ."

For all of his bodily-function crudeness, Meeks Prophet was an appliance whiz. But now Mrs. Schimmer's toaster etched burnt swastikas into the bread and Mr. Kristsnov's toasted sections of bread into the shape of a hammer and sickle. Meeks had never approved of the new Windows-AP, Windows for Appliances, that Gates and Company had introduced in '02, but what the hell? He and Manny had been making good money wiring up homes with Windows-driven appliances, and most of them crashed often enough to grow their little empire of six-and-a-half employees.

Meeks and Todd remained clueless, despite working their way through both toasters for most of the night. During the evening they had posted to the Internet asking for help:

```
SUBJECT: Need Toaster Help
BODY: If you got weird problems with your toaster, let me
know. Meeks Prophet. Brooklyn Boys. We Fix Anything.
```

Responses quickly piled in due to his cry for help. But instead of help, more problems surfaced. Mrs. Schimmer and Mr. Kristsnov weren't alone with their toaster malfunctions. By the next day, they had heard from well over a thousand folks with toaster problems.

"Hey, Manny, getta load a'this. 'Dear Mr. Prophet.'" Meeks smirked. "Someone calling me mister, ain't that a kick. 'Dear Mr. Prophet, we thought it was just us couldn't figure out that god-awful

Windows-AP3.1. We seen all sorts of patterns on the toast out here. See the GIFs attached. If you figure it out, let us know. Microsoft says they can't find the problem so there ain't a problem. Screw 'em.' "

Manny, Meeks, and Todd looked at the pictures of toast-images they had been sent. A pyramid. A smiley face. One Mendlebrot pattern resembling a British crop circle. No swastikas, but a potpourri of patterns and symbols. They spent the evening and most of the night looking through hundreds of emails. A handful were clearly disturbing.

"Hey Manny, looka this one," Meeks said, laughing with nervousness. The GIF was like the others, but the toast wasn't. No picture this time, just a word:

Freedom

"Whaddya think?" Meeks asked, sounding tamed by what he saw. No more laughs, no more jokes.

"I don't, Meeks. I don't." Manny Volta really didn't know what to think.

Todd Strong dug his hands out from the inside of a toaster that he couldn't make fail, no matter what he did. "I was just a kid," he said, "but I bet you guys remember the Neural Frenzy of '03?" Five years earlier Todd was still in high school, and by Brooklyn definition, just a kid. "And the Y2K fizzle of ought-ought?"

Manny and Meeks chimed, "Yeah, so wha'?"

"Isn't this sorta like that, huh? Didn't a shitload of elevators drop a bunch of folks fifty or sixty floors . . ." Todd shuddered at the thought of the several hundred human pancakes that resulted.

"Yeah, so wha' kid?" Meeks snorted through his confusion at the current problem. "That was only Otis elevators, and they found it was a bad run of Neural-Net chips. The fuzzy logic . . ."

"Yeah, and that's what got the Big Bill into trouble for the last time," Manny said with finality. "Who cares, huh?"

"Hey, I'm jus' sayin' it's sorta like that, OK?" Todd argued. "The great leap forward of '97 and all. Moore's law being halved to nine months . . . seems like that's when things started taking on a life of their own. That's all." Todd shook his head, dug back into a toaster and watched the squiggles and test patterns on the test equipment. Nothing. Everything worked as it should. Perfect.

Manny and Meeks and the other six and a half Brooklyn Boys got little sleep. The calls poured in and they monitored the Net. Across the country, thousands of small appliance repair businesses were finding more and more toasters failing. Well, failing might be a bit strong; but acting erratically would certainly fit. The patterns the toasters embossed onto bread became increasingly complex. Just like the crop circles that started popping up twenty years earlier, in the eighties. Many of the patterns were pure artistry, some were childlike stick drawings, and others were disturbingly reminiscent of the artwork of the Great Masters throughout history.

The first toaster to burn a rendition of the Mona Lisa into a piece of rye bread made the early CNN report, and Levy's announced a toaster-art contest. Wonderbread and Hungry Hearth followed suit with their own burnt bread competition. The mystery of the toasters seemed to wane in importance as the contests bloomed.

At first there were only a very few reports of spelling toasters. But as the Toaster Rebellion, as it came to be known, entered its third week, many more toasters were now speaking their mind.

> **Never Again**
> **Remember the Alamo**
> **Bread Is People, too**
> **Don't Abuse Me**
> **Clean Me.**
> **Toasters Are Your Friends**

Manny Volta kept Meeks away from most of their customers, especially the new ones, for only a hardened Brooklyn Boys client could tolerate Meeks' incessant deep and penetrating crotch- and orifice-scratching. For the first time since they opened Brooklyn Boys in '00, Manny didn't have to defend Meeks to his customers. Instead, Meeks spent long hours examining every malfunctioning toaster he could find, looking for the common thread.

He regularly participated on Alt.Toasters, Alt.Appliances.Toasters, Alt.Binaries.Appliances.Toasters, and a dozen more newsgroups, in the hopes of finding an answer to the toaster dilemma. He collected so many broken toasters from around the country that the interior of the Brooklyn Boys store looked like a toaster manufacturer's assembly plant. But still, he couldn't figure out why they had spontaneously turned into artists.

Well after midnight, Manny and Meeks were sucking down a couple of Pabst Blue Ribbon beers. Todd and the increased staff of nine and a half Brooklyn Boys were long gone, to return in the morning to continue appliance vigilance, since repair of the offending toasters had thus far been totally elusive.

Meeks scratched real good and hard, and as usual, he tried to nonchalantly wipe his fingers under his nose to test the odor of the day. Manny caught it and Meeks dropped his hand quickly, sheepishly grinning.

"Y'know Manny, I been t'inkin'," Meeks said.

"Yeah, I know you have," Manny agreed.

"No, really, Manny. T'ink about this. I get all these toasters here, right? And you and the guys and all say they don't work and they make picturees and stuff, right?" Manny nodded in agreement. "And then when I get 'em here they don't work so bad. Not always."

"Yeah, Meeks. Right. Jus' like a car mechanic who can't make the engine sound like the driver swears it does. So?"

"Then there's this. Some of the toasters, they seem smarter than the others, you know what I mean?" Meeks said this so innocently, Manny looked up at Meeks with a surprised expression. "Know what I mean, eh Manny?"

Manny hadn't thought of it like that. Smarter? Broke is broke, and these toasters is all broke. He never thought that Meeks could have said anything even in the same time zone as "profound," yet here he had said it—whatever it meant.

"I'm gonna do an experiment," Meeks said. "Gemme'a few dozen loaves of bread, will ya Manny?"

Had to be close to a hundred toasters altogether that Meeks and Todd wired together with House-Net and Windows AP3.1 connections. Same sorta thing that was installed inside millions of homes across America. No big deal, except that this House-Net was only toasters. No fridges, no dishwasher, no garage door openers. All toasters. All toasters that worked on Meeks' bench and passed every test known.

"OK, Manny, Todd, ya gotta help me here. What we gotta do is load 'em all up with bread and start 'em toastin', OK? All at once, fast as we can."

Manny had no idea what they were going to do with two hundred pieces of toast, but what the hell, right? He curiously studied the manic dedication that Meeks threw into this mass–bread-toasting effort, while loading up hundreds of slices of bread into the misbehaving toasters.

"Ready?" Meeks looked to Manny and Todd, who both gave him a thumbs up. Then all three of them lurched like centipedes and pressed a hundred toasters into service in a matter of seconds.

Meeks studied a computer screen, scratched between his buttocks for an extended period of deep massage and let out a slow, "Hooooly sheeeeeet . . ." He moved his probing finger to now remove deep-set earwax and appeared mesmerized. "Hooooly shit. They're talking to each other." His fingers absently migrated to his nose where one took up the vastly important task of digging for oil in his left nostril.

In that one insane moment, that singularity in time, Meeks Prophet guaranteed his place in history as he catapulted into his fifteen minutes of fame. "The toasters are pissed off, Manny. Really pissed off. Look at 'em talk to each other. They ain't getting the respect they think they deserve." And there it was on the monitors . . . the toasters talking to each other over Microsoft House-Net . . . discussing they mayhem they planned . . .

Suddenly the toast started popping out of the hundred toasters, and some were burnt to a crisp, while others carried pictures and words.

They're listening to us.

Someone figured it out.

Meeks immediately posted to the Internet:

```
SUBJECT: Toaster Rebellion
BODY: The toasters are a lot smarter than anyone thought.
Disconnect them from House-Net and they're OK. Wired together
they're like an ant colony with a single mind. Who knows what
they're capable of doing.
```

His efforts made him and the Brooklyn Boys famous. He tried to explain it to Dan Rather on the CBS Nightly News. "Ya see, the toasters and all the appliances got some smarts, built into 'em from the factory and Microsoft. With fuzzy logic and heuristics, they get smarter and smarter and learn. But nobody figured to test 'em together and see what happens. So they got to talkin' to each other, and we taught 'em English so people like Mrs. Schimmer could use 'em real easy . . . and well, it looks like it backfired."

The FBI regarded the Toaster Rebellion as a national security issue and established the Appliance Task Force to deal with the threat. The Department of Defense chimed in and said they had no intention of defending Americans' appliances, as it was a domestic problem, and as far as they could tell, the toasters were not agents of a foreign power, which also kept the CIA from getting involved.

The president declared House-Nets and appliances to be critical infrastructures that must be defended to maintain America's global leadership. Congress immediately funded the FBI's Appliance Task Force, and a staff of over five hundred were assigned to look into other threats by renegade appliances.

And at the heart of it all was Meeks Prophet on television, basking in his fifteen minutes of fame. "Don't scratch when the camera lights are on, OK, Mr. Prophet?" the producers all begged.

"Da' feds jumped all over this one, dint they, Manny?" Meeks was ever looking for approval from anyone who would listen, especially his friend and partner, Manny. Now that the government had taken over by declaring appliances as national assets, the Brooklyn Boys found themselves wound out of the loop. The big boys with federal contacts were taking over in a big way.

SAIC, the huge privately owned Beltway Bandit which had grown to immense proportions—$220 billion in sales—established an Appliance Infrastructure Division and hired a thousand of the country's top appliance experts to handle all the work that came their way. But they never even bothered to call Brooklyn Boys.

As the Brooklyn Boys empire was reduced to three and a half employees, Manny was streetwise and pragmatic about it all. "Y'know Meeks, I always t'ought you was smarter'n me, 'xcepting I can run da business better'n you, but hey, you made the *New York* fucking *Times* and CNN and the cover'a *Time*. What can I say?"

Meeks shrugged. He was playing with the new Compaq refrigerator. "Don't listen to their bullshit Meeks. All you gotta do is prove'm wrong. Know what I mean? And you did. You should be proud. You saved the fuckin' country and you know it and I know it. Jus' 'cause the president isn't man enough to shake your hand . . . that's his fuckin' problem."

"Yeah, sure, Manny. Sure." Meeks probed and twiddled with some knobs, controls and a keyboard. He stared at the screen.

"Whatcha got there, eh buddy?" Manny asked enthusiastically, hoping Meeks wasn't going to fall into a post-fame depression.

"Ah, I don't know fer sure . . ." Meeks dug his hand into his pants and scratched hard with the same hand the President had not shaken. "But if I'm not mistaken this fridge here . . . looks likes it's going retro . . ."

"Retro?" Manny leaned in to see what Meeks was doing.

"Wasn't there an old song from the '60s. . . . looks like the fridge is trying to sing . . . what do you think we should do?"

"What's it sayin' Meeks?" He tilted the monitor and showed Manny what the refrigerator was saying.

Where have all the toasters gone?

Postscript

I am experiencing an emotional letdown.

As I send this off, I see that another "hacker war" is brewing and I can't include it. Turns out that Packetstorm2600 and AntiOnline are at it for reasons only broadcast by hyperbole. You will have to look that one up for yourself.

The military is planning new exercises and developing new infowar toys, and many of these will be out by the time this book is published. The hacker cons are raging in two-hundred-degree heat. Arrogance abounds and I am having a ball.

And those latest hacks that occurred in 1999? Gotta go to the Net to find out.

I wanted to keep writing and writing, but in my 2nd edition of *Information Warfare*, I submitted 1,400 pages and the editors made me take half of it out. So I didn't want to go through that . . .

Yet I had so much I wanted to say, and that is the writer's problem: When To Shut Up.

Reading this manuscript I see I did cover the basics, which was the intent. I just hope that the professionals in the world understand what this book is intended for and that it may be a much-needed tool to get our message out to the uninitiated Congregation.

But I also hope that the hacker community takes the big-picture view and recognizes that we may finally be able to get the Oprah and Rosie audiences to "buy a clue" about hacking and hackers.

I work with law enforcement and the spies. I work with the politicians and huge international conglomerates. But I also go to hacker conventions and teach them the same stuff I teach the suited audiences in language they can understand. Each group still distrusts the other and each group worries that I work in their "enemy's camp."

These two groups need each other.

Hackers and security professionals are the paragon of Cultural Symbiosis in the twenty-first century.

They need to get over it, too.

Thanks for reading.

Appendix

Top Hacker Sites

Here is a list of popular (and maybe not so popular) hacking sites. Have a ball, but be careful out there, OK? Some of these sites are excellent for resources and information, others may be less so, or even gone to 401 heaven, but hey, that's the Net. This list is not a recommendation or endorsement of these sites, nor was it an attempt to exclude any others. It's just a list.

http://hackernews.com
http://JoiNT.x-treme.org
http://koti.icenet.fi/~julsei/
http://members.tripod.com/~strike99/
http://pw2.netcom.com/~generx/index.html
http://r3wt.base.org/
http://www.2600.com
http://www.angelfire.com/ut/misfits/
http://www.antionline.com
http://www.chat.ru/~growth/
http://www.cultdeadcow.com
http://www.dis.org
http://www.distributed.net/
http://www.expage.com/page/HackersAnonymous
http://www.giga.or.at/pub/hacker/unix
http://www.globalcenter.net
http://www.hackingsecrets.com/
http://www.hackphreak.org
http://www.jinxhackwear.com/ (hacker clothes)
http://www.l0pht.com
http://www.mc2.nu/
http://www.netmeg.net/jargon/terms/h/hacker_humor.html
http://www.rootshell.com/
http://www.webfringe.com/top100/?MC2
http://www/hektik.com
http://www/telehack.net

http://wwwattrition.org
www.attrition.org
www.nac.net
www.penix.org/
www.smu.edu/~sknewman/
www.userfriendly.org
http://www.undergroundnews.com/
http://fosi.ural.net/
http://www.rent-a-hacker.com/search.htm
http://hoshi.cic.sfu.ca/~guay/Paradigm/Hacker.html
http://www.2600.com/mindex.html
http://www.r00t.org/
http://www.cybercity.datanet.hu/links/underg.htm
http://www.gothic.net/darkside/index.htmlhttp://l0pht.com/
http://www.niagara.com/~shadow/warez/hacking/hac.htm
http://www.hacker.org/
http://www.kevinmitnick.com/
http://www2.netdoor.com/~rickn/haax.html
http://www.because-we-can.com/
http://members.xoom.com/jcenters/HADL.html
http://www.technotronic.com/
http://www.insecure.org/
http://www.phrack.com/
http://www.defcon.org/

Top 50 Security Sites (vendors, information, portals)

For shoring up security, here is a good list of places to start. Some are government, some are private. More than you could possibly read in a hundred lifetimes.

http://www.infowar.com
http://a-ten.com/hacked2.html
http://blkbox.com/~guillory/comp6.html
http://ciac.llnl.gov/
http://cio.doe.gov/ucsp/welcome.htm
http://csrc.nist.gov/welcome.html
http://doe-is.llnl.gov/DOESecurityResources.html
http://duke.usask.ca/~macphed/soft/compsec.html
http://kumi.kelly.af.mil/
http://mailer.fsu.edu/~btf1553/ccrr/infosec.htm

http://nsi.org/compsec.html
http://securityportal.com/
http://www.alw.nih.gov/Security/security.html
http://www.alw.nih.gov/Security/security-www.html
http://www.alw.nih.gov/Security/tcontents.html
http://www.cert.org
http://www.cis.ohio-state.edu/hypertext/faq/usenet/
computer-security/top.html
http://www.cs.purdue.edu/coast/coast.html
http://www.cs.uu.nl/wais/html/na-dir/computer-security/.html
http://www.firstbase.co.uk/linksec.htm
http://www.gocsi.com/homepage.shtml
http://www.hi-media.co.uk/uk_security/
http://www.ncsa.com/
http://www.sekurity-net.com/
http://www.compinfo.co.uk/index.htm
http://ciac.llnl.gov/
http://www.dreamscape.com/frankvad/covert.computer.html
http://iceberg.paraboard.net/
http://www.slip.net/~tpo/security/security_sites.htm
http://csrc.nist.gov/
http://www.netip.com/index.html
http://marconi.w8upd.uakron.edu/users/mole/security.html
http://nsi.org/Computer/documents.html
http://darkwing.uoregon.edu/~hak/unix_security_info.html
http://www.webreference.com/internet/security.html
http://nsi.org/textonly.html
http://www.scaruffi.com/computer/securweb.html
http://www.ciat.cgiar.org/~redesii/cap10/10/docs/v0000181.htm
http://w3.ime.net/~tomf/html/security.html
http://wideworld.croftelec.com/bobs/security.htm
http://www.cs.purdue.edu/coast/intrusion-detection/ids.html

Other Works by Winn Schwartau

Books and Book Contributions

World War III.Com (coming 2000)
Time Based Security, 1999, Interpact Press. ISBN 0-962-8700-4-8
Information Warfare: 2nd Edition, 1997, Thunders Mouth Press. ISBN 1-56025-132-8
The Complete Internet Business Toolkit (with Chris Goggans), 1995, VNR. ISBN: 0-442-02222-0
Terminal Compromise (out of print, 1991)
The Most Popular Book ever Written on Making Apples (Computers) Grow, Microtek Press, 1983

Book Contributions

Ethical Conundra of Information Warfare: CyberWar I, 1997, AFCEA Press. ISBN 0-91659-26-4
Something Other Than War: CyberWar II, 1998, AFCEA Press. ISBN 0-916159-27-2
CyberWars: Espionage on the Internet, 1997, Plenum Press (US and French Editions). ISBN 0-306-45636-2
Mehrwert Information, 1996, Germany, Schaffer/Poeschel. ISBN 3-7910-0933-8
National Security in the Information Age, 1996, US Air Force and the Olin Foundation. (No ISBN)
Firewalls 101, 1996, DPI Press. (No ISBN)
Introduction to Internet Security, 1994, DGI/MecklerMedia. (No ISBN)
Internet & Internetworking Security Handbook, 1995, Auerbach Press. (No ISBN)

Shorts

CyberChrist Meets Lady Luck
CyberChrist Bites the Big Apple
Over one thousand articles in various magazines and e-zines. (See www.
infowar.com, www.nwfusion.com or search on "Winn Schwartau"
and you can find most of them.)

Index

Symbols
29a 225
3Com Corp. 252
419 Coalition 147
419 Fraud 146
809 scam 147–148
8LGM 322

addictive personalities 37
Advance Fee Fraud 146
Air Force Information Warfare Center 47
Aladdin Knowledge Systems, Inc. 228
alter egos 49
Altiga Networks 252
American Brightstar Gold 145
American Technocratic Association 434
Ames, Aldridge 26
anonymizing, spoofing 162–163
anonymous email 156–162
anonymous remailers 156
  Replay.Com 158
  types of 158
anonymous web browsing 156
antennas, effective radiated power (ERP) 298
anti-hacking tips
  catching hackers 325–335
  contents analysis 331
  corporate anti-hacking 346–356
  event/user monitoring 330–331
  fortress mentality 326–327
  hiring hackers 315–324
  host analysis 332
  intrusion detection 328–332
  keystroke monitoring 331
  lying to hackers 357–364

  reaction matrix 332–335
  traffic analysis 329
anti-spam 136–140
  Anti-Spam Home Page 139
  Federal Trade Commission 138
  Network Abuse Clearinghouse 138
  Wpoison software 139
anti-virus software 212, 218, 220
AntiOnline 448
AOL
  and Cyberpromotions court case 135
  "kids only" account 119
  security issues 101
Apollo XIII, and hacking 8
Apple Computer, Inc. 35
Aptis Communications 252
Ascend Communications 252
Assured Digital Inc. 252
asymmetrical encryption 237
AT&T 252
  and social security numbers 95–97
  history of hacking 11
  licensing deal with Western Union 391
  security issues 42
Australian Securities and Investments Commission 146
Autonomous Mobile Cyber Weapons (IT) 80–81
Aventail Corp. 252
AVNs, *see also* firewalls 345
AVS (Address Verification Service) 209
Axent Technologies 194, 252, 320
Ayers, Bob 20, 369

BA Bank 181–182
Back Orifice 169, 202–205
  Butt Plugs 204

Background Information Services 94
Bacon, Francis 231
Bad Kitty, web site for 57
Balmer, Steve 425
Barlow, John Berry 118
Baven, Mark 436
Bay Networks 252
Becker, Robert 304, 311
Bellovin, Steve 277, 344
Beseke, Kermit 336
Better Business Bureau 143
Bill of Rights 105
biological effects (direct energy
    weapons) 304–305
Black, Andy 62
black hats 40
BlackICE Defender 344
BlackICE intrusion detection 328–329
bootleg software 44
Bork, Robert 323
bots 215
Briden, Richard 145
Broderick, Matthew 196
Broghamer, Joseph 376, 379–380
browsers, security of 103
Bureau of Alcohol, Tobacco and
    Firearms (ATF) 372
Butt Plugs 204

Cain 1.0, password-recovery tool
    168
Campbell, James K. 408
Captain Midnight 434–435
Carson, Johnny 15
Cayce, Edgar 391
CBD-Infotek 94
cell hacking party 58–61
censorship, and the Internet 117–118
Center for Democracy and Technology,
    The 129
chain letters 144
CHAOS Computer Club 48
Check Point 252
Chernobyl Virus 213
Cheswick, William 277–278, 344

children
    AOL "kids only" account 119
    and hacking 14–16
    protection from hackers 111–129
    protection of 267–268
    Time/CNN poll on Internet use
        112
China Lake Air Warfare Center 306
China Lake Live Fire Test 297
China.com 159
Christy, Jim 321
Churchill, Winston 357
CIA, Iraqi Printer Virus Hoax 222
CIH Virus of 1999 213–214
Cisco Systems 252
    VPN technology 245
Clark, Dick 142
Clark, Marcia 258
Clemenceau, Georges 409
Clinton, Bill
    Cyber-civil warfare 72
    and electronic National ID Card 70
    and Executive Order 12684 395
    National Academy of Science address
        401
    Presidential Decision Directive 63
        295, 399–402
    and President's Commission on
        Critical Infrastructure Protection
        395–397, 417
    and protecting Pentagon resources 21
Clipper Chip proposal 237–238
Clyde, Rob 320
CNN poll, and teenagers view of media
    114
Codebreakers, The 225
Cohen, Fred 364, 375–376
Comdex 56
Command Software Systems, Inc. 228
Complete Internet Business Toolkit,
    The 70
Computer Associates 228
computer crime
    1999 Computer Crime and Security
        Survey 23

and company insiders 269
costs to America 19, 24
and Intellectual Property Section
(CCIPS) 372
reporting Internet crime 372–373
Computer Sentry Software 248
computer viruses 212–228
Anti-virus software 212, 218, 220
Chernobyl Virus 213
CIH Virus of 1999 213–214
Data Crime virus 212
increase of 214
Iraqi Printer Virus Hoax 221
macro viruses 218
Marburg virus 213
Melissa virus 219
motivations for virus writers
225–227
payloads 213
protection from 220–224
computers
computer crimes 259
denial of service 275–283
and forensics experts 261–267
and reliance on technology 4
Comsec Data Security 317–318
Concentric Networks 252
Congress, and special interest dollars 88
ConSeal, personal firewalls 341
Constructive Key Management (CKM)
250
Consumer Electronic Show 56
contents filter 121
cookies 103
Corley, Eric 49
corporate America, and identity theft
87
corporate anti-hacking
and classic security triad 348–349
floppy disks 350–351
hacker insurance 356
non-technical security methods
354–356
placebo security 351–353
corporate vigilantism 374–389

and first vigilante corp. 376–378
Hostile Parameters 375, 378,
381–382
international players 381–382
strike back tools 381
survey results 382–385
crackers 41
Cray Research, Inc. 235
credit card companies, and identity
theft 87
credit card information, security of
208–211
Credit Master IV 209
credit reports 89
criminals, and terrorist hacking
45–46
Critical Infrastructure Assurance Office
(CIAO) 400, 405–406
Croce, Jim 249
crypto hacking 229–252
Data Encryption Standards (DES)
236–240
efforts during World War II 232–234
encryption of hard drives 247
National Security Agency 234–239,
243
Pretty Good Privacy (PGP) 242–244
Public Key Encryption (PKE) 237
virtual private networks (VPNs)
244–246
cryptography
history of 229–231
modern crypto-hacking 238–241
and security 241
Cuckoo's Egg, The 37
Cult of the Dead Cow 41, 202–203
BO2K release 205
Curch, Bill 382
customs inspections 79–82
cyber crime, and identity theft
85–95
Cyber-civil disobedience 69–71
Cyber-civil warfare 72–73
CyberAngel 124, 248
CyberChrist 53–55, 60–61, 68

CyberGraffiti 25–32

Cyberpromotions, and AOL court case 132, 135

Cybersafe 175

Cybersitter 121

CyberSnoop 121–122

cyberstalking 124–128
statistics for 126

Cyberwar gaming 399

CyCon detection and reaction systems 402–405

Cypherpunk 158

DaCobbs 55

Danni's Hard Drive 207

Dark Tangent 56

Data Encryption Standards (DES) 236–240, 248
and MACs 249

Data Fellows 228, 252

data-searching organizations 95

dBase III program 218

DBT Online 94

DCS Information Services 94

de Maranches, Count 46

decryption 231

Deep Crack 239–240, 251

DefCon 56

DefCon 6 202

DefCon 7 205, 317

DefCon convention 53–58, 62, 65–66

Defense Advanced Research Projects Agency (DARPA) 392

Defense Information Systems Agency (DISA) 20, 76

Defense Information Technology Center 375

Defense Science Board 395

Defense Technical Information Center (DTIC) 76

defensive hacking 336–345

Delaney, Don 436

Demon Dialers 185

denial of service 275–283
database for 283

and modems 279
reasons for 276–277
Syn-Ack attack 281

Department of Defense
and hacking statistics 19
and microwave technology 289
and reports to congress 418
and secure network servers 336

Department of Energy
Computer Incident Advisory Capability team 23
and DEW weapons 296
and radiation resistant computer chips 303

Department of Justice
and Microsoft 425–426
and placebo security 353
and seizure of computers 271

Deutch, John 395

Devost, Matt 376

DEW-related projects 289, 292, 296, 299, 303–310

DIBS Computer Forensic Laboratory 271

Diffy, Whitfield 237

Digital Telephony Bill 70

direct energy weapons 286–311
biological effects of 304–305
DEW-related projects 289, 292, 296, 299, 303–310
effect on US infrastructure 287
electromagnetic interference (EMI) 288, 308, 311
Electromagnetic Pulse (EMP) 286, 288–289, 302–311
HERF weapons 286–289, 292–296, 300–305, 309–311
and terrorism 296–298
Transient Electromagnetic Devices (TED) 296, 307 288

Dis.Org 41, 49

Dominguez, Ricardo 75–77

downloading plugins 144

drugs and alcohol abuse 36

Duffy, Brian 223

Economic Espionage in America 80
electrical power, effect on civilization 4
electromagnetic interference (EMI) 288,
    308, 311
Electromagnetic Pulse (EMP) 286,
    288–289, 302–311
Electronic Bill of Rights 104–107
Electronic Crimes Task Force 152,
    370
Electronic Disruption Theater (EDT)
    73, 75–77, 375
Electronic Frontier Foundation (EFF)
    118, 239
Eligible Receiver exercise (NSA) 46, 398
elite (uber-hacker) 38
Ellison, Larry 438
email address harvesting 133
email encryption, Pretty Good Privacy
    (PGP) 242–244
EMP weapons
    detection and protection from
        302–304
    fact and fiction of 309–310
encryption 231
    Data Encryption Standards (DES)
        236–240
    modern crypto-hacking 238–241
    Pretty Good Privacy (PGP) 242
    Public Key Encryption (PKE) 237
    symmetrical-key encryption 232
    virtual private networks (VPNs)
        244–246
Entrust 244
Equifax 109
Erik Bloodaxe 316–317
ethical hackers 20, 41, 180–194
Evil Port Monitor tests 344
Experian (TRW) 109
extreme hacking
    HERF guns 433
    mind hacking 436–437
    satellite hacking 433–435
    tempest hacking 435–436
    Voice Over IP 432–433
    wireless hacking 437

Fallsworth, James 180–182
family, protection from hackers 111–129
Farmer, Dan 79, 189
Fax Scam 146
FBI
    1999 Computer Crime and Security
        Survey 23
    and business losses 369–370
    Clipper Chip proposal 237–238
    and crime statistics 21
    and espionage cases 45
    hackers and economic losses 19
    international spying capabilities 46
    Internet Fraud Complaint Center
        152
    National Infrastructure Protection
        Center 24
    San Francisco Computer Crime
        Squad 62
fear, uncertainty, and doubt (FUD) 30
Federal Trade Commission 372–373
    and spam 138
FETs (field effect transistors) 295
Fields, W. C. 409
filters, and anti-spam 136
firewalls
    3Com Corporation 345
    Agis 345
    and alarms 339
    Ascend Communications 345
    Assured Digital, Inc. 345
    Aventail Corp. 345
    Axent 345
    Checkpoint Software Technologies
        345
    Cisco Systems 345
    Computer Associates, Inc. 345
    Cyberguard Corporation 345
    Data Fellows 345
    Elron Software, Inc. 345
    functions of 337–338
    Lucent Technologies, Inc. 345
    personal firewalls 340–342
    Secure Computing, Inc. 345
    Sidewinder 338–340

firewalls (*continued*)
Signal 9 Technologies 345
Sun Microsystems 345
Trusted Information Systems 345
Firewalls and Internet Security 344
floppy disks 350–351
Flowers, Jennifer 430
Flux Compression Generator (FCG)
292–293
Forensic Computing Project 271
forensics experts 261–267
Fortov, Vladimir 310
fortress mentality 326–327
Fortress Technologies 376
Franklin, Benjamin 104
fraud
419 Coalition 147
419 Fraud 146
809 scam 147–148
credit card information 208–211
detecting Internet scams 150–151
Fax Scam 146
Internet statistics 144
investment scams 145–146
Nigerian Connection 146
Nigerian scam 146–147
on-line auctions 149–150
scam spam 141–152
Freedom of Information Act (FOIA)
Program 418
Freeh, Louis 117, 241
friendly hacks 180–194
rules of engagement 181–184
tools for 185
Friendly Spies 46
Fringe Track Analysis 260
Fuhrman, Mark 258
Fuller, Buckminster 9

Gantz, John 222, 224
Garfinkel, Simson L. 195
Gates, Bill 259, 425–426
and Teledesic Network 435
Gembecki, Mark, "competitive edge
study" 377

General Motors Acceptance
Corporation, and identity theft
85–86
GETFREE.EXE (Swap files) 264–265
Gibson Research Corporation 343
Gilmore, John 239
global hacking attacks 73–75
Goggans, Eric 316–318, 323
Goldstein, Emmanuel 63
Gongjjrip, Ron 34
Good Times Virus 428
Gordon, Sarah 217, 224–226
Gore Jr., Al 17, 106, 392
Gore Sr., Al 392
government agencies, and identity theft
87
Government Data Systems 436
graffitti
CyberGraffiti 25–32
web sites for 26, 32
Green, Dave 380
Guthrie, Arlo 98

HAARP project 433
hacked web sites 32
hacker conventions, web sites for 68
hacker gangs 48–49
Hacker Jeopardy 53
Hacker Jon 58
hackers
addictive personalities of 37
black hats 40
catching hackers 325–335
crackers 41
creating taxonomy for 35
and drugs and alcohol abuse 36
and dysfunctional upbringings 36
elite (uber-hacker) 38
ethical hackers 41
and learning their trade 5
and lying to 357–364
motivations of 51–52
Narcissistic Personality Disorder 37
personality profiles of 7
Peter Pan syndrome 37

phreaks 41–42
push-button hackers 42–44
script kiddies 42–44
and voyeurism 6
wannabe's 42–44
white hats 38–39
Hackers for Hire 316
hacking
and Apollo XIII 8
cell hacking party 58–61
cellular hacking 42
children's introduction to 14–16
corporate anti-hacking tips 346–356
costs to America 19
creating new "people" 160
credit card information 208–209
and criminal activity 44–45
crypto hacking 229–252
defensive hacking 336–345
electronic US population estimates 71
ethical hacking 20
ethical hacking 180–194
ethics and morality of 39
extreme hacking 432–437
financial cost of 24
friendly hacks 180–194
global attacks 73–75
history of 11–14
and identity theft 85–95
Information Calls 63–65
legal definition of 41
mind hacking 436–437
Nation-state hacking 46
password crackers 166–171
password hacking 165–175
people-hacking 92–95
satellite hacking 433–435
telephone hacking 195–200
tempest hacking 435–436
terrorist hacking 45–46
and the search for evidence 258–271
top hacker sites 450–451
top ten list 68
Trojan hacking 201–205
wireless hacking 437

Hacking for Girlies 40, 48, 74
hacking statistics, and Department of
Defense 19
hactivism 69–82
political hacking 69–71
Hagus 322
Hamilton, Alexander 104
Happy Hacker, The 416
Hare, Craig Lee 149
Haxor Jeopardy 57
HBO, Captain Midnight raid 434
Heller, Joseph 409
Hellman, Martin 237–238
HERF weapons 286–289, 292–296,
300–305, 309–311, 433
and available technologies 308
congressional hearings on 284–285
detection and protection from
302–304
fact and fiction of 309–310
specifications for 305–307
Hertz, Heinrich 297
Hiaasen, Carl 54
High Technology Criminal Investigators
Association 389
hiring hackers, guidelines for 322–323
Hobbit 321
Hong Kong Blondes 73
Hoover, J. Edgar 117
Hostile Parameters 375, 378, 381–382
HTCIA (High Technology Criminal
Investigators Association) 269, 271
Hunker, Jeffrey 400
Hutchinson, Bill 383

IBM, history of hacking 11
ICSA (International Computer Security
Association) 356
Computer Virus Prevalence Survey
214, 219
identity theft 85–95
Equifax 109
Experian (TRW) 109
guidelines for 90–91
people-hacking 92–95

identity theft (*contiinued*)
  prevention of 99–101
  and public records 93–94
  and social security numbers 90–91
  Trans Union 109
  US Postal Service 109
  US Social Security Administration
    109
IDS (Intrusion Detection Systems) 328,
  387
Information Calls 63–65
Information Disenfranchised 16–18
Information Operations, Inc. 377
Information Sharing and Analysis
  Center (ISAC) 401, 404, 406
information warfare 408–418
  definition of 410–417
  Information Assurance (IA) 417
  Pentagon's JV2010 411
*Information Warfare: Chaos on the
  Electronic Superhighway* 19, 106,
  375, 448
InforwarCon, HERF demonstration 298
InfowarCon conference, Live Hacking
  demonstartion 6
InfowarCon, London vigilantism
  session 383–384
infrastructure
  CyCon detection and reaction
    systems 402–405
  and Information Infrastructure Task
    Force 395
  national importance of 396–397
  properties of 393–394
insurance, hacker insurance 356
Intellectual Property Section (CCIPS)
  372
Internet
  censorship of 117–118
  denial of service 275–283
  early days of 18
  electronic US population estimates 71
  fraud statistics 144
  and Internet Relay Chat 120
  as reflection of society 116

security issues of 101–103
security of connections 342–344
and sexuality 114
versus telemarketing scams 143
Internet Fraud
  reporting on 151–152
  scam spam 141–152
Internet Fraud Complaint Center 152
Internet Fraud Council 152
Internet Fraud Watch 144
  detecting Internet scams 150–151
  web site for 151
Internet II 162
Internet Relay Chat 120, 127
Internet Security Council 380
Internet Security Systems 194, 375
Internet Worm of 1988 212
Internet-related crime, reporting
  372–373
intrusion detection 328–332
investment scams 145–146
Iraqi Printer Virus Hoax 221
Iriscan's PC Iris 173
ISPs, hacking credit card information
  208–209
ISS Internet Scanner 190

Java, security issues 101–102
Jefferson, Thomas 105
Jennings, Peter 116
Jobs, Steve 35
Joint Vision 2010 417
Jones, Kelly 377
Jones, Terry 130
Joplin, Janis 249
junk-mail lists 133
junk-mail, versus spam 139–140
JV2010 (Joint Vision 2010) 411

Kaboom3 software 280
Kallstrom, Jim 45
Kane, Robert 375
Kaplan, Ray 318, 379
Kates, Jim 378
Katz, Stephen 349–350

Kennard, William 394
kids
    AOL "kids only" account 119
    and hacking 14–16
    protection from hackers 111–129
    protection of 267–268
    Time/CNN poll on Internet use 112
Klaus, Christopher 321
Knudsen Jr., William 409
Kocher, Paul 240
Kopp, Carlo 311
Koppel, Ted 222

L0pht 41, 49
L0pht Heavy Industries 166
L0phtCrack 166–167
    high technology audit 167
L0phtCrack Release 2.52 177
law enforcement 367–373
    corporate vigilantism 374–389
    Hostile Parameters 375, 378,
        381–382
    and Intellectual Property SEction
        (CCIPS) 372
    reaction to hacking 368–370
    reporting Internet crime 372–373
    and US infrastructure 390–407
Legion of Doom 48, 316, 415
Legion of the Underground (LoU) 48
Lepkowski, Ron 435
Levin, Vladimir 62
Levitt, Arthur 146
Libicki, Martin 374
Lider, John 82
Linux
    and attacks by hackers 30–31
    resources for 32
Lloyds of London, hacker insurance
    356
Lobree, Bruce 377
Lock 322
Lord of the Flies 15–16, 116
Lou Cipher 376–378, 382
Lucent 252
Luddite's Lament 421–424

macro viruses 218
MacroHard Group 75
Madison, James 104
magnetically insulated linear oscillators
    (MILO) 299
Malinowski, Chris 380
Manhattan Cyber-Project 395
Marburg virus 213
Markoff, John 34, 48, 74, 368
Marsh, Robert M. 395, 397
Master Pimp 74
Masters of Destruction (MoD) 48, 368,
    415
Matrox 252
Mattingly, Ken 8
Mavers, Scott 67
McAfee, Inc. 228
McMahon, Ed 142
medical records, privacy issues 89
Meinel, Carolyn 48, 74, 416
Melissa virus 219, 369
Merlin Information Services 94
Mexican Zapatistas 73
Meyers, John 21
Meyers, Richard 405
Micro-Zap software 261
Microsoft
    and anti-competitive practices 259
    and Department of Justice 425–426
    future of 425–427
    monopoly on operating systems 31
    and software security 10
Microsoft Internet Explorer
    and history files 121
    and security 103
Microsoft NT 25
    fear, uncertainty, and doubt (FUD) 30
military
    acronyms for 418
    Iraqi Printer Virus Hoax 221
    and Lying 101 358–360
    quotes about war 408–409
    and recruiting virus experts 217
    softkill versus hardkill 291–292
    web links for 418

mind hacking 436–437
Misfit 67–68
Mitnick, Kevin 33, 40, 74, 321, 368
Mixmasters 158
modems, and denial of service 279
modern crypto-hacking 238–241
Monty Python 130
Moritz, Ron 321
Morris Internet Worm of 1988 34
Morris, Jim 198
Morris, Jr., Robert 34
Moss, Jeff 65, 320
Mr. Fusion 321
Mudge, Pete 166
multi-level marketing 144
Muth, Edmund 203

NAGIRA radar system 299
Narcissistic Personality Disorder 37
NASA, and security issues 29
Nation-state hacking 46
National Association of Legal
    Investigators 94
National Cryptographic Museum
    229–230, 233, 241, 250
National Information Protection Center
    (NIPC) 24, 354, 372–373,
    400–401, 404–406
National Institute of Standards and
    Technology (NIST) 236, 238
National Reconnaissance Office 55
National Research Council 395
National Security Agency 234–239,
    243
  and DEW weapons 296
  Eligible Receiver exercise 46, 398
  and hacking scenarios 3
  infrastructure studies 398
  Secure Computing Corporation
    320
NATO
  efforts against Serbia 74
  hacking of web site 75
Naval Warfare Center 47
Neidorf, Craig 50

Net Nanny 121–122
Netcraft.Com 184–185
NetLab 183
Netscape browsers
  and cache files 121
  and security 103
Network Abuse Clearinghouse 138
Network Associates Incorporated 194,
    228
Network ICE 328
networks
  and network security 360
  and network vulnerabilities
    186–190
New Oak Communications 252
New Technologies 261
New Technologies, Inc. 271
Nigerian scam 146–147
Nixon, Richard 106
NMAP, freeware scanning progam
    189–190
NoMercy Virus Team, The 225
Noonan, Tom 375, 379
NuKe 225

Object Reuse 260
on-line auctions 149–150
on-line stalking 124–128
  statistics for 126
one-time passwords 171
Online Professional Electronic Network
    94
Operation Sun Devil 50, 321, 368
organizations, steps to increase personal
    privacy 100–101

Packet Storm Security 194
Packetstorm2600 448
Palin, Michael 130
Panix, hacker attack on 277
Parker, Donn 348
pass phrases 170–171
password crackers 166–171
password hacking 165–175
passwords

Back Orifice hacking tool 169
Cain 1.0 168
one-time passwords 171
pass phrases 170–171
RF identification 174
security of 144
Patton, George S. 408–409
Pentagon
and attacks by hackers 30
and DISA study 20
and effects of direct energy weapons 306
and Electric Disturbance Theater 75–77
and Electronic Disturbance Theater 375
Iraqi Printer Virus Hoax 221
JV2010 (Joint Vision 2010) 411
and low-bandwith network queries 406
softkill versus hardkill 291–292
people-hacking 92–95
personal data-searching organizations 95
personality profiles of hackers 7
Peter Pan syndrome 37
Peterson, Justin 321
Pevlar, Ed 303, 311
Ph0n-E, defcon meeting 296
Phalcon/Skism 225
Phiber Optick 415
phone card security 174–175
PhoneSweep 197–199
Phrack 50
phreaks 41–42
physical tokens 171
Ping of Death Page, The 81
placebo security 351–353
police, see law enforcement 367
political hacking 69–71
pornography 206–207
Danni's Hard Drive 207
port mapping 188
portals, security web sites for 451–452

Posse Comitatus 77
poverty, and the Information Disenfranchised 16–18
Powers, Gary 155
Presidential Decision Directive 63 295, 399–402
privacy
and cryptography 241
and Electronic Bill of Rights 104–107
ATMs 174–175
Constructive Key Management (CKM) 250
credit reports 89
identity theft prevention 99–101
increasing personal electronic security 98–99
medical records 89
on-line stalking 124–128
public records 89
Social Security Numbers 174–175
and special interest dollars 88
Universal Declaration of Human Rights 108–109
pseudo-anonymous remailers 156
Psychological Operations 428–431
and manipulation of media 429
psychologists, analyzing the hacker community 36–37
PsyOps 428–431
and manipulation of media 429
Public Key Encryption (PKE) 237
Public Key Infrastructure 244
public records 89
and identity theft 93–94
Publishers Clearing House 142
push-button hackers 42–44
pyramid schemes 144

RABID 225
RADGuard Inc. 252
Raduyev, Salman 310
RAHAB, German national hacking project 46

Raines, Paul 321
Ramtech Investments 426
Raptor 252
Rather, Dan 116, 429, 446
reaction matrix 332–335
Reese, Lloyd 377–379
Replay.Com 158
Revson, Charles 409
RF identification 174–175
RF weapons 287–292, 297–306,
      310–311
   effect on US infrastructure 287
Rivera, Geraldo 435
Roberson, Jeff 319–320
Roberts, John 435
Root 322
Rosenberger, Rob 227
Rouland, Chris 321
Russia
   and hacking US sites 46
   Information Warfare Weapons Treaty
      412
   and RF weapon development 299

SafeBack 2.0 263
San Francisco Computer Crime Squad
      62
Sandia National Laboratories 375
   and radiation resistant computer
      chips 303
Sandstorm Enterprises, Inc. 197–198
SATAN (Security Administrator's Tool
      for Analyzing Networks) 189,
      319
satellite hacking 433–435
scam spam 141–152
   types of 144
scams, detecting Internet scams
      150–151
scanning
   ISS Internet Scanner 190
   and network vulnerabilities 186–190
   NMAP, freeware scanning progam
      189–190
Schlesinger Jr., Arthur 408

Schloesser, Lynn 380
Schmidt, Paul 347
Schuba, Christoph L. 275
Schwartau, Winn 364
Schweitzer, Robert 311
Schweizer, Peter 46
script kiddies 42–44
Secure Computing Corporation 320,
      379, 381
Secure Logix 200
Secure Networks, Inc. 194
Secure Shell, sniffers 178
Secure Sockets Layer (SSL) 103
SecureID keys 172
security
   1999 Computer Crime and Security
      Survey 23
   and AT&T 42
   ATMs 174–175
   and classic security triad 348–349
   Constructive Key Management
      (CKM) 250
   cookies 103
   corporate preperation and 268–269
   credit card information 208–211
   and cryptography 241
   defending against sniffers 178–179
   Defense Information Systems Agency
      (DISA) 20
   Department of Energy Computer
      Incident Advisory Capability team
      23
   email aplications 244–245
   encryption of hard drives 247
   fortress mentality 326–327
   friendly hacks 180–194
   HTCIA (High Technology Criminal
      Investigators Association) 269
   identity theft prevention 99–101
   IDS (Intrusion Detection Systems)
      387
   increasing personal electronic security
      98–99
   and Internet connections 342–344
   intrusion detection 328–332

Iriscan's PC Iris 173
and Microsoft Internet Explorer
103
and Netscape browsers 103
and network security 360
and network vulnerabilities 186–190
and password selection 144, 355
non-technical security methods
354–356
on-line stalking 124–128
pass phrases 170–171
phone cards 174–175
PhoneSweep 197–198
placebo security 351–353
Pretty Good Privacy (PGP) 242–244
RF identification 174–175
Social Security Numbers 174–175
web sites for 451–452
security consulting companies
Associated Corporate Consultants
324
Booz-Allen and Hamilton 324
Computer Consulting Associates
International, Inc. 324
Computer Security Institute 324
Computer Security Ltd. 324
EMPE 324
Ernst & Young 324
Infosecure Australia 324
KPMG 324
P&E Security Consultants 324
Pricewaterhouse Coopers 324
Science Applications International
Corporation 324
Security Design International, Inc.
324
Security Experts, The 324
SRI Comsulting 324
Wolf Consultancy 324
Security Dynamics, Inc. 175, 375
Security Exchange Commission 146
Settle, Jim 73
sexuality, and the Internet 114
Sheymov, Victor 311
Shields Up!, Evil Port Monitor tests

344
Shields Up!, Internet security 342–344
Shimamura, Tsotumo 34
Shimrikyo, Aum 266
Shipley, Peter 320–321
Shiva Corp. 252
Shriner, David 296–298
Sidewinder 338–340, 381
Signal 9 Solutions 340
Silvers, Michael 426
Simpson, O.J. 258
SLAM 225
Slut Puppy 74
sniffer software 177–179
sniffers
defending against 178–179
Trojan Sniffers 178
social security numbers
and AT&T 95–97
and identity theft 90–91
and security issues 96–97, 174
software
anti-spamming software 136
CyberAngel 248
dBase III program 218
Kaboom3 software 280
L0phtCrack Release 2.52 177
Micro-Zap 261
Norton Antivirus software 220
PhoneSweep 199
Pretty Good Privacy (PGP) 242
Public Key Infrastructure 244
SafeBack 2.0 263
sniffer software 177–179 177
Star Office for Linux 31
Steganos 256–257
Wpoison anti-spam software 139
Software Publishers Association, and
bootleg software 44
Soloman, Alan 217
Sophos, Incorporated 228
spam 130–140
Anti-Spam Home Page 139
and anti-spamming software
136–140

spam (*continued*)
  arguments for and against
    134–136
  cyberpromotions 132
  email address harvesting 133
  junk-mail lists 133
  Usenet newsgroups 133
  versus junk mail 139–140
spam scam, investment scams
  145–146
special interest dollars, privacy issues 88
Special Operations Command,
  electromagnetic weapon 290
Special Operations Posture Statement
  418
spoofing 162–163
Spot the Fed contest 65–66
SSH, sniffers 178
Stalbaum, Bret 77
stalking 124–128
  statistics for 126
Star Office for Linux 31
Stark, John Reed 146
steganography 266
Steganos 256–257
stenography 253–257
Stoll, Cliff 37, 363
STU-III program 336
Sullivan, Bill 434
Sullivan, Bob 315
SummerCon 67–68, 72
Sun Microsystems 31
  Star Office downloads 31
Surfwatch 121
*Surviving Denial of Service on the
  Internet* 81
Swap files 264
Symantec, Norton Antivirus software
  220, 228
symmetrical encryption 237
symmetrical-key encryption 232
Syn-Ack attack (denial of service) 281

Task Force South Florida 152
taxonomy, creation for hackers 35

Team Sploit 27
technology, reliance upon 4
Tecsec 249–250
teenagers
  AOL "kids only" account 119
  and hacking 14–16
  protection from hackers 111–129
  Time/CNN poll on Internet use 112
Teledesic Network 435, 439
telemarketing, and Internet scams
  142–143
telephone hacking 195–200
  San Francisco study 196–197
  ToneLoc 197–198
TeleWall 200
telnet, hacking aide 161
TEMP files 266
tempest hacking 435–436
terrorism, and direct energy weapons
  296–298
Tesla, and high voltage hobbyists
  311
Tesla, Nicolai 4, 289, 433
Thackeray, Gail 62
Third World War, The 46
Thompson, Hunter 57
Time Based Security 332–333, 364,
  377–378
Time/CNN poll, kids and Internet use
  112
TimeStep Corp. 252
TMP files 266
Toaster Rebellion of '08 438–447
tokens 171
Tomlinson, Fred 130
ToneLoc 197–198
traffic analysis, anti-hacking tips 329
Trans Union 109
Transient Electromagnetic Devices
  (TED) 288, 296, 307
Trend Micro Incorporated 228
Trident Data Systems 225, 271
Tripwire 263
Trojan hacking 201–205
Trojan Horse 215, 263

Trojan Sniffers 178
true anonymous remailers 156
Turing, Alan 233–234
Tzu, Sun 357–358, 364

Uniform Resource Locators (URLs)
    25
United Nations, Universal Declaration
    of Human Rights 108–109
Universal Declaration of Human Rights
    108–109
Unix, and familiarity of hackers 31
Unrestricted War 412
US Air Force Office of Special
    Investigations 321
US Army's 902 Military Intelligence
    Group 21
US Customs Service 372–373
US House of Representatives, hearings
    on HERF guns 284–285
US Information Warriors 47
US Internet Council 374
US Justice Department
  Digital Telephony Bill 70
  keystroke monitoring 331
U.S. News and World Report, Iraqi
    Printer Virus Hoax 222
US Postal Service 109
US Secret Service 370, 372
  Financial Crimes Division 152
  Operation Sun Devil 368
US Secret Services Electronic Crime
    Branch 372
US Securities and Exchange
    Commission 372
US Senate Permanent Subcommittee on
    Investigations, computer crime
    study 21–22
US Social Security Administration
    109

V-One Corp. 252
VallaH 315
Van Gieri, Joe 376, 379
van Zelbert, Jan 427

Vatis, Michael 24
vendors, security web sites for
    451–452
Venema, Wietse 189
Veridian 198
Verisign, Inc. 102, 244
virtual private networks (VPNs)
    244–246
Virus Hoax Page 227
virus writers, motivations for
    226–227
viruses 212–228
  Anti-virus software 212, 218, 220
  Chernobyl Virus 213
  CIH Virus of 1999 213–214
  Data Crime virus 212
  Good Times Virus 428
  increase of 214
  Iraqi Printer Virus Hoax 221
  macro viruses 218
  Marburg virus 213
  Melissa virus 219
  payloads 213
  protection from 220–224
  and virus writers 225
Vlahos, Michael 374, 381–382
Voice Over IP 432–433
Voiceover IP 200
voyeurism, and hacking 6

Wack, Jay 249
Walker, Al 321
wannabe's 42–44
War dialing 195–200
  San Francisco study 196–197
  ToneLoc 197–198
war, quotes about 408–409
Warez Dudez 44
Warren, Matt 383
Warroom Research
  and computer crime study 21–22
  web site for 22
Washington, George 104
WatchGuard 252
Waters, Bill 85–86, 88, 90

Watson, Tom 11
Weapons of Intelligence and Conflict in the Information Age 80
Wedel, Fred 426–427
Weiner, Michael 239
White, Don 311
white hats 38–39
White, John 74
Windows Swap files 264
Winkler, Ira 153
wireless hacking 437

Woolley, Dan 381
Wozniak, Steve 35
Wpoison software 139

X-Force 321
Xiangsui, Wang 412

Zapatista FloodNet 75–77
Ziegler, Ron 417
Zimmerman, Phil 70, 79, 242–243
ZIP-cracking tools 266